T0304319

Generating Predictability

Human behaviour is infinitely complex, the result of thousands of interactions between predispositions, external factors, and physical and cognitive processes. It is also highly unpredictable which makes meaningful social engagement difficult without the aid of some external framework such as that offered by an institution. Both formal and informal institutions can provide the element of predictability necessary for successful, complex interactions, a factor which is often overlooked by institutional analysts and designers. Drawing on a wide range of disciplines including psychology, economics, and sociological and political studies, this book develops a coherent and accessible theory for explaining the unpredictability of individual behaviour. The author then highlights the danger of institutional reforms undermining the very capacity to generate predictability which is so central to their success. This book will appeal to academics, researchers and professionals in the fields of judgement and decision-making, forecasting, management studies, behavioural economics and the new, interdisciplinary field of institutional design.

CHRISTOPH ENGEL is Director of the Max-Planck-Institute for Research on Collective Goods in Bonn and Professor of Law at the University of Bonn. He has published in both German and English.

Generating Predictability

Institutional Analysis and Institutional Design

Christoph Engel

CAMBRIDGE
UNIVERSITY PRESS

CAMBRIDGE
UNIVERSITY PRESS

University Printing House, Cambridge CB2 8BS, United Kingdom

Cambridge University Press is part of the University of Cambridge.

It furthers the University's mission by disseminating knowledge in the pursuit of education, learning and research at the highest international levels of excellence.

www.cambridge.org
Information on this title: www.cambridge.org/9780521851398

© Christoph Engel 2005

First published 2005
First paperback edition 2011

A catalogue record for this publication is available from the British Library

ISBN 978-0-521-85139-8 Hardback
ISBN 9/8-1-107-40599-8 Paperback

Contents

Preface

Surprise is a necessary member of a research team. My group conducts research on collective goods, like clean air, fisheries or the radio spectrum. We are interested in institutional design. The standard models for understanding our issue are economic. These models are admirably clear and advanced. But they are not interested in some phenomena that are crucial for our class of goods from a policy perspective. For example, people possess highly sensitive mechanisms for detecting cheats, and reactions to cheats are likely to be driven by individually quite irrational, but socially powerful punitive sentiments. Such findings have led us to a shift in the agenda. We now focus on fleshing out the implications of behavioural research for institutional design in the area of collective goods.

Not all of us were specialists in behavioural research at the outset of our work. The group therefore went through an extended exercise in collective learning, guided by those specialists who had been willing to join us for the purpose. Starting with the biases literature, we made ever more daring forays into behavioural territory. On doing this, one cannot but be overwhelmed by the richness of findings. This experience turned out to be the surprise cause for this book: if the human mind, at least at the symbolic level, is such a mixed bag of forces and effects, how on earth can we ever interact in a meaningful way? My intuition was: it is due to institutions. This book explores the hypothesis.

Not surprisingly, I am not the first to have this intuition. But none of those who previously looked at the issues examined here combined the three bodies of literature that I rely on: psychology for problem definition; game theory for generating a benchmark; institutional phenomenology for finding solutions. None of these authors had written for the institutional designer either; they all focused on the institutional analyst. As a result, they neglected one latent policy issue: institutional reform, undertaken with the best intentions, can hamper the hidden function of existing institutional arrangements for the generation of predictability.

Throughout the course of writing this book, many have given valuable advice. Elke Weber and Eric Johnson invited me to Columbia University to present an earlier version of the book and discuss it with the audience. The late Margaret Gruter enabled me do the same at the last Squaw Valley Conference she was able to chair. Bruno Frey and Gérard Hertig asked me to Zurich for the purpose. Arno Scherzberg and Gerhard Wegner invited me to Erfurt, and Karl Christoph Klauer to the Bonn Psychology Department. Roland Czada (Osnabrück) pointed me towards more of my predecessors. Burkhard Schipper (Bonn) was willing to read entire parts of the book critically. My most radical, and most elucidating, critics, however, have been the members of my own group: psychologists Martin Beckenkamp and Stephanie Kurzenhäuser; economists Heike Hennig-Schmidt, Frank Maier-Rigaud, Chrysostomos Mantzavinos and Dorothee Schmidt; political scientist Margaret McCown; and lawyers Thomas Baehr, Guido Kordel, Jörn Lüdemann, Stefan Magen, Indra Spiecker and Stefan Tontrup. Rosel Porcas has typed the whole volume with admirable speed and accuracy. Darrell Arnold has carefully checked and improved my English. Brigitte Martin has done the final layout. I am most grateful to all of them.

CHRISTOPH ENGEL
BONN

Notation

Basic notation

c	cost
ε	add on (to a term, typically small)
g	fair gain
gg	unfair gain
l	loss
p	Ego's subjective probability of Alter being beneficial
q	Ego's subjective probability of finding a signal that rationally makes him more optimistic
r	Alter's expectation about Ego co-operating
s	side-payment
v	expected value of the game for Ego

Suffixes for persons

c_A or g_A	Alter
c_E or g_E	Ego
c_{E+A}	Ego and Alter jointly
c_{TP}	third party
c_{SV}	sovereign intervention

Suffixes for types of cost

c^{G2}	out of pocket or opportunity cost of second game in a repeated or nested game
c^{In}	cost of insurance
c^s	cost for getting a signal about Alter's type

c^{SQ} cost of improving or reducing the quality of a signal sent out by
            Nature
c^{Tx} cost of a tax/subsidy scheme

Suffixes for alterations

p' or r'or v' updating of prior beliefs

$\bar{p}$ or $\bar{r}$ second-guessing
$\underline{p}$ social assessment

Bayes' Rule: generic notation

o object
P probability
σ signal

1 Introduction

1.1 The puzzle

The obvious is often not self-explanatory. We obviously interact with others in a meaningful way. This presupposes that we can predict reasonably well what another person is going to do, and how he is going to react to our own moves. Yet psychology demonstrates the almost unlimited plasticity of human behavioural dispositions.[1] Why are we nonetheless able to interact successfully? This book claims that, to a substantial degree, it is because of institutions.

To use a metaphor: wild animals have fur to survive hostile weather. Humans are left naked by nature. They must sew clothes for the purpose. Likewise, animals have instincts to make their behaviour predictable to their peers. Humans again are forced to take recourse in artefacts for the purpose.[2] In both domains, the paucity of their natural endowment makes humans more needy. But they need not wear their fur when they move from Scotland to Sicily. Their less ready-made endowment thus makes for greater adaptability. The same holds for the mental endowment of humans. To a very high degree, it consists not of hard-wired solutions, but of the ability to find appropriate solutions in reaction to a permanently changing environment. But the Scots do wear furs (or modern equivalents). Likewise, humans often have to seek out mental clothing if they want to interact. This book purports to show that, and how, institutions provide humans with a rich wardrobe of mental clothes, all making them more predictable.

---

[1] The term is used in psychology, see e.g. Mischel and Shoda 1995: 246; it will be further fleshed out below, see in particular 2.1.3. NB. For ease of use, the masculine pronoun is employed throughout the book.

[2] The point has frequently been made. A characteristic voice is Anderson 2000b: 1: 'humans are exceptional in how plastic they are behaviourally'. For a stimulating account of the neurological bases, see Hebb 1949: 166–7. Consequently, for predicting human behaviour it is not sufficient to know the (human) species. One must know the history of the individual being, since, via learning, it has made an impact on its behavioural dispositions. Hebb 1949, 166.

Let's be a little more explicit with respect to the elements of our puzzle, although a thorough analysis is to follow in later chapters. From the ancient Greeks onwards, observers have been overwhelmed by the unpredictability of their fellow humans.[3] For centuries, René Descartes' dualistic concept of human nature provided scientists with an intellectual tool to cope with the problem. In his perspective, all human behaviour is either one way or the other: either deterministic or volitional; either driven by reflex or an exercise of free will.[4] More than two hundred years later, scientists such as Ivan Petrovich Pavlov[5] and Charles Scott Sherrington rejected dualism.[6] For them, at closer sight, all human behaviour was deterministic. It was all reflexes. At least at the neurological level, the predictability problem then fades away. Today's neurobiologists also claim monism, but the other way round. For Paul Glimcher, all behaviour is probabilistic, even if it looks highly determined to an observer who sees only behaviour, not how that behaviour is generated mentally.[7] At least at the neurological level, the predictability problem then becomes pervasive. And the overview presented in chapter 2 of this book will demonstrate that the neurological plasticity to a remarkable degree translates to the symbolic level, that is, to human behavioural dispositions.

Predictability is paramount for co-ordination. If Ego has no clue as to how Alter is going to behave, Ego is better off staying as far away from Alter as possible. In economic terms, one can say precisely why. Humans are not born with identical endowments. Some have greater physical forces, others have quicker minds, to name only one dimension. By division of labour, they can exploit this diversity and make both co-operating individuals better off.[8] But the division of labour can only work if it makes sense for Ego to use some of his endowment on Alter's behalf. It does if Ego can reckon on Alter reciprocating. If the transaction is on the spot, Ego may be able to withhold his own contribution until Alter delivers. But often, simultaneous exchange is not within reach. Ego offers Alter a favour today, but he expects Alter to respond with a favour later. Economists have studied this situation at length.[9] But they have focused on a different aspect of the problem. They have asked

---

[3] The fascinating history of the neurosciences in Glimcher 2003 can also be read as a history of conceptualising human unpredictability; explicit references to predictability are to be found on, among others, pages 13, 27, 39, 272–3.

[4] Descartes 1664.

[5] Pavlov and Anrep 1927.

[6] Sherrington 1906.

[7] Glimcher 2003: 273 and *passim*.

[8] A much more elaborate account is to be found in Engel 2002b.

[9] A prominent contribution is from Williamson 1985.

why Alter should have any interest in keeping his earlier implicit or explicit promise. But even if Alter is an honourable and caring citizen, the enormous plasticity of human behavioural dispositions might make it difficult for him to keep his promise. More importantly even, a breach of contract may not result only from outright 'opportunism'.[10] It suffices if Alter does nothing to counteract the low natural predictability of his own future behaviour. And, of course, not all human interaction involves mutual exchange. Pedestrians must predict whether cars are likely to stop at a red traffic light. Government must predict whether consumers are likely to drive less, and hence help the ailing atmosphere, if government doubles the price of petrol. These few examples should make it clear that human interaction could not be anywhere near as manifold as it is, had human beings not found ways drastically to narrow down the natural plasticity of their behaviour.

Predictability is thus defined very broadly here. It encompasses any situation where Ego would wish to know how Alter is going to behave in the future. Specifically, full predictability is defined as follows: Alter's behaviour is fully determined; Ego has access to the information about the determining mechanism, and about the presence of the input necessary from the environment to get the mechanism going. It is obvious from this definition that full predictability is extremely rare. The predictability problem, thus defined, is pervasive. This breadth is nonetheless justified. First of all, the most prominent model in the social sciences, the rational choice model, makes exactly this assumption. For it is a pure motivational model. Social interaction fails because the interaction partners are driven by conflicting interests. Any cognitive problem is assumed away. Moreover, it is true that institutional intervention typically creates no more than what will be called soft predictability.[11] But understanding why such prudence is warranted presupposes that the analysis starts from the idea of generating the maximum, that is, full predictability.

Finally, the basic claim of this book is the following: institutional analysts have fallen prey to their own role as actors within environments shaped by institutions. They have thus implicitly confounded the roles of observers and actors. In real-life environments, the predictability problem is indeed often not grave. Ego can take it for granted that the behavioural space of Alter is severely reduced. Ego can reckon that Alter will exploit almost none of the plasticity of his behavioural dispositions

---

[10] Williamson 1985: chapter 2, appendix has coined this term for the deliberate breach of promise.
[11] See below 3.2.9(e).

in the situation at hand. Consequently, Ego can rightly focus on the remaining uncertainty, and on Alter's interests in particular. When they designed their research questions, institutional analysts wrongly started from their own real-life experiences. But the neatness of this situation is not natural. It is generated by heavy institutional intervention. Put differently, most context is not simply out there. It has been generated by institutions. This neglected institutional task becomes visible if the analysis starts from the broad concept of predictability just presented.

There are two qualifications. Predictability is not always a good thing. If Alter risks being Ego's prey, Alter is clearly better off not being predictable. Nature has even endowed animals with mental tools for generating randomness for the purpose. The classic example is the hare darting back and forth. Likewise, humans change their itineraries if there is a risk of being robbed. Alter's unpredictability can even be to Ego's benefit. If birds of prey were able to extinguish the target population, they would starve in the long run. Having a hard-to-hit target thus helps sustain the natural equilibrium between both populations.[12] A second benefit of unpredictability is more complicated to demonstrate. The full demonstration will be made in the rational choice part of this book. Suffice it at this point to mention the basic intuition. Egoistic actors can be caught in stalemate. Both would be individually better off if they co-operated. If, however, only one of them does, he becomes vulnerable to being exploited by the other. In such contexts, adding some uncertainty can make it rational to co-operate.[13]

The second qualification concerns sources of unpredictability. Although the character of behavioural dispositions is the most important source practically speaking, it is not the only one. Other sources include an overwhelming degree of complexity that goes beyond the cognitive abilities of Ego,[14] the neglect of available information,[15] or the inappropriate weighing of recent, salient information, at the expense of information about the past.[16] More generally, the limitation may lie not only in Alter's behaviour, but also in Ego's limited ability to cope with it. This point will be taken up at the end of this book.[17]

---

[12] The idea has been fleshed out in resource economics, see e.g. Hartwick and Olewiler 1998.

[13] More below 3.2.3(c).

[14] Elster 1989: 4; Glimcher 2003: 39–40; an interesting example is discussed by Walker et al. 2000: 218.

[15] Elster 1989: 8.

[16] Elster 1989; see also below 2.2.3(c) on deviations of standard subjects from statistical norms.

[17] See below, chapter 5.

This book not only uses a broad definition of predictability. It also defines institutions in a liberal way.[18] Any outside intervention that impacts on behaviour is here seen as an institution.[19] The intervention need not be legal or in other ways formal. In order to qualify as an institution, there are no particular requirements for structure.[20] The impact on behaviour can be the side-effect of activities aimed at other purposes. The behavioural effect can rest on the interaction between several co-ordinated or unco-ordinated interventions. The institution can, and indeed often will, comprise an entire institutional arrangement, rather than one single intervention.[21] The concept used here includes symbol systems, cognitive scripts and moral templates. It thus does not make a distinction between institution and culture.[22] The institution need not be purposively designed; it can result from some form of evolution, the course of which no single planner has directed. Only one definition offered in the literature is excluded: mere regularities of behaviour are not seen here as institutions.[23] This follows from the purpose of this book. It aims to understand how the individual obtains help from the outside – i.e. from institutions – to solve problems he could not solve on his own.

Again, this breadth is necessary to capture the essence of the problem. In reality, sometimes there is indeed ad hoc, targeted intervention to overcome one specific reason for unpredictability. For instance, untrained persons make many mistakes in using information on probabilities.[24] They do much better if this same information is given to them in the form of natural frequencies.[25] They then are told that, say, 5 cases out of 1,000 fall into some category, rather than 0.05 per cent of them.[26]

[18] For an overview of the many possibilities for defining institutions, see DiMaggio and Powell 1991; Hall and Taylor 1996; Peters 1999; Engel 2001b: 1–5; cf. also below, chapter 7.
[19] In this, the book follows North 1990: 3, who defines institutions as the 'rules of the game in society or . . . these humanly devised constraints that shape human interaction'; Sweet 1999: 150 explicitly embraces this definition; Nee 1998: 12 similarly notes: 'Sociology as a discipline has specialised in the study of humanly devised constraints'; in line with this, according to Nee 1998: 8, 'institutions, defined as webs of interrelated rules and norms that govern social relationships, comprise the formal and informal social constraints that shape the choice-set of actors'; the criterion is also implicit in Peters 1999: 146, who finds it as common ground of all competing strands of institutionalist thinking.
[20] On this, see Peters 1999: 18.
[21] Cf. Hodgson 1988: 179, pointing to this implication of North's definition.
[22] Hall and Taylor 1996: 947 see this as a characteristic of sociological institutionalism rather than political science institutionalism.
[23] This definition is prominently used by Hodgson 1998: 179 and *passim*. It goes back to Veblen 1919: 239 and to Hamilton 1932: 84.
[24] For an overview, see below 2.2.3(c).
[25] Hoffrage et al. 2002.
[26] This is particularly helpful for the correct treatment of conditional probabilities.

But most cases are different. Intervention is much more diffuse. Predict-ability is increased in many respects at a time. Moreover, the interven-tion often does not only affect predictability. It also changes incentives. A characteristic example is the imposition of professional training. If a layman interacts with a professional, he comes with a whole set of expectations, and most of them are warranted most of the time. More-over, being a member of the profession changes the opportunity struc-ture. The individual professional knows that he will have to interact with his peers for decades, and that they will have joint interests in defending themselves from outside actors such as the government.

In its analytic part, the mission of this book is to reconstruct insti-tutions rationally. Many of them serve a purpose that is typically neg-lected by institutional analysis: the generation of predictability. In order to make this claim, the book follows three indirect routes. Relying on evidence from the behavioural sciences, it demonstrates that the human mental endowment is a source of dramatic unpredictability. Relying on a game theoretic model, it demonstrates the limited ability of interaction partners to solve the predictability problem from scratch. Relying on institutional phenomenology, it demonstrates how many existing insti-tutions can be interpreted as tools for easing the predictability problem.

Scientists from a culture of rigorous empirical testing will see all this as an exercise in generating hypotheses. They would want to test these hypotheses in experiments, or at least in meticulously controlled fieldwork. This is not done here. It would be beyond this author's competence. But it might also be difficult to do for reasons of principle. The basic hypothesis is that it is largely because of institutions that humans can interact in a meaningful way. In an institution-free en-vironment, the problem of generating predictability would be over-whelming. How could this hypothesis be tested? In theory, the test is easy to design. Put a number of individuals in an institution-free en-vironment, and observe what happens. According to the prediction, they would either fail to co-operate, or they would start creating their own institutions. But it is not easy to design such an environment. Not many subjects would be willing to stay in the laboratory long enough. If they know that the experiment is short-lived, they are likely to behave differently than they would otherwise. It would not be easy to control for the presence in the laboratory of informal institutions that subjects bring from their culture of origin. The very design of the experiment could serve as an informal institution that makes the pre-dictability problem easy to solve for the participants. But other research-ers may be more optimistic, and they may know after the fact that they were right.

1.2   The policy problem

The topic of this book is a puzzle. Is it also a policy problem? Do the existing institutions fail to allow individuals properly to predict the behaviour of their interaction partners? Does individually or socially beneficial interaction fail to take place? Are the existing institutions unduly costly, or do they take suboptimal form?

Since prediction is fundamental to co-operation, it should not come as a surprise that the predictability problem is more often solved than not. Consequently, the contribution of this book to institutional analysis is more profound than its contribution to institutional design. But the implications for design are not negligible.

The design task is most visible if interaction takes place in an almost clean, context-free environment. Currently, the most prominent example is interaction over the Internet. On the Internet, people from the other side of the globe are just a click away. One usually has never seen those with whom one is interacting, and this is not expected either. One often has not even seen the face of one's online interlocutor, and only a webcam makes it possible to observe his reactions. Often nicknames even conceal the identities of those communicating. If an Internet user wants to go further, he can rely on encryption and remailing services.[27] Yet people use the Internet for a host of purposes, including trading goods. How do they overcome the predictability problem? They rely on the services of intermediaries. If the seller is a firm, the typical intermediary is a credit card organisation. For the credit card companies have chargeback systems. If the seller does not deliver on his promises, the buyer is reimbursed by the credit card company. This company disciplines the seller.[28] If consumers sell some of their property, they typically go through an Internet auction service such as eBay. This does two things for predictability. It offers a trading platform, thereby narrowing mutual expectations down to what can be done within this framework. More importantly, eBay also offers a technical tool for generating a reputation. Despite these interventions, the willingness to co-operate over the Internet is much smaller than in face-to-face interaction.[29]

---

[27] For an overview, see Engel 2000: 204–12.
[28] The European Commission, DG Internal Market, Payment Card Chargeback when Paying over Internet, First Sub-Group meeting of the PSTDG and PSULG held on 4 July 2000, Markt173/2000, S.3, http://europa.eu.int/comm/internal_market/en/media/elec-comm/chargeback.pdf; Perritt 2000: 689–94.
[29] More from Ockenfels 2003.

In a second class of situations, the design task is a result of external shock. Before this shock, the predictability problem had basically been solved by the existing institutional arrangements. But redesign is necessary, since the earlier framework no longer performs adequately after the shock. This is what happens in situations of imposed decontextualisation. Many fear that the Internet has this potential. They see it as a threat to 'national values'.[30] If that really were to happen, the effect certainly would not be confined to the predictability problem. The erosion of social norms would also hamper traditional solutions to social dilemmas by informal institutions. But lower predictability would be an important portion of the problem. Nations might want to take action, for instance, by attempts at renationalising the Internet.[31]

Finally, the increased predictability problem can result from purposeful intervention. This is straightforward if lower predictability is in the interest of powerful actors. It may, for instance, help them escape otherwise stringent regulation. But not so rarely, the predictability problem is just a side-effect of an act of intervention with different goals. Again, the Internet may serve as an illustration. Especially during the Internet bubble on the financial markets, many countries felt that opening themselves up to the Internet was paramount for national growth. They proactively promoted the access of their populations to the Net. If the above-mentioned concern were real, they then would have deliberately taken the ensuing predictability problem into account. More generally, any deliberate decontextualisation has this effect. Two prominent examples are globalisation and the promotion of a multicultural society. But simple physical mobility can also be brought under this rubric. It exposes travellers to foreign mores, and it brings people with different cultural backgrounds in. It therefore is not difficult to tell a story of progressive decontextualisation.

One can even go a step further. Humans and animals have to survive in the same natural environment. Biologists sometimes speak about institutions in animals, like the 'state of bees', with a queen and her subjects. If one looks at primates, one might even find the equivalent of deliberate institutional design. But even if the difference in the end is one of degree rather than of principle, it would still be huge. The comparison supports a claim: 'natural' complexity is not the issue. Humans outperform animals, because a greater part of this complexity matters for them.[32] In our modern times, more and more of this complexity is even

[30] The concern has been addressed in National Research Council 2002.
[31] For more on the technological options, and the ensuing social cost see Engel 2003c.
[32] Cf. Bartlett 1932: 210.

endogenous, resulting from other humans, not from nature. The enormous plasticity of their mental apparatus is only a necessary, not a sufficient condition for the ability of humans to handle this complexity. The sufficient condition, this book claims, is a set of institutions for nonetheless generating an appropriate degree of predictability. From this angle, improving the pertinent institutions is a way of safeguarding survival, welfare and social betterment.

Analytically, making behaviour predictable and changing behaviour do not collapse. In a rational choice perspective, predictability is a matter of information. If an institution makes behaviour predictable, an outsider learns how an actor may behave. But the actor keeps his freedom of choice. Likewise, predictability is not a mere matter of compliance with cultural or social standards. The behaviour of those at the fringe of society is often easy to predict, even if it is highly inappropriate.

The analytic distinction between predictability and normative desirability makes an option for institutional choice visible. Institutional designers can adopt a one-level or a two-level approach.[33] In the former case, generating greater predictability and changing incentives are done simultaneously, in one and the same act of intervention. In the latter case, one set of institutions sees to predictability. To the extent that predictable behaviour is socially undesirable, another set of institutions intervenes in the interest of changing incentives. In this case, the predictability problem is only indirectly present at the second level. It adds a criterion to institutional comparisons. Institutions aiming at social betterment may be ranked according to the degree of predictability they presuppose. The more they presuppose, the greater their demands for first-level institutions.

If institutional designers follow the one-level approach, one and the same institution serves both purposes. It sees to predictability in that it makes addressees behave in the socially desirable way. This option for institutional design has an important analytic consequence. It tremendously increases the set of institutions that can be interpreted as tools for making behaviour more predictable. Specifically, every institution that is not exclusively symbolic must have this effect.[34] This insight might also explain why the role of institutions in generating predictability has attracted fairly little academic interest so far.[35] The interest of researchers may have been siphoned away by a concern with understanding how

---

[33] More on one-versus two-level institutions from Engel 2003d.
[34] The classic text on symbolic policy-making (and hence the symbolic character of institutions, if institutional design is the political output) is Edelman 1964; see also Hansjürgens and Lübbe-Wolff 2000.
[35] For an overview of earlier attempts, see below 1.4.

social betterment can be brought about. Again, description and prescription are closely related. The possibility of a one-level approach adds an important dimension to institutional comparisons. If the institutional designer opts for a one-level approach, the comparative assessment of options must start with predictability effects.

1.3   An interdisciplinary approach

A single discipline would not be able to analyse the predictability problem in a satisfactory way. This book draws on three bodies of knowledge. In order to understand why low predictability would be pervasive in a world without institutions, it presents a host of findings from both psychology and experimental economics.[36] Both fields do also help understand how existing institutions are able to make behaviour more predictable. Insights from these fields can also be used to assess suggestions for institutional design.

The second body of knowledge is economics, and, more specifically, game theory. Game theoretic tools make it possible to generate a conceptual benchmark. How would two individuals be able to co-ordinate behaviour, if Ego knows that Alter can exhibit either of two kinds of behaviour? This is visibly a rigorous simplification of the actual predictability problem. But even in this extremely well-behaved environment, it is a serious challenge to overcome the predictability problem. This analysis thus allows a much clearer definition of the institutional task. And it generates valuable insights for institutional design. It points to additional options, like leaving the predictability problem as is, or insuring Ego against the behavioural risk. And it teaches institutional designers how to assess institutional options comparatively.

The third body of knowledge is institutional phenomenology. It is partly taken from law, but it also encompasses non-legal formal and informal institutions. This work not only provides ample evidence for institutions that actually do lower the predictability problem. It also offers criteria for systematising the evidence, and for assessing the comparative performance of different solutions.

1.4   Related approaches in the literature

The impact of institutions on the predictability of behaviour has never been a fashionable topic, at least not among economists and

---

[36] See chapter 2 below.

psychologists. But there are, of course, predecessors.[37] Starting with Adam Smith, researchers have pointed to the low predictability of behaviour:[38] 'The other [fellow], acts variously and accidentally, as humour, inclination, or interest chance to be uppermost.'[39] Differential psychologists, i.e. psychologists interested in understanding different personalities, were even on the brink of abandoning their field, since they were overwhelmed by the variance of behaviour across time and context.[40] Others have stressed that predictability is crucial for social interaction,[41] but almost impossible to attain.[42]

Actually, the problem is even graver. In truth, it is not predictability that matters, but prediction. For the individual interaction partner, it is irrelevant whether other, more gifted, well-trained or better informed people can make better predictions. It is even less relevant whether scientific observers have a greater ability to correctly predict behaviour. For social interaction to be effective, the individual interaction partner must himself be able reliably to predict what the actor is going to do. Thereby, our topic is linked to one of Herbert Simon's basic puzzles: How is it possible for decision-makers to make reasonable choices, given their limited cognitive abilities?[43]

Other predecessors do link predictability and institutions. Psychologists and behavioural economists investigate the rationalising effect of institutions.[44] Others see institutions as 'passive decision support' that 'encourages more accurate strategies by making them easier to

---

[37] Some of them do not share much more than the term predictability with this book. Morgenstern 1935 aims at assessing the assumption of perfect information, including perfect foresight, in neoclassical economic thinking. Grunberg and Modigliani 1954 are concerned with an agent's reaction to a published prediction.

[38] 'There are an infinite number of ways of being nonperfectly rational,' says Scharpf 1997: 108. The possibilities of governing behaviour 'from the exterior' are limited, says Weck-Hannemann 1999. Ripperger 1998: 17 speaks about 'endogenous uncertainty', resulting from the multitude of behavioural options. These are only some of the many voices.

[39] Smith 1790: III.v.2; 'The coarse clay of which the bulk of mankind are formed, cannot be wrought up to such perfection.'

[40] See for the moment only Bem and Allen 1974; Mischel and Shoda 1995; see also 2.5.

[41] Kunda and Nisbett 1988: 326.

[42] One characteristic voice is Epstein 1979: 1123: To predict individual behaviour with reasonable accuracy, a correlation between some observable signal and actual behaviour must be in the vicinity of .8 or .9. But such correlations are almost never generated in the laboratory. For an even more explicit treatment, see another characterstic voice: Rostain 2000: 986. She speaks of the 'fundamental unpredictability of human action', which will persist for ever (984).

[43] For a summary of his thinking, see Simon 1987.

[44] Particularly noteworthy are V. Smith 1991: 879–94; Frey and Eichenberger 1994; Slembeck and Tyran 2002.

execute'.[45] In a way, one can also bring the work on debiasing[46] and on trust under this rubric.[47] For debiasing often reduces behavioural variance.[48] From the perspective of trust, low predictability is seen as a risk. The interaction partner decides whether taking this risk is worthwhile, given the expected gain from interaction.

The classic equivalent to the approach adopted here comes from sociologist Arnold Gehlen. He is interested in the supportive effect of institutions.[49] Institutions protect the individual from the need to take too many decisions. They give him orientation when tossed around by impressions and stimuli.[50] Institutions are reliable for outsiders, since they gain autonomous power vis-à-vis the individual. As a result of this, knowing the institutional framework suffices to predict behaviour.[51] Gehlen thus makes the same claim as this book. In line with his sociological background, however, he is only interested in highly aggregate, 'social' institutions. And he offers no micro analysis for his ideas.

One of the key works on social constructivism also ties into the agenda of this book. Peter Berger and Thomas Luckmann see institutions as tools for social construction. In this way, institutions help the actor overcome a double problem of predictability: both about the character and evolution of the context, and about the way his social counterparts

---

[45] Payne et al. 1997: 201.

[46] Psychology and behavioural economics speak of a bias if a population systematically deviates from a normative behavioural standard, like rationality (more below 2.2.2). Consequently, debiasing implies intervention aimed at bringing behaviour closer to the standard. From the many voices, see only Camerer 1995: 587: he professes a 'strong intuition' that the 'thickness of institutional veils is important' in wiping out the errors people make; Frey and Eichenberger 1994.

[47] For an overview of the abundant literature, see Hardin 2002 and Lahno 2002; my own (provisional) position is to be found in Engel 1999.

[48] Occasionally, however, debiasing can even have the opposite effect. This is the case, if the concrete bias which exists is particularly stable; see also 2.2.3(b). In that case, debiasing can result in opening up the general variance of human behaviour.

[49] The German original is more graphic. Gehlen 1960: 70 speaks of the 'Entlastungswirkung der Institutionen'.

[50] The German original reads: 'Solche kulturellen Verhaltensmuster oder Institutionen bedeuten für das Individuum eine Entlastung von allzu vielen Entscheidungen, einen Wegweiser durch die Fülle von Eindrücken und Reizen, von denen der weltoffene Mensch überflutet wird', Gehlen 1960: 71. 'Sie [sc.: die Institutionen] sind die Formen, die ein seiner Natur nach riskiertes und unstabiles, affekt-überlastetes Wesen findet, um sich gegenseitig und um sich selbst zu ertragen, etwas, worauf man in sich und den anderen zählen und sich verlassen kann' (71). On this account, Gehlen has two predecessors: Plessner *Stufen des Organischen* 1928; Scheler *Die Stellung des Menschen im Kosmos* 1928.

[51] In German: 'Institutionen, die schließlich den Individuen gegenüber etwas wie eine Selbstmacht gewinnen, so dass man das Verhalten des einzelnen in der Regel ziemlich sicher voraussagen kann, wenn man seine Stellung in dem System der Gesellschaft kennt, wenn man weiß, von welchen Institutionen er eingefasst ist', Gehlen 1960: 71.

see this context. Via institutions, the actor thus not only gives the context meaning; he also does so in the same way as all others under the spell of this institution. Specifically, institutions differ from mere habituation by bringing third parties in as guarantors. This feature makes them much more reliable, and hence more powerful in solving the predictability problem.[52] The approach differs from the one offered here in two respects in particular. The authors only very briefly allude to micro foundations.[53] And they are not interested in going into institutional detail.

Another intellectual neighbour is Jon Elster. In his thinking, there are two fundamental social problems. The first, the co-operation problem, is amply studied by economists. But the second, the predictability problem, looms equally large.[54] Unlike most others who have done work on social norms, Elster sees their main function as consisting in solving the second problem, not the first one.[55] This book shares the conviction that people need institutions to overcome the predictability problem. It also agrees with Elster that social norms have an important role to play in this. But it differs on two accounts in particular. It does not analyse the predictability problem within the rational choice framework,[56] but exploits psychological findings for that purpose. And it does not restrict the choice of institutions to social norms. It rather assembles a whole array of institutional responses, and offers guidance to policy-makers on how to choose among them. This policy orientation is not present in Elster's book.

One further neighbour is Uwe Schimank. Like Elster, he sees a double social problem: stabilising expectations and overcoming social dilemma situations.[57] He distinguishes between two situations. In the first case, there is an institution out there for stabilising expectations. But this institution is precarious. It erodes if the individuals do not make contributions to the provision of this collective good. But, as is usual for collective goods, each individual is best off if all the other members of the community make their contribution and he free-rides.[58] In the second case, there is no institution in the first place. The individuals' problem then is twofold. They must co-operatively generate a sufficiently stable social environment. But they also pursue their egoistic goals within that framework.[59] Co-operation and conflict thus go

---

[52] Berger and Luckmann 1967, in particular 70–85.
[53] Berger and Luckmann 1967: 74–6.
[54] Elster 1989: 1 and *passim*.   [55] Elster 1989: 97.
[56] Elster 1989: 3.   [57] Schimank 1992: 182–9.
[58] Schimank 1992: 189–95.   [59] Schimank 1992: 195–8.

hand-in-hand.[60] Schimank models the first case as a prisoner's dilemma, and the second as a battle of the sexes.[61] Both games will be introduced in greater detail below.[62] Suffice it at this point to highlight the differences to the approach pursued here. This book is not concerned with the first case. It (analytically) starts from an institution-free situation. Put differently, it wants to generate a benchmark for institutional analysis and institutional design that abstracts from institutional history at the moment of institutional intervention. Like Schimank, the model used here often finds the players in a second-order game.[63] But it is more radical in that it does not see the generation of predictability as a co-operative problem in the first place. It rather starts from a situation where Ego considers whether it is worthwhile to embark on interaction with Alter, given the predictability risk. The model used here thus digs one step deeper and treats predictability as an information asymmetry. All this, of course, has to be fleshed out in much greater detail.

A number of economists also link institutions to predictability, Ronald Heiner being the most notable.[64] 'Social institutions evolve because of uncertainty.'[65] They 'enable each agent in the society to know less and less about the behaviour of other agents'.[66] This approach does thus take behavioural unpredictability as a given. It is interested in how an interaction partner best behaves, given that the behaviour of the actor is not predictable. Using jargon from the climate change negotiations, one might thus state: The economic approach reported here is exclusively interested in adaptation, not in the mitigation of the predictability risk. Other voices add: The task of institutions is not to drive out human irrationality.[67] What they ought to achieve is a change of the environment such that it does not matter whether people behave rationally or not.[68] This option is further pursued below, but it is contrasted with

---

[60] On markets, this situation has meanwhile been dubbed 'co-opetition'; see, for example, Brandenburger and Nalebuff 1996.

[61] Schimank 1992: 192 and 195 respectively.

[62] See below, 3.2.3(b) and (c).

[63] But this game is formally characterised as a chicken game, not as a battle of the sexes; see below, 3.3.3(b).

[64] Heiner 1983; see also his later papers elaborating on the idea: Heiner 1985a, 1985b, 1989. In a way, Alchian 1950 and Becker 1962 can be interpreted as predecessors; see also Satz and Ferejohn 1994: 81: the view that 'interests . . . are determined by features of the agent's environment' implies that altering the environment is a way of changing interests.

[65] Heiner 1983: 573.

[66] Heiner 1983: 580.

[67] Becker 1962: 2.

[68] Becker 1962: 4, with respect to markets.

institutional interventions that address the problem directly and aim at generating greater predictability.

In a way the predictability problem can also be seen as having triggered the evolution of game theory.[69] Back in 1928, Oskar Morgenstern observed that rational action presupposes a prediction of how other individuals react to the action. Now this problem is reciprocal. A outguesses B, and B outguesses A. Morgenstern saw this is as a serious policy problem.[70] One may claim that this unsolved problem led Morgenstern to co-operate with John von Neumann and develop game theory.[71] This book, in chapter 3 on rational choice, heavily draws on game theory. But it does so from a different angle. Classic game theorists have been interested not in deviations from *Homo oeconomicus*, but in how fully rational, but incompletely informed, players could nonetheless interact successfully.

Yet another approach reinterprets predictability problems in terms of game theory. In this perspective, low predictability engenders multiple equilibria, and hence a problem of equilibrium selection. Institutions are consequently seen as tools that select one equilibrium, to the detriment of its competitors.[72] The game theoretic part of this book also addresses a second-order problem of equilibrium selection. It originates in the fact that both Ego and Alter would prefer co-operation to the status quo. But each of them would rather have the other incur the cost of generating as much predictability as is necessary for the purpose. But this book does not see the predictability problem itself, i.e. the first-order problem, as one of equilibrium selection. It rather interprets it as a problem of information asymmetry.

A related approach is also to be found in political science. Simon Jackman and Paul Sniderman see it as the task of political institutions in general, and party competition in particular, to narrow down spaces for choice. If, but only if, choices are watered down to a simple selection between A or B, voters can be expected to choose rationally.[73] This is an interesting application of the general ideas developed in this book. But for the sake of parsimony, the bulk of this book is concerned with a much poorer environment, where just two persons want to interact: Ego and Alter.

---

[69] Burkhard Schipper pointed me to this.
[70] Morgenstern 1928: 5–6, 97; see also Morgenstern 1935.
[71] Von Neumann and Morgenstern 1944.
[72] Bohnet and Cooter 2001; on governmental institutions as tools for equilibrium selection see also Guesnerie 2001.
[73] Jackman and Sniderman 2002; see also Heiner 1983: 586: political institutions are particularly simple, because of the inherent complexity of political reality.

Finally, there are related concepts in law. Lawyers from the systems theory tradition see the main task of the legal system as consisting of stabilising expectations.[74] Others distinguish between first- and second-order decisions. The latter are seen as a tool for simplifying the actual decision, in reaction to the boundedness of human rationality.[75] This is done by limiting options or limiting information.[76] This work ties into the last, phenomenological part of this book. But here the focus is broader in that non-legal institutions are considered as well.

1.5   Organisation of the book

The book is organised as follows: chapter 2 presents the psychological predictability problem. Chapter 3 takes the problem as a given, but seeks a rational reaction to it. Chapter 4 drops the rationality assumption on the part of the informed actor, but keeps it on the part of his uninformed counterpart. Chapter 5 also drops the latter assumption. All this assumes a precisely defined situation. Ego interacts with one *ex ante* defined actor, called Alter, in one unrepeated instance. Chapter 6 looks at other constellations. It allows for Alter to be uninformed. It looks at a reciprocal predictability problem. It allows for multiple instances, groups of Egos, groups of Alters, chance interaction partners; it allows for Ego to bind himself and for situations with externalities. Chapter 7 is the conclusion.

This book does not look at two things. It does not look at collective or corporate actors, but looks exclusively at individuals.[77] With respect to solutions, it looks only at tools, not at political institutions designing them.[78]

---

[74] See e.g. Luhmann 1986: 126: 'Durch die zweiwertige Codierung des Rechtssystems [sc.: in den Code Recht oder Unrecht] wird die Sicherheit erzeugt, dass man, wenn man im Recht ist, im Recht ist und nicht im Unrecht. Rechtsunsicherheit gibt es dann nur noch in prinzipiell behebbarer Form, nämlich in Bezug auf Entscheidungen, die im Rechtssystem selbst getroffen werden können. Diese Sicherheit ist jedoch innerhalb der Gesellschaft nur erreichbar, wenn allein das Rechtssystem über Recht und Unrecht befindet und dies nicht außerdem noch abhängen kann von Stand oder Schicht, von Reichtum oder politischer Opportunität . . . Die unbestreitbaren gesellschaftlichen Auswirkungen des Rechts beruhen darauf, dass dies *im Rechtssystem* geschieht' (emphasis in the original).

[75] Sunstein and Ullmann-Margalit 2000: 187.

[76] Sunstein and Ullmann-Margalit 2000: 190.

[77] For definitions, see Scharpf 1997: 54–8.

[78] For more on the distinction between 'inner' and 'outer' institutions see Lachmann 1963; the distinction is also present in Scharpf 1997: 38, although the term is not used. For my own position see Engel 2001b: 3–5.

1.6   Addressees

Who can put this book to good use? There is some potential for second-ary uses. Chapter 2 might prove useful for social scientists who are interested in behavioural foundations. There are quite a number of synthesis reports dealing with these issues.[79] But this one might be interesting in that it is written from the perspective of institutional analysis. Chapter 3 adds to the rather small amount of literature on asymmetric prisoner's dilemma games. And chapters 4 and 5 may also be read as a contribution to the growing literature on the interaction between formal and informal institutions. For most institutional arrangements that prove instrumental for generating predictability combine inputs from both sources.

The book also, and more specifically, is part of a fairly recent move-ment that is involved in trying to flesh out the relationship between human behavioural dispositions and institutions. The bulk of this litera-ture is written by lawyers. Many of these authors either come from the law and economics tradition, or are in opposition to it.[80] This book differs from the mainstream in two respects. Its scope of observation is broader in that other formal and informal institutions are included. And chapters 2, 4 and 5 deliberately avoid rational choice analysis. Chapter 3, of course, employs a rational choice model. But here, the behavioural findings are restricted to just one variable, i.e. whether the actor is of a beneficial or a detrimental type. Here, the interest is thus not in being behaviourally informed, but in using the rational choice framework to understand the strategic implications of unpredictability.

This book, however, primarily addresses institutional analysts and institutional designers. Both are alerted to a frequently overlooked insti-tutional task: generating predictability for humans who are born with an extremely plastic mental apparatus. It is the taken-for-grantedness of this function that makes it so susceptible to neglect. Happily enough, our day-to-day experience as citizens is not one of pervasive chaos. We seem to live in a fairly ordered and hence predictable environment. This makes us free to direct most of our attention to the pursuit of our own interests, often in interaction with others who are doing this as well. Occasionally, decontextualisation makes the underlying predictability problem visible. If we then look back, or start comparing our environ-ment with other environments, we realise that the general illusion of

---

[79] See, for example, Conlisk 1996; Jolls et al. 1998; Selten 1998; Tirole 2002.
[80] For a characteristic contribution, see Sunstein 2000a.

predictability is generated by a dense network of formal and informal institutions.

Normally, if academics address the institutional designer, they are striving for social betterment. Why bother if the institutional framework is *grosso modo* in good shape? Part of the answer is offered in the section of this introduction on policy-making. Not so rarely, generating predictability is one of the true tasks of current institutional design. More importantly, however, this book wants to alert institutional designers to a likely side-effect of their intervention. They run the same risk as academic institutional analysts. They may confound their personal role as social actors with their professional role as detached observers of social phenomena. If they do, they are likely to overlook, or to underestimate, the role of existing institutions in generating predictability. When they redesign, the expected effect of social betterment may well be outweighed by the generated lack of predictability.

There are certainly various possible explanations for the failure of the market economy in most of Eastern Europe. But one interpretation is highly pertinent, and it can serve as an illustration for the normative claim of this book. When Westerners came to newly liberalised Eastern Europe – and most of them with the best intentions – they just transposed the set of formal institutions that worked well in their respective country of origin. They forgot, however, the dense network of institutional arrangements that provided predictability back home. And they were not aware of the entirely different arrangements that generated at least some predictability under communism. This is certainly not to say that Eastern Europe would have been better off by maintaining communism. But the example shows the need for much more modesty and prudence in attempts at fundamentally redesigning institutions. Such natural experiments can easily have devastating consequences if reformers do not provide predictability, be that before or while striving for social betterment.

Predictability is not only crucial in the transition from planned to market economy. Overlooking the effects on predictability generally is one of the prime perils of deregulation. The deregulation movement tends to see product regulation as a costly burden and as an unjustified limitation to firm inventiveness. Both are true. But product regulation also increases competitive pressure on every producer. It becomes more difficult for individual producers to define their niche. In the technical language of competition theory: monopolistic competition becomes less likely.[81] This effect is a result of increased predictability. Since

---

[81] The classic text is Chamberlin 1933.

consumers expect every producer to deliver the same quality, price elasticity of demand increases. If one producer raises prices, consumers are more likely to switch to a different provider. Put differently, there is thus a close link between predictability, generated by product regulation, and market organisation.[82]

One of the most popular targets of the deregulation movement is the dense regulation of the liberal professions. In countries like Germany, comparable regulation affects most crafts as well. Why not open these services up for unfettered innovativeness? Here the key problem is what economists call an information asymmetry. Most of these services are at best experience, if not trust goods. These terms mean that the consumer only learns after the fact whether he has spent his money well, and whether any collateral damage has occurred. Not so rarely, even after the fact there is at most suspicion. The consumer sees the unwanted outcome. But he may not be sure whether it has indeed been caused by poor service quality, or rather by some uncontrollable event from the environment. For instance, if the patient is still ill after she has seen the doctor, this may, but need not be the doctor's fault.[83] In our language, deregulating these rules thus generates a predictability problem for consumers. While before they had more reason to trust any provider, they must now fend for themselves.

Deregulation is more prominent currently than regulation. This is why predictability problems resulting from deregulation spring to mind first. But regulation can easily have the same negative effect. This is particularly likely if actors have previously co-ordinated expectations informally. Take the introduction of explicit, sporadic controls by management where behaviour had previously been monitored informally by peers. This intervention need not increase predictability. Some may indeed dread formal sanctions and become more rule-abiding. But others may perceive the new controls as a shift in regime. They may no longer feel morally obliged to play by the rules, but rather calculate the risk of being sanctioned.[84] If this is a realistic scenario, overall predictability decreases because of regulatory intervention.

---

[82] On the latter see Engel and Schweizer 2002.
[83] The seminal paper is Akerlof 1970.
[84] A related problem in voluntary contributions to the provision of public goods has been dubbed 'crowding out' by Frey and Jegen 2001.

2   The psychological predictability problem

2.1   Introduction

2.1.1   *Making predictability problems visible*

Epistemology teaches: he who wants to see everything will see nothing.[1] Understanding why it is so difficult to predict behaviour is no exception to this rule. Like a magnifying glass, theories make visible what is in their purview. But this greater visibility comes at a price. The fringe of the field of observation is blurred. Rational choice theory is a strong magnifier. It makes one class of predictability problems crystal clear. The theory allows for random preferences.[2] It demonstrates how interaction is nonetheless possible, with or without institutions. One can even interpret recent economic theory as concentrating more and more on the predictability problem. For information economics has assumed centre stage. Mechanism design demonstrates the conditions under which rational actors can overcome information asymmetries.[3] But when employing this magnifying glass, a large environment remains invisible. It assumes full rationality, of both the informed and the uninformed actor. Both possess well-behaved utility functions. They optimise anew from scratch, whenever new information comes up. Their computational capacities are unlimited.[4]

This part of the book uses a different magnifying glass. Many proponents of the approach on which this book draws tell a story of fact versus fiction. They criticise rational choice analysis for being purely

---

[1] See, for example, Albert 1978.
[2] In order not to be misunderstood: rational choice theory is full of strictures for the composition of individual utility functions. They have to be 'well-behaved', in order for the mechanics of the model to work smoothly. But the model takes individual preferences as a given. It is not interested in where they come from, and it allows individuals to be as idiosyncratic as they wish.
[3] For an overview, see Schweizer 1999.
[4] For a criticism of rational choice from these angles, see Gigerenzer et al. 1999: 8–12.

speculative. They contrast it with what they claim is a realistic approach.[5] The rhetoric of this criticism is epistemologically naïve. Perfect realism would imply a one-to-one description of reality. Even if that were technically feasible, it would not allow the observer to give the observed object any meaning. Without glasses, we at most receive useless sensual input. Or, to use a saying famous among economists: Assumptions may even be counterfactual, as long as they yield useful explanations or predictions.[6]

But if I stand at the shore and want to scan the horizon for arriving ships, an electron microscope is the wrong tool. Rhetoric aside, the critics of rational choice analysis do thus claim that this intellectual tool is inappropriate for understanding problems of social interaction. Or they pretend, less radically, that rational choice analysis makes many features of social interaction invisible. This book focuses on one of the areas left rather dark by rational choice analysis: the predictability problem resulting from behavioural dispositions.

2.1.2   A unified theory of the mind?

'Can behavioural economics generate a unitary theory of behaviour, or is it an unruly collection of effects?'[7] This sigh of one close observer of the field will be shared by most who begin studying behavioural dispositions. All the more so if they come from rational choice analysis. When first reading texts from psychology or behavioural economics, neoclassical economists suffer from a cultural clash. Yet some psychologists have made highly sophisticated attempts to generate unified theories.[8] Economists interested in deviations from the behavioural assumptions underlying their model have found highly systematic ways of integrating them into their thinking.[9] At closer sight, the apparent difference between rational choice analysis and behavioural approaches is thus rather one of strategy than of principle. To date, most behavioural researchers are more interested in the fit of their conceptual tools than in their

---

[5] From the present rich literature, see Hogarth and Reder 1986; Smith 1991, 1994; Camerer 1995; Conlisk 1996; Rabin 1998, 2002; Fehr and Falk 2002.

[6] Friedman 1953; see also Hammond 1990.

[7] Sunstein 2000c: 9.

[8] Currently, the three most prominent attempts are labelled ACT-R 5.0: Anderson et al. 2004; Soar: Newell 1990; Laird et al. 1991; Lehmann et al. 1998; and (with a somewhat narrower field of observation) EPIC: Meyer and Kieras 1997; for a stimulating earlier attempt, see Hebb 1949.

[9] The most systematic is Tirole 2002.

parsimony.[10] In line with this, most of these researchers are much more willing to accept a considerable plurality of concepts, and they are reluctant to define their field by one generally accepted paradigm.

This book takes an intermediate position. It is not interested in explaining an isolated effect. But neither does it need a grand theory. It must help the reader understand why the behavioural dispositions of humans generate a predictability problem. Not each and every behavioural effect outlined below is present in every practical instance of interaction. But there is hardly any instance where at least one of these effects is not present. Quite often many of them are combined.

Moreover the book wants to demonstrate how institutions are able to address the psychological predictability problem. Not all available or imaginable institutions will be able to address all sources of unpredictability at once. The picture drawn here must therefore be sufficiently detailed. But it must also enable us to see links between behavioural dispositions. For such links generate hypotheses about the performance of different institutions.

The following is thus an attempt to provide a systematically structured picture of findings from psychology and behavioural economics. It does not claim to offer a causal explanation for the position of each and every element within the overall picture. One might also characterise the approach by evoking a strategy used by many political scientists. They deliberately forgo the search for all-encompassing theories, and replace these with what they call theories of middle range.[11] In a similar vein, in the following presentation, multiple theoretical approaches are used. Given the research question of the book, they are usually not fleshed out in detail. It suffices for the present purposes if the reader gains a systematic understanding of the many behavioural reasons for low predictability.

2.1.3   Micro-nano-pico analysis

Economists routinely distinguish micro from macro analysis. While the former looks at individual interaction, the latter is interested in aggregates. A classic issue is the impact of inflation on the employment rate. For their purposes, political scientists often add a third, intermediate

---

[10] See Harless and Camerer 1994: 1285: 'the best theory depends on one's trade off between parsimony and fit'; and for an explicit treatment, see Elster 1989: 250: 'Ultimately, parsimony must take second place to realism'; for an application to legal policy, see Engel 2002a: 31–3.

[11] For a characteristic treatment, see Sil 2000.

Macro	Meso	Micro	Nano	Pico	Femto	Atto
		10^{-6}	10^{-9}	10^{-12}	10^{-15}	10^{-18}
Economics Political science						
			Psychology			
				Neurosciences		

Figure 2.1. Levels of analysis.

dimension, called the meso level. It looks in particular at corporate and collective non-state actors. Those who come from any of the above-mentioned backgrounds see behavioural analysis as decreasing the grain size even further than microeconomics or the analysis at the level of individual behaviour does. This is why the analysis that investigates where a certain behaviour mentally comes from is occasionally dubbed pico analysis.[12] Actually, this is bad mathematics. Mathematicians use the term micro for 10^{-6}. Pico is defined as 10^{-12}. The correct term for pushing the analysis just one level below micro analysis is thus nano. In mathematics it stands for 10^{-9}.

This may sound pedantic, since the terms are used metaphorically anyhow. But having a term for yet another level of analysis is helpful. The layer directly leading to behaviour may be called behavioural dispositions,[13] or the nano level. Below this is another layer, explaining how behavioural dispositions come into being, and how they play themselves out. This level can, by analogy, be called the pico level. And one can dig even deeper. There is a neurophysiological level and, inevitably, a molecular or an atomic one.[14] If one wishes to push the terminological metaphor that far, one might use the terms femto or 10^{-15}, and atto, or 10^{-18}, for the purpose. Figure 2.1 illustrates the approach.

Interaction partners ultimately are interested in behaviour. They are strongly interested in how behaviour is influenced by behavioural

---

[12] Tirole 2002: 652: 'I think we should go "pico" where we currently go "micro" '; I used the same term in Engel 2003a; we were both inspired by Ainslie 1992.
[13] The term is used in psychology, see e.g. Mischel and Shoda 1995: 246.
[14] See Mischel and Shoda 1995: 252; Anderson and Lebiere 2003: part 4.2 with refs.

dispositions. This is why this book focuses on the nano level. It takes a short, clarificatory look at the pico level, but does not dig deeper.

2.1.4   Actor constellations

What can Ego and Alter do individually to overcome the psychological predictability problem? When do they need institutional help? How can these institutions be designed? These are the questions this book intends to deal with. The answers depend on actor constellations.[15] The book starts by looking at a very simple actor constellation: one actor (Alter), one interaction partner (Ego), one instance, no outside effects.

2.2   The nano level

2.2.1   Introduction

What makes people behave as they do? On the most abstract level, it is the interaction of two elements: the situation and the behavioural dispositions of the actor.[16] Both elements can exhibit high or low variance. In some contexts, situations vary rapidly and in unexpected ways. Travelling across unfamiliar countries is a case in point.[17] This book looks at the other element, behavioural dispositions.[18] Their variability is what is meant by the psychological predictability problem.

Why is it that this element varies so visibly? This book looks only at the proximate cause, the plasticity of behavioural dispositions.[19]

---

[15] Scharpf 1997: 69 uses the term somewhat differently. He looks at game structures, and also includes what he calls 'interaction orientations'. The latter is placed here under the rubric of motivation; see below, 2.2.7.

[16] This distinction is in the focus of psychological research into personality. It frequently adds personal history as a third element. But analytically, this history has itself been the outcome of situation and behavioural dispositions interacting; see, for example, Bem 1972; Bem and Allen 1974; Mischel and Peake 1982; Mischel and Shoda 1995. See also 2.5.4.

[17] The situation itself does often result from human behaviour. This is different only if the situation consists of nature untouched, a rare event these days. But the distinction between behaviour and situation makes sense nonetheless. For the behaviour part should be narrowed down to the behaviour of the one actor with whom the interaction partner currently interacts.

[18] But see below, 2.5.3, on a behavioural theory of situations, and 4.3.8(e) on shaping situation, rather than behavioural dispositions, in the interest of making behaviour more predictable.

[19] A good alternative source for a systematic presentation of human behavioural dispositions is Antonides 1996. It is, however, not organised in reference to the predictability problem.

A good candidate for the remote cause is investigated by evolutionary psychology. These scholars claim that behavioural plasticity either is adaptive today, or was adaptive when the human genetic programs were hardwired.[20]

A proviso is in place. When compared with the behavioural construct underlying rational choice analysis, the *Homo oeconomicus*, the following sketches a picture of much greater variance and hence lesser predictability. But when considered in isolation, individual elements of the following picture can even be seen as generators of higher, not lower predictability. An example is what first made rational choice theorists interact with psychologists: the so-called biases, i.e. systematic deviations from the predictions of rational choice theory.[21] Some of them are not only widespread, but they have also been demonstrated to resist training. A case in point is the so-called hindsight bias.[22] Once people learn *ex post* that a risk has materialised, it is almost impossible for them to make a fair *ex ante* assessment of its likeliness.[23] If Ego holds this piece of generic knowledge, this allows him to make a fairly reliable prediction of Alter's behaviour. But most behavioural traits listed below are also individually generators of lower predictability, not only as part of a person's entire behavioural endowment.

Moreover, many mechanisms uncovered by experimental research are contextual.[24] For instance, psychologists have known for decades that operant conditioning affects humans, not just animals. If a certain reinforcer, over an extended period, appears closely enough connected to some kind of behaviour, the individual subconsciously learns the association and moulds his behaviour accordingly.[25] This piece of generic knowledge would, however, only help Ego in predicting Alter's behaviour if he also had the opportunity to observe the actor over a long period. Even if the effect itself is straightforward, exploiting it can thus entail information requirements that are almost impossible to meet.

The following is a systematic description of what makes human behaviour so malleable. The following elements have to be taken into consideration: the fact that humans possess a plurality of mental tools (2.2.2); the mechanisms playing themselves out in cognition (2.2.3) and judgement (2.2.4); the impact of memory (2.2.5) and learning (2.2.6);

---

[20] See Cosmides and Tooby 1992.
[21] For the time being, see, for example, Kahneman and Tversky 2000a; much more below.
[22] Rachlinski 2000.
[23] On attempts at 'debiasing', see Sanna and Schwarz 2003.
[24] Stephanie Kurzenhäuser pointed this out.
[25] See Anderson 2000b: chapters 3–4.

the role of motivation (2.2.7), emotions (2.2.8), and how everything listed so far impacts on choice (2.2.9). Finally, risk as a situational feature warrants special treatment (2.2.10).

2.2.2   Plurality of mental tools

The human mind is not a general purpose computer. My mind does not work the same way when grasping the coffee mug in front of me, driving to work in the morning, or designing my next article. While psychologists agree on this level of generality, there is lively controversy about the details. Dual process theorists claim that the human mind has two cabinets. The first, called system one, is a mixed bag of ready-made behavioural rules. I want some more coffee and grab the mug without further ado. The second cabinet, called system two, is reserved to conscious, elaborate mental action. I go a long way mentally before writing down the first sentence of my next article.[26] Others distinguish between a reflective and impulsive system. In their view, the borderline between the two systems is not watertight. There is the possibility of behaviour without previous reflection. But reflection is not thought to be free from impulses. Instead, reflection is modelled as tightly interacting with impulses.[27] Yet another group of scholars denies the special role of reflection. These researchers rather see the mind as an adaptive tool box.[28] Depending on the situation, people pick an appropriate tool from this box.[29]

In principle, this might be an ontological problem. Much in the same way as the computer industry offers task-specific central processing units, parts of the brain could be reserved for some tasks, and different regions for others. Mental mapping is indeed currently a hot issue in the neurosciences. But the evidence uncovered so far does not seem to point in this direction. To use the terminology introduced above, the link between parts of the brain and tasks seems to be at the pico, not at the nano level.[30] If this turns out to be true, we are in the realm of modelling. The question is not whether one of these approaches is false. What matters is how appropriate they are, given a research question.

---

[26] For a classic treatment, see Stanovich and West 2000; see the comments published thereafter for a critical discussion; see also Evans and Over 1997; Chaiken and Trope 1999; Bohner 2001.
[27] Strack and Deutsch 2002.
[28] This is the term used by Gigerenzer et al. 1999: 141 and *passim*.
[29] Other scholars from this school include Payne et al. 1988; Blais and Weber 2001.
[30] A fascinating analysis is provided by Anderson et al. 2004.

We are interested in the psychological predictability problem. For this purpose, there is no need to take sides in the dispute among psychologists. It is important, however, to understand the effects of the plurality of mental tools on predictability. More sharply: the predictability problem does not disappear if the apparent plurality of mental tools turns out to be an epiphenomenon of a single mental machine for judgement or decision-making.[31] This statement holds as long as an interaction partner has no chance to observe, or to second-guess, how this pico level mechanism works. Put differently, governing the reactions of mechanisms at the nano level from without is already difficult. For the nano level is not likely to play itself out directly at the micro level, i.e. in behaviour. But since the interaction partner can often observe behaviour, this may, in appropriate circumstances, allow him educated guesses about what happens at the nano level. Predicting mechanisms at the pico level from data at the micro level is, however, not likely to be successful in most cases.

Correctly identifying the mental tool used by Alter is of paramount importance for Ego. For the differences between these tools are huge. The degree of elaboration characteristic of the decision-making process is a first dimension on which these tools differ. There are radically simple tools. By employing rules for guiding and stopping search, they deliberately ignore most of the information available.[32] If they use more than a single cue, these cues are often organised in a lexicographic manner. The mind thus proceeds along a decision tree, and it never looks back.[33] That way decisions become quasi-automatic.[34]

Part of the dispute among psychologists concerns principle versus degree. Many feel models to be overly strict if they only allow for a distinction between automatic action and fully conscious and reflective behaviour. These critics rather see mental apparatuses as entailing different degrees of generality,[35] resulting in a continuum.[36] This approach seems plausible, since it would be inappropriate to classify habits and routines as either fully automatic or fully conscious and reflective.[37]

---

[31] This is indeed the position of Anderson et al. 2003.
[32] Gigerenzer et al. 1999: 4–5, 10, 16–17.
[33] Gigerenzer et al. 1999: 4, 81–2.
[34] On quasi-automaticity, all psychological schools agree: Stanovich and West 2000: 658; Bohner 2001: 242, 260; Strack and Deutsch 2002: 6; the observation dates back to James 1890; see also Bargh et al. 1996; consequently, economists see heuristics as deviations from optimisation: Tirole 2002: 640.
[35] Cosmides and Tooby 1992: 165.
[36] Newstead 2000.
[37] A standard text on routines is Ronis et al. 1989; for habit formation, interpreted as expertisation, see Anderson 2000a: chapter 9; research into routines has much older roots, see e.g. Bartlett 1932: 205; Weber 1976: 570.

The less elaborate the mental tool, the faster it usually works.[38] Since such simple tools demand little computational capacity,[39] they may also be expected to work reliably under suboptimal conditions,[40] i.e. if the individual can only muster few cognitive resources, or if information about the context is scarce.

The more that decision rules are ready-made, the more they also have to be domain specific.[41] It then is paramount for an interaction partner to get the interpretation of the situation just right.

The latter is an instance of a more general problem for interaction partners. If humans can appropriately be described as possessing many mental tools, Ego must predict which tool Alter will use in the situation at hand.[42] This is a multi-faceted problem. As of yet, even science is only beginning to learn how heuristics are selected.[43] Moreover, the ready-made solutions do not seem to be stored in memory in a consistent way. A new situation can thus simultaneously trigger problem solutions that point in different directions. They might even be contradictory.[44]

The individual also possesses the ability to change heuristics while making his decisions. He does so by editing, i.e. by selectively processing information available from the context.[45] An individual can, of course, deliberately switch from ready-made solutions to a more conscious and elaborate mode of judgement and decision-making.[46] The individual need not necessarily choose between different mental tools. He can also use them in parallel. Thus using one tool does not necessarily block access to competing mental tools.[47] This compounds the predictability problem. For the impulses generated by the different tools can be antagonistic.[48]

When institutional analysts look at the plurality of mental tools, they usually are attracted by biases.[49] The term means systematic deviations from some normative standard of judgement or decision-making. Biases

---

[38] This dimension is fleshed out by Newstead 2000: 690; see also Anderson et al. 2004: 1042.
[39] Stanovich and West 2000: 658.
[40] Strack and Deutsch 2002: 6.
[41] From the many voices, see Cosmides and Tooby 1992: 164–6, 178–80, 193–9; Cosmides and Tooby 1994: 328–9; Goldstein and Weber 1997: 585–91; Gigerenzer et al. 1999: 41.
[42] Payne et al. 1988: 184.
[43] Some very tentative comments are to be found in Gigerenzer et al. 1999: 32.
[44] Mantzavinos 2001: 24.
[45] Payne et al. 1988: 198.
[46] Kühberger 2000: 685.
[47] Stanovich and West 2000: 659; Strack and Deutsch 2002: 6.
[48] Strack and Deutsch 2002: 5–6, 13; see also Friedrich 2000: 672; Wilson, Lindsey and Schooler in Psychological Review 2000.
[49] See, for example, Sunstein 2000c: 3–5.

are to be distinguished from mere errors. The latter term characterises either occasional outliers, or mistakes that are wiped out in the aggregate.[50] Heuristics and biases are often mentioned simultaneously in the literature.[51] Yet they are not the same thing. To say that the human mind is biased is to make a statement about performance. To say that we use a heuristic is to make a statement about which mental tool is used. But there is some overlap. The use of ready-made, simple mental tools can result in the human mind deviating from norms. How much deviation is found obviously depends on the norm. Much of the controversy in the literature is about the appropriate norm. Those who compare actual human decision-making with the expectations derived from rational choice theory find many biases.[52] The opponents of this view point to the fact that human decisions are hardly ever taken in environments as stable and predictable as those assumed by rational choice theory. What looks like a bias in a rational choice perspective may be highly adaptive under less certain circumstances.[53]

Again, we need not take sides in that dispute. For we are interested not in rationality, however defined, but in predictability. If a deviation from rational choice theory is stable, behaviour remains as predictable as it would be for the textbook *Homo oeconomicus*. And indeed many biases have been found to be highly stable. The already-mentioned hindsight bias fits here. The patent evidence makes us grossly overestimate the *ex ante* likelihood.[54]

The hindsight bias is thus an instance where a bias does not create a predictability problem. But not all biases are of this kind. Others depend on context or personality. For instance, most people exhibit overoptimism. They see themselves as above average in almost all tasks. Obviously, if all people do, this cannot be true.[55] If there is some individual or social reason why we want people to assess their abilities correctly, this is a bias. Yet overoptimism can be trained away.[56] This is

[50] See, for example, Tversky and Kahneman in Science 1974; for summaries of the literature on biases, see Conlisk 1996: 670–1; Korobkin and Ulen 2000: 24; Stanovich and West 2000: 645–6.
[51] See, for example, the title of the influential book by Kahneman et al. 1982.
[52] This is basically the Kahneman and Tversky research programme. For summaries, see Kahneman et al. 1982; Kahneman and Tversky 2000b.
[53] The most prominent proponent of this idea is Gigerenzer; see Gigerenzer et al. 1999; Gigerenzer 2000a.
[54] Rachlinski 2000: 96–8; another example is known as the Allais paradox: people consistently value certainty much higher than a gamble with the same priors, but only an ounce of risk: Allais 1953.
[55] Miller and Ross 1975; Svenson 1981; Kaplan and Ruffle 2001; Brocas and Carillo 2002; for a treatment from the perspective of institutional design, see Farnsworth 2003.
[56] Jolls et al. 2000: 39.

visible in police officers or fire-fighters. If they are to survive, they have to learn which risks they should not take.

Since human beings possesses a variety of mental tools, a full account of behavioural dispositions would require that each of them be analysed separately. But this would not only go beyond the scope of this book. It would also demand more than psychology can give to date. The following is thus inevitably simplified.

On the most abstract level, any mental tool that leads to an observable reaction must at least possess the following four modules: input, elaboration, decision and output. Through one of his senses, the individual receives input from the environment. His mind elaborates on this input. It draws a consequence. This consequence translates itself into some action, involving the motoric system. Yet in simple (decision) heuristics, the intermediate steps collapse. Input directly yields output. A cue directly triggers behaviour. This is different in conscious decision-making. Here, all four steps remain distinguished. Cognition determines whether and how impulses from the environment are taken into consideration. The individual elaborates on them, bringing judgement about. He takes a conscious decision, called choice in psychology. Based on this choice, the individual generates an output, namely behaviour. Conscious choice thus has many more degrees of freedom than simple heuristics do. Each of these degrees of freedom generates a new predictability problem for interaction partners.

As reported, there is controversy among modellers about whether one should allow for intermediate mental tools, characterised by a degree of complexity somewhere between that of simple heuristics and that of fully reflective and conscious decision-making. The foregoing adds an additional argument to this debate. The intermediate tools could be understood as mechanisms exhibiting some, but not all degrees of freedom present in fully elaborate decision-making. But again, we need not decide the controversy. It is enough for our purposes to point out these additional degrees of freedom. This is done in the following sections, starting with cognition.

2.2.3   Cognition

Cognition consists of at least three elements: (a) attention, (b) perception and (c) elaboration. One might also add memory,[57] but this is treated further below.[58]

---

[57] Bohner 2001: 267 has all four elements in his model.
[58] See below 2.2.5.

(a) Attention   A music CD needs about the same storage space as 600–700 megabytes of data. Even with the most elaborate word processor, this is the equivalent of thousands of pages of text. Yet the playing time of the music CD is no more than some 70 minutes. Nobody is able to read or even peruse thousands of pages in such a short time. The example demonstrates that humans could not survive without ignoring most of the information available in their environment. Their attention is perforce limited and selective.[59] Moreover, all humans take thousands of decisions a day. Their minds would never be able to handle all this input by conscious reflection. Attention thus also serves a second purpose. It helps select issues that are important enough to be treated by a more elaborate mental tool.

Both are important for Ego. If he wants to predict behaviour, it is not enough to know which information is available to Alter. Ego must also predict whether Alter will take it into consideration. To the degree that outcome depends on which mental tool is used, Ego should also predict whether Alter is likely to process this information in a reflective manner. The latter is also important, since, as demonstrated, the degrees of freedom for Alter are greater in the latter case.

Understanding attention is the mission of a whole sub-field of psychology.[60] It must suffice here to point to the role of attention heuristics. Heuristics, or mental shortcuts, are thus not confined to decision-making. They can intervene at any point of the – otherwise – reflective reasoning. This is true for attention as well. By way of attention heuristics, the context has an impact on attention.[61] Attention heuristics make features from the environment salient.[62] A well-studied example is the availability heuristic. It links attention to memory. The individual pays greater attention to features of the environment it has encountered before, or it has understood well.[63] As with decision heuristics, what is adaptive in general can be inappropriate in specific instances. Concentrating all mental and physical resources on a risk to which one just has been alerted is often wise. But it is no longer beneficial if policy-makers exploit or even generate a scandal in order to divert attention away from much more problematic risks.[64]

---

[59] See Bohner 2001: 268; Gifford 2001.   [60] For an overview, see Pashler 1998.
[61] Goldstein and Weber 1997: 593, with refs.
[62] Goldstein and Weber 1997: 602, with refs; Hogarth et al. 1997: 259–60, with refs.
[63] The classic text on the availability heuristic is Kahneman and Tversky 1973. But it focuses on judgement, not on attention. The link to attention is present in Noll and Krier 2000: 344–5.
[64] Cass R. Sunstein takes this as a reason for promoting systematic cost–benefit analysis instead: Sunstein 2000b: 15–16.

(b) Perception If I do not become attentive, I ignore a piece of information entirely. That I pay attention, however, does not determine how I perceive the information.[65] Ego can by no means take it for granted that he and Alter perceive a given situation the same way. Put differently, bringing a piece of information to Alter's attention is not enough to make Alter's cognition predictable.

Again, the features of perception potentially causing a predictability problem cannot be exhausted here. Pointing to some of the most obvious must suffice. If the individual uses a simple decision heuristic, distinguishing attention from perception is not of great importance. Perception boils down to a pattern of activation. If the individual realises the cue to be present, the heuristic fires.[66] The less contextual the mental tool, however, the more pronounced the need for mentally representing the information from the environment.[67] In the interest of getting to the essence of an issue, the individual must literally abstract away from many features.[68] He must attempt to give the observations meaning.[69] Perceptual input must be linked to a semantic category.[70] In order to generate a representation, input from the environment and knowledge already stored in the actor's mind must interact. Representation is a hermeneutical task.[71] This inevitably adds an idiosyncratic element to representation. A possible psychological explanation can be found at the pico level. The specific knowledge stored in memory that is activated by the sensual input depends on both the base rate of activation and the activation rate in the near past.[72]

A particular technology of mental representation is called editing.[73] By way of editing, elements of the environment are not evaluated in isolation, but lumped together.[74] It makes a difference whether consumers see a purchase in isolation, or whether they prepare for a more extended consumption path. In the latter case, they would typically not

---

[65] As often, one may quarrel about terminology. If one defines perception as mere sensory input, it is a more general concept. Attention in this perspective is a technology for selecting some of this input for further mental processing. One could avoid this misunderstanding by talking here about representation. But this would generate another source of misunderstanding. It might make the reader feel that only conscious mental processes are considered.

[66] Strack and Deutsch 2002: 6.

[67] Anderson 2000a: chapter 8; Rachlin 2001: 10, 26.

[68] Goldstein and Weber 1997: 580.

[69] The link between cognition and meaning is the topic of Turner 2001.

[70] Strack and Deutsch 2002: 4–5.

[71] At this point, an old philosophical discussion and psychology are linked. A philosophical classic on hermeneutics is Dilthey 1923.

[72] For a formal treatment, see Anderson 2004: 1042–3; see also Strack and Deutsch 2002.

[73] Payne et al. 1997: 198.   [74] Simonson 2000: 735.

exclusively go for the item they prefer most. They would rather seek some variety.[75] Likewise, in isolated choices, the discount rate of typical individuals is high. They find possessing a good today much more attractive than getting it tomorrow. If, however, they see the purchase from a long-term perspective, the effect reverses. For most people prefer to be better off in later moments of life.[76] Most people even keep different 'mental accounts'. Whether a choice seems attractive or not depends on the account into which it is mentally booked. Saving $5 by a twenty-minute detour seems attractive, if the good in question costs $10. But it seems unattractive if the good costs $1,000. Likewise, an over-priced meal seems acceptable when on holiday, but outrageous in the canteen.[77] In order to predict Alter's behaviour correctly, Ego must not only second-guess whether the actor has had recourse to any of these forms of editing. He also has to know their precise delineation. He has to know, for instance, how many mental accounts the actor holds, which is their current balance, by which factor the actor evaluates the action at hand.

Moreover, the way that an evaluation is elicited has an impact on its contents. This has been well studied in connection with the distinction between choice and matching tasks. In a choice task, all parameters necessary for making the choice are given. From two or more options thus presented, subjects choose the one they prefer. They state, for instance, whether they want to buy good A at price X, or good B at price Y. In matching tasks, one element of information is missing. The individual, for instance, knows the price of good A, but not of good B. The subject is asked to state the appropriate price of B, given the price of A. If one has two groups, selected by the same criteria, the outcomes to these tasks differ markedly. In a choice task, individuals are willing to buy goods at a price they would not find appropriate in a matching task.[78] Such psychological findings do at least make prediction more demanding for an interaction partner. For he must possess the generic knowledge uncovered by psychologists. Moreover, how these generic effects play themselves out in concrete cases typically depends on context and on personality.

Editing can be seen as a particular instance of a more general phe-nomenon called framing.[79] Framing means that two alternatives are logically, but not transparently equivalent.[80] Preferences are thus not

---

[75] Simonson 2000: 735 and *passim.*   [76] Loewenstein and Prelec 2000.
[77] Thaler 1999; see also Heath 1995.   [78] Tversky et al. 2000.
[79] Such is the interpretation of Goldstein and Weber 1997: 582.
[80] I owe this definition to Heike Hennig-Schmidt; see also Conlisk 1996: 670: answers are sensitive to logically irrelevant changes in the questions.

invariant, but are susceptible to description and procedure.[81] In the elicitation process, they are often constructed, not merely revealed. These constructions are contingent on how the context frames the problem.[82] Cover stories matter.[83] The semantic context impacts on behaviour. A graphic example of framing-effects is contained in the following joke. A bishop comes to the Pope and asks: Is it allowed to smoke while praying? As one would expect, the Pope is shocked and rejects the idea. Some days later, another bishop approaches the Pope with the following question: Is it allowed to pray while smoking? What would you expect the Pope to answer?

How people perceive a problem is thus highly contingent on how it is presented to them.[84] Typically, this presentation serves as a reference point.[85] One such reference point has attracted particular attention. It makes a fundamental difference whether subjects perceive a change as a gain or as a loss. This is important, since avoiding a loss is a much stronger motivator than forgoing a gain.[86] If interaction partners know the effect, they can sometimes even exploit it. Suppose a firm wants to discourage clients from using credit cards. It can either promise them a bonus if they pay cash, or it can impose a penalty on them if they pay by card. Obviously this is nothing but two ways of framing the same choice. But the second frame is likely to have a much stronger effect.[87] Likewise, it should make a difference whether yoghurt is presented as 95 per cent fat free, or as containing 5 per cent fat.[88]

Moreover, adding logically irrelevant alternatives to the choice set can have an impact on choice. This is because of contrast effects. If the actor has to compare option A with option B, the implicit reference point is somewhere in between. If an alternative is added that is clearly less attractive than A, this can shift the reference point closer to A.[89]

Particularly powerful perceptual tools are anchors. They are used when an individual is faced with a quantitative task, like determining

---

[81] Slovic 1995.   [82] Tversky and Simonson 2000: 526.
[83] Goldstein and Weber 1997: 566 and *passim*; a graphic example is provided by Wagenaar 1997.
[84] Kahneman 2000c: xv.
[85] Loewenstein and Prelec 1992: part IV; see also Tirole 2002: 635–6.
[86] For a basic treatment, see Kahneman and Tversky 1979.
[87] McCaffery et al. 2000: 262.
[88] Kahneman et al. 2000c: 645; in the latter example, a second effect might contribute to the outcome. If the yoghurt is presented as (largely) fat-free, this resonates with a positive norm. If the yoghurt is presented as (substantially) fat, this may bring the respective negative norm into play. Indra Spiecker pointed me to this.
[89] A more elaborate treatment of contrast effects is to be found in Tversky and Simonson 2000.

the size of an object, or a percentage.[90] They have been demonstrated to
be highly robust against generic knowledge about the effect, admonition
and even longer training.[91]

Framing does not only result from how information is presented
to the actor. It also rests on how the actor himself constructs
reality.[92] Many individuals, for instance, have a tendency to view cases
in isolation, rather than to see them as part of a broader perspective.[93]
And the selection of frames tends to be self-serving. For instance,
anti-abortionists typically perceive themselves as 'pro-life', not as
'anti-choice'.[94]

Some of the examples have already pointed to the possibility that
Ego has of exploiting generic knowledge about framing. But even if
he relies on this knowledge, the contextual and the idiosyncratic elements of framing are pronounced. Even in this optimistic case, the information requirements are thus pronounced. This causes a predictability
problem.

In sociology, problems of perception are typically discussed under
a different heading. Constructivists claim that individuals do not have
direct access to reality. They can only make sense of their environment if
they rely on a specific conceptual framework.[95] Obviously, Ego and Alter
need not start the process of understanding from the same conceptual
background.[96] Ideas filter how reality is perceived.[97] This too generates
a significant predictability problem.[98]

Just as there are heuristics for attention, there are also heuristics
for perception. Those who have investigated them have mainly been
interested in deviations from rationality. They have thus looked for
perceptive biases.[99] They have found that humans are overly influenced
by vivid, but unrepresentative personal case evidence, and under-
influenced by more representative and diagnostic, but pallid statistical

---

[90] Chapman and Bornstein 1996; Strack and Mussweiler 1997; Chapman and
Johnson 1999.
[91] Mussweiler et al. 2000; Epley and Gilovich 2001.
[92] Kahneman 2000c: xiv.
[93] Kahneman and Lovallo 2000: 396–400.
[94] Quattrone and Tversky 2000: 461.
[95] For a classic treatment, see Berger and Luckmann 1967.
[96] Understanding the impact of this observation on policy-making is the intention of
cultural theory; for a classic treatment, see Thompson et al. 1990; my own position is
to be found in Engel 2001d.
[97] Singer 1993.
[98] The point has been made in psychology: Goldstein and Weber 1997: 600-1; in economics: Bohnet and Cooter 2001: 25, and Slembeck and Tyran 2002: 17; and in law:
Rostain 2000: 986.
[99] For an explicit treatment, see Sunstein 2000c: 3.

evidence.[100] Humans also have a tendency to see design and pattern in situations that are unpatterned, not designed, or just random.[101] And there is the confirmation bias.[102] Adam Smith graphically called it 'the misrepresentations of self-love'.[103] Problem definition is interest driven. People tend to see those problems which they can handle. They project their own opinions on others too often.[104] But none of this is more than a tendency. Even if Ego knows about the bias *in abstracto*, this does not thus allow him reliably to predict behaviour.

   (c) Elaboration   If an actor is to decide how to react to a situation, it often is not enough just to perceive it. The actor must also manipulate the information generated by perception. In so doing, the context, and how the actor has perceived it, play an important role.[105] Many have observed that humans fail to live up to the standards of rational choice theory on that account.[106] The deviations from the norms of statistics are particularly striking. Humans fail to understand co-variation. They make errors in updating probabilities on the basis of new information. They fail to recognise stochastic dominance. They fail to appreciate the law of large number effects. They mistake random data for patterned data and vice versa. And they misunderstand statistical independence.[107] When elaborating perceptions, humans frequently use approaches that deviate from statistical standards. In particular, they rely on analogies and associative clusters.[108]

   From the perspective of predictability, the picture is again ambivalent. Some deviations from rational choice standards are common. But they are not ubiquitous. Otherwise there could be no trained statisticians. And how actors actually elaborate the perceived information is not easy to assess. For there is more than one non-standard mechanism available. And within themselves these mechanisms are hard to calculate *ex ante*. This is obvious in the case of analogies. Which analogies the actor will draw largely depends on his personal previous experiences.

---

[100] Stanovich and West 2000: 647.   [101] Levinson 1995.
[102] Stanovich and West 2000: 645.
[103] Smith 1790: III.iv.12; see also III.iv.4: 'It is so disagreeable to think ill of ourselves, that we often purposely turn away our view from those circumstances which might render that judgement unfavourable.'
[104] Stanovich and West 2000: 650 speaks of a 'false consensus effect in opinion prediction'.
[105] Goldstein and Weber 1997: 593, with refs.
[106] The idea is prominent in the work of Herbert Simon; see e.g. Simon 1957; see also Gigerenzer et al. 1999: 10–14; Jolls et al. 2000: 14–15.
[107] Findings on all these shortcomings are reported in Conlisk 1996: 670.
[108] For a comprehensive treatment, see Gentner 2001.

Elaboration typically is not confined to the individual information unit. It rather consists of integrating these units into higher mental aggregates. There are many ways of conceptualising these aggregates. Stereotypes are even accessible in choices made using rigorously simple mental tools. If an element characteristic for the stereotype is found, the complete stereotype is automatically activated. This is also true if the individual uses a more elaborate mental tool.[109]

'Mental models' is a term often used in institutional analysis, and in economics more generally.[110] But it can also be introduced into psychological modelling.[111] It then characterises information aggregates that are conscious.[112]

The concept of schema lies somewhere between the concept of stereotypes and that of mental models.[113] If the individual uses a schema, he no longer simply reacts to a stimulus.[114] A schema is 'an active organisation of past reactions'.[115] Thereby, schemata are highly plastic. New information can simply be assimilated to them. A more elaborate option is tuning. In tuning, the new information is brought into the purview of an existing schema by readapting it. Finally, new information can induce the individual to construct an entirely new schema from this and other bits of information stored in the memory.[116] Tuning and construction are facilitated by the fact that schemata are interwoven, creating in the mind what one might call networks.[117] Comparing humans with instinct-driven animals thus reveals that a schema is a mental tool for freeing up the individual.[118] Given their complexity, it is obvious why schemata are particularly cumbersome for predicting the behaviour of an actor.

The concept of blending pushes the analysis of plasticity even further. It is meant to explain the cognitive foundations of human creativity.[119]

---

[109] Strack and Deutsch 2002: 23; see also Bargh et al. 1996: 230, with refs.

[110] A comprehensive account of the concept is to be found in Mantzavinos 2001: 65–82; see also Johnson-Laird 1989; Denzau and North 1994.

[111] See Gentner and Stevens 1983; Johnson-Laird 1983; Devetag 2000; more from http://www.tcd.ie/Psychology/Ruth_Byrne/mental_models/(25/10/2003).

[112] See also 4.3.3(a) for *shared* mental models as a way of making behaviour more predictable.

[113] For a basic treatment, see Bartlett 1932: chapter 10; see also the definition by Goldstein and Weber 1997: 598: 'We employ the notion of "schema" as an overarching or generic knowledge structure that provides the mental representation and organization of declarative information of all types.'

[114] Bartlett 1932: 200.

[115] Bartlett 1932: 201, 203.

[116] I owe this conceptualisation to Martin Beckenkamp.

[117] Bartlett 1932: 212.

[118] Bartlett 1932: 206.

[119] It thus provides the micro (or nano) foundations of a topic that is central to evolutionary economics; see Wegner 1996.

The essence of conceptual integration [i.e. blending] is its creation of a new mental assembly, a blend, that is identical with neither of its influences and not merely a correspondence between them and usually not even an additive combination of some of their features, but is instead a third conceptual space, a child space, a blended space, with new meaning. This new meaning is 'emergent' meaning, in the sense that it is not available in either of the influencing spaces but instead emerges in the blended space by means of blending those influencing spaces.[120]

Or shorter: blending is 'conceptual sex'.[121] Blending is necessarily selective.[122] It is a dynamic process[123] that runs at high speed.[124] The outcome is not predetermined.[125] As a result of this mental mechanism, it is likely that the individual changes his worldview in unexpected ways and at unexpected moments. Typically, this will have repercussions for future behaviour. The resulting predictability problem could not be more obvious.

2.2.4   Judgement

It is not easy to say where precisely perception and elaboration end, and where judgement begins. Nor is it easy to draw a strict line between judgement and motivation. This conceptual uncertainty is less bothersome if we remind ourselves that we are talking not about ontology, but about models.[126]

If one talks about judgement, this typically means one of two things. Firstly, one may be characterising a task. If that is the case, judgement tasks are typically distinguished from choice tasks.[127] An example would be the opinion most Catholics hold about priests being married, although they pursue different careers, and although they do not seriously consider converting to a different religion for that reason. Since this is a book about prediction, however, pure judgement tasks are not of interest. The distinction is nonetheless important if judgement and choice happen at two separate points of time.

Yet a second use of the term judgement is more important here. In accord with this use, judgement is the terminal point in a process of perception (and elaboration). Judgement is the mental step in which people integrate all the available, often conflicting, information

---

[120] Turner 2001: 17.
[121] Turner 2001: 140; one may also link this to the idea of competition leading to 'recombination', as developed by Schumpeter 1912: 100.
[122] Turner 2001: 19, 71, 81.   [123] Turner 2001: 19.
[124] Turner 2001: 65.   [125] Turner 2001: 74, 99–100.
[126] See above 2.1.1.   [127] Goldstein and Hogarth 1997: 4.

to forge an evaluation of the situation.[128] In so doing, the subjects often also normatively assess the situation, a potential outcome or their own conduct.

As we will see, the mechanisms for passing judgement are particularly rich. Judgement thus generates a pronounced predictability problem. Again, only the most important features can be highlighted here.[129]

First of all, there is more than one evaluation mode.[130] Alternatives can be evaluated jointly or separately.[131] They can be ranked before taking a judgement or not.[132] Judgement can be exclusively based on memory. Or it can be taken in direct interaction with the environment.[133] The judgement can content itself with classifying a prototype, or it can assess each member of a class of objects separately.[134] Likewise a representative moment can be constructed that stands for the entire outcome.[135] All this has been demonstrated to have an impact on the outcome.

More fundamentally even, there is rich evidence that judgement is directly linked to context, and to how context is perceived. A whole school of psychologists focuses on this contextuality. After their founder they are called Brunswikians.[136] Contextuality, for instance, means that valuation follows context,[137] and that people have adaptive expectations.[138] Of course, if Ego knows the context well, or if he is even in a position to shape context at will, this contextuality can ease the predictability problem. But for outsiders, the pronounced contextuality of behaviour generates a strong predictability problem.[139]

The prime mental tools for judgement are attitudes. Attitudes already have an impact on perception.[140] They can also generate behaviour automatically.[141] But they also enter into conscious judgement.[142] This

---

[128] See the definition in Goldstein and Hogarth 1997: 4.
[129] A succinct presentation, from which the degree of the predictability problem can be derived, is to be found in Goldstein and Hogarth 1997: 6–9.
[130] The point has often been made, see e.g. Hastie and Park 1997: 438; Gigerenzer et al. 1999: 54; Friedrich 2000: 672.
[131] Hsee 2000.
[132] Ofek et al. 2002.
[133] Hastie and Park 1997 call the latter 'on-line' judgement.
[134] Kahneman et al. 2000c: 650–1.
[135] Kahneman 2000a: 694.
[136] Comprehensive Brunswik 2001.
[137] Fischhoff 2000: 624–5 for instance demonstrates that two equally conducted surveys of general happiness yield almost diametrically opposite results if applied to different contexts.
[138] For a demonstration, see Smith 1988.
[139] Goldstein and Weber 1997: 593.
[140] Bohner 2001: 240.
[141] Bohner 2001: 242, 280; this is stressed by Fazio 1990, 2001.
[142] On the interaction between conscious and subconscious mechanisms in attitude formation and retrieval, see Betsch et al. 2001.

generates a predictability problem, since attitudes are not deterministic. 'An attitude is a psychological tendency that is expressed by evaluating a particular entity with some degree of favour or disfavour.'[143] An attitude is 'a summary evaluation of some object'.[144] 'Attitude names a complex psychological state or process which it is very hard to describe in more elementary psychological terms. It is . . . very largely a matter of feeling, or affect.'[145] It should therefore not come as a surprise that 'attitudinal ambivalence' is a frequent phenomenon.[146]

In judgement, heuristics play a particularly large role.[147] Subjects have recourse to mental shortcuts, even if judgement is part of deliberately choosing action. Judgement heuristics can thus be part of a more complex mental process relying on several mental tools. Frequently these heuristics are not aligned with the precepts of rational choice norms. Bias researchers have therefore been particularly interested in them. But they often are adaptive, in particular in uncertain environments.[148] Again, a number of examples must suffice.

When judging frequency and probability, people often rely on the availability heuristic. What they have seen or recalled recently is judged to be more frequent or probable.[149] Memory is thus used as a guide to judgement.[150] If the judgement object has multiple attributes, subjects often base their judgement on one of them exclusively. They scan the attributes for those that they think are characteristic for a stereotype. This implies that they neglect the remaining information and, in particular, the base rates.[151] People also tend to be overly confident in their own abilities.[152] The effect is corroborated by a frequent illusion of control.[153]

The already-mentioned prospect theory can also be brought under this rubric.[154] Depending on where they see the reference point, people

---

[143] Bohner 2001: 241; see also Kahneman et al. 2000c: 644.
[144] Bohner 2001: 241.
[145] Bartlett 1932: 206–7.
[146] Bohner 2001: 244–5 offers an illustrative example.
[147] For a recent overview, see Nisbett and Ross 1980: 17–42; Strack and Deutsch forthcoming.
[148] The general normative discussion on heuristics and biases does thus apply; see above 2.2.2.
[149] Tversky and Kahneman 1973; on normative criticisms, see e.g. Noll and Krier 2000: 331: miscalculation; Korobkin and Ulen 2000: 37–8: violation of Bayes' rule.
[150] Hastie and Park 1997: 435–6.
[151] Kahneman and Tversky 1972; Grether 1980, 1992; on base rate neglect, see also Kahneman and Lovallo 2000; if the base is a reference group, it sometimes is called reference group neglect; see e.g. Camerer and Lovallo 1999: 311.
[152] For a recent summary of literature, see Kahneman and Tversky 1995: 46–50.
[153] Langer 1975; Presson and Benassi 1996; see also Brocas and Carillo 2002.
[154] For a basic treatment, see Kahneman and Tversky 1979.

evaluate changes as gains or losses. Losses loom larger. In evaluating judgement objects, people are also influenced by self-esteem.[155] A good example is the false consensus effect. In one experiment, subjects were asked to walk around a university campus with a big signboard reading 'Repent'. Some agreed to do so, others declined. Later all subjects were asked how many they would expect to have agreed. Those who had agreed themselves said 62 per cent; those who had declined said 29 per cent.[156] More generally, judgement is influenced by emotions. This can cut both ways. For instance, if the subject expected a sad story, he may be angry if the story turns out to be hilarious. His anger may make him rate the experience negatively.[157]

Finally, heuristics can also help the individual apply multiple criteria to an evaluation object. They do so if these criteria are ranked in a lexicographic manner. This is, for instance, the case if a subject thinks: 'This medical procedure is quite painful, but it is short.' In that case, the primary criterion elicits a prototype, the evaluation of which serves as a baseline. The second criterion is seen as a relative movement, up or down with respect to this baseline.[158]

As with heuristics used for different purposes, the effect on predictability depends on two elements: how stable the heuristic is across situations and personalities; and how much additional information Ego needs to know that a particular heuristic cuts in.

2.2.5 Memory

The human mind tries to save cognitive capacity. A major tool for doing that is memory.[159] Ready-made decision rules are stored and recalled if the cue is present.[160] But memory also plays a key role if the individual uses more elaborate mental tools. It then taps the vast knowledge base contained in memory, and it retrieves heuristics for intermediate tasks. All this introduces an endogenous component into behaviour. Behaviour does not only respond to sensory input from the context. It can also be determined partly by preconfigured components stored in memory. The elements that are retrieved from memory depend upon their activation rate. The following elements have an impact on this rate:

---

[155] For self-esteem as a motivator, see below 2.2.7.   [156] Ross et al. 1977.
[157] More on the interrelationship between emotions and judgement from Strack and Deutsch forthcoming.
[158] The example is taken from Kahneman et al. 2000c: 654.
[159] From the rich literature, see, for example, Bartlett 1932; Weber et al. 1995; Anderson 2000a: chapters 6–7; Mullainathan 2002.
[160] Smith and Decoster 2000; Strack and Deutsch 2002: 5, 10.

the recency and frequency of usage; an associative component; the degree to which a chunk from memory matches current retrieval specifications; and a noise component, giving it an element of stochasticity.[161] If the individual retrieves not only factual knowledge, but also a decision rule, the latter typically only partly matches the task at hand. This causes additional variance.[162] If the individual attempts to recall a whole event from the past, the outcome is an imaginative reconstruction, not a one-to-one representation of the knowledge present previously.[163] Finally, there are close links between memory and attitudes,[164] resulting in a tendency to search memory for information that supports a view the individual wants to hold.[165] All this results in a severe predictability problem. It would not even be enough for Ego to know the observable history of Alter. He would also have to be informed about how Alter has stored bits and pieces from these experiences in his mind. And he would need knowledge about the factors influencing current retrieval.

2.2.6   Learning

Learning is one of the most disputed issues among psychologists.[166] Consequently, some sketchy remarks must suffice to illustrate the ensuing predictability problems.

Learning is important for predictability, since humans have a rich array of learning mechanisms at their disposal.[167] They share the learning tools of animals.[168] In classical conditioning, a stimulus directly causes behaviour. The proverbial Pavlovian dog produces saliva when the bell rings, even if this time it is not accompanied by food.[169] Put differently, classic conditioning is a way of building behaviourally relevant associations. This also holds for operant conditioning.[170] Like classical conditioning, it is a subconscious mechanism. But in operant conditioning, the link between the stimulus and the response is less direct. The subject learns about reinforcers. If learning has been effective, the

---

[161] Anderson and Lebiere 2003: part 4.2.   [162] Anderson et al. 2004: 1044.
[163] Bartlett 1932: 207.   [164] Bartlett 1932: 197–8.
[165] Babcock and Loewenstein 2000: 360.
[166] For an overview of the plurality, see http://tip.psychology.org/theories.html (8/2/2003); see also Anderson 2000b for a systematic presentation and Fudenberg and Levine 1998 and Brenner 1999 for (different) economic perspectives.
[167] In keeping with the organisation of this chapter, the following remarks are confined to the nano level. For models of what happens in learning at the pico level, see Hebb 1949: 181 in particular; Anderson 2000b: 30–6 and passim.
[168] For a comparative treatment, see Domjan 1998; Anderson 2000b.
[169] For an extensive treatment, see Domjan 1998: chapters 3–4; Anderson 2000b: chapter 2.
[170] It is sometimes also called instrumental conditioning.

presence of the stimulus makes the conditioned behaviour more likely.[171] Reinforcement need not affect the learning individual himself. It can be enough if the individual observes the reinforcer working on other individuals in comparable situations. More generally, learning can be social, i.e. by imitation.[172] And learning can be cognitive.[173] In the latter case, learning is a conscious mental exercise. Individuals can rely on learning heuristics for the purpose. They may, for instance, rely on the precepts of those whom they accept as experts. Or they can do the analysis themselves and store the result in memory. Finally, introspection can serve as a learning tool. This is, for instance, the case in a mechanism well studied by social psychologists, called the reduction of cognitive dissonance. An individual is forced by his environment to behave in some way. In the interest of preserving self-esteem, the individual comes to view his behaviour as aligned with what he always wanted. This reduction of cognitive dissonance can thus be interpreted as a tool for learning one's own wishes.[174]

Depending on the learning mechanism at work, the mental availability of the learning result and its robustness to external shocks differ largely. To give only one example: if the stimulus disappears, the conditioned behavioural trait fades away. If the individual has been thoroughly convinced that it is in his long-term interest to behave in some way, another behavioural trait can remain stable without stimulus or reinforcers over decades. It is thus not enough for Ego to observe a behavioural trait. If he wants to predict the actor's behaviour, he also needs to know how this trait came into being.

2.2.7 Motivation

What drives human judgement and decision-making? Economic models often assume it is money. They do so for good reason. For such a uniform, infinitely separable, easily exchangeable and storable currency makes their models much more tractable. This makes effects visible that would otherwise remain hidden. And market exchange demonstrates that the assumption is not far-fetched. On markets one indeed frequently meets profit maximisers. Yet even on markets, not all participants maximise profit. Some are content with their niche. Others grudgingly work for a living, but aim at subsistence, rather than maximisation. Profit

---

[171] Domjan 1998: chapters 5–10; Anderson 2000b: chapter 3.
[172] For a classic treatment, see Bandura 1977.
[173] On cognitive learning, see Krause 1991, 1992; Collins and Bradizza 2001.
[174] For a basic treatment, see Festinger 1957; I owe the link to learning mechanisms to Eva Jonas.

maximisation is even less of a guide outside markets. If Ego wants to predict behaviour, he must thus guess which motivational forces are at work in Alter's mind.[175]

They can be very basic, like appetite or instinct.[176] Humans can be driven by momentaneous impulses.[177] Even the overall goal is unclear. Is it indeed utility, or is it rather happiness?[178] Put differently: Are individuals after decision utility, as (implicitly) assumed by standard economics, or are they after experience utility?[179] Actually, things are even more complicated. For psychological research demonstrates that most subjects are not good at predicting what will make them happy later.[180] This apparent defect might actually be a very healthy mental mechanism. For it allows people to readjust their expectations to dire circumstances.[181] Happiness is thus an adaptive concept.[182] One could even see it as a mental immune system. Or as Adam Smith once put it: individuals have an interest in preserving a positive sentimental balance.[183] Accordingly, judgement and choice are not causally linked. When they try rationally to make a choice, humans are likely to mistake the assessment of current happiness for happiness at the moment of future consumption.[184] Moreover, happiness does not only result from the degree of pleasure. It also has a relative component. Humans compare their current pleasure with earlier experiences stored in memory. This can even yield perverse effects. If the individual once relished extraordinary pleasure, this can spoil agreeable, but less outstanding experiences in the future.[185] Even if Ego has been alerted to the difference between utility and happiness, he will have a hard time predicting how it will play itself out in concrete instances. For that presupposes knowing how well Alter has understood the difference, and how apt he is at parrying it while choosing.

A powerful competitor to utility as a motivator is self-esteem.[186] It can mean two different things. The individual can be driven by managing a

---

[175] There are many attempts to classify human desires. A well-known scheme is the one offered by Maslow 1954.
[176] Bartlett 1932: 212–13.
[177] Sunstein and Ullmann-Margalit 2000: 206.
[178] For more see Frey and Stutzer 2002.
[179] Kahneman and Snell 1997; Kahneman 2000b.
[180] Kahneman and Snell 1997: 393; Mccaffery 2000: 283.
[181] McCaffery 2000: 284.
[182] Kahneman 2000b: 686.
[183] Smith 1790: I.ii.V.3.
[184] Tversky and Griffin 2000: 721–2.
[185] Tversky and Griffin 2000: 709 and *passim*.
[186] From the many voices, see Bem 1967; Mischel and Shoda 1995: 252; Baumeister 1998; Brennan and Pettit 2000; Tirole 2002: 642–6.

self-concept.[187] Or the subject can seek social approval.[188] Adam Smith already fleshed out the links between the two concepts: 'We desire both to be respectable and to be respected. We dread both to be contemptible and to be contempted.'[189] 'The chief part of human happiness arises from the consciousness of being beloved.'[190] Yet 'man naturally desires, not only to be loved, but to be lovely; or to be that thing which is the natural and proper object of love.'[191] 'Self approbation' is the highest goal.[192] The 'jurisdiction of the man without' ranks below the 'jurisdiction of the man within'.[193] It presupposes that one is the observer of one's own action.[194]

Self-esteem plays itself out in many instances. It makes people strive to demonstrate their skills to others,[195] to save face,[196] to care for sunk cost[197] and to align their behaviour to custom.[198] Self-esteem does thus clearly matter. But it does not matter equally for all individuals. And it may play itself out in very different ways. Put differently: it compounds the predictability problem for Ego.

People do not care only about themselves. They also care about others. The weakest form of this is a desire for reciprocity.[199] It is the classic *do ut des*. Fairness is stronger.[200] This is quite apparent in the extensively studied ultimatum game.[201] In this game, two persons have to decide how to divide a fixed sum. The proposer is free to propose any division. The responder can accept or refuse. If he refuses, the bank keeps the money. If he accepts, the bank distributes according to the proposal. If both players were rational, as assumed by economic models, the proposer should make a highly asymmetric offer. Actually, in experiments proposers give the responders much more. But there are

---

[187] Hogarth et al. 1997: 246 speak of 'internal incentives'.
[188] More from Fehr and Falk 2002: 704–13; psychologists often call this impression management; for a basic treatment, see Tedeschi 1981.
[189] Smith 1790: I.iii.III.2.
[190] Smith 1790: I.ii.V.1; see also VI.i.3.
[191] Smith 1790: III.ii.1.
[192] Smith 1790: III.ii.3, III.vi.13.
[193] Smith 1790: III.ii.32.
[194] Smith 1790: III.i.6.
[195] Deci and Ryan 1985.
[196] Bohner 2001: 243 speaks of 'ego defence' more generally.
[197] Rachlin 2001: 5–6.
[198] Schlicht 1998: 2.
[199] From the growing literature, see Fehr and Tyran 1996: 69–70, 79–80; Fehr, Gaechter and Kirchsteiger 1997; Fehr and Falk 2002: 689–704.
[200] From the rich literature, see Kahneman 1986; Smith 1994: 124–6; Young 1994; Fehr and Tyran 1996; Fehr and Schmidt 1999, 2000; Farnsworth 2001.
[201] The game was invented by Güth et al. 1982.

differences among individuals. And there are pronounced differences among cultures.[202]

Fairness considerations can also explain why many are willing to defend a commons, like a communal pasture or a fishing ground, against free-riders.[203] This is not rational in the economic sense. For each peasant or fisherman does best individually if he exploits the commons to the maximum degree individually possible. In terms of game theory, a commons thus has the character of a prisoner's dilemma.[204] Even worse, the original prisoner's dilemma repeats itself at the implementation stage. This is why, in a world of hard-nosed rationalists, agreeing on a regime for the exploitation of the commons would be useless. For such an agreement must be policed. Yet if one contracting partner sees to it that the other partners keep their promises, this is to the advantage of all partners. By agreeing to joint provision, the social dilemma does not change for rational actors.[205] Happily enough, though, in reality it often has. This is because of empirically quite pronounced punitive sentiments.[206] But they are, of course, not present in all individuals. And they hinge upon how individuals represent the situation mentally. For instance, it makes a difference whether they treat the case as one of contract, rather than of order.[207]

Predictions based on fairness considerations are also risky, because there is more than one fairness norm. Is it fair to distribute according to outcome, to effort or to needs?[208] Not surprisingly, empirical fairness concepts echo the philosophical discussions on distributive justice.[209] And they are tilted by individual position. Those who stand to gain the most from one fairness concept do not only tend to adhere to it. They often also, in all honesty, think it to be the only sensible one.[210] The least Ego must know is how Alter perceives himself if he wants to predict his personal fairness concepts. And there is, of course, additional variance among individuals.

---

[202] A stimulating account of the evidence across cultures is to be found in Henrich and Boyd 2001.
[203] Ample material is provided by Ostrom 1990.
[204] For a classic treatment, see Hardin 1968.
[205] Scharpf 1997: 117.
[206] Hirshleifer 1987; Fehr and Tyran 1996: 79; Schlicht 1998: 137; Fehr 2000; Kahneman et al. 2000b: 328–9; Carpenter 2002: Price et al. 2002.
[207] Those interested in the difference speak of deontic reasoning; see Cosmides and Tooby 1992: 193–206 (on cheater detection mechanisms).
[208] Babcock and Loewenstein 2000: 357.
[209] For a precise treatment, see Kersting 1997.
[210] Wade-Benzoni et al. 1996; Babcock and Loewenstein 2000: 366.

Fairness is a conditional concept. It seems fair to treat another person in a non-egoistic way, since he deserves it. He has done me a favour earlier. I expect to do him a favour in the future. We are both part of a social setting where such behaviour is mutually expected. But there is also true, unconditional altruism in the world.[211] Distinguishing it from conditional fairness, reciprocity or mere error is, however, often hard to do, generating yet another predictability problem.[212]

Empirically, people do not only care for others in a benevolent sense. They also are sensitive to a relative position when they assess their own wishes.[213] This makes them care for status, and it can make them envious.[214] But not all people do care for these things, let alone in each and every situation.

Reciprocity, fairness, altruism and envy are all instances of simple give or take. Human interaction is often of a more complex nature. It is embedded in rich environments. Which action the actor feels compelled to take depends on how he interprets this situation. The more complex the situation, the more closely cognition and motivation are thus intertwined. This explains why ideas cut both ways. They do not only give the individual a tool for understanding the situation. They often also urge him to take some action. Ideas do thus matter, and they are not the same as interests.[215] They can take the form of religious beliefs or ideologies.[216] More generally, the multiplicity of fundamental social value orientations plays itself out.[217] Related to this is the observation that people care not only about utility, but also about an identity.[218] The identity can change with context. Sociology then talks about roles.[219] Again, predictability problems abound. To which ideas has the actor been exposed in the past? How strongly does he feel about

---

[211] See only Simon 1993; Stark 1995; Gérard-Varet et al. 2000; Harbaugh and Krause 2000; Charness and Haruvy 2002.

[212] Anderson et al. 1998.

[213] The point has been stressed by Frank 1985; Tirole 2002: 635 speaks of 'flow utility [that] may depend on the consumption of other individuals'.

[214] On envy, see, for example, Mui 1995.

[215] The point has been independently made by Vanberg and Buchanan 1989; Yee 1996.

[216] For a stimulating treatment of ideology, see North 1981: chapter 5.

[217] For a psychological treatment, see Liebrand and McClintock 1988; Fiske 1991: chapter 16; from sociology, see, for example, Thompson et al. 1990.

[218] For a psychological view, see Turner 2001: 116; this is an old topic of philosophy, see e.g. Jakobs 1999. There is a link between self-esteem and identity. But both concepts focus on different aspects. Identity is by definition social. If one looks at self-esteem, 'other-esteem' is one source of it. In self-esteem, the social dimension is thus not necessarily constitutive, or at least only indirectly, in that the individual might need (social) communication to obtain a benchmark for self-assessment.

[219] See, for example, Linton 1945; Parsons 1951; Goffman 1956.

them? Is he firmly embedded in one single identity, or does he play several roles? If the latter, which role is he likely to play in the concrete instance?

The rational choice model assumes that more is always better. Actors are, of course, modelled as optimisers. But they are only willing to accept less than the maximum, since getting one good has an opportunity cost. Consequently, the individual must implicitly pay by getting less of another, equally desired good. And rational choice models typically include the idea of diminishing returns. Having ten items of a good is typically seen to be less valuable than having the very first item. Psychological research makes it more likely that for many goods individuals hold bliss points. There is a most desirable quantity, and more is less, irrespective of any opportunity cost.[220] If so, Ego faces yet another predictability problem. He ought to know where exactly Alter's bliss point is, and how quickly the good is depreciated if it falls below or goes beyond this point.

People do not only have wishes for goods or services. They also care about consistency,[221] coherence,[222] regularity,[223] clarity[224] and, of course, predictability itself.[225] But they are also driven by curiosity,[226] resulting in a preference for variety,[227] and occasionally even unpredictability.[228] To arrive at correct predictions, Ego must therefore find out whether Alter feels any of these urges and, if so, how strongly they intervene in his wishes for goods, services or identity.

Related to this is the observation that people do not seek only outcomes, but also ways to achieve them. There are thus independent preferences for institutions.[229] If Ego wants to predict Alter's behaviour, he can thus not confine himself to an estimation of Alter's ultimate goals. He must also understand how strongly Alter values specific procedures.

To sum up, individuals are torn between competing motivational forces.[230] The forces sometimes are even contradictory.[231] Hence it

---

[220] Allison 1989.   [221] Ofek 2002; Strack and Deutsch 2002: 8.
[222] Schlicht 1998: 21.   [223] Schlicht 1998: 21.
[224] Schlicht 1998: 2, 79 and *passim*.
[225] Kiesler 1973.
[226] Turner 2001: 102 points this out.
[227] Simonson 2000: 736–8.
[228] Kiesler 1973: 354.
[229] This observation is prominent in the work of Bruno Frey; see Frey 1999a: 25, 38, 153, 165–72; Frey and Stutzer 2001; Benz et al. 2002; see also Lind and Tyler 1988; Tyler 1997; Hayashi et al. 1999; Benz and Stutzer 2002; Coglianese 2002; and see Dalton 1996: 340–1 with refs. from the discussion in political science.
[230] Mischel and Shoda 1995: 252; Conlisk 1996: 677; for a formal treatment, see Güth and Kliemt 2003: part 6.1.4.
[231] Tirole 2002: 636 with an example.

often is not possible to reconstruct motivation from observed behaviour.[232] Moreover, the individual motivating forces change over time.[233] All this makes prediction a hazardous enterprise.

2.2.8 Emotions

Humans are often not rational, but emotional. In David Hume's famous words: 'Reason is and ought only to be, the slave of the passions.'[234] Men are tempted[235] and sometimes become addicted.[236] They can be full of fear and panic. And they can be driven by spite and enmity.[237]

But emotions do more. They are not only motivators; they can interfere with all mental processes.[238] They can alert the individual to a situation and thereby work as an attention heuristic.[239] They can guide perception in that they make the individual focus on some elements of the environment.[240] In other instances, the individual's judgement is guided by emotion.[241] They improve elaboration and thus learning, and they influence which information is retrieved from memory.

For a long time, moralists have taught that taming passion is the true problem.[242] But it is not as simple as that. Not only are emotions highly useful, as demonstrated. They also can make behaviour more, not less predictable. To use an obvious example: if I know that the actor suffers from some phobia, it can be quite easy for me to predict what he will do next. But on average, it is true, it will not be easy to estimate which mixture of emotions will interact in which way with the mental tools of the actor.

---

[232] Tirole 2002: 637.
[233] Kahneman and Snell 1997.
[234] Hume 1739: II.iii.3; see also Frank 1988.
[235] On the antagonistic force of temptation, see Strack and Deutsch 2002: 5–6.
[236] On addiction, see e.g. Fehr and Zych 1998; Korobkin and Ulen 2000: 1113–19; Strack and Deutsch 2002: 28.
[237] See, for example, Handerich 1985; Farnsworth 2002; Falk et al. 2003.
[238] Elster 1998; Hermalin and Isen 1999; Kaufman 1999; Hsee et al. 2003; a good overview is provided by Hanoch 2002.
[239] Hanoch 2002: part 5.1.
[240] Hanoch 2002: part 6.
[241] Strack and Deutsch forthcoming: part 6.1.1; see also Bartlett 1932: 206–7 on the interaction between attitudes and emotions; and Schlicht 1998: 3: 'custom arises from the intermeshing of behavioural, emotional, and cognitive elements'.
[242] See, for example, Smith 1790: III.iv.12, III.iv.4; see also Sunstein 2000b: 8, who recommends cost–benefit analysis as a remedy.

2.2.9   Choice

Not all mental activity leads to action. The individual hesitates. He cannot make up his mind. He does not think the time is ripe. Something else is more urgent. His attention is diverted. He forgets his original intention. Or he never wanted more than to consider a proposition. But often, central input does indeed generate an output. In that case the individual must make a choice.

Humans have a rich array of mental tools for that purpose.[243] Some of them are entirely subconscious. Like animals, humans have reflexes.[244] The ideo-motor principle means that behaviour may be elicited by the mere presence of a cue.[245] Basic needs, like thirst or hunger, may drive a person to act against his own better judgement. An often-cited example is a shipwrecked person drinking salt water.[246] People can subconsciously imitate what others do.[247]

Moreover, decision-making is often guided by heuristics. Parsimonious decision rules fit choice tasks particularly well. For choices usually are to be taken under time constraints. Often, at least some degree of uncertainty is also present.[248] There are many choice heuristics. People, for instance, follow a custom,[249] or they trust another person's advice.[250] They can also rely on an automated routine.[251] If this is opted for, the original decision was fully conscious. But the conscious decision process is not repeated. The individual may even have become unable to recall the original learning process.

Even if the decision-making process is otherwise deliberate, the individual can use mental shortcuts in between. He can, for instance, rely on stereotypes,[252] or on schemata.[253] Yet another option is associations. If the individual relies on them, he does not actively guide the process of deliberation by following a well-defined procedure.[254]

---

[243] A systematic overview is provided by Goldstein and Weber 1997: 594; Weber and Lindemann 2002.

[244] Strack and Deutsch 2002: 3.

[245] James 1890.

[246] Strack and Deutsch 2002: 3.

[247] Strack and Deutsch 2002: 3.

[248] Gigerenzer et al. 1999: 164.

[249] Schlicht 1998: 12.

[250] Ripperger 1998: 258.

[251] Strack and Deutsch 2002: 21; more on routines above at 2.2.2.

[252] Goldstein and Weber 1997: 594–5; more on stereotypes above at 2.2.3(c) and 2.2.4.

[253] Bartlett 1932: 206, 208; Goldstein and Weber 1997: 598–9; more on schemata above at 2.2.3(c).

[254] Goldstein and Weber 1997: 595; for a formal treatment, see Busemeyer and Townsend 1993.

Even if humans engage in 'rational' decision-making, this differs from the precepts of rationality theory in the social sciences. They have discernible intentions.[255] They can also engage in analytic reasoning.[256] But the process is adapted to the rapidly changing world that humans populate.[257] It is rational, given the limitations of the human mind.[258]

When humans deliberate about choice, they want to solve problems.[259] They limit the information taken into account, as well as the solutions considered. Defining the problem is itself a wilful act.[260] The deliberation process is terminated once the aspiration level of the individual has been satisfied.[261]

Most of the time, humans are satisficers, but not always. They sometimes do indeed tally pros and cons carefully.[262] In the end, however, they typically do not use any of the norms taught in the social sciences. They rather engage in what has been dubbed 'reason-based choice'.[263] They want to convince themselves, perhaps also outsiders, that they made a reasonable choice.[264] They thus pick reasons[265] as the context seems to dictate.[266] Again, a self-serving bias is present.[267] And the richer the context, the more reasons the individual has at his disposal.[268]

One frequent technique employed when taking decisions consists of constructing plausible narratives.[269] Individuals begin the decision-making process by constructing a causal model to explain the available facts.[270] The individuals are more convinced the more coherent this story sounds.[271] If they are able to make up several stories, individuals decide by judging which of them sounds best.[272] Individuals do thus link choice with an attempt to give the evidence 'meaning'.[273] Decision-making turns out to be the 'backward invention of the story'.[274]

---

[255] Strack and Deutsch 2002: 14.   [256] Goldstein and Weber 1997: 596.
[257] Evans and Over 1997: 406 and *passim*.   [258] Stanovich and West 2000: 648–9.
[259] Newell and Simon 1972.
[260] More from Mantzavinos 2001: 7–8 and *passim*.
[261] For a definition of the famous concept of satisficing, see Simon 1990: 9; see also Gigerenzer et al. 1999: 351 on the origin of aspiration levels.
[262] Goldstein and Weber 1997: 586.
[263] Shafir et al. 2000.
[264] Pennington and Hastie 1993, 1997.
[265] Goldstein and Weber 1997: 592.
[266] Evans 1993: 19.
[267] Babcock and Loewenstein 2000: 360.
[268] Goldstein and Weber 1997: 592.
[269] Pennington and Hastie 1997; Dawes 1999.
[270] Pennington and Hastie 1997: 454.   [271] Pennington and Hastie 1997: 455.
[272] Pennington and Hastie 1997: 474.   [273] Pennington and Hastie 1997: 468.
[274] Turner 2001: 112.

Some of these decision modes are highly predictable in and of themselves. If I hit your knee at the right point, your leg will go up.[275] If it does not, I know you are ill. But most other decision modes do already engender a pronounced predictability problem in isolation. Which reasons will the actor be able to contrive? Which one is likely to gain the upper hand mentally? These isolated predictability challenges are compounded by the observer's need to imagine which decision mode will be selected by the actor. Thus far, psychology has been able to do no more than indicate some of the factors influencing that selection. If incentives rise, individuals tend to work harder on their choices, but they do not necessarily become smarter.[276] For incentives basically work by focusing attention and prolonging deliberation.[277] The expected liability to error and the need to justify the decision work into the same direction.[278] Negative affect also has a role to play. It signals to the individual that the issue is serious, and it makes him increase his cognitive effort. Positive affect, on the contrary, signals that everything is fine, and it induces the individual to lower his decision-making effort.[279] But the choice among decision modes is also adaptive.[280] It thus partly depends on the decision-maker's expertise in the specific field. The greater this experience, the richer the set of available decision modes. In particular, experience can enable the individual to decide by category or schema.[281] Other decision modes need more time. If time is scarce, it becomes particularly unlikely that individuals will construct narratives.[282]

2.2.10 Behaviour under perceived risk

In a way, all life is uncertain. This explains why it has not been possible to avoid occasional allusions to behaviour under uncertainty in earlier sections. All the more so, since a growing school in psychology postulates that understanding all human mental tools should start from that assumption.[283] Yet many psychological observations focus specifically

---

[275] Depending on how narrowly one defines a decision, one might even say that a reflex is not a decision at all. It is integrated here, since it still involves an output by the individual to an input from the environment.
[276] Payne et al. 1997: 200.
[277] Tversky and Kahneman 2000: 222.
[278] Payne et al. 1997: 182.
[279] Strack and Deutsch forthcoming: part 6.1.1.
[280] Payne et al. 1988.
[281] Goldstein and Weber 1997: 598–9.
[282] Goldstein and Weber 1997: 599–600.
[283] See again Gigerenzer 1999; Brunswik et al. 2001; Glimcher 2003; more above at 2.2.2.

on decisions under risk and uncertainty. Another way of characterising this class of observations is that they look at decisions under perceived risk.[284] For our topic this implies that Ego ought to know whether Alter sees himself as facing a risky choice. If so, Ego must not only be aware of the psychological implications. He also ought to predict correctly how they will play themselves out in the instance.

If we freeze in front of the proverbial snake, a very simple heuristic is at work: snakes are dangerous and irascible: don't move. If the others jump into the lake, I follow. Instead of calculating depth, temperature and hostile fish, I just imitate.[285] If I drive to work by car, I do not check death statistics and weigh the ensuing risk for life and limb against the loss of time and comfort involved in taking the tram. I just follow my routine.

But not all risky choices are taken by using ready-made, issue-specific mental tools. If not, all the mental steps laid out above have their own specific features for choices under risk. Does the individual see the risk component involved in the concrete choice? Is he attentive to this risk at all? Typically not. Ironically, we succeed in living in a world full of risks by ignoring most of them most of the time. This explains why we tend to overreact if an event, or a mere hype in the media, brings a risk to the forefront of our attention.[286]

Risk perception deviates from the normative standards of the social sciences in quite a number of degrees. It is highly sensitive to representation. For instance, untrained people are poor statisticians if the evidence is presented to them in the way statisticians are used to it, i.e. in the form of percentages and probabilities. They are, however, significantly better at handling the evidence if it is presented in the form of natural frequencies instead.[287] More generally, people typically attach subjective probabilities to events. In so doing, they often ignore base rates, and they typically give insufficient weight to the size and the representativeness of the sample. But they overestimate information that is easy to retrieve from memory, and vivid information more generally.[288] People usually do not update expectations as statisticians would when new

---

[284] A classic is Kahneman et al. 1982; see also Frey 1999a: 195–211.

[285] Admittedly, a fully rational individual might do the same. He might take the fact that the other individual is willing to jump as a credible signal of how this first individual assesses the danger of doing so. Indra Spiecker pointed me to this. Yet in actual fact such a fully rational calculation is not very likely in such choices.

[286] This phenomenon has attracted more scientific interest in sociology, see e.g. Japp 2002; Schulte 2002; see also Sunstein 1996: 266; Noll and Krier 2000: 331, linking the observation to the availability heuristic.

[287] Hoffrage et al. 2002.   [288] Evans 1993: 9.

information becomes available.[289] They draw a distinction between the perception of identifiable versus statistical risks.[290] And they perceive risks differently if they are voluntary, as opposed to being imposed on them.[291]

The latter elements also enter into the decision about whether a risk is worth taking. Such judgement is highly sensitive to reference points. People dislike suffering a loss much more than they regret a forgone opportunity. This is the basic tenet of prospect theory.[292] But the status quo is not the only possible reference point.[293] People are prepared to accept almost any (quantitative) information they take from the context as an anchor.[294]

It is rational to value future consumption less than present consumption. For in a world of scarcity, waiting until later entails an opportunity cost. For a profit-maximising individual, the discount rate is identical to the interest rate on capital markets.[295] Empirically, however, the discount rates of most individuals are hyperbolic. People value consumption now much higher than consumption in an hour. Consumption today is valued much more than consumption tomorrow. Yet, consumption anywhere this week is already not so sharply preferred to consumption next week. The larger the distance in time, the less pronounced the difference in valuation.[296]

Not all individuals value risk alike. Rational choice theorists speak about risk preferences. They typically assume subjects to have a risk preference that is constant across issues. They are thought to be either risk loving, risk averse or risk neutral, whatever the risk they face. Empirically, however, there is variance in respect to the type and degree of the risk.[297]

Risk assessment is often driven by emotion, rather than calculation.[298] In line with this, people tend to be overly optimistic. They see themselves as less prone to risk than the average citizen.[299] This can be interpreted as a mechanism for preserving self-approbation.[300]

[289] Noll and Krier 2000: 329.
[290] Noll and Krier 2000: 327.
[291] Noll and Krier 2000: 328.
[292] See again Kahneman and Tversky 1979.
[293] More from Kahneman 1992.
[294] Tversky and Kahneman 1974; Wilson et al. 1996.
[295] This is a standard approach in resource economics, see e.g. Ströbele 1987.
[296] Ainslie 1992; Loewenstein and Prelec 1992; Laibson 1997.
[297] Kahneman 2000c: xii.
[298] Loewenstein et al. 2001.
[299] See again Miller and Ross 1975; Svenson 1981; Kaplan and Ruffle 2001; Brocas and Carillo 2002.
[300] On self-approbation as a motivator, see above at 2.2.7.

Economists conceptually distinguish risk from uncertainty. In the former case, both the problem space and probabilities are known. If one also knows the individual risk preference, the decision can be calculated. In the case of uncertainty, probabilities are not known. A rational decision-maker must then find other criteria on which to base his decision. One option is to have recourse in his subjective expectations.[301] Yet in reality, the problem space is often not well defined.[302] Economists then often speak of decisions under ignorance.[303] To a degree, human decision-makers can again step in with what they expect to be the problem space. But there are limits to such educated guesses.[304] Psychologically, it therefore makes a pronounced difference whether the individual sees the choice as one under risk or under ignorance. In the latter case, a random element is introduced into choice. It becomes paramount for the individual to justify his choice to himself, perhaps also to others.[305] Individuals switch to reason-based choice and they pick whatever argument seems to support their intuitions and to allow them to ignore conflicting arguments.[306]

If the actor is likely to see himself in a situation of risk or even ignorance, the predictability problem for Ego is thus compounded. He would have to know how Alter does indeed see the situation, and he must second-guess at which point one of the mechanisms just described cuts in.

2.3   The nano/micro divide

Our presentation of the psychological predictability problem has started with remarks on the conceptual status of the observations. They are not ontological, but models, offering ways to organise the empirical evidence. But in modelling, it seems appropriate to distinguish a micro and a nano level. Behaviour is not causally linked to behavioural dispositions.

In the psychological literature, one element of this nano/micro divide has attracted particular attention. Originally, psychologists were

---

[301] The classic source is Knight 1921; on subjective probabilities, see Savage 1954; for an alternative approach, allowing for ambiguity, see Schmeidler 1989; Eichberger et al. 2003.

[302] The point is prominently made by Shackle 1992; Langlois 1986: 228 calls this 'structural uncertainty', as opposed to mere 'parametric uncertainty'.

[303] Another way of conceptualising these tasks has them as decisions in a situation of which the actors are partly unaware: Dekel et al. 1998; Heifetz et al. 2003.

[304] Another option is precautionary. The individual focuses on avoiding what he expects to be the worst imaginable outcomes. Technically speaking, he then follows a maximin strategy.

[305] Hogarth and Kunreuther 1997: 484, with refs.

[306] Hogarth and Kunreuther 1997: 504.

surprised that attitudes quite often do not determine behaviour.[307] Having been through our analysis of the predictability problem, this should not come as a surprise. Behaviour can be entirely automatic, meaning that attitudes have no opportunity to play themselves out.[308] Competing, stronger motivators, like addiction, can outperform attitudes.[309] The individual may have used a narrative mode of decision-making to build up a competing causal story, and so on.[310]

Obviously the distinction between attitude and behaviour is a specific instance of the more general difference between behaviour and behavioural dispositions. It stems from the plurality of mental tools, and from the richness of many of these tools once the individual has opted for them.

2.4   The pico level

Digging deeper is another story. In all likelihood, at the pico level one does not arrive at ontology either – if that is ever possible. But if one is willing to look at the dispositions of behavioural dispositions, one can explain the predictability problem in another, more elegant language. One particularly impressive approach will be presented here,[311] that of John R. Anderson and his school.

The model is known under the name adaptive character of thought or ACT. The model has been revised several times.[312] The current version is labelled ACT-R 5.0.[313] It is an attempt to arrive at one integrated theory of the mind.[314] The model has three layers. Modules are linked to productions by way of buffers. The production is where the mind actually makes a difference. Some input yields some output. The modules provide this input. But they are not doing so directly. They must go through the buffers.

The model has at least four modules. But further modules can be integrated into it. In the current version, these modules are called the intentional, the declarative, the visual and the manual. The modules are

---

[307] LaPiere 1934; Wicker 1969; Fishbein and Ajzen 1975; Ajzen and Fishbein 1980; Bohner 2001: 270–81.

[308] Bargh et al. 1996: 231.

[309] Strack and Deutsch 2002: 28.

[310] See also Bartlett 1932: 199: 'By means of perpetual alterations in position we are always building up a postural model of ourselves which constantly changes.'

[311] On competing approaches, see above note 8.

[312] A brief overview of the evolution of the theory is provided by Anderson et al. 2004: 1036–7.

[313] More technical details are provided at http://act-r.psy.cmu.edu/tutorials/ (12/1/2003).

[314] See, for example, the programmatic title of Anderson 2003.

allowed to work autonomously and in parallel. The visual module can thus scan the landscape, while the manual module cuddles the dog, the intentional module sketches the next article, and the declarative module is busy finding the name of a neighbour encountered minutes ago.

How is man, nonetheless, despite all this parallel mental activity, able to behave in a meaningful way? The model says: because of powerful filters. For the productions do not directly interact with the modules. They only process what these modules deposit in their respective buffers. The intentional module thus has its goal buffer. The declarative module has a retrieval buffer. The visual module has a visual buffer, and the manual module a manual buffer. The model is even more restrictive. It claims that, at any given point of time, each individual buffer can not hold more than one unit of knowledge, labelled a chunk. This rigorous limitation ensures that the productions are not confused with each other. They try to make sense of what is currently available in the buffers. If this does not work, they give it back to the buffer, asking for different input.

Productions can themselves be stored in the declarative module. This explains why humans apparently have a plurality of mental tools. Human rationality is a fall-back option. But there are more specific tools that are genetically determined or acquired by earlier experience. However, the model does not presuppose that such ready-made productions entirely match the input from the external world. Rather, the model allows for partial matching. This is one way to explain how associations and blending work. Whether declarative knowledge and productions are retrieved from the declarative modules depends on two factors: a base rate, and the recent history of activation. This explains how behaviour becomes adaptive.

This rough picture of a much richer theory deepens the understanding for the fact that human behaviour is so utterly unpredictable. The human mind is purposively made not to be deterministic. There is a fundamental plasticity built in, cleverly combined with a mechanism that prevents the individual from being tossed around by inputs and intentions.

2.5   Effects

2.5.1   Introduction

It is time to sum up: What do all the effects listed above mean for the predictability of human behaviour? Predictability is a relative concept. Ego must be able to predict what Alter is likely to do in one given situation. Predictability does therefore not require the stability of behaviour across contexts. It is enough if Ego foresees a change in behaviour, or its variance across contexts. But if behaviour is stable, it also is predictable.

The psychological predictability problem is also related to the characteristics of psychology as a science. This science is permanently uncovering new behavioural dispositions, new effects or new interactions between known elements. The body of generic knowledge is thus growing continually. Today's established truth can be refuted tomorrow. Old predictions can lose their conceptual base. Moreover, psychology is no different from other fields in that a good deal of the knowledge is disputed.[315] The uncertainty of generic knowledge does, however, not translate itself automatically into a predictability problem for Ego. This is so, since eventually Ego is interested only in behaviour, not in behavioural dispositions, and even less in the dispositions of behavioural dispositions. Practically speaking, Ego is thus able to formulate an educated guess about the behaviour of Alter without much knowledge or expertise in psychology. The latter may, of course, be of help. This is obvious, if an insight at the nano level plays itself out at the micro level in a more or less straightforward way. Even if the interplay between behaviour and behavioural dispositions is not linear, however, the possession of generic knowledge may help Ego formulate helpful hypotheses. Generic knowledge thus serves as a guide to the search. Ego can make more productive use of the information available to him. But much less elaborate approaches will often do a reliable job too. 'Having experience with a person' would not be regarded so highly were this not the case.

Within the architecture of this book, behavioural dispositions are viewed as generating a predictability problem, and institutions are expected partially to solve it. This occurs frequently, but it is neither logically nor practically the only possibility. Institutions do not always make behaviour more predictable. On the contrary, they can aggravate the predictability problem. Because of the just mentioned uncertainty about the underlying mechanisms, it is possible that institutions will engender counterproductive effects. If such counterproductive effects occur, it shows that the institutional designer has only partly understood the predictability problem. One particularly acute risk is called 'overfitting' by evolutionary theorists. In that case, a solution perfectly fits the problem present in the training ground. But when applied to the field,

---

[315] For an illustrative account, see Anderson 2000b: 72: 'a symposium was held to commemorate the twenty-fifth anniversary of that theory [sc.: the Rescorla/Wagner theory of classic conditioning]. Few theories survive that long in psychology.'

the standard conditions of the training ground are no longer present. Intervening variables that were not investigated or manipulated during training play themselves out in unexpected or even counterproductive ways.[316] The negative effect on predictability can also be a side-effect of institutions meant to solve a different social problem. For instance, financial innovations can generate excess liquidity and thereby increase the tendency of hyperbolic discounting.[317]

The predictability problem plays itself out in variance over time (2), across contexts (3) and across individuals (4).[318]

2.5.2 Variance over time

Empirically, behaviour varies greatly over time.[319] More precisely, it varies, although the situation remains stable.[320] Economists often refer to this by speaking about the time inconsistency of behaviour.[321] Any of the components of the mind analysable at the nano level can be responsible for this variance.[322] The individual may have used different mental tools in the two situations. He may have been attentive to one, and inattentive to the other. He may have perceived them differently. He may have elaborated his perceptions in one case and forgone the opportunity in the second. If the situation called for judgement, he may, or may not, have used a judgemental heuristic. He may have activated different elements from his memory. The situations may have occurred at different moments of the individual learning history. Different motivators may have played themselves out. Emotions may have intervened in one situation and not in the other. The individual may have used different approaches to choice. If the situations were characterised by risk, the individual may have assessed the risk in many different ways.

The richness of behavioural dispositions is the most important, albeit not the only reason for the time inconsistency of behaviour. A second reason is the development of behavioural dispositions themselves. The individual learns a new heuristic by imitation. He adopts a new routine.

---

[316] On overfitting, see Weigend 1994.
[317] Laibson 1997: 446; on hyperbolic discounting, see above 2.2.10.
[318] For a similar typology, see e.g. Shoda 1999: 364; see also Funder and Colvin 1991; Mischel and Shoda 1995.
[319] From the many voices, see only Hogarth et al. 1997: 256.
[320] Shoda 1999: 365–6.
[321] Refs. at Tirole 2002: 638; from the psychological literature, see e.g. Slovic 1995; Loewenstein and Thaler 1997: 369.
[322] For a narrower treatment, see Kahneman and Snell 1997: 396: time inconsistency can have a cognitive or a motivational source.

Trauma makes him shy away from a class of experiences in the future. Professional training allows him to use state-of-the-art statistical tools.

A third possibility does not speak directly to the time inconsistency of behaviour, but to how it is mirrored in actual prediction by Ego. The predictability problem can also rest on limited knowledge about behavioural dispositions. If Alter has never played a hidden disposition out, this is as surprising for Ego as if he had newly acquired it.

2.5.3   Variance across contexts

Behaviour is not stable across contexts.[323] Cross-situational predictability is even lower than temporal predictability.[324] This finding has been particularly troublesome for differential psychology. This sub-field of psychology is interested in understanding personality. It has been puzzled by the persistent variance of behaviour with context, which apparently refutes the hypothesis around which the whole field is organised: that people have distinguishable personalities.[325] A different strand of psychology not only welcomes the news. It has built its whole approach on the fundamental contextuality of behaviour. As mentioned earlier, those adhering to this view call themselves Brunswikians, after Egon Brunswik.[326] From a totally different angle, evolutionary economists reach similar conclusions. They stress the 'co-evolution of knowledge and acquired wants'.[327] Accordingly, these scholars deviate from a fundamental feature of the economic model. The economic model draws a line between preferences and restrictions. It is not interested in preferences. They can be random. What the model wants you to understand is how individuals holding different preferences do interact. Evolutionary economists, however, tend to endogenise preferences. They are interested in preference learning.[328] Others go even further and claim that preferences are constructed while they are elicited.[329]

---

[323] From the many voices, see, for example, Payne et al. 1997; Kahneman 2000: 657.

[324] Mischel and Peake 1982: 749.

[325] See Shoda 1999: 364–5 for an analytic treatment; other voices include Hartshorne et al. 1928; Newcomb 1929; Allport et al. 1933; Dudycha 1936; Bem 1972; Bem and Allen 1974; Mischel and Peake 1982; Wright and Mischel 1987; Funder and Colvin 1991; Ross and Nisbett 1991.

[326] Brunswik et al. 2001; see also Goldstein and Hogarth 1997: 8; Kahneman and Snell 1997: 401.

[327] Witt 2000b: 22; on evolutionary economics as a field, see Nelson and Winter 1982; Nelson 1995.

[328] Witt 2000b: 23; see also Ripperger Vertrauen 1998: 203; Tack 2003: 107.

[329] Payne et al. 1992: 89 and *passim*; Slovic 1995; Tversky et al. 2000: 517; Tversky and Simonson 2000: 526.

Accordingly, despite the same deep structure of a situation, subjects behave differently depending on the surface structure. Put more bluntly: cover stories matter.[330] Even more important is the impact of local culture.[331]

The list of context effects is long. Some illustrations must suffice at this point. Individuals behave differently when they are asked to decide repeatedly compared with when one decision applies to many cases.[332] As a rule, subjects exhibit an ambiguity aversion.[333] If they are allowed to choose between a clear and a vaguer prospect, a large majority prefer the clear prospect.[334] The aversion disappears, however, when the subject does not have to choose between two prospects, but has to evaluate the less safe prospect independently.[335] The aversion also fades away in areas where the subjects consider themselves to be experts.[336]

2.5.4   Variance across individuals

This is a section on the interaction between two well-defined persons (Ego and Alter) in a well-defined single instance. Variance across individuals is thus only indirectly relevant for Ego. He does not want to apply a standard response to a whole class of actors.[337] But he might be interested in exploiting generic knowledge about human behavioural dispositions. Of course, the typical interaction partner does not consult psychological literature. But some psychological findings do even become public wisdom in the long run. Most newspaper readers have come across the concepts of self-fulfilling prophecies, group think and cognitive dissonance, to name only a few examples. More importantly, humans are good at exploiting their individual experiences. The greater the variance across individuals, the less valuable experience with other actors is.

Actually, this variance is remarkable. Good psychological experiments generate reliable evidence. But it is rare indeed that 100 per cent of the subject pool behaves alike. A two-third, one-third distribution often seems acceptable evidence.

---

[330] Wagenaar et al. 1997: 552 and *passim*.
[331] This has already been observed by Smith 1790: V.i.6; see also Schlicht 1998: 273.
[332] Redelmeier and Tversky 1992.
[333] The point has already been made by Ellsberg 1961; Burkhard Schipper pointed me to this.
[334] Fox and Tversky 2000: 528–9.   [335] Fox and Tversky 2000: 528.
[336] Fox and Tversky 2000: 530.   [337] On this case, see below, chapter 6.

As mentioned, a whole sub-field of psychology, differential psychology, investigates these differences across individuals.[338] Pointing to this variance has been a weapon in the ongoing fight about the concept of biases. Opponents have demonstrated that quite a number of biases are correlated with low intelligence.[339] Other biases are shown to disappear with more information or training.[340] Individual abilities do also have an impact on the likeliness of subjects to use a more elaborate mode for judgement or choice.[341] The ability to exploit a rich array of mental tools has been interpreted as an element of human capital.[342] Variance across individuals can thus partly be seen as the difference between mental haves and have-nots. The extreme case is the one outstanding individual able to impose his will on the whole community. In that instance, one charismatic leader is able to change the behavioural dispositions of all his followers.[343] But there are more reasons for variance.[344] An obvious example is the 'abnormal' behaviour, like phobic behaviour, generated by mental defects.[345]

Differential psychology is not only interested in mere variance. The driving force of the sub-field is the attempt to link this variance to personality.[346] Put differently, the field has been searching for personality as a sort of a prototype.[347] It has been plagued and stimulated alike by what has been dubbed the personality paradox. Intuitively, most people believe in the concept of personality. Yet there is compelling evidence of fairly little consistency of behaviour across situations.[348] Technically speaking, the unconditional correlation between personality and behaviour is low.[349] This finding has led the field to reconceptualise personality.[350] Personality now is predominantly seen as a characteristic

---

[338] Characteristic texts include Brown 1991; Funder 2000; Stanovich and West 2000; Brandts et al. 2002; see also Simon 1990.

[339] Funder 2000: 674; Stanovich and West 2000: 651–2.

[340] Stanovich and West 2000: 652.

[341] Stanovich and West 2000: 659.

[342] Payne 1997: 195; the classic text on the concept of human capital is Becker 1993.

[343] A good example is already to be found in Smith 1790: V.i.7. Culture largely defines what is thought to be valuable, e.g. in the fine arts. But an 'eminent artist' can change fashion such that his individual style becomes the future norm.

[344] For example, see Quattrone and Tversky 2000: 468 (on prospect theory); Stanovich and West 2000: 656–8 (on framing).

[345] Strack and Deutsch 2002: 29.

[346] For an overview, see e.g. Epstein 1979; Mischel and Shoda 1995.

[347] Mischel and Peake 1982: 730, 750 and *passim.*

[348] Epstein 1977: 97; Epstein 1979: 1097; Mischel and Peake 1982: 730; Wright and Mischel 1987: 1173, 1175; Mischel and Shoda 1995: 246–7; Shoda 1999: 361–2.

[349] Epstein 1979: 1097, 1098–102, with many refs.

[350] For an explicit treatment, see Mischel and Peake 1982: 731, 748.

interaction between the person and the situation.[351] 'Behavioural signa-
tures' are thus unstable.[352] The fact that people nonetheless see themselves as having a personality rests on an exercise in constructing
consistency *ex post*.[353]

There is even a second layer to the predictability problem. The behaviour of some people is more predictable than the behaviour of
others. Predictability is thus itself an important personality trait.[354] But
the first-order predictability paradox repeats itself at this second order.
For observers frequently agree on whom they see as particularly predictable. This consensus, however, often cannot be replicated by rigorous
empirical methodology.[355]

Based on the overview of behavioural disposition outlined above, it
is not difficult to understand why there is variance across individuals.
None of the many mental tools is purely objective. This is even true
for elaborate, decontextualised reasoning. As demonstrated, in such
situations humans characteristically do rely either on reason-based
choice or on narrative reasoning.[356] The decisive reason they choose,
or the precise story they develop, largely depends on their individual
history, and on the context within which they have interacted before.
The contextual element is even more pronounced in the less elaborate
mental tools. These tools adapt not only to the context, but also to the
current capabilities of their user.[357] The information that triggers the
actor's attention is also influenced by his earlier experiences. If a family
member has passed away after a furious horse has tramped over him,
this event becomes part of the mental family history. An individual with
such a family history is likely to be very attentive to the sight of horses
that an average individual would find quite uninteresting. Some people
are better than others in combining scattered pieces of information
into a consistent mental story. Those who have learned economics or
statistics are much more likely to represent quantitative data according
to the norms of these fields. Personality differences can thus also rest in
perception and elaboration. Attitudes are idiosyncratic from the very
beginning. Other elements of judgement have a personality trait too.
An obvious example is personal 'thinking dispositions', used as an
evaluation mode.[358]

---

[351] Bem 1972: 20; Wright and Mischel 1987; Mischel and Shoda 1995: 251, see also 246,
       255–6; Shoda 1999: 379–80 and *passim*.
[352] Shoda 1999: 366–7.
[353] Mischel and Peake 1982: 750.
[354] Epstein 1979: 1124; Underwood and Moore 1981: 785 and *passim*.
[355] Mischel and Peake 1982: 749.   [356] See above 2.2.9.
[357] Gigerenzer et al. 1999: 32.   [358] Friedrich 2000: 672.

Idiosyncrasy is quintessential for memory. Since people live their independent lives, not only the individual bits and pieces of information differ. More importantly even, memory works by *ex post* reconstruction at the moment of recall.[359] Memory is personal 'not because of some intangible. . . "self" . . . , but because the mechanism of adult human memory demands an organisation of "schemata" depending on an interplay of appetites, instincts, interests and ideals peculiar to any given subject'.[360] Learning also creates variance, since every individual has a different learning history. Not all individuals are driven by the same motivators. Some seek profit. Others do care more for a peaceful life. While most individuals are influenced by fairness considerations, they adopt different fairness norms.[361] Many individuals can be characterised as multiple selves, with these different selves playing themselves out in an idiosyncratic way.[362] The differences in the emotional make-up of individuals are even greater. Individuals have their personal decision-making habits. They thus differ regarding when and how they have recourse to the multiple decision modes.

The impact of the individual mental history on behaviour is thus the most important source of individual differences. This should not come as a surprise, given that the high degree of plasticity is the most prominent feature of human behavioural dispositions. But there are also genetically coded differences. Some are born with a higher potential for intelligence than others. And the individual mental development plays itself out. The most important element is imprinting. Early in life children are thereby put on mental tracks that distinguish them from others[363] – one more reason why predictions are difficult, and not the least important.

---

[359] This is the basic tenet of Bartlett 1932.

[360] Bartlett 1932: 213.   [361] Wade- Benzoni et al. 1996.

[362] Conlisk 1996: 677.   [363] Delgado 2000.

3   Rational choice responses

3.1   Introduction

What would a fully rational actor do after he has read the foregoing chapter? In a nutshell, this is what the present chapter investigates. Another way of putting this is: this chapter is looking for behaviourally safe solutions. It takes the findings about behavioural dispositions as a given, as well as the knowledge about how they play themselves out at the behavioural level. Ego is thus assumed to be fully aware of the predictability problem generated by the high plasticity of human behavioural dispositions. He is further assumed to be a classic *Homo oeconomicus*.[1] At a later stage in the chapter a third assumption is added. Alter is also assumed to be rational in so far as he responds to the action of Ego. In so doing, the chapter follows an approach frequently used in work by economists on irrational behaviour.[2] Finally, for the purposes of this chapter, human behavioural dispositions and the ensuing predictability problem are seen as exogenous. This chapter thus only looks at institutional reactions to a predictability problem that is 'out there'. In keeping with methodological individualism, it does not consider intervention that aims at proactively changing behavioural dispositions.[3]

Ironic critics see this as the approach of rational demons.[4] And indeed, the idea of having rational reactions to one's own irrationality is highly counterfactual. But there is value in the approach. The strongest argument stems from the philosophy of science. Developing a powerful paradigm is a demanding social exercise. Over more than a hundred years, nearly all economists all over the world have been united by their adherence to one paradigm, the rational choice model. Accordingly, the model is in excellent shape. It is not wise to switch to another paradigm, even if it seems to fit a class of problems better. The shift

---

[1] For details, see Becker 1976.
[2] For examples, see Fehr and Tyran 1996: 79; Mullainathan 2002.
[3] Chapter 4 will drop this assumption.
[4] Outspoken on this are Gigerenzer et al. 1999: 10–12.

would only be justified if one can expect the substituted new paradigm to be even more powerful in the foreseeable future. This is the basic message of Thomas Kuhn.[5]

A second, related argument is less powerful. It dates even further back in history, to the medieval monk William of Ockham. He taught that 'One should not increase, beyond what is necessary, the number of entities required to explain anything.'[6] The principle goes by the name 'Ockham's razor', or the principle of parsimony.[7] The rational choice model explains social interaction by the interplay between preferences and restrictions. Preferences can be random. The model thus entirely cuts out behavioural dispositions. In that respect it is highly parsimonious. But parsimony is no value as such. There is a never-ending tension between parsimony and fit.[8] Or in Albert Einstein's words: 'Everything should be made as simple as possible, but not simpler.'

A third argument is pragmatic. Because of the high degree of evolution of the rational choice model, dropping the rationality assumptions one by one is a clear way of structuring the book.

A fourth argument is normative. In its simplest form, it takes rationality as the benchmark for behaviour. Deviations from this benchmark are seen as individual or social problems. From the perspective of an institutional designer, any gap between reality and the rational choice model is seen as a problem to be solved.[9] This is acceptable, however, only in so far as it can be ruled out that behaviour chosen without recourse to rational reasoning performs even better than rationality. Those conducting research into heuristics have made a point of finding instances where fast and frugal decision-making is indeed even better than fully rational decision-making.[10] We will have to come back to this.[11] But this is not the norm. Usually, it is much easier to justify deviations from the precepts of the rational choice model by referring to cognitive and computational limitations or the prohibitive decision cost of a more elaborate approach.[12] When this is feasible, rational choice can still legitimately be used as a benchmark.

The legitimacy of relying on the rational choice model increases even more if deviations from the benchmark are taken as a justification for

---

[5] Kuhn 1962.
[6] The Latin original reads: 'Entia non sunt multiplicanda praeter necessitatem.'
[7] Thorburn 1915.
[8] Harless and Camerer 1994: 1285.
[9] Even fervent critics of the rational choice model are willing to use it in that function, see e.g. Martignon and Blackmond Laskey 1999.
[10] A graphic example is to be found in Gigerenzer et al. 1999: 3–5.
[11] See below 4.3.   [12] Gigerenzer et al. 1999: 8–15.

central intervention. This is typically what institutional design is about. For institutions typically are not chosen in full freedom. This is obvious if the institution is established by law. For law rests upon the sovereign powers of the state. Rationality is helpful for that purpose, precisely because it totally disregards context. This makes it possible that the design of general rules makes no exception for chance or privilege. The law, or justice more generally, can keep its proverbial blindfolded eyes.

The last set of arguments is empirical. Obviously not all actors respond rationally to the predictability problem. But for a cognisable part of them, the assumption of rationality is not far-fetched. They may not exactly behave as assumed by the theory. But they may still come close enough for the theory to have predictive power. This is particularly likely for professionals and within institutionalised settings. Traders in markets and police officers come to mind as examples. More generally, Ego should be more strongly motivated to deal with the predictability problem in a rational way than Alter himself. For Alter, at least in principle, is always able to override behavioural dispositions by employing a more elaborate decision-making procedure. Ego, however, is the victim of the ensuing variance. This argument should, however, not be overstated. Gaining a more realistic view of how actors are likely to react to the predictability problem will be the topic of another chapter.[13] Even more counterfactual is the idea that Alter, who is irrational in the first place, reacts rationally to his own behavioural variance. There are instances of this. We will treat them under the heading of the Ulysses problem below.[14] Alter might also be excluded from desirable types of interaction because of the low predictability of his behaviour. That might make him anticipate the response of Ego and strive for higher predictability in the first place. But such foresight is rather exceptional.

The present chapter thus aims to answer a descriptive and a prescriptive question. The descriptive question asks how far rational choice analysis can be pushed. The prescriptive question is interested in the extent to which institutions can be based on the finding of a deviation from rational choice expectations. The latter implies that institutions work by deliberate and purposeful intervention, be it by one or both of the players, or whether they encompass some activity of outsiders.

In a rational choice perspective, the predictability problem is best analysed in a game theoretic model (3.2). Within this conceptual framework, the parties have at their disposal four different possible ways to

---

[13] See below, chapter 5.   [14] See below, chapter 6.

overcome the problem. They can try to establish a mechanism by which Ego receives credible information about Alter's type (3.3). A subsidy or a tax can make it irrational for Alter to exploit the plasticity of his behavioural dispositions (3.4). Likewise, Ego can be insured against the risk of behavioural variance (3.5). Finally, a risk premium can make Ego willing to assume the behavioural risk inherent in unpredictability (3.6).

3.2   Game theoretic model

3.2.1   Introduction

In a rational choice framework, the most elegant way of casting the predictability problem consists of interpreting it as an information asymmetry. Because of the plasticity of human behavioural dispositions, observing past or present conduct is not enough for Ego. Alter still retains a huge potential for behavioural variance. Note a methodological implication: rational choice is a pure motivational theory. This holds for cases in which there is an information asymmetry as well. Modelling predictability as an information asymmetry is thus a way of artificially transforming a cognitive problem into a motivational one.

Economists model information asymmetries as relationships between informed agents and uninformed principals.[15] The application of the model thus entails an assumption about the abilities of Alter. It is not necessary that Alter be able to control his own future behaviour. The model is thus open to the Ulysses problem. But Alter must know what he will do in the future, and he must be able to impart this knowledge to Ego. Psychologically, this is not always the case. Alter may, for instance, not always predict which emotions will play a role at a certain point in time. But the assumption is not grossly misleading. More importantly even, seeing the predictability problem as an information asymmetry makes it possible to capture the essence of the problem for Ego.

This interpretation is in line with one strand of economic thinking. Economists repeatedly have pointed to the fact that bounded rationality can largely be transformed into perfect rationality under conditions of imperfect information.[16]

---

[15] The starting point of this strand of economic thinking was Akerlof 1970. For a recent presentation, see Furubotn and Richter 1997: chapter V, and (more elaborate, but in German) Schweizer 1999.
[16] Characteristic pieces include Banerjee 1992; Bikhchandani et al. 1992; Welch 1992; for a theoretical treatment, see Conlisk 1996: 680.

Ego is interested in the future behaviour of Alter. He needs this information to decide rationally how to pre-empt this action by his own activity or by remaining inactive. The principal–agent model thus implicitly reduces the predictability problem to one of actual prediction. Put differently, this truly is a model for one instance. Within this model, predictability is only of interest if it actually allows true predictions. In that case, Ego is fully informed. The principal–agent relationship disappears. But the model is open to rational expectations. It thus can compare two situations. In the first situation, the principal is fully uninformed. He has no clue how Alter is likely to behave. In the second situation, the principal–agent relationship persists. But it is less pronounced in that the principal can rely on secondary information. This secondary information allows him to form rational expectations about what Alter is likely to do.

If the predictability problem is modelled as an information asymmetry, Ego is assumed to have no direct interest in understanding the behavioural dispositions of Alter. What he wants to predict is future behaviour. In the language introduced above, the model is thus exclusively interested in the micro, not in the nano level, and even less in the pico level. Put differently, in this model Ego has no direct interest in understanding why there is so much behavioural variance. All he wants to do is correctly predict behaviour.

The model is interested in the distinction between private knowledge and the knowledge that is common to Alter and Ego. The model does not presuppose that this knowledge is accessible to outsiders. It is thus open to the orthogonal distinction between explicit and implicit knowledge.[17] Put differently, the model itself is decontextual. But it does not presuppose a decontextualised reality. It simply is not interested in this context.

A further distinction is important for the model, however; namely the one between specific and generic knowledge. The psychological findings on behavioural dispositions provide such generic knowledge. They are published in journals and books open to the public. If Ego finds this sufficiently valuable, he could receive training to understand the mechanisms and map them to reality. Directly, the model speaks to none of this. It can be seen as a pure model of the additional specific knowledge about Alter needed to exploit this generic knowledge. But the more generic knowledge Ego possesses, and the better he is able to manipulate it, the less specific knowledge he will need. The scope of the principal–agent problem thus shrinks.

---

[17] For a basic treatment, see Cowan et al. 2000.

The principal–agent model presupposes that gaining access to the private information of the agent makes a difference to the principal. Put differently, the model presupposes that decisions made by Alter and decisions made by Ego are strategically linked. This is not always the case. The classic exception is market exchange. If a buyer and a seller meet in the marketplace, they lack a great deal of private information about each other. All they know is the price at which the seller is willing to sell, and the price at which the buyer is willing to buy. As long as the quality of the good is fully and unequivocally determined, this is all they need. Of course, both act strategically. The seller will typically demand a price above marginal cost. And the buyer will make an offer below what he is marginally willing to pay for another unit of the good. But this does not matter, since workable competition forces both partners to come close to revealing their private information.[18]

This beneficial effect disappears, however, if at least one of the partners no longer has a credible outside option. This is true under conditions of monopoly and oligopoly.[19] But strategic interaction can even result from an exchange that originally took place on a fully competitive market. This is the case if the interaction between the two contracting partners is not concluded on the spot. This is obvious if both parties have agreed to interact over an extended period of time, with elements of the exchange and payments being protracted.[20] Such contracts have been graphically dubbed relational.[21] But the same holds if Alter promises today to deliver a well-defined good on some well-defined day in the future. This is obvious if Ego is obliged to pay in advance. But even if he is not, a situation of strategic interaction ensues once Ego makes an investment in his sphere in reliance on the contract.[22] At closer sight, even spot exchange often has a strategic element. For usually the buyer cannot be fully sure *ex ante* whether the product does indeed possess the promised quality. Once the contract is struck, however, the buyer loses his original outside option to go to another seller. The interaction thus becomes strategic, since the buyer anticipates the possibility of later being at the seller's mercy when the good turns out to be defective.[23]

---

[18] In game theoretic language: workable competition imposes a game against Nature on the agents; Scharpf 1997: 5.
[19] For a rigorous, game theoretic treatment, see Tirole 1988.
[20] For a basic treatment, see Williamson 1985.
[21] MacNeil 1971.
[22] Understanding of this type of strategic interaction is behind the rich literature on the 'efficient breach of contract'; see e.g. MacNeil 1982; Friedmann 1989.
[23] Classic texts on this problem include Priest 1981; Quillen 1988.

On a more abstract level, the interaction between two persons becomes strategic if at least one of them incurs an opportunity cost for ending the relationship.[24] In economic relations, this typically results from an investment that is not only market- or relation-specific, but even transaction-specific.[25] Economists also often refer to this situation as one where a partner must sink cost.[26] Actually, in a fixed bilateral relationship, sunk cost is not itself the problem. The problem is the asymmetry between the partners. If both are forced to sink costs symmetrically, these costs even serve as hostages for the legitimate expectations of the other party to the contract.[27]

A contract with asymmetric sunk cost is not the only situation in which predictability matters for Ego. It also matters in Ego's decision concerning whether to conclude the contract. If Ego acts rationally, he anticipates the future asymmetry and insists on safeguards or he shies away from the contract. Actually, this is the decision institutional economists are truly interested in. But similar situations arise even if Ego has never considered concluding a contract. For predictability to matter nonetheless, Ego must be vulnerable. The information asymmetry then has an impact on the decision of Ego to shy away from a contact, or to protect himself proactively against intrusion by Alter. Analytically, this class of situations resembles the interaction between an interaction partner and chance actors. The difference lies in the fact that, in the latter case, not only the action, but also the actor is unknown. Since this latter situation is investigated separately below,[28] the following concentrates on contractual relationships.

3.2.2   The model

The technical tool used by economists to analyse situations of strategic interaction is game theory.[29] This section looks at a situation characterised by one actor, one interaction partner and one instance, i.e. a two-player, one-shot game. Seemingly, a model with two players should thus suffice. A more powerful model, however, introduces Nature as a third actor. It is a sequential game. Nature moves first. Nature matches Ego (or shorter E) to an actor Alter (or shorter A) from the population, with high or low behavioural risk. At stage 2, Ego moves. When he does,

---

[24] On the crucial role of opportunity cost in social interaction, see Siebert 1996.
[25] More from Furubotn and Richter 1997: chapter IV.2.
[26] More from Baldwin 1989.
[27] More from Williamson 1985: chapters 7.3 and 8.2.
[28] See below, chapter 6.
[29] Standard texts include Rasmusen 1989; Kreps 1990.

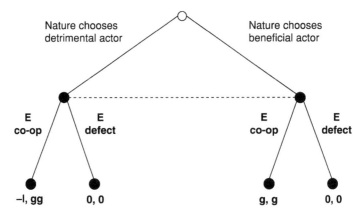

Figure 3.1. Base game.

Ego does not know the type of the actor he is dealing with. Neither does he know the (objective) probability that Alter is of one rather than another of these types. The probability distribution is thus not common knowledge. Ego then can choose between co-operating with Alter or refraining from co-operation. Alter moves at stage 3. If he presents a high risk, he will harm Ego. If he presents a low-risk player, he will not, and interaction pays for both players.[30] In the following, the fact that Alter is a high-risk actor is called detrimental and denoted A^-. If Alter is low risk, he is called beneficial and denoted A^+.

Figure 3.1 illustrates the situation. The dotted line linking the two actor types indicates that E cannot observe Nature's move. In this figure, the actor types are depicted by the following pay-offs: if Ego co-operates with a beneficial actor, both make a symmetrical gain of g. If, however, Ego co-operates with a detrimental actor, he incurs a loss of $-l$, while Alter makes an even larger gain of gg.

Formally, the relationship between gains and losses is as in Equation 1:

$$gg > g > 0 > -l. \tag{1}$$

---

[30] For an easily accessible introduction to sequential games, and their presentation in extensive form, see Baird et al. 1994: chapter 2. The idea of modelling information asymmetries by introducing a move of Nature was introduced by Harsanyi 1967–8. Technically speaking, it converts a game of incomplete information into one of imperfect information. In the former case, one player does not know the structure of the game or the pay-offs of the other player. In the latter case, all this is fully specified, but one player does not know the entire history of the game when he moves. The latter game is open to a solution in game theoretic terms.

If it becomes necessary to distinguish between both players, the fair gains of Ego and Alter respectively are occasionally denoted g_E and g_A. This is in keeping with an axiom of neoclassical economics. It assumes utility to be strictly subjective. One of the tasks of the model, however, is to make different solutions comparable. This presupposes the ability to compare gains and losses across parties. It also presupposes the possibility of sharing the cost of intervention such that it is paid out of the expected gains from trade. For these reasons, it is further assumed that gains can be expressed in a uniform currency accepted by both parties. Of course, these gains could differ. Co-operating could be more beneficial for one player than for another. But since the model is interested in the asymmetric distribution of information, not of (fair) gains, the second assumption is

$$g_E = g_A. \tag{2}$$

A third assumption becomes understandable in the light of the following considerations. Individually, in this game, E will not want to co-operate with A−. For E then faces a loss of $-l$. But if $gg - 2g > l$, it would still be socially advantageous for A− to impose this loss on E. For there would still be a surplus. According to the Kaldor/Hicks criterion, allowing A− to do so would even be defined as efficient. The competing Pareto criterion is more demanding. Under this criterion, exchange is only beneficial if no party is worse off and at least one is better off.[31] But under this criterion, it is still possible that E would agree to A defecting, provided A makes him whole. These additional complications are excluded by the third condition. It assumes l to be larger than $gg - 2g$. By basic transformation, this yields

$$2g + l - gg > 0. \tag{3}$$

Game theoretic models generally analyse the interaction between two or more rational actors. This model is interested in a different type of interaction, where only Ego acts fully rationally, while Alter is driven by a mixed bag of behavioural dispositions. But the model of a sequential game can be adapted to this. One drops the analysis of stage 3. It is replaced by an outcome that has already been determined by Nature's selection of type. Specifically, the pay-offs for both players are given by what a rational observer would expect *ex ante* when Nature moves. By assumption, this is identical to what Ego himself would have expected had he known Nature's move when he moved himself.

---

[31] For a succinct presentation of the two criteria from welfare economics, see Feldman 1980: 140–4.

To be explicit: the model thus assumes behavioural dispositions to be deterministic. This is the price one pays for conceptually transforming bounded rationality into a problem of imperfect information.[32] But this is less of a limitation than it might seem at first glance. For the model is open to more than two actor types. Every single behavioural disposition could be portrayed as a different type. Even every possible combination of different behavioural dispositions could be modelled that way. The model only needs the *ex ante* definition of an outcome for each of these actor types.

Game theorists solve sequential games by backwards induction.[33] They start at the end of the game and work themselves back to the beginning. Since Alter is assumed to be the victim of his behavioural dispositions, the analysis can go directly to stage 2. Ego's problem is to find out whether the balance of the interaction is positive. If not, he would rather shy away from the action. In game theoretic language: he would choose not to co-operate. But how shall he know? Nature has drawn Alter's type, but Ego does not know this part of the history of the game. A term from the literature on insurance offers a graphic description: Ego must thus rely on the pooling equilibrium.[34]

Put differently, Ego must decide under conditions of uncertainty. The good news is that within the model, the uncertainty is not extreme. For the model assumes that each behavioural disposition, as well as each combination of the same, translates itself into an *ex ante* defined outcome for both parties. The solution space is thus well defined.[35] But the model says nothing about probabilities, i.e. the distribution of actor types within the population. In the terms of Frank Knight, Ego thus faces a decision under conditions of uncertainty, not risk.[36] The inter-action partner is thus confined to attaching subjective probabilities to the different actor types. Formally, Ego's problem can thus be written as:

$$pg_E - (1 - p)l > 0, \tag{4}$$

where p is the subjective probability Ego attaches to Alter being beneficial. Since, within the model, Alter can be only one of these types, the two probabilities must add up to 1. Accordingly, the corresponding

---

[32] See again note 30 and accompanying text.
[33] See again Baird et al. 1994: chapter 2.
[34] More from Baird et al. 1994: 83 and *passim*.
[35] On the possibility of an open solution space, see Spiecker gen. Döhmann 2001. Dekel et al. 1998 and Heifetz et al. 2003 struggle over integrating it into the rational choice model by interpreting the open solution space as unawareness.
[36] Knight 1921; on modern attempts at modelling uncertainty as ambiguity, see Schmeidler 1989; Eichberger et al. 2003.

probability of Alter being detrimental is $1 - p$. This implies that a rational interaction partner will not only look at probabilities. He will also take the difference between g and l into account. The greater l is, compared with g, the larger the subjective probability of A being beneficial must be if he is to co-operate.

The foregoing makes it possible to extend the scope of the analysis. A strategically equivalent situation is the following: the actor has indeed moved before Ego, and he may have co-operated or defected. But Ego cannot observe the actual move. He only has expectations about the distribution of actor types in the population.

3.2.3   Types of games

(a) Introduction   Predictability does not have value for Ego as such. This may, of course, be different. Ego can rely on the services of an independent information intermediary, say a credit information bureau.[37] The relationship between the information intermediary and Ego can itself be portrayed in game theoretic language. Alter and Ego can also split their interaction up into two levels themselves. At level 1 they overcome the predictability problem. At level 2 they interact on this basis.[38] But both are already ways to overcome the predictability problem, not descriptions of the problem itself.

If these options are assumed away for the moment, the decisive question is how low predictability changes the equilibrium of the original game. As modelled above, the issue of high versus low predictability is a question of perfect versus imperfect information. When Ego acts under conditions of low predictability, he does not know Alter's type. But, by assumption, he does know exactly the sequence of moves, and the pay-offs for both parties resulting from each possible combination of moves. As mentioned above, game theorists solve this class of games by backwards induction. Depending on the character of the game, the difference between high and low predictability is therefore more or less important.[39]

There are games of pure harmony. They allow each player to obtain his best outcome without coming into conflict with the other player.[40] At

---

[37] On information intermediaries as a response to the predictability problem, see below 3.3.5.

[38] On a two-level game as a joint response by both players, see below 3.3.4.

[39] For a most elucidating typology of games, written from the perspective not of game theory, but of applied sciences relying on this conceptual tool, see Holzinger 2003.

[40] Technically, such an extreme game has a unique equilibrium: it is a Pareto-optimal solution; there is no conflict between the players over the evaluation of the outcome, or over their distribution; Holzinger 2003: 9, 11.

the extreme opposite end, there are games that keep the players in strict conflict.[41] By intuition one sees that giving Ego more or less information does not matter in either of these situations. Harmony cannot be disturbed in the first case, and the conflict cannot be overcome in the second case.

Moving away from these extreme cases makes it possible to ask the relevant questions. Which games are robust to changes in predictability? Which of them yield the same outcomes, irrespective of the type of actor, expressed in his degree of predictability? One can even translate the question of principle into a question of degree. A specific degree of irrelevant unpredictability can be attached to each class of games. The smaller this degree, the more the predictability problem matters for the game. For predictability has been modelled above as measurable in reference to the variance in Alter's response. A rational interaction partner wants to know whether co-operating with Alter is going to be beneficial. Given the make-up of the model, this is even the only question he is interested in. For the model looks at a world populated by just these two players. Co-operating with Alter thus entails no opportunity cost for Ego. He does not have to pay for this co-operation by forgoing other opportunities to co-operate.[42]

Actually, in some games unpredictability is even beneficial, be it for one of the players or for the little economy consisting of both of them. At this point, a non-technical example must suffice. One can model the interaction between a bird of prey and its potential victim in game theoretic terms.[43] It is well understood that the victim is better off individually if it succeeds in making its behaviour unpredictable to the bird of prey.[44] This result typically remains the same even if one looks not at the individual victim in isolation, but at the victim plus the entire species of aggressors. For low predictability of the victim might help maintain an equilibrium. Aggressors are in the same situation as humans exploiting a natural resource. In the long run, they do best if they keep the natural resource at its maximum sustainable yield. If individual aggressors, in the aggregate, are technically able to go beyond this point, they run the risk of extinguishing the resource on which they live.[45] A

---

[41] This holds for the game that goes by the name 'matching pennies'. Its only equilibrium is in mixed strategies where both players randomise; Fudenberg and Levine 1998: 16–17.

[42] A functionally equivalent statement is: the full opportunity cost is already contained in Ego's pay-offs.

[43] For a classic treatment, see Stephens and Krebs 1986.

[44] The point has been made by Glimcher 2003: 274–5; see also 300, 310.

[45] More from Hartwick and Olewiler 1998.

certain degree of unpredictability in the victim's behaviour can thus be a functional equivalent of regulation that limits catch.

It is beyond the scope of this book to assess the value of predictability in all the many types of games. But since the remainder of this book will look at one specific game only, it seems important to show at the outset that the value of predictability entirely hinges upon the character of the game and why. Two classic examples will illustrate the point. The first is what game theorists call a battle of the sexes (b), the second a (symmetrical) prisoner's dilemma (c). This formal presentation also serves a second purpose. It will make it possible to determine precisely the character of the game analysed here (d).

(b) Battle of the sexes   Game theorists call the first game a battle of the sexes. The cover story is a bit old-fashioned. A married couple want to spend an evening together. The husband would prefer to see a football game, while his wife would rather go to the opera. But both dislike being in splendid isolation even more. They would rather forgo their first preferences than miss the other's company.[46] Game theorists have general solution concepts to determine the outcomes of their games. The easiest concept is dominance. One player knows what to do, irrespective of what the other does.[47] This is a result of the fact that this strategy will always yield him or her a strictly higher pay-off than any other strategy. But in this game, neither player has a dominant move. The utility of each player entirely depends on how the other behaves. The solution concept for that type of interaction is the Nash equilibrium. Each player determines a best response, given a certain move of the other player.[48] Not so rarely, this intellectual trick alone is enough to give the game a unique solution. But the battle of the sexes is different. It has two Nash equilibria.[49] If the husband has the upper hand, the wife will join him in the stadium. If the wife gains the upper hand, the husband will join her in the opera house. The game thus poses a problem of equilibrium selection. The problem is compounded by the fact that the man would rather go to the game, while the woman would rather go to the performance. The spouses thus have a distributional problem.[50] If

---

[46] More illustration from Baird et al. 1994: 41–2.

[47] See also Baird et al.1994: 12 on iterated dominance.

[48] More from Baird et al. 1994: 19–28.

[49] Actually, it even has a third Nash equilibrium. Game theorists call it an equilibrium in mixed strategies, as opposed to the two equilibria in pure strategies described in the text. The third equilibrium implies that both players play one strategy with some probability, and the other with the remaining probability; more from Fudenberg and Levine 1998: 18–23.

[50] This feature of the game is exploited by Knight 1992: chapter 3.

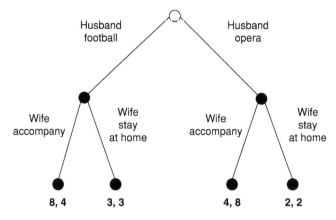

Figure 3.2. Battle of the sexes extensive form: husband moves first.

both spouses behave fully rationally, and nothing else is given, it is a mere coincidence whether they succeed in spending the evening together or not. Put differently, adding a little context is necessary to solve this type of game successfully. Game theorists call the elements taken from context 'focal points'.[51]

Game theorists often present their games in matrix form. The matrix implicitly has both players move simultaneously. In a battle of the sexes, switching to a predetermined sequence of moves solves the problem of the parties altogether. Sequential games are portrayed by a decision tree. Figures 3.2 and 3.3 are the two alternative trees for this game. Note that, in contrast to the base game, here the two options, football and opera, are not linked by a dotted line. According to game theoretic conventions, this implies that the second mover can observe the first move when it is his turn. Actually, it is not the sequential character alone, but the observation that does the trick.[52] To see why, have a look at the game tree in Figure 3.2. By way of illustration, and somewhat artificially, numerical pay-offs are added to the different outcomes. The left-hand number is the first mover's pay-off, the right-hand number the second mover's pay-off.

If the husband is allowed to move first, given his preferences, he will obviously go for football. The decision tree implies that he can credibly commit to this strategy, e.g. by buying the tickets. Since his wife would

---

[51] For a basic treatment, see Schelling 1960.
[52] Not to be misunderstood: this change also makes for a different game.

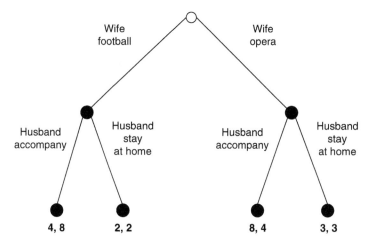

Figure 3.3. Battle of the sexes extensive form: wife moves first.

rather go to the stadium than spend the evening in isolation, the game is easily solved. So too, if the wife has the first-mover advantage, her husband will follow her to the opera house.

These obvious solutions, however, only follow if the second mover knows the first move when he decides. If this is not the case, the second mover is back to the original situation. This is why game theorists say that simultaneous games are functionally equivalent to sequential games without knowledge about the history of the game.[53] Above we have already apostrophised this situation as one of imperfect information.

Depending on the structure of a battle of the sexes, the spouses do or do not know what the other has done or is going to do. One might call this a problem of predictability. But it has nothing to do with the predictability problem of this book. Both spouses are strict utility maximisers. Their preferences are fully determined *ex ante*. They exploit all the information available. They optimise their behaviour, given the restrictions. What happens if one adds a predictability problem of the kind investigated here? Since we have interpreted this problem above in game theoretic language, we now can simply combine the two pieces. One possible outcome appears in Figure 3.4. Of course, one could draw three more pictures. One could have the wife move first. And one could have the first mover exhibiting behavioural variance, rather than the second.

[53] Baird et al. 1994: 53.

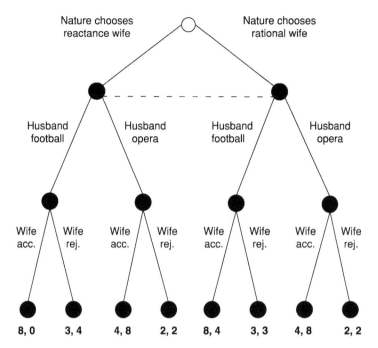

Figure 3.4. Battle of the sexes extensive form: Nature selects actor type.

In actual fact, however, the number of possible pictures is almost infinite. This becomes obvious once we have a closer look. The right-hand side of Figure 3.4 is identical with Figure 3.2. If the husband knew that he was in this situation, he would play his first-mover advantage out. The situation depicted on the left-hand side, however, is different. It can be interpreted in line with a well-known psychological mechanism. The wife is furious that her husband solves their conflict so egoistically. She exhibits reactance.[54] She would rather stay at home and shout at her husband than join the egoistic monster at his football game. Cold-blooded economists depict this by a small change in pay-offs. The utility of the wife for going to the game has dropped to zero. If she does not really feel like shouting, her utility for not having an outing today might even increase a little more. If her husband remains even-tempered, he could still play his first-mover advantage. Now his first choice would also be to go to the opera house. Look at the pay-offs to see why. If the husband commits to the football game, his wife will stay at home. The

---

[54] See above 2.2.7.

husband's utility is 3. If he offers an evening in the opera house, however, he receives 4. By anticipating the irascible temper of the wife, the solution to the game is a unique Nash equilibrium.

Of course, the problem is prediction. Even irascible people do not exhibit reactance all the time. For a host of reasons, they might prefer to be gentle to their spouses. If the husband has no way of finding out how his wife will react, he must make the decision under conditions of uncertainty described above. In short: if the original game is a battle of the sexes, predictability matters a lot.

(c) Prisoner's dilemma   Of the many two-by-two games, one has attracted by far the most attention among social scientists – the prisoner's dilemma.[55] The cover story runs as follows. Two criminals have jointly committed a crime. They are caught by the police and questioned separately. The police officer starts the interrogation by telling each of them the rules of the game. If both confess, they are given a moderate sentence. If both remain silent, they receive a light punishment. If one of them confesses, however, and the other remains silent, the first receives crown witness treatment. He goes without punishment, while the other receives the most severe sentence. Figure 3.5 shows an example in matrix form.

This game has very different properties from the battle of the sexes. If both parties behave fully rationally, the game is easy to solve. Both confess. There is not even a need for recourse to the concept of a Nash equilibrium in order to solve the game. For each player has a dominant strategy.[56] As mentioned, dominance is a game theoretic solution strategy. It is applicable if one player does better by choosing one option, whatever the other player does.[57] If prisoner 2 confesses, prisoner 1 must confess too. Otherwise he suffers his worst outcome. If prisoner 2

		Prisoner 2	
		Silent	Confess
Prisoner 1	Silent	−2, −2	−10, 0
	Confess	0, −10	−6, −6

Figure 3.5. Prisoner's dilemma normal form.

---

[55] Standard references are Rapoport and Chammah 1965; Poundstone 1992.
[56] But if one uses the Nash equilibrium as the solution concept, the result is the same. Both players' dominant strategies are also the unique Nash equilibrium.
[57] Baird et al. 1994: 11; see also 12 on iterated dominance.

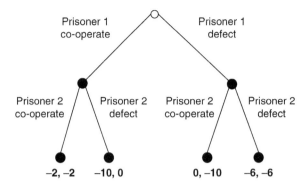

Figure 3.6. Prisoner's dilemma extensive form: prisoner 2 can observe.

remains silent, prisoner 1 might also remain silent. This would be the best outcome for the little society of two prisoners. But in this outcome, prisoner 1 would miss the even better outcome that he now can achieve by confessing.

Like any game, a prisoner's dilemma can also be written in extensive form. One of the two possibilities is presented in Figure 3.6. Of course, one could also have prisoner 2 move first. For simplicity, the following only looks at the first option.

If prisoner 2 does not know what prisoner 1 has done, this sequential game is strategically equivalent to the simultaneous game shown in the matrix. The only interesting case is thus the one in which prisoner 2 can observe prisoner 1's move before he moves himself. This situation is demonstrated in Figure 3.6. There Prisoner 1's two options are not linked by a dotted line.

In the battle of the sexes, this change in the game was beneficial for the parties. In a prisoner's dilemma, the change is irrelevant. It does not bring both prisoners any closer to the social optimum of their little society, i.e. both remaining silent. This is obvious if prisoner 1 confesses. Game theorists then speak of defection. The only sensible thing for prisoner 2 is to confess as well. The two prisoners end up with the same outcome as before. Intuitively, one might think that the sequential structure of the game allows them to do better. For now prisoner 1 can signal his willingness to co-operate by remaining silent. Game theorists have indeed investigated this option at length. But strictly speaking, it does not even help if the two parties interact repeatedly. If all players are fully rational, such a game should unravel from the end, and result in

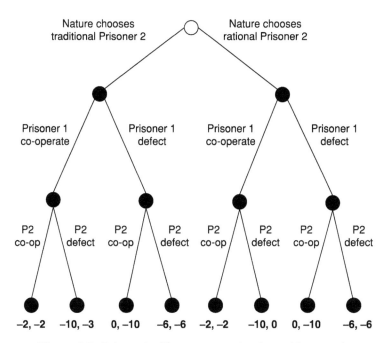

Figure 3.7. Prisoner's dilemma extensive form: Nature selects actor type.

defection from the very beginning.[58] This holds even more in a one-shot game. For prisoner 2 is assumed to be a utility maximiser. If he could observe prisoner 1's move, he would know for sure that prisoner 1 had remained silent. Within the model, prisoner 1 also has no opportunity to revise his choice. Prisoner 2 now knows that by confessing himself, he can go home free of punishment. A utility maximiser does not miss an opportunity to obtain his best outcome.

What happens if one of the players' behaviour is not fully predictable? This can be modelled the same way as in the battle of the sexes. The resulting decision tree is presented in Figure 3.7.

Again, the right-hand side of the tree is identical to Figure 3.6. The left-hand side has somewhat vaguely been called traditional behaviour. This vagueness suffices at this point. It brings a slight change in the pay-offs. If prisoner 1 co-operates and prisoner 2 defects, prisoner 2 no

---

[58] The classic reference is Selten 1978. For a stimulating treatment, juxtaposing game theoretic and psychological insights, see Beckenkamp 2003.

longer receives 0, but -3. That is, if prisoner 1 co-operates and prisoner 2 defects, prisoner 2 no longer receives his best outcome. Now, for him the best situation is one in which he and prisoner 1 co-operate. Note that the change is not symmetrical. For prisoner 1, it still would be best to defect, while prisoner 2 co-operates. But because of the sequential character of the game, this is not an equilibrium. When prisoner 2 moves, he can observe what prisoner 1 has done. If prisoner 1 has defected, prisoner 2 will defect too. In this transformation, the game thus exhibits a second-mover advantage. For prisoner 1 anticipates the reaction by prisoner 2. He therefore co-operates. Co-operation becomes the unique equilibrium of the game.

In psychological terms there are many possible explanations of where such a traditional attitude of prisoner 2 might come from. He simply might follow a heuristic saying that a criminal should never confess. This is quite plausible, since prisoners are hardly ever involved in the situation modelled by the game. Prisoner 2 might also consider it unfair to confess. Precisely this could be the case, since his own confession would also lead to the conviction of the other prisoner. A third explanation relies on honour among thieves. Since they receive a moderate punishment if they both confess, they reckon on coming back to the criminal community. Even if this were not the case, they might rightly fear sanctions from this community within prison.

If prisoner 1 knows prisoner 2's type, he can thus rationally decide what to do. If prisoner 2 is a rationalist, prisoner 1 will defect. If prisoner 2 is a traditionalist, prisoner 1 will co-operate. But in the game modelled here, Nature conceals prisoner 2's type. Prisoner 1 must thus decide under conditions of uncertainty. He faces a difficult choice. If he confesses and prisoner 2 is rational, both receive a moderate sentence. If he confesses, and prisoner 2 is traditional, the outcome is the same. But the outcome differs markedly if prisoner 1 remains silent. If prisoner 2 is traditional, this leads to the best outcome provided by the game. Both receive a light sentence. But this strategy of prisoner 1 can go badly wrong. For if prisoner 2 behaves rationally, this results in the worst of all situations for prisoner 1. He receives the most severe punishment.

Economists assess risks as the product of two components: the potential damage, and its probability. Given the structure of the game, prisoner 1 is completely aware of this damage. It is the difference between a moderate and a high degree of punishment. Similarly, prisoner 1 can calculate the potential gains of co-operation. If prisoner 2 is traditional and prisoner 1 remains silent, prisoner 1 receives a moderate rather than a light punishment. The potential harm is thus -4, the potential gain $+4$. At this point, prisoner 1 is assumed to be fully rational. His decision thus entirely hinges upon the subjective probabilities attached to the two actor types.[59]

Predictability does thus also matter in a prisoner's dilemma. But the effect of behavioural variance is entirely different. Depending on the precise distribution of pay-offs, a small amount of behavioural variance can already be enough to ensure that the parties reach the social optimum. Since the unique rational equilibrium is a social dilemma, behavioural uncertainty can be irrelevant. The right kind and degree of unpredictability can even be beneficial.[60]

(d) *Character of the standard predictability game* Based on the foregoing, the character of the standard game presented in 3.2.2 can finally be determined. The prisoner's dilemma from Figure 3.6 can also be written in generic form as Figure 3.8.

The concrete numbers −10, −6, −2 and 0 have been replaced by generic notation. The line between gain and loss has moved: what was previously denoted as −6 has now become 0. But the ranking has

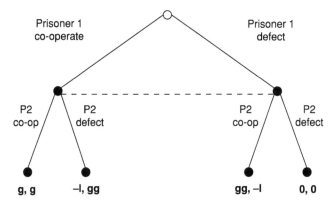

Figure 3.8. Symmetrical prisoner's dilemma extensive form: generic payoffs.

---

[59] Economists often allow for risk preferences that deviate from risk neutrality. In that case, losses or gains would have to be weighted with the risk preference of prisoner 1. Psychologically, loss-aversion might play a role, provided prisoner 1 sees the neutral priors of the game as a reference point; see above 2.2.4. In that case, prisoner 1 would have to find it much more likely that prisoner 2 is traditional, if the uncertainty is to be of help to the parties.

[60] Elster 1989: 3 and chapter 3, also observes that unpredictability can be socially beneficial.

remained the same, which means that Equation 1 holds. It is repeated here for convenience:

$$gg > g > 0 > -l.$$

This minor change in notation shows that the game analysed in this chapter, and presented earlier in Figure 3.1, actually is also a prisoner's dilemma. Proof is the fully analogue presentation in Figure 3.9.

But there are two differences between this and the earlier version of the prisoner's dilemma. The prisoner's dilemma presented in 3.2.3(c) is symmetrical. Each player is in precisely the same situation. Put differently, each player is at the other player's mercy. Each can, and given the rationality assumption will, choose the dominant move and defect. The game analysed in this chapter, however, is characterised by an asymmetry.[61] Only Ego stands to loose, not Alter. As will be demonstrated later, this makes for a different incentive structure. The prime difference, however, is not the one between a symmetrical and an asymmetric game. The prime difference rests in the additional move by Nature at the outset of the game, which picks Alter from one of two types: i.e. beneficial or detrimental.

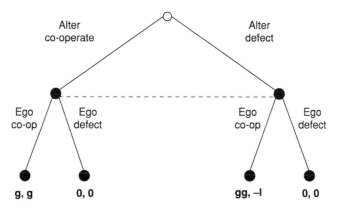

Figure 3.9. Predictability game: Nature's move omitted.

[61] It appears that asymmetric prisoner's dilemmas of this kind have not been studied in the literature, the closest analogue apparently being Engelmann 2001; see also Kandori 2002 and the papers following this introduction to a special issue of the journal; Eriksson and Lindgren 2002; short remarks are also to be found in Poundstone 1992: 221–2; finally, Sheposh and Gallo 1973 is interested in an asymmetric distribution not of information, but of pay-offs.

3.2.4 Artificially increased unpredictability

Behavioural dispositions are not iron-clad. Below, the power of institutions to mould behavioural dispositions will be investigated.[62] Alter can rely on many of these interventions autonomously. And reducing behavioural variance is not the only option. To quite a degree, Alter can increase behavioural variance instead. He, for instance, can undergo training and acquire a new behavioural routine.

The model used here assumes that Alter takes these decisions in a fully rational manner. Alter, when deciding about increasing unpredictability, is thus aware of the structure of the base game. He will only decide to increase unpredictability if the balance of the shift in predictability is positive. Trivially, if the benefit for both parties in this game is greater, the more predictable Alter is; he will not increase unpredictability instead. The latter observation often even holds if Ego gains even more from the predictability of Alter than Alter himself. For a rational actor is not interested in distributional gain as such. His individual utility is not influenced by how well the other player does. Preferences are not relative. Alter is not envious. He simply looks at how he can do best individually.[63] Why might Alter be better off if he allows Ego to make a distributional gain? This is a result of the fact that the behaviour of Alter and Ego is strategically linked. Put differently: if Ego is fully rational, he anticipates the effect that the low predictability of Alter's behaviour has on his own utility. And if Alter is rational, he anticipates that Ego will anticipate this effect.

A reader not accustomed to rational choice models is likely to find all this amazing. If Alter purposefully makes his behaviour less predictable, does he not do so because he wants to deceive Ego? Does rational choice analysis thus model away the essence of the problem studied in this

---

[62] See below 4.3.

[63] For some readers, it might be easier to understand the foregoing if one also assumes a uniform currency, say price. In that case, growth can be written as a measurable increase in the gross product of the economy (here assumed to be composed of the two players exclusively). The actor will not reduce the predictability of his behaviour if the ensuing opportunity for exploiting Ego eats up the increase in welfare that would otherwise result from co-operation.

An example could be the following: the gains from trade with full predictability are 20 currency units, equally distributed between both players. If Alter strategically decreases predictability, he can expect to get three-quarters of the gains from trade. He will not do so, however, if lower predictability also decreases growth below 15 currency units. While this presentation of Alter's problem is more graphic, it is not fully in line with the simple game theoretic model used here. For a uniform currency unit implies a more complex game, allowing Ego to compensate Alter for his willingness to exhibit greater predictability.

section? Yes and no. Within the game modelled here, there is indeed no room for unanticipated surprise. But the model is open to an increase in anticipated uncertainty. The potential intervention of Alter is thus portrayed in yet another combination of pay-offs for the two parties. Since the change comes as a surprise for Ego, it translates into yet another part of the history of the game Ego has not been able to observe. In the language of the game, Nature has yet a richer pool of actor types from which to draw. In the first approximation, actor type 1 is fully predictable. Actor type 2 exhibits 'natural' unpredictability. On top of the natural unpredictability, actor type 3 also exhibits artificial unpredictability. Actually, within the model, the latter type is presented by adding yet another set of pay-offs to the game. The rational reaction of Ego remains the same as before. He must attach subjective probabilities to each of these sets of pay-offs, and calculate his response from there. The ensuing structure of the game is as shown in Figure 3.10.[64]

In reality, it is not very likely that an actor will be able to manipulate the predictability of his behaviour for just one case of application. If, for instance, he acquires a new behavioural option by training, he will be able to use that option in many more cases. A rational actor then faces a problem of indivisibility. It is particularly relevant if more unpredictability is good for the actor in one instance, but bad in another. This is a likely scenario. For it has been demonstrated that it depends on the character of the base game whether behavioural uncertainty is beneficial for the actor or not. If the actor is unable to customise the manipulation of his predictability, he is forced to play a nested game. Game theorists speak of nested games if single games are part of larger complexes of games.[65] The actor then faces a trade-off. If he increases unpredictability, he arrives at a more beneficial equilibrium in the game of origin. But he pays for this benefit by a less beneficial equilibrium in another game.

---

[64] Another way of modelling the ability of Alter strategically to increase unpredictability would come even closer to reality. Nature would draw twice. Nature would first pick one of two pools. In the first pool, actors never exhibit more than 'natural' unpredictability. In the latter pool, if they are unpredictable, they also increase the natural predictability strategically. At step 2, Nature would then pick an actor from within the pool determined at step 1. If Alter drawn at step 2 is of the predictable type, the difference in pools does not play itself out. It only does if Nature at step 2 picks an actor of the unpredictable type. But since Ego cannot observe the history of the game anyhow, both steps collapse as shown in Figure 3.8, without a loss of explanatory power.
      In order to leave the character of the base game and the way that it is transformed by unpredictability, the pay-offs are not specified in the figure.
[65] For an introduction to the study of nested games, see Baird et al. 1994: 191–202.

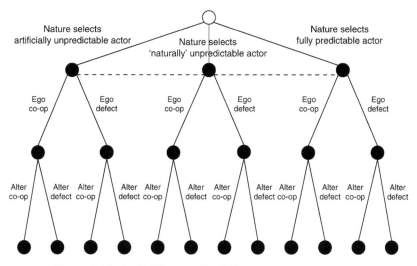

Figure 3.10. Artificial unpredictability.

3.2.5   Signals

Empirically, people can 'fake an attitude'. They are able to engage in 'impression management'.[66] There is no place for this within the simple model used thus far. The interaction partner has been assumed to be fully ignorant of Alter's type. In the language of the game: Ego is unable to observe the history of the game. It is precisely during this history that Nature has determined Alter's type. But models of asymmetric information can be enriched if it is possible for the informed agent to send out a signal. Introducing a signal into the model can have one of two purposes. In one, the information itself is not verifiable. Even if the informed agent wants to impart this information directly to the uninformed principal, he has no way of doing so. Of course, the agent could make a statement. But given that there is no outside possibility to assess the truth of the statement, it is meaningless to rational actors. That being the case, rational actors have an incentive to search for ways to transmit the non-verifiable information indirectly. Put differently, they have an incentive to try to change the game cleverly so that the informed agent can send a credible signal.[67]

---

[66] Bohner 2001: 267.
[67] For an informal treatment and examples from the law, see Baird et al. 1994: 125–42.

But there is also a second reason for using the concept of signal. This applies to situations in which the informed agent transmits a signal that improves the access of the principal to information, without removing the information asymmetry altogether. If used under these conditions, the signal has some, but not full informational value. The principal is no longer confined to subjective probabilities. He can use the signal to make a better-informed guess.[68]

'Impression management' can thus be interpreted in game theoretic language as a technique whereby Alter sends out signals about his behavioural dispositions. In and of itself, this can make a lot of sense. For if Ego trusts the signal, he will move away from a decision based on his prior beliefs. He will start from behavioural assumptions that more closely mirror what Alter is really likely to do. But would a rational actor not rather send out a false signal about his behavioural dispositions? At first glance, this option seems attractive for Alter. By sending the incorrect signal, he can make Ego more vulnerable. But we assume that Ego is fully rational. If this is the case, signals are only sent out if they are fully credible. This should not be misunderstood: their informational value can be below 1. Even in a one-shot game, a signal that reduces behavioural uncertainty without removing it entirely remains valuable. But signals are useless if it cannot be ruled out *ex ante* that they are faked. For a rational interaction partner would anticipate that possibility and ignore the signal.

Of course, in reality there are faked signals about behavioural dispositions. But the foregoing analysis points to an important implication. Faked signals only make sense for Alter if one of two possibilities holds. Either Ego does not behave fully rationally. Or Alter and Ego are not playing a one-shot game.

3.2.6   Alternative languages

Game theoretic language is not the only language that can be used to define the predictability problem. In the following, some alternative languages will be used. They help highlight additional aspects of the predictability problem.

An initial set of terms looks at a particular class of predictability problems. If two persons have concluded a contract, they must ask

---

[68] Schweizer 1999: 143–6 uses the concept in that way. A more technical way of making the point would be: the presence of the signal allows the principal to update his prior beliefs. The conceptual background of this idea is Bayesian updating. For an accessible introduction, see Martignon and Blackmond Laskey 1999.

themselves how likely it is that the other will deliver on his promises. The predictability problem is then a problem of deviation. The problem is real whenever a contract is incomplete. Incompleteness has two aspects. The parties may have left a contractual risk without a specific solution. Or some element of contract fulfilment can be non-self-enforcing.[69] Institutional economists point to the fact that non-self-enforcing contracts engender the risk of opportunism.[70]

The predictability problem described by these terms originates in imperfect commitment. But the idea can be extended to cases without explicit or implicit commitment. It is enough that Ego has expectations about Alter's behaviour and that Alter knows about these expectations. The parallel becomes visible if one interprets this situation as a non-binding, implicit contract, which is incomplete. The predictability problem can thus be characterised in more general form as a risk of a breach of expectations. These expectations can result from legal contractual commitment. But they can also result from other legal obligations, e.g. regulation. Or they can originate in the private, non-binding, but explicit co-ordination of behaviour, or the non-explicit co-ordination of behaviour. An example of the weakest form of this would consist of Alter, who knows that Ego sees him as a member of a class, but cannot be sure whether Alter performs true to type.

If one interprets the predictability problem as a breach of expect-ations, one also establishes a link to the rather encompassing extensive literature on trust.[71] If there is no way to make expectations safe, Ego faces a hard choice. Gains from trade are only to be had if he is willing to trust Alter. The willingness to take a behavioural risk becomes a precondition for mutually beneficial interaction.

A key concept of institutional economics is property rights.[72] Insti-tutional economists are particularly concerned with attenuated pro-perty rights. By this, institutional economists mean a situation where outsiders have a say about how a good is used, whether it is abused, whether yet more outsiders can have access to it, or whether it can be sold off. They see attenuation as detrimental to allocative efficiency. For outsiders can use valuable components of the good without paying for them.[73]

---

[69] The theory of incomplete contracts is an important part of institutional economics. For a summary, see Furubotn and Richter 1997: chapter V.5 and 6; Schweizer 1999: 239–83.
[70] The term was coined by Williamson 1985: chapter I.3 and *passim*.
[71] For references, see above, chapter 1, note 47.
[72] For a basic treatment, see Eggertsson 1990.   [73] Eggertsson 1990: 38–40 and *passim*.

This concept can be used in several ways to describe the predictability problem. The first is identical to the interpretation just presented. A contractual right can be interpreted as a relative property right. If the holder of this right, because of unpredictability, is not sure about delivery, this can be seen as an attenuation of the relative property right. A second interpretation looks at the actor. The concept fits if the behavioural predictability problem is natural, not strategic. For this means that the actor is unable to issue fully enforceable promises. The individual ability to fulfil a promise can be interpreted as a good. The individual has recourse either to his fortune or to what economists call his human capital.[74] Unpredictability here means that the individual does not have complete property rights over his own human capital. If Ego is rational, Alter pays for this incompleteness because Ego has a smaller willingness to pay.

To the extent that Alter is able credibly to make his own behaviour more predictable, one can use the concept of property rights the other way round too. One can interpret the natural degree of unpredictability as an implicit property right of Alter, which he can trade. At closer sight, however, this interpretation does not fit well with the situation investigated here. For this section looks at voluntary co-operation between Alter and Ego. In such cases, being unpredictable in the first place is not a valuable good for Alter. This is different in torts. There, the threat of unpredictable intrusion serves as the baseline for potential victims.[75]

Finally, there is a defined relationship between the two rational choice explanations of the predictability problem discussed in this book. Both are reasons for behavioural risk. If Ego is unable to contain this risk, he must live up to it or abstain from interaction. But in these two cases the behavioural risk has a different origin. If the predictability problem originates in an information asymmetry, the problem is solved once the partners themselves or an intermediary intervening from the outside make it possible to impart the missing information credibly. This strategy is not available if the behavioural risk originates in the indeterminacy of behavioural programme. In that case, to reduce the risk the behavioural dispositions have to change themselves. If this is not feasible or acceptable, the only remaining strategy consists of bearing the risk.

3.3   Type revelation

When faced with information asymmetry, players have a whole set of options, which will be discussed in this chapter. Each of them can react

---

[74] For a basic treatment, see Becker 1993.   [75] See below 6.

individually: Ego (3.3.1) and Alter (3.3.2). They can also join forces, be that by sharing the cost of unilateral technologies (3.3.3) or by using joint technologies in the first place (3.3.4). They can rely on the services of a third party (3.3.5), or a sovereign can intervene on their behalf (3.3.6). Before the parties do any of this, they will, however, want to consider additional problems originating in natural or artificial links between issues or persons, on the one hand (3.3.7) and in problems of power, on the other (3.3.8). Based on this, they will be able to make their institutional choices (3.3.9).

3.3.1   Unilateral response by Ego

(a) Introduction   There are many ways of defining institutions.[76] For the purposes of this book, it is not necessary to take sides in this dispute. The book is open to formal and informal solutions. And it does not confine its interest to responses by outside actors, be they the law, government more generally, or private parties. In order to make this openness explicit, the book rather speaks of responses to the predictability problem, and it makes explicit who will become active. This section starts with unilateral options for Ego.

This part of the book is interested in situations where mutually beneficial co-operation between Ego and Alter would in principle be possible. The problem of Ego can thus be described in terms of an opportunity cost. Ego always retains the option of abstaining from co-operation with Alter. The *status quo ante* is thus his outside option. Rational choice bargaining theorists also call it the breakdown value.[77]

At the outset, the problem of Ego is compounded by the fact that he faces a game with a pooling equilibrium.[78] We have seen that this element of uncertainty can even be beneficial. But the following only looks at the flipside of the coin, i.e. at situations where generating more certainty would be beneficial for both parties. In the stronger case, for Ego the breakdown value is higher than the expected value from co-operation, should the pooling equilibrium persist. In the weaker case, generating more certainty would make co-operation even more beneficial for Ego. In both cases, Ego will consider intervention that is likely to generate greater certainty.

---

[76] Overviews of the discussion are to be found in Hodgson 1988: 123–38; Knight 1992: chapters 1 and 3; Furubotn and Richter 1997: chapter I.1 g; Scharpf 1997: 38.
[77] For a succinct presentation of rational choice bargaining theory, see Knight 1992: chapter 5.
[78] On the concept of a pooling versus a separating equilibrium, see above, 3.2.3(a).

As pointed out above, unilateral reactions by Ego are not the only option in such a situation. Ego and Alter can join forces. Outside actors such as government can step in. And it can be rational for Alter to make his own behaviour more predictable. Since Alter is assumed to deal rationally with his own unpredictability, he is also likely to do so. Ego will anticipate this. Before he takes action on his own, he will compare his course of action with all these other options. But for analytic purposes, this section only looks at what Ego can do unilaterally. This part of the book thus makes an additional assumption. It assumes that Ego believes that no other person will intervene in the interest of making Alter's behaviour more predictable.

Ego, intervening unilaterally, has the following options at his disposal: inspection (b), a direct mechanism (c), the exploitation of signals (d) and screening (e). In the last two cases, the behavioural uncertainty is not removed, but only reduced. A rational reaction to this change is Bayesian updating (f).

(b) Inspection   If I know less than I want to, the easiest thing to do is engage in inspection. Ego searches for (direct)[79] information about Alter's type. Inspection presupposes, however, something that is rare in the area of behavioural uncertainty: the information sought after must at least be observable. Information economics distinguishes three classes of information: verifiable, observable and non-observable information. In the first case, even an outsider can verify the correctness of a statement. In the case of observable information, only the interacting partners can do so. In the case of non-observable information, not even the direct interaction partners can distinguish a true from a false statement.

The distinction between verifiable and observable information is obviously only of importance if a third party wants to intervene. It can be ignored at this point. But statements about future behaviour are typically not even observable. Even if we are truly acquainted with another person, we could not say whether he is telling the truth about his future behaviour. This can be different, however, if the object of the statement is not behaviour itself, but the ability to behave in a certain way. The information asymmetry typically persists for negative statements about behavioural dispositions. If a good friend says he is unable to engage in revenge, this may sound plausible to our ears. But actually, the most we could assess is that we have never observed any sign of vindictiveness. But positive statements about behavioural dispositions

---

[79] Otherwise, one is in the realm of signalling and screening, investigated below.

could be another matter. If our friend says he is a trained statistician, we might be able to verify this statement. Since very few people are, this might be important information for us if we have to interact with this friend in a situation that involves calculable risk.

In the world of rational choice models, nothing is free of charge. Inspection is no exception. In reality, the additional cost for the generation of information may sometimes be negligible. Ego may possess this information anyhow, since he could not avoid collecting it. This is often the case if Alter and Ego have been part of the same context for a while. Put differently, assuming the inspection cost to be zero can be a way of modelling contextual interaction in a parsimonious way.

But also in reality, the inspection cost will often not be zero. It can come in two parts. Learning more about Alter's behavioural dispositions can come at an out-of-pocket cost. Ego must invest time or money for the purpose. Often, the opportunity cost will be more relevant, however. Closely observing or even proactively testing Alter is often not without risk. Many people see such action as unfair or as a breach of trust. Rationally, Ego anticipates such reactions. He weighs the pros and cons of inspection. In economic language: he calculates the inspection cost.[80]

If one translates the foregoing into game theoretic language, the possibility of inspection generates a more complex game. Ego still cannot directly observe Alter's type. He still ignores the history of the game when he is first allowed to move. But he now has two sequential options. He must first decide whether to invest in inspection. If he declines the option, he goes directly to his final move. If he seizes the opportunity, he may learn something about the history of the game afterwards. The ensuing structure of the game is presented in Figure 3.11.

This game is an enriched version of the base game presented in Figure 3.1. The additional option of inspection that is open to Ego is portrayed as an extra stage of the game. If Nature chooses a beneficial actor, Alter responds to the move of Ego in a fully symmetrical way. If Ego co-operates, Alter also co-operates. If Ego defects, Alter also defects. If both defect, no change in utility occurs. If both co-operate, there are gains from trade. These gains are shared symmetrically between the players. Since inspection is costly, a rational interaction partner will not be interested in inspection if Nature has chosen a beneficial actor. For Ego would then lose money, regardless of how he himself moves at stage 3. If he defects, Alter also will. But Ego then incurs a loss, namely the inspection cost. If Alter now co-operates, the balance may

---

[80] For economists, this line of reasoning is so obvious that it is rarely mentioned, but see Eichenberger 2002: 84.

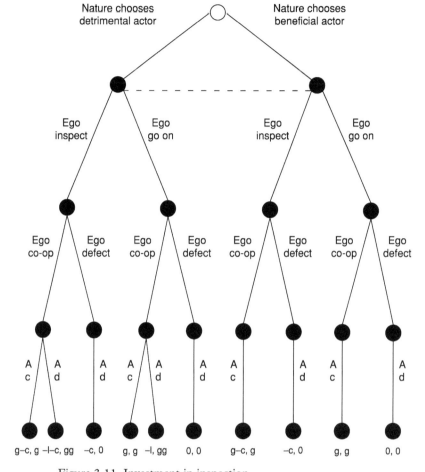

Figure 3.11. Investment in inspection.

still be positive. This depends on whether Ego's share of the gains from trade is higher than the inspection cost or not. But had he not inspected, he would have received the full gain.

But of course, Ego does not know Nature's move. If Nature has chosen a detrimental actor, inspection can indeed be beneficial for Ego. The explanation comes in two steps. Step 1 shows that Ego is better off defecting if Nature has chosen a detrimental actor. Since, with a beneficial actor, co-operation is beneficial, knowing the type of actor matters. Let us see why. If Ego co-operates with a detrimental actor, this actor could co-operate too. If that happens, the outcome will be the same as with a beneficial actor. The gains from trade will be split evenly among the players. But if Ego co-operates, a detrimental actor can do even better. He can keep all the gains from trade for himself, and inflict a loss on Ego. Since all actors are assumed to be rational, the detrimental actor will do this if it is possible. If Ego knew the type of actor he was dealing with, he would anticipate this outcome and defect. If that occurred, there would be no gains from trade. Both players would keep their *status quo ante*.

But again this is only part of the story, for inspection comes at a price. If Ego wants to protect himself by learning the type of actor that he is dealing with, he will never be able to obtain the best outcome, which would be an even split of the gains from trade. The best he can obtain is the following. If he learns that Alter is beneficial, he will co-operate. He will receive the gains from trade, minus the cost of inspection. If he learns that Alter is detrimental, he will defect. In that case, he will incur the cost of inspection as a loss.

If we further assume risk neutrality, Ego's decision about inspection essentially boils down to a comparison of three parameters: the share in the gains from trade, the cost of inspection and the potential loss. If the cost of inspection is larger than the share in the gains from trade, the solution is simple. Even if, after inspection, Ego finds out that Alter is beneficial, he will no longer want to co-operate. Ego will defect. Formally, this condition can be written as:

$$g - c > 0, \tag{5}$$

where g is Ego's maximum gain from trade, and c the cost of inspection. Likewise, learning Alter's type at a cost only makes sense if the potential loss from co-operating with a detrimental actor is larger than this cost. Otherwise the cost for learning Alter's type is prohibitive. Formally,

$$l - c > 0, \tag{6}$$

where l is the maximum loss for Ego. If Ego learns by inspection that Alter is detrimental, he will not co-operate. It is assumed here that the inspection technology with certainty allows Ego to learn Alter's type. Accordingly, his decision about investing this cost can be expressed in the following equation:

$$pg - c > 0, \tag{7}$$

where p is the subjective probability of Alter being beneficial, as in Equation 4.

Before he takes action, Ego will compare this potential cost with the cost of remaining inactive. If he does nothing, from Equation 4, he expects

$$pg - (1-p)l.$$

If he invests and gains certain knowledge of Alter's type, from Equation 7, he expects

$$pg - c.$$

Accordingly, investment pays under the following condition:

$$(1-p)l - c > 0. \tag{8}$$

Ego must thus compare the expected loss as a result of co-operation with a detrimental actor, multiplied by the *ex ante* probability of this happening, with the cost of investment.

(c) *Direct mechanism*   In reality, there is often no real possibility of learning Alter's type by inspection. We cannot open people's heads. And not even brain imaging, fashionable among neuroscientists nowadays, enables us to determine behaviour. Typically, the best option available is to observe a person for a while, and to try to deduct personality traits from those observations. If also coupled with a correct assessment of the psychological situation, this may work.[81] But it often will not. In the language of game theorists, Alter's type then is not observable. Such situations are studied by a branch of economics called mechanism design. Researchers of mechanism design try to design institutions such that the best response of the informed agent is to reveal his private information truthfully to the uninformed principal. It is thus the design of the institution that makes the information credible.[82]

A classic example is workable competition.[83] Gains from trade presuppose that the buyer values the good higher than the seller. Obviously, both sides want to find out how much so. Put differently, there is more than one price for striking a deal. A rational buyer wants the seller to believe his willingness to pay to be as low as possible. Likewise, a rational seller wants the buyer to believe his willingness to sell is as high as possible. The respective willingness is private information. But workable

---

[81] More above, 2.5.3.
[82] For a succinct presentation, see Schweizer 1999.
[83] The classic reference for this norm for competition policy is Clark 1961; for an overview of competing proposals, see Bartling 1980.

competition forces both partners to reveal this information.[84] If the
buyer states a lower willingness to pay, the good goes to another buyer.
Likewise, if the seller states a willingness to sell only at exaggerated
prices, the buyer goes to another seller.

In such cases, game theorists speak of a direct mechanism, since
the institution forces the agent to reveal his private information fully.
Such mechanisms need not be imposed on the parties from outside.
They can design them on their own. Specifically, uninformed Ego can
make Alter an offer that is conditional upon the revelation of Alter's
private information. If the offer is designed cleverly enough, Alter may
be unable to resist. They must be designed so that Alter is worse off if he
remains unwilling to impart his private knowledge truthfully.

Within the model, one can say precisely how large the cost at the end
of the game must be for Alter for not co-operating. If Ego co-operates,
and Alter defects, Alter gains gg. If Alter co-operates, he receives g. The
potential gain from defection thus is $gg - g$. Accordingly Alter is indifferent about both co-operation and defection if Ego can credibly threaten
Alter with a loss of $gg - g$ should he defect at the end of the game. If
Ego wants to be sure that Alter will co-operate, he must impose a loss
that transcends $gg - g$ at least a little. Formally, the credible threat of a
punishment must thus be $gg - g + \varepsilon$.

Within the environment fully devoid of context that is depicted in our
base game, Ego has no possibility to impose such a mechanism on Alter
against his will. Put differently, a direct mechanism is a unilateral option
for Ego only if, given elements from a richer context, Alter is vulnerable
to his intervention. If so, Ego can exploit the fact that, after Alter has
moved, Ego also knows what type of an actor he is. For a beneficial actor
will not defect, whereas a detrimental actor will. He can credibly
threaten Alter with punishment, should he turn out to be of the detrimental type. If the punishment makes Alter worse off than his outside
option of a zero gain, Alter will rather reveal what type of an actor he is.

(d) Exploitation of signals   Conceptually speaking, a direct
mechanism exploits a one-to-one correlation between two facts. If the
correlation is that strong, an observation of the first fact suffices to
predict the second. In reality, for behaviour, the correlation is typically
weaker. If Ego observes some signal, there is a given probability
that Alter will behave in a given way, but no certainty. This weaker

---

[84] Actually things are usually a little more complicated, since sellers are typically not able
to implement full price discrimination; they mostly sell their standard goods even at a
uniform price.

correlation is much more frequent, precisely because human behavioural dispositions are so malleable. Even if Alter intends to tie his future behaviour to this one signal, this plasticity often prevents him from doing so. Observing this signal thus does not free Ego from the need to make a risky choice, based not only on information, but also on prior beliefs. Yet another way of making the point is as follows: knowing the signal reduces the behavioural space of Alter that is to be taken into account, but it does not narrow it down to zero. Or in shorthand: direct mechanisms are deterministic, signals are probabilistic.

This probabilistic character makes Ego's problem more complex. But it does not make it fundamentally different from the problem studied under a direct mechanism. Ego will believe signals only if they are credible. If he tries to make Alter send signals, he thus must design the mechanism as cleverly as with a direct mechanism. Sending the signal out must be the best response for Alter, given the restrictions introduced by this mechanism. Since at this point only mechanisms that do not involve third parties are considered, there is no need for the signal to be verifiable by outsiders. It is enough if the signal is observable.

As with direct mechanisms, allowing Alter to have behavioural limitations enlarges the scope for signalling. For these limitations may force Alter to send out signals, even if this is not beneficial for him in concrete instances. Signals can thus be imposed on Alter by Nature. In truth this is rather frequent. This explains why signalling in reality is a powerful tool for alleviating the predictability problem.

Actually, the whole idea of distinguishing a micro and a nano level fits here. For even if Ego learns about behavioural dispositions of Alter, he cannot linearly translate this into predictions about behaviour. If he gets the behavioural disposition right, he can, at most, make a better educated guess about behaviour.

By implication, observing earlier behaviour is not in and of itself enough to allow future behaviour to be predicted; in this, behaviour at most conveys a signal about some behavioural disposition. In the next instance, this disposition can play itself out differently, since it interacts with the context or with other behavioural dispositions in new ways. It also can be outperformed by a different behavioural disposition. Put differently, Ego is forced to interpret previous behaviour. He must assess how good a signal for future behaviour it actually is. But all this said, the information value of earlier behaviour is not zero. On the contrary, it typically remains the best predictor available for future behaviour.[85]

---

[85] Mischel and Peake 1982: 748.

Not all previous behaviour is equally informative. The more behaviour is patterned, the more informative it is. The more an actor becomes an expert in an area, the more likely it is that some cues will have high predictive power. Actually there is a direct link between the idea of patterned behaviour and the work on differential psychology discussed above. *In abstracto*, there are two sources that make behaviour more predictable: context and personality.[86] Since Ego is not interested in either of them in isolation, he is even better off. He can search directly for specific combinations of personality and context. Put differently, if this one actor is exposed to a well-defined context, and if he is an expert in that area, this can allow a rather reliable prediction of his behaviour.

Sometimes, just knowing the context is in itself an informative signal. Low stakes are one example. They make it much more likely that actors will be willing to listen to their conscience, or to moral norms to which they are exposed.[87] Likewise, personality traits can be so powerful that they are very likely to play themselves out, whatever the context. Strong emotions can fit in here as well. If Alter is known to be choleric, a little disturbance of his expectations is likely to trigger aggressive reactions in most contexts.

Not so rarely, Ego meets actors pre-selected according to their behavioural dispositions. A professional fire fighter is not likely to be a coward. The litigation specialist of a big law firm is likely to act as strategically as he can. A nun is likely to be more compassionate than the ordinary citizen. Professional training, and group membership more generally, are thus good signals for behavioural dispositions. But Ego must be aware that actors are able to play several roles. They can easily be multiple selves.[88] This, in return, weakens signal quality.

The more selective a group, the stronger the predictive power. But even membership in less exclusionary groups may still convey valuable information. Even the most general, the culture into which Alter is embedded, may make some behaviour more likely than others. Alter's adherence to a certain ideology can also be important information. Of course, outspoken social democrats sometimes exhibit little solidarity. But they are still more likely to be driven by solidarity than people from the right wing, at least vis-à-vis outsiders.

---

[86] See above 2.5.3–4.
[87] The point is made by Weck-Hannemann 1999: 76–8, relying on work by Kirchgässner on behaviour in low-cost situations: Kirchgässner 1992, 1996; Kirchgässner and Pommerehne 1993.
[88] Roberts and Donahue 1994.

(e) Screening Game theorists terminologically distinguish signalling from screening. In the first case, the agent, i.e. the informed party, takes the initiative. In screening, the principal, i.e. the uninformed party, exposes the agent to a context that forces him to convey an informative signal.[89] A graphic example is the following. An employer has a pool of applicants for a post. He wants to omit those with bad backs from his selection, since he is afraid they will be ill too often. He has all applicants go through an assessment centre lasting several days. He offers two types of chairs, a highly uncomfortable one and an orthopaedic chair good for ailing backs. He expects the applicants to react rationally. If they do, they ask themselves why these two types of chairs are present. Those with the ailing backs realise that picking the orthopaedic chair will reveal private information to the future employer. But they see going through the assessment centre with an awfully ailing back as even worse. Provided those with healthy backs have equal prevoyance, those with the ailing backs indicate their health problem by their behaviour. But if the pool of applicants is large enough, the employer need not worry. He can simply discard all applications from those who have chosen the orthopaedic chair. In that case, the signal is not fully informative. But it conveys enough information for the employer to make a rational choice.[90]

(f) Bayesian updating If the correlation between the observed information and the behavioural disposition is not deterministic, Ego faces a risky choice. Bayes' rule states how a rational actor should go about making such a choice. He should start by using the base rate. He should thus rely on as much information as he can about the distribution of behavioural dispositions in the population from which Alter is taken. Using this information is important, since it allows Ego to generate better-informed prior beliefs. He is no longer confined to fully subjective probabilities. Specifically, the Bayesian rule wants Ego to exploit statistical findings, rather than gut feelings.[91] This recommendation even holds if Ego is an expert in this type of risky choice. For there is ample evidence that statistics outperform professional experience.[92]

But the base rate is only the starting point for prediction. The more information Ego uncovers via signalling or screening, the more he is able

---

[89] For an overview, see Baird et al. 1994: chapter 4.
[90] The example is close to the one presented by Baird et al. 1994: 125–42.
[91] The classic reference is Bayes 1738. For a modern introduction, see again Martignon and Blackmond Laskey 1999.
[92] Meehl 1954 is a basic treatment; for a recent example, see Meadow and Sunstein 2001.

to update his prior expectations. His final assessment thus has two components: the base rate, and the more specific information. A rational interaction partner weighs these two elements according to the expected reliability of the information. The less certain he is about the quality of the additional information, the more important it is that he weighs the base rate. Specifically, if the concrete information is not fully reliable, Ego must cater to two opposite risks: either relying on the signal, although it did not correctly predict the outcome; or not relying on the signal (but on the base rate), although the signal correctly predicted the outcome. Ego must thus keep in mind that the signal can have false positives and false negatives.[93]

Consequently, Bayes' rule reads:

$$P(o|\sigma) = \frac{P(\sigma|o)P(o)}{P(\sigma)},$$ (9)

where $P(o|\sigma)$ is the conditional probability of the outcome o, given the presence of the signal. $P(o)$ is the unconditional probability that outcome o is present in the environment, i.e. the base rate. $P(\sigma|o)$ is the conditional probability that the signal σ is present if outcome o has been observed. And $P(\sigma)$ is the unconditional probability of the signal being present in the environment, whether connected to the outcome o or not. $P(o|\sigma)$ can thus also be interpreted as a measure for the reliability of the signal.

The Bayesian approach makes it possible to develop further the game theoretic model presented in Figure 3.11 above. If Ego cannot be certain of Alter's type, calculating the value of generating type information becomes more complicated. First of all, the signal as such does not help Ego. For it is correlated to Alter's type only in a probabilistic manner. Ego will therefore want to update his prior beliefs about Alter's type in the light of this additional information. According to Bayes' rule, he therefore needs two more pieces of information: the unconditional probability of the signal being present in the environment, and the conditional probability of the signal being present if Alter is beneficial. Generating these two pieces of information, on top of the signal itself, makes this option more costly for Ego. The overall cost of generating the signal and these additional pieces of information is denoted as c_E^s.

What about benefit? Despite the fact that the signal is only probabilistically correlated to Alter's type, the signal is informative. It therefore allows Ego rationally to update his prior beliefs about Alter's type. While

---

[93] More on this from Lübbe 2002.

the prior belief p could only exploit information about the base rate, his updated belief p' is less error prone. This helps Ego in two respects. Since it is a signal about Alter being beneficial, Ego becomes less likely to miss out on co-operation, although this would have been beneficial. But the model only allows for two actor types. If Alter is not beneficial, he is detrimental. Consequently, updating p logically also makes it possible to update $1 - p$. Hence, Ego's new decision problem can be written as:

$$p'g - (1 - p')l > 0. \tag{10}$$

Comparing this new problem with the original problem taken from Equation 4 makes it possible to determine how to calculate the benefit expected from generating the signal. For that purpose, one may rewrite Equation 4 as

$$v = pg - (1 - p)l, \tag{11}$$

where v stands for the expected value of co-operation. By the same token, Equation 9 can be rewritten as

$$v' = p'g - (1 - p')l, \tag{12}$$

where v' stands for the expected value of co-operation, as updated upon generation of the signal. If Ego actually finds the signal, the benefit of this operation is thus $v' - v$. But of course Ego cannot be sure *ex ante* whether he will find the signal. To make his decision about the investment in the search, he must therefore again have recourse to a subjective probability. This time, he must estimate the subjective probability of actually finding the signal. This subjective probability is denoted as q. Accordingly, Ego will invest in generating the signal if

$$qv' - v - c_E^s > 0. \tag{13}$$

3.3.2   Unilateral response by Alter

The previous section has assumed Ego to believe that Alter and all outsiders will not become active in order to make Alter's behaviour more predictable. This section looks at the symmetrical situation for Alter. He is thus assumed to believe that neither Ego nor any outsider will make an effort to generate credible information about what type of an actor he is. Note that Alter's problem is not symmetrical to Ego's problem, because of the asymmetry characteristic for the predictability problem: Alter has no doubts about Ego's type, for the latter is assumed to be a rational utility maximiser.

Alter must calculate whether generating or transmitting type information is in his best interest. This first presupposes that he assess the expected gains should he remain inactive (a) and should he invest in type revelation (b). Alter must compare these two expected outcomes in order to find out whether the investment in any technology for transmitting type information pays (c). There are several technologies for this. The credible transmission of type information by Alter is the functional equivalent of inspection by Ego. If this is not feasible, Alter may send out a signal that at least has some information value (d). It may also make sense for Alter to embed the game in a larger context. He can strive to repeat it several times, and use that feature to develop a reputation (e). And he, finally, can strive to transform it into a more complex, nested game (f).

(a) Utility under inactivity   We are looking here at a situation of potential co-operation, which results in gains from trade. We also assume Ego to be fully rational. In such a situation, being unpredictable is also a problem for Alter himself. For Ego always retains the outside option of abstaining from co-operation. If he does not reveal type information, Alter thus potentially loses gains from trade. How much so depends on Ego's problem under inactivity, taken from Equation 4:

$$pg_E - (1-p)l > 0.$$

Two parameters in this equation, g_E and l, are common knowledge. But the subjective probability attached by Ego to Alter being beneficial, or p, is not. Logically, the corresponding subjective probability attached to Alter being detrimental, or $1 - p$, is also unknown to Alter. He therefore must second-guess these parameters. These guesses are denoted by $\bar{p}$ and $1 - \bar{p}$ respectively. If he remains inactive, Alter expects an outcome of 0, should Ego defect. If Ego co-operates, a beneficial actor expects g; a detrimental actor expects gg. These elements allow Alter to calculate the expected benefit of inactivity. All he needs is to assess the probability of Ego co-operating, or r.

Formally, this parameter is defined as follows:

$$r =: prob\{\bar{p}g_E - (1-\bar{p})l > 0\}. \tag{14}$$

Alter thus expects Ego to co-operate if the present value of doing so is positive. Whether this is the case depends on two things: the difference between the potential loss as a result of co-operating with a detrimental actor and the potential gain as a result of co-operating with a beneficial one; and the expected distribution of these actors in the population.

Based on r, thus defined, a beneficial actor's expected gain should he decide on inactivity is rg, and a detrimental actor's expected gain should he remain inactive is rgg. Note that both terms can be zero if r is zero. This is the case if Alter does not expect Ego to co-operate, given Equation 4.

(b) Investment in the transmission of type information   Against this backdrop, Alter must decide whether it is worthwhile to engage in the transmission of type information. As with inspection, the transmission of type information is typically not free of charge. Therefore, Alter faces an investment decision similar to the one analysed for Ego. It is portrayed in Figure 3.12.

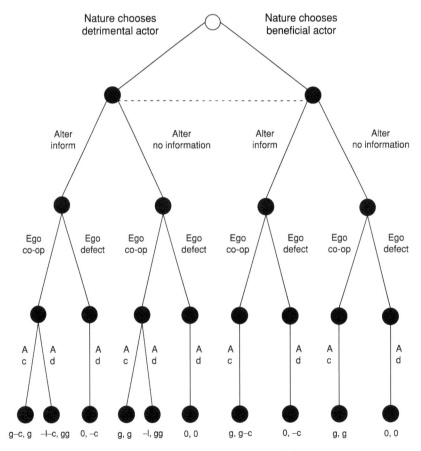

Figure 3.12. Investment of Alter in type revelation.

Nature still matches Ego with one of the two types of actors. But, at a cost, this actor can inform Ego about Nature's move. This way of modelling the problem fits the behavioural assumptions. Alter is assumed to be driven by his behavioural dispositions in the first place. But he then is thought to be able to act rationally, given Nature's move.

Actually, solving Alter's investment problem is fairly simple. For Ego will never co-operate with a detrimental actor, and he will always co-operate with a beneficial actor. Consequently, it never pays for a detrimental actor to invest in type revelation. The statement even holds in the extreme case in which the detrimental actor expects Ego to believe that the population consists only of detrimental actors. Even in this case, the detrimental actor is not indifferent about the choice between investment and non-investment. In this borderline case, he can indeed not lose any expected gains from trade. But he still incurs the investment cost as a loss. Formally, even if

$$\bar{p} = 0,$$

and hence

$$r = 0,$$

it still holds that

$$rgg > rgg - c_A.$$

For in this constellation,

$$rgg = 0,$$

whereas

$$rgg - c_A < 0,$$

whenever

$$c_A > 0.$$

Let us now look at the problem of a beneficial actor. It is also fairly simple, because of the make-up of the model. If Ego learns by some credible means that Alter is beneficial, he will always want to co-operate. For he then can be certain of the fair gain g_E, which is larger than the breakdown value of 0. Hence, the beneficial actor's problem reads:

$$g_A - c_A > 0. \tag{15}$$

This actor invests in type revelation whenever the investment cost is smaller than his expected gain from trade.

(c) Comparing type revelation to inactivity   Based on this, an actor can decide whether investing in type revelation is worthwhile. As stated earlier, a detrimental actor never will. A beneficial actor has to make the following comparison. Inactivity yields

$$rg_A.$$

Investment will make Ego certain to co-operate. But it comes at a cost. It thus yields the outcome described in Equation 15. This must be larger than the expected outcome under inactivity. By basic transformation, the beneficial actor's problem thus reads

$$g_A - rg_A - c^{TR} > 0, \tag{16}$$

where c^{TR} is the cost of type revelation.

(d) Signal   Observable information need not be deterministically linked to the unobservable information about the type of actor. Actually, in reality it typically is not. But there are many probabilistic links. If Alter exhibits a certain behaviour now, he is more likely than an average actor to behave beneficially or detrimentally later. Why this is often the case has been demonstrated when describing Ego's parallel problem.[94] Sometimes Alter can generate such a signal ad hoc at a cost c_A^s. A detrimental actor will not want to do that. For sending out an informative signal would be a way of reducing the likeliness of Ego's co-operation. But sending out such a signal is in principle in the interest of a beneficial actor. He then faces an investment problem. He can go about it in a way that is fully analogous to the parallel problem of Ego.

Upon receiving the signal Ego can update his prior beliefs about Alter's type in accordance with Bayes' rule.[95] Alter must second-guess this exercise. This leads to Equation 17:

$$\bar{p}'g - (1 - \bar{p}')l > 0, \tag{17}$$

where $\bar{p}'$ is in Ego's updated belief about the likelihood of Alter being beneficial, as second-guessed by Alter. $1 - \bar{p}'$ is the corresponding, updated and second-guessed likelihood of Alter being detrimental. From this equation, Alter can derive the updated likelihood of Ego's co-operation. It can be written as

$$r' =: prob\{\bar{p}'g - (1 - \bar{p}')l > 0\}. \tag{18}$$

---

[94] See above 3.3.1(d).
[95] For a formal presentation of Bayes' rule, see above 3.3.1(f).

Under inactivity Alter expects

$$rg_A.$$

If he invests in the generation and distribution of the signal, he expects

$$r'g_A - c_A^s.$$

Investment pays if the following equation holds:

$$r'g_A - rg_A - c_A^s > 0. \tag{19}$$

So far, Alter's problem could have been treated in a manner fully parallel to Ego's problem. This parallel ceases if one considers a further possibility. Not so rarely, a signal about Alter's type is available, although Alter has not purposefully generated it. In such instances, the behavioural link is no longer fully natural. Practically speaking, there is typically no such signal unless Alter has contributed to it. Take the example of professional training.[96] Normally, such training has not been imposed on Alter by some irresistible outside force. But the important thing is that, in the concrete situation, Alter cannot decide about the presence of this signal in the environment. For the purposes of his current problem, the presence of the signal can therefore be treated as exogenous, or sent out by Nature.

If Alter has no chance to do anything about the signal, it is just part of his opportunity structure. But not so rarely, this is not the case. Although Alter cannot now decide upon the presence of the signal, he retains the ability either to improve or to reduce the quality of the signal by costly effort. In such instances, the behavioural link is no longer fully natural. Metaphorically speaking, Nature writes a first draft. But Alter has the ability to rewrite it. In this context, quality is measurable in relation to the reliability of the signal for Ego. A better signal has a higher correlation with Alter's type.

This is not an academic question. The example of professional training makes it possible to illustrate the point. We all have talked about professional deformation with tongue in cheek. The trained economist starts analysing a matrimonial conflict in terms of game theory. Not such a good idea, our experience in life would tell us. Most spouses would not be pleased to learn that they are pushed like pawns around the chess board by their partners. And they might react in quite irrational, harmful ways. A reasonable spouse will thus try to customise his behavioural dispositions to his context. But the more advanced his game theoretical

---

[96] For more examples, see above 3.3.1(d).

abilities, the more difficult it will be for him to think and feel entirely differently. His mind will always plot a rational game for him. He must therefore make an extra effort to customise his behavioural dispositions, or even to unlearn the earlier disposition entirely.

In such a context, Alter faces an investment problem. The solution to this problem will be sketched under the following simplifying assumptions. Alter has just one option for investment. Ego knows Alter has this option, and he knows the investment cost involved. This assumption makes it possible to avoid the additional need of basing Ego's ensuing problem on mere expectations. Secondly, it is assumed that the signal itself is transmitted by Nature free of charge. The only investment decision Alter has thus concerns the investment in blurring the signal or in making it less noisy, respectively. This assumption prevents Alter from having to take two investment decisions at a time: Should he transmit the signal at all, and should he invest in changing its validity? The third assumption is about the prior knowledge of Alter. Alter is assumed to possess certain knowledge of his own type.[97]

The ensuing problem will first be analysed for a beneficial actor. He is interested in improving signal quality. Such improvement comes at a cost, denoted c^{SQ}. The improvement pays off for Alter under the same conditions that were present when he was able to generate a signal in the first place. Formally, the problem can be written the same way as in Equation 19. The only difference is in the cost parameter. c_A^s is replaced by c^{SQ}. This makes for Equation 20:

$$r'g_A - rg_A - c^{SQ} > 0. \tag{20}$$

A detrimental actor would not generate the signal on his own initiative. But it may well make sense for him to reduce the quality of a signal sent out by Nature. Note that in this constellation Nature must send out a signal that allows Ego to become more pessimistic. This is because of the assumption that the signal is informative. If Alter reduces the quality of a pessimistic signal, he pushes Ego further back to his prior beliefs. By doing so he makes Ego somewhat more optimistic. Whether such effort pays off for a detrimental actor depends on Equation 21:

$$\bar{r}'gg - \bar{r}gg - c^{SQ} > 0, \tag{21}$$

where $\bar{r}$ and $\bar{r}'$ are defined as before. For Ego is still not certain of Alter's type, but the signal allows him to update his prior beliefs. The effect of

---

[97] This avoids the additional problems present in a situation where Alter must decide whether to invest in learning his own type.

this updating must be second-guessed by Alter. Of course, a detrimental actor will spend c^{SQ} not for improving, but for deteriorating signal quality. There is a borderline case too. If the detrimental actor succeeds in destroying the signal, his investment problem simplifies to

$$rgg - c^{SQ} > 0. \tag{22}$$

The foregoing, however, has implicitly made an additional assumption: Ego can observe only the result of the activity, not Alter's activity itself. If Alter remains inactive, Ego views the signal as sent out by Nature. If the beneficial actor has invested, Ego sees the signal as improved by this activity. Likewise, if the detrimental actor has invested, Ego sees the signal as reduced by this action. With this additional assumption, the investment opportunity changes only Alter's problem, while Ego's problem remains unaltered. If this additional assumption is dropped, the players' problems become more complicated.

First note a technological limitation. If a detrimental actor's investment is observable, the investment opportunity fades away. By the very fact that Alter reduces the quality of the signal, Ego learns his type. Accordingly, the following analysis is confined to a case where Ego can observe activities that corroborate an optimistic signal.

In this case, the additional complications stem from the following fact: Ego will be alerted if Alter does not make the investment. For this inactivity might be telling. If it is, Ego ought to update his beliefs. Specifically, he ought to decrease the subjective probability of Alter being beneficial. For in principle, a beneficial actor has an interest in seizing the opportunity to strengthen Ego's belief in Alter's beneficial type. Alter is thus faced with what game theorists call a signalling problem. But Alter will not invest at any cost whatsoever. He will only do so under the conditions laid down in Equation 20. If Alter does not invest, Ego's problem thus consists of second-guessing Alter's calculation under Equation 20. Formally, he updates under the condition laid down in Equation 23:

$$r'g - rg - c^{SQ} > 0, \tag{23}$$

where r and r' correspond to Equations 14 and 18, as second-guessed by Ego. Inevitably, this leads to a ping-pong game. For Alter will anticipate this update and make that a part of his own decision about investment. Ego will also anticipate this anticipation and so forth.

(e) Repeated game   Let's repeat it! This is a standard response of game theorists to problems of co-operation.[98] Psychologists join in and

---

[98] For an overview, see Baird et al. 1994: chapter 5.

stress that repeated interaction is less plagued by the predictability problem.[99] Games that have a repeated character from the outset are investigated separately below.[100] But turning a game that originally was a one-shot game into a repeated game is one of the options available to the players themselves if they want to overcome a dilemma situation. This is why repetition must be looked at here.

Of course, game theorists know that repeating a prisoner's dilemma does not help if the number of rounds to be played is determined *ex ante*. With fully rational players, this leads to the chain store paradox.[101] If the game is characterised by a last-mover advantage, the disadvantaged player will not want to be suckered in the last round and defect in the penultimate round, and so on and so forth. But the result[102] disappears if the game is not infinite, but of unknown duration, or if any other light uncertainty is introduced into the structure of the game.[103] In reality, this last condition tends to be easy to meet. This problem aside, repetition is helpful, since it makes it possible to invest in reputation.[104] Sociologists of the rational choice brand then also speak of social capital.[105] One might therefore expect all this to work in our context too. One might even surmise two possibilities: a reputation that Alter is fair, or a more modest reputation that he is predictable.

At first sight, one might think that building on this strand of game theoretic thinking is not that easy in our case. For at this point the predictability problem is assumed to be unilateral. Ego does not know *ex ante* Alter's type, but Alter does not have a similar predictability problem. But even a detrimental actor should prefer the opportunity to obtain his fair gain *g* in later rounds to his smaller outside option of 0.

One might think that repetition can help Ego in yet another respect. It might not only help bring a detrimental actor under the shadow of the future. Repetition might also be a tool for generating type information. This seems to be the case if Ego can legitimately expect Alter's type to be stable over all rounds of the repeated game. Psychologically, this is not unlikely. For in a repeated game, not only the personality, but in principle also the situation, remains stable. This seems to allow Ego to use the first round of the game as an opportunity to learn Alter's type. Playing round 1 would then turn into an investment decision. Since all Ego risks is losing −*l* once, the investment seems small.

[99] Epstein 1979: 1097, 1105, 1123.   [100] See below, chapter 6.
[101] Selten 1978.
[102] Much criticised by outsiders anyhow, characteristically Turner 2001: 105–18.
[103] Baird et al. 1994: 159–65.
[104] Baird et al. 1994: 178–86.   [105] Coleman 1990: 300–24.

At closer sight, however, this does not work that easily. The behavioural assumptions have been the following: a detrimental actor behaves opportunistically; a beneficial actor keeps his promises. A beneficial actor will therefore co-operate in the first round. But this observation only helps Ego if he can prevent a detrimental actor from co-operating as well. If the detrimental actor defects, he obtains his unfair gain gg in this round, and nothing in later rounds. In a repeated game, this is not the detrimental actor's best outcome. He would prefer to have his fair gain g in all earlier rounds, and the unfair gain gg in the last round only. In principle, a detrimental actor thus has an incentive to co-operate in earlier rounds. From the perspective of information transmission, one may also say that a detrimental actor has an incentive to mimic the behaviour of a beneficial actor in earlier rounds.

This analysis, however, ignores a further element of the model. Ego has also been assumed to be a rational utility maximiser. Rational actors solve games by backwards induction. If Ego expects Alter to be detrimental, Ego should not want to co-operate in the penultimate round. Alter will anticipate this behaviour and defect in the second round before last. Ego will anticipate this fact in turn, and so on and so forth. Logically, this seems to imply that co-operation in the first round actually is telling. Only beneficial actors would do that, while detrimental actors would anticipate Ego's reactions in later rounds and defect from the very beginning.

But at closer sight, this analysis is dubious. First of all, both intuitively and empirically, the unravelling just described is unlikely; actually this is what generated the already mentioned chain store paradox. The doubts are even stronger if both players know from the very beginning that Alter will move last. This is a plausible assumption, given the interest in predicting Alter's behaviour.[106] For Ego does not interact with an actor whom he knows to be detrimental. Consequently, if Alter co-operates in all earlier rounds, this can mean one of two things: that Alter is beneficial and will also co-operate in the last round; or that he is detrimental, wants to obtain his fair gain in all earlier rounds, and the unfair gain in the last. More importantly, the detrimental actor knows this element of behavioural uncertainty. He can therefore anticipate it when he decides upon his behaviour in earlier rounds. Even a fully rational detrimental actor can therefore legitimately engage in early co-operation.

Within the confines of the model, co-operation in early rounds is therefore indeed without informational value. If one allows for a little

---

[106] Specifically, allowing Ego to move last is already a tool in his hands for partly solving the predictability problem.

more realism, however, the picture looks different. Experimental evidence shows a very stable effect: close to the end of the game, co-operation rates drop, and depending on the character of the experimental setting, they even drop dramatically.[107] Intuitively, this makes sense. Most untrained people are poor chess players. Their ability to anticipate further moves is limited. If one introduces this element, co-operation becomes more telling, the closer the round is to the end of the game. Co-operation in earlier rounds is then no longer a mechanism for transmitting certain type information. But it has signal value, and more, the closer that one is to the end of the series.

So far, it has been assumed that Alter's type will be stable over all rounds. Is this a strong assumption? It seems rather realistic to assume away random variance between rounds of a repeated game. For in such a scenario, not only the personality persists, but also basically the situation. Such a context typically makes for rather stable behaviour.[108] Put differently, even the repeated game can arguably be modelled such that Nature moves first, and determines the actor type for the first and later rounds simultaneously and identically. The only important source of behavioural variance is the larger context into which the individual game is embedded. If, for instance, Alter changes his profession between two rounds of the game, this might make him see in an entirely different light what otherwise is an identical situation. A change in perceived context might also serve as an explanation for the already mentioned end-round effect. For the situation close to the end of a series of repeated games is not the same as at the beginning of this series.

There are, of course, less rigid ways of modelling repeated interaction. In a second case, Alter's type is indeed fixed. But Ego is not sure about this. If we further assume that Alter himself is certain about the stability of his type, he gains an opportunity for strategic action. If Alter is of the detrimental type, he will, of course, not want to move. But if he is of the beneficial type, it helps him if he has an opportunity to convince Ego of the stability of his behavioural dispositions. In the language used above, this is a way of corroborating a signal sent out by Nature. It has been formally described in Equation 20. Practically speaking, this would be easier in environments where outsiders could enforce a commitment against Alter. In such cases, he could promise to indemnify Ego, should his behaviour change in later rounds. But we are looking here at a situation devoid of outside intervention. In such cases, the only option for Alter is to sink costs for all later rounds.

---

[107] A survey of the experimental evidence is provided by Ledyard 1995.
[108] See above 2.5.

Things look a little brighter if Ego is not as fatalistic as that. He might not be willing to believe a mere statement of Alter. But he might be willing to become more and more assured, the more rounds Alter has indeed co-operated. But strictly speaking, this violates the assumption that Ego is fully rational. For the only information Ego obtains is statistical. But co-operation in some rounds of a repeated game is far from being statistically significant.

Let us now move on to the assumption that Alter's behaviour is not fixed. As assumed throughout this book, Alter is not able fully to control his own behaviour. But, as in the models of the single-shot game investigated above, Alter might be able safely to predict his own future behaviour. He would for instance know that he will defect only once, and co-operate in all other rounds. In such a case, it would be good for Alter if he could credibly transmit this knowledge to Ego. Unfortunately, given the framework conditions, again, the only option is to sink costs.[109] But Ego need only lay down that sum for rounds where he predicts that he will defect. Again, the situation improves if Ego is willing to update his belief in the credibility of Alter's statements the more often they have been true. If that is the case, a side-payment, decreasing from round to round, will be sufficient.

(f) Nested game   Games cannot only be repeated. Single games can also be part of larger complexes of games. Game theorists then speak of nested games.[110] In principle, there are two possibilities. The players can remain the same as in the base game. But they know from the outset that they will be playing more than one game. And, in contrast to repeated games, these later games are not identical to the first one. The second possibility is that more actors can enter the scene. This makes a difference if what a player does in the first game has repercussions on later games he plays with other players.

Again, the more complex structure is not in and of itself the topic here. This section is confined to simple games between only two actors. But in their interest in overcoming the predictability problem, these two actors might consider making the game more complex. Specifically, this section looks at unilateral options of the informed actor. But assessing these options presupposes that we have a preliminary look at nested games as such.

---

[109] One might also see insurance as an option. But in this book, insurance is treated as a technology of a different kind. It ignores type information, rather than exploiting the existing knowledge about type distribution, and about the type of the concrete actor.

[110] For an overview, see Baird et al. 1994: chapter 6.

We start with a situation in which the set of players remains the same in all games. Moreover, Alter's type is assumed to be stable over all games. Nature has created the embedded structure. Ego then has two different choices. Does he want to co-operate? And does he want to continue playing? Figure 3.13 assumes that Ego will take these two decisions simultaneously.

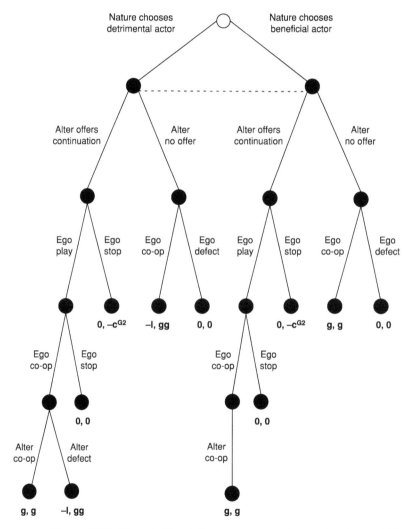

Figure 3.13. Repeated/nested game: same actors, actor type stable, Nature embeds, Ego decides simultaneously about continuation.

Note that this figure only shows the first round; the second and final rounds are not specified here. They are compressed to the parameter c^{G2}, to be explained below. The simplest case for the final round would be a game as shown in Figure 3.1.

These assumptions result in four options for Ego. He can co-operate once, but finish the interaction. He can co-operate and continue. He can defect but continue. And he can defect and step out of the interaction. Ego has all four options, irrespective of Alter's type. If Ego decides to discontinue the relationship with Alter, pay-offs are like those in the base game used throughout this book. If the game continues, rational players will not only look at the pay-offs in this first game. What will count for them is the overall gain or loss. It obviously depends on the character of the other, later games. Since Ego decides whether to continue, he will assess this overall outcome. If he only partly knows the history of these other games, he will have to rely on his prior beliefs.

Thus far, the assessment would have been the same, if Ego had had an option to play a number of totally disconnected games. The nested character would be devoid of strategic implications. This can differ for one of two reasons. The nested character can change the opportunity structure for the first game. Or it can allow Ego to generate information or Alter to transmit it.

As in a repeated game, the former possibility is easier to assess. The nested character of the game can bring Alter under the shadow of the future. Even if he is a detrimental actor, it may no longer be in his interest to exploit Ego in the first game. Specifically, a rational actor will not seize the opportunity to exploit Ego in the first game if the condition laid down in Equation 24 holds:

$$gg - g - c^{G2} > 0. \tag{24}$$

c^{G2} is a generic term that stands for the cost Ego can inflict on Alter by moving on to the other games, or by declining Alter access to them. This parameter can thus stand either for an out-of-pocket cost or for an opportunity cost. It is an out-of-pocket cost if Ego has the ability to punish Alter in later rounds, should he defect in the first round. c^{G2} signifies an opportunity cost if Alter forgoes an opportunity for further gains, should Ego decide not to continue the game.

Equation 24 makes two statements. The simpler statement is that gg must be larger than c^{G2}. Otherwise, co-operation in the first round is a dominant strategy for Alter. Irrespective of Ego's move, Alter can never do better than co-operate at this point. But Equation 24 is more complex. For if Alter does not co-operate in the first round, he also loses the fair gain g. Put differently, defection is only rational if the unfair gain is larger than the fair gain plus c^{G2}.

Can a beneficial actor rely on these insights for making co-operation more likely? One possibility is the following. Alter offers Ego the possibility of playing a second game where the fair gain is larger than g, but smaller than gg. The second game offers no opportunity for exploitation. There is thus no unfair gain. Alter offers to pay the entire gain from the first gain to Ego if Ego moves on to game 2. Such an offer is rational for beneficial actors. For they gain more in the second game than in the first. Making the same offer, however, would be irrational for detrimental actors. For they would be less well-off than if they simply defected in the first game.

It is, however, not easy for a beneficial actor to rely on this technology. The offer is only rational if a beneficial actor is better off by making such an offer. This may, but need not be the case. Alter's total gain from both games must be larger than $gg - \varepsilon$, where ε can be any parameter that keeps the offer below the unfair gain.[111] Moreover, there is no possibility of making the initial offer credible without outside enforcement. To be sure, Alter can hand over the difference between gg and g as a deposit. He would state that he is prepared to receive the difference between this deposit and the additional gain from game 2, once the latter is played. But such a deposit assumes away the possibility that Ego will not hand over the difference to Alter once he has co-operated in the second game.

As with repeated games, the alternative route exploits the nested character as a tool for generating type information. In order to be effective, Alter's behaviour in the first round must allow Ego to find out Alter's type, or at least to receive an informative signal. This only works if a detrimental actor cannot successfully mimic a beneficial actor's behaviour. In principle, the considerations that have been raised for understanding the parallel problem in repeated games apply. In the first step, the crucial parameter consists of comparing Alter's best outcome in both stages of the game. If the potential gain from defecting at the second stage is larger than that from defecting at the first stage, there is an incentive to mimic. In the second step, the behavioural assumptions for Ego play themselves out. If the detrimental actor has to contend with Ego to anticipate being exploited at the second stage of the game, mimicking no longer pays. In step 3, however, anticipation can become less likely because of the uncertainty about Alter's type.

In the model used thus far, Nature moves once and for ever. Alter's type is thus assumed to remain stable over the whole game. In repeated

---

[111] By way of illustration: if the second game were identical to the first, the beneficial actor would expect a total gain of $2g$. Equation 3 allows for $2g > gg$, only if either l is small or g is fairly close to gg.

games, the same assumption did not seem too strong. In a nested game, it is stronger. For in this game, not only the larger context may change from round to round. The game itself differs. This makes it fairly likely that, psychologically speaking, the situation differs enough that the personality plays itself out in different ways.[112] If this is sufficiently likely in the case at hand, the advantage of the single game being nested evaporates. Ego is back to the options available for single-shot games. At most, he might gain information from different sources as to how Alter is likely to behave in one of the subsequent (psychological) situations.

Let us now move on to the second class of nested games, the ones involving additional players. In principle, these can be either additional informed actors or additional uninformed actors. The distinction between several independent games and a nested game rested on the impact of Ego on the continuation of the game. He must be able to make it more or less likely that Alter will interact with other uninformed actors. Likewise, Ego must have a say about the interaction between the first round and other actors involved in later rounds. The parameter c^{G2} in Equation 24 then stands for this impact. If Ego can make it more likely that others inflict damage on a defecting actor, c^{G2} is this out-of-pocket cost. It is an opportunity cost if Ego can make it less likely that Alter will receive a benefit from different players in later rounds.

Again, in this context, the ensuing options for Alter individually are of interest. These options rest on the opportunity that a beneficial actor has to commit unilaterally to the continuation of the game. There are many possibilities for this. Alter can allow a second uninformed actor to inflict a punishment on him in a later round, or to withhold a benefit. Likewise, Alter can bring himself under the spell of other actors, should he not be as beneficial as promised. Visibly, a nested game is thus a way of modelling third-party involvement or a privately run institution. These options will be further investigated in the following sections.

3.3.3   Joint decision about individual type revelation

The foregoing sections have artificially narrowed the scope of the analysis. When analysing the individual options for Ego and for Alter, an additional assumption has been added: namely, both players have made their decisions under the assumption that the other will remain inactive. Put differently, the previous analysis has presumed that both partners will not play a second-level game when deciding who will intervene and who will bear the cost. This assumption will now be dropped.

---

[112] See again above, 2.5.

This extended analysis first presupposes a benchmark, which is the social gain from co-operation, not the individual gain (a). Moreover, the parties must understand the strategic character of this second-level game (b). And their decision is affected by the strategic character inherent in the original game (c). At closer sight, however, the fact that both strategic interaction problems are compounded turns out to offer a solution to both of them.

(a) Social benefit When assessing the social benefit of type revelation, rational parties will engage in cost–benefit analysis. They will thus compare the expected outcome under inactivity with the expected outcome under type revelation. Since they employ a decision-oriented perspective when making this comparison, it is the *ex ante* assessment that matters. They must thus compare the expected social values of the available solutions.

Calculating the expected value of inactivity is straightforward. When this is done, the distribution of the actors in the population, and hence the likeliness of Alter being beneficial or detrimental, is given by Nature. The only parameter Ego takes into account is the assessment of this distribution. It is thus transformed from Ego's subjective assessment to a parameter invoked to decide upon social benefits. It is transformed as follows: if

$$pg + (1 - p)l < 0,$$

Ego defects. Accordingly, social welfare is zero. No gains, no losses. If

$$pg + (1 - p)l > 0,$$

Ego co-operates. This does not, however, mean that this co-operation is socially beneficial. It is if Alter is actually beneficial. Then both parties receive a fair gain g, and no one incurs a loss. When that is the case, the gains from co-operation are $2g$. If Alter is detrimental, however, Alter gains gg, whereas Ego incurs loss l. By definition, $gg - 2g < l$; see Equation 3. Accordingly, in the latter case, co-operation is detrimental not only for Ego, but also for the economy, composed of both parties. Co-operation then is inefficient.

Now when the parties assess whether to take action, Ego does not know Alter's type. In order to be able to compare the options, inactivity and type revelation, the parties must thus generate a benchmark. This presupposes a deviation from the strict idea of subjective utility. For cost and benefit must be compared across parties. At this point, one has to assume that there is a uniform currency for comparing the gains of both parties. Likewise, one must assume that it is possible to compare the transaction cost necessary for type revelation with the same currency. Moreover, calculating the gains from trade presupposes that there is some way to assess the *ex ante* probability that Alter will be beneficial or detrimental. These probabilities can be as subjective as before. But such a calculation will not work if Alter can do no better than second-guess the subjective probability that Ego attaches to his type. For Ego, in turn, could only second-guess this guess, and so forth. Practically speaking, the parties must thus find a way to standardise the definition of this probability. In order to distinguish it from the individual guess of Ego, the standardised probability that Alter will be beneficial is denoted by $\underline{p}$. Accordingly, the corresponding probability that Alter will be detrimental is written as $1 - \underline{p}$.

Of course, this is a somewhat peculiar assumption if one also assumes that Alter is certain of his type. One way of making the assumption a little more palatable is to interpret $\underline{p}$ as the distribution of actors in the population from which Nature draws Alter. The following calculation appears fully natural if one further assumes that, when deciding whether to invest in type revelation, Alter does not know his type either. The following calculation, however, would best be interpreted as depicting the view of an omniscient and omnipotent social planner who advises the parties of their joint best choice. Put differently, the following is a hypothetical exercise, meant to give the parties a benchmark for their joint decision.

Based on this, remaining inactive is socially rational if

$$2\underline{p}g + (1 - \underline{p})(gg - l) > 0. \tag{25}$$

The parties can take this as a benchmark for comparing inactivity with type revelation. If they use one of the technologies for generating and distributing type information, this comes at the cost c_E^{TR} or c_A^{TR} respectively. If they do, no co-operation with a detrimental actor comes about. Accordingly, investment is rational in isolation if

$$2\underline{p}g - c_E^{TR} > 0, \tag{26}$$

or if

$$2\underline{p}g - c_A^{TR} > 0. \tag{27}$$

But rational parties will compare this with the expected social gain should they remain inactive. If they do, investment pays if

$$-(1 - \underline{p})(gg - l) - c_E^{TR} > 0, \tag{28}$$

or if

$$-(1 - \underline{p})(gg - l) - c_A^{TR} > 0. \tag{29}$$

Despite what one might expect at first glance, this is a meaningful question. For by definition, in Equation 3, l is larger than gg. Accordingly, the term $gg - l$ is negative, which makes $-(1 - p)(gg - l)$ positive. The social planner's problem thus boils down to the following: which is larger, the expected loss from inadvertent interaction with a detrimental actor, or the cost necessary for type revelation?

Moreover, and obviously, the players will compare the two individual technologies and pick the cheaper one. They will thus opt for type revelation by Alter if

$$c_E^{TR} - c_A^{TR} > 0. \tag{30}$$

And they will decide otherwise if

$$c_A^{TR} - c_E^{TR} > 0. \tag{31}$$

But this is less likely, given that Alter is certain of his type.

Pulling the bits and pieces together yields the overview in Figure 3.14, which should be read in the following way. The players generate a benchmark. E means that both parties agree on Ego becoming active. A means that both agree on Alter becoming active.

A comparison of this analysis with the one in the foregoing sections shows that this one does more than just get rid of a restrictive assumption. For individually, an interaction partner will only invest in type revelation if his expected personal gain is larger than the cost. He thus has the problem described by Equation 7, repeated here with the enriched notation:

$$pg - c_E^{TR} > 0.$$

Socially, the expected gain from this activity, however, is $2\underline{p}g$. Despite the difference between p and $\underline{p}$, this term will typically be larger. Formally, it is, whenever

$$2\underline{p}g - c_E^{TR} > pg - c_E^{TR} \Rightarrow$$

Social assessment	Inactivity	Type revelation
E	$2\underline{p}g + (1 - \underline{p})(gg - l)$	$2\underline{p}g - c_E^{TR}$
A	$2\underline{p}g + (1 - \underline{p})(gg - l)$	$2\underline{p}g - c_A^{TR}$

Figure 3.14. Social assessment inactivity and type revelation, Ego and Alter.

$$2\underline{p}g - pg > 0,$$

or shorter:

$$2\underline{p} - p > 0. \tag{32}$$

The following example illustrates the point. Assume p to be 0.5. In that case, Ego's prior belief is that, since he knows nothing, it is equally likely that Alter will be beneficial or detrimental. Further, assume that the omniscient social planner is somewhat more pessimistic. Jointly deciding about type revelation still matters as long as the social planner assesses the probability that Alter will be beneficial to be above 0.25. Put differently, the parties can still afford a more expensive technology for type revelation, as long as the social planner estimates more than one of four actors in the population to be beneficial.

Making the same comparison for a beneficial actor's individual action yields a different result. His individual problem can be taken from Equation 15:

$$g - c_A^{TR} > 0.$$

Jointly deciding to use this same technology yields the outcome described in Equation 27:

$$2\underline{p}g - c_A^{TR} > 0.$$

Jointly deciding is thus able to enhance social welfare if

$$2\underline{p}g - g > 0. \tag{33}$$

Put differently, welfare increases only if the standardised *ex ante* probability that Alter will be beneficial is above 0.5. It thus only works out if Ego is sufficiently optimistic. This is because of the fact that the beneficial actor is certain about his own type, whereas the standardised probability must mirror the fact that Ego can only rely on his prior beliefs.

Another way of making the foregoing claim is as follows: if one partner takes care of type revelation, this has a positive externality. All members of this little economy, i.e. both players, obtain the benefit. This conceptualisation helps clarify another implication. The expectation of rational choice theory is that positive externalities lead to underproduction. Since the one person who becomes active cannot cash in on the entire benefit of his intervention, he is likely to do less than would socially be beneficial.[113]

---

[113] And efficient in the sense of the Kaldor-Hicks criterion.

(b) Strategic interaction over gains from type revelation   Of course, there is no social planner. This has even been deliberately assumed away at the outset, since this section looks at options Ego and Alter have if they do not rely on outside intervention. The foregoing thus has only generated a normative benchmark. The parties now know what they best could achieve by individually or co-operatively generating type information. Were the parties able to interact on a market, i.e. under workable competition, they might well also expect to reach this outcome without further ado. Yet unfortunately this is not the case. The game is plotted such that they interact strategically.

From this observation, one limitation of the analysis in the previous sections becomes apparent. These sections have deliberately ignored the fact that rational players do not look at their own opportunities in isolation, but actually know that they are in strategic interaction with the other player. This does not matter for a detrimental actor, since he will not transmit type information. But a beneficial actor is aware that Ego has an interest in reducing the predictability risk. Likewise, Ego knows that Alter, if he is beneficial, has an interest in transmitting type information in a credible way. This reciprocal awareness matters, since increasing predictability unilaterally comes at a cost. Each player would rather have the other bear that cost. Actually, Ego and (beneficial) Alter are thus engaged in a second-level game about cost attribution. The structure of this game is presented in Figure 3.15.

In this game, as previously, c_E^{TR} and c_A^{TR} signify the transaction cost involved in credibly transmitting type information at Ego's and Alter's initiative respectively. Accordingly, if Ego takes the initiative, both part-ners expect the fair outcome g in the final game, with probability p.[114] But since Ego bears the cost of generating credible type information, his

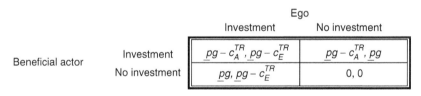

Figure 3.15. Second-level game over cost of type revelation.

---

[114] Actually, at this point, the analysis could even do without standardising subjective probabilities across players. Instead of weighting the gain with $\bar{p}$ for both parties alike, it thus could use p for Ego and $\bar{p}$ for the (beneficial) actor. But since the same analysis also holds, if both players invest jointly, by way of simplification $\underline{p}$ is used from the outset.

overall gain is reduced to $\underline{p}g - c_E^{TR}$. Likewise, if the (beneficial) Alter takes the initiative, his overall expected gain decreases to $\underline{p}g - c_A^{TR}$. This description also demonstrates that this second-order game is a zero-sum game. In order to bring co-operation about, both parties would wish to use the least costly technology. And each would rather have the other bear most or all of this cost.

Most of the technologies for generating credible type information presented above are mutually exclusive. For instance, screening (at Ego's initiative) is not easily wed with signalling (at Alter's initiative).[115] But there may be other technologies for the transmission of information that can be combined without the two involved players disturbing each other. It is thus theoretically possible that both Ego and Alter will bear a transaction cost for the transmission of type information. But both players have been assumed to be rational. Specifically, it has been assumed that Alter will deal with his own behavioural limitations in a rational way. If one of the players knew that the other would bear the transaction cost anyhow, he would not make any effort on his own.[116] If they are rational, neither Ego nor Alter would want to forgo the transmission of type information, provided the cost of transmission is below the total expected gain both parties stand to have from co-operation. For by definition, g is larger than zero. This would only be different in the extreme case where Ego believes that there are only beneficial actors in the population. Likewise, (beneficial) Alter would have to believe that Ego holds this extreme belief.

Rational players would thus not want to end up in either of the investment/investment or no investment/no investment cells of the matrix in Figure 3.15. In game theoretic terminology, none of these outcomes is a Nash equilibrium. None of these outcomes is thus the conditionally best response, given the other actor's move.

But the game has a Nash equilibrium or, more precisely and worse, three of them. If Ego bears the cost, Alter receives a free lunch. The same is true for Ego if Alter invests. Game theorists call these 'equilibria in pure strategies'. By this they mean that each player always plays one well-defined strategy. The third equilibrium goes beyond this: it is an equilibrium in mixed strategies. This means that there is a

---

[115] See above 3.3.1(d), 3.3.1(e) and 3.3.2(d); screening or signalling agreed upon by both players is a different story.

[116] This would be different, however, if one player believed the technology used by the other to be incomplete. It then would be fully rational to add his own efforts, in the interest of generating fully credible, or more credible information. But this assumption would not add additional insights into the character of the interaction. This is why it is not further pursued at this point.

	Player 2 Option 1	Option 2
Player 1 Option 1	0, 0	2, 1
Option 2	1, 2	0, 0

Figure 3.16. Battle of the sexes: generic notation.

	Player 2 Option 1	Option 2
Player 1 Option 1	−1, −1	2, 1
Option 2	1, 2	0, 0

Figure 3.17. Chicken game: generic notation.

given probability that each player will play one strategy, and the corresponding probability that they will play the other strategy.[117]

This second-level game closely resembles the battle of the sexes game presented earlier.[118] In generic form, a battle of the sexes game is characterised by the matrix in Figure 3.16.

The second-level game between Ego and a beneficial Alter shown in Figure 3.17, however, looks slightly different.

Game theorists call this type of game 'chicken'. The cover story is rather out of date. Two lads expect to impress a girl by the cold-blooded way they drive their cars. Both start at opposite ends of a small lane. If neither of them stops, there will be an accident and both will die, or at least suffer serious injury. If both stop early, they lose face among their friends (they are 'chickens'). If one of them stops at the very last moment, this is seen as honourable behaviour. But it is the other, the one who has not been swerving, who wins the girl's heart. Like the battle of the sexes game, the chicken game is thus characterised by a distributional conflict. The difference between the two games is off the equilibrium path.[119]

We now can also say more about the comparison between individual and social type revelation technologies. Such comparisons are feasible, and have been undertaken from the perspective of an omniscient and omnipotent social planner. They can thus be undertaken in the interest of assessing the social benefit inherent in each of these options. But

---

[117] For an easily readable introduction to the concept of mixed strategies, see Baird et al. 1994: 37–9.
[118] More on this class of games above, 3.2.3(b).
[119] More from Fudenberg and Levine 1998: 18–20.

this does not help the individual player to make his own decision. Equation 28, written in generic form, describes the expected social benefit of type revelation as

$$-(1 - \underline{p})(gg - l) - c^{TR} > 0.$$

But an individual player, be it Ego or Alter, cares only about individual gain, not social gain. What he wants to know is how much of this social gain goes into his individual purse. Now, if they co-operate, the parties are entirely free to distribute the social gain, or, equivalently, to allocate the cost of type revelation as they will. Accordingly, from an individual point of view, there is no meaningful way of comparing individual and social type revelation technologies. An extended version of Figure 3.14 therefore comes in two parts, as in Figure 3.18.

(c) Strategic interaction inherent in the base game In principle, a chicken game only poses an efficiency problem if both players have to play simultaneously. If the game is transformed into a sequential game, the first mover defines the equilibrium. This first-mover advantage, of course, has implications for distribution. But rational players are certain to reach the efficient outcome. For given the move of the first player, it is the second mover's best response to go for the equilibrium with a distributional loss. This outcome directly follows from the fact that both[120] combinations in which only one player invests in type revelation are Nash equilibria. One might therefore think that the parties could solve the problem by switching to a sequential game. But

Individual assessment	Inactivity	Type revelation
E	$pg_E - (1 - p)l$	$pg_E - c_E^{TR}$
A+	rg_A	$g_A - c_A^{TR}$
A-	rgg	-
Social assessment	Inactivity	Type revelation
E	$2\underline{p}g + (1 - \underline{p})(gg - l)$	$2\underline{p}g - c_E^{TR}$
A	$2\underline{p}g + (1 - \underline{p})(gg - l)$	$2\underline{p}g - c_A^{TR}$

Figure 3.18. Individual and social options: inactivity and type revelation: ego, alter.

---

[120] More precisely, if one includes the equilibrium in mixed strategies, all three outcomes.

when they decide about the sequence of moves, both players obviously know about the first-mover advantage. Each will therefore want to move first. The original chicken game repeats itself.

But the players have a second option. They can exploit the fact that the first-level game and the second-level game are nested. By clever design, they can exploit the potential gains from trade if one partner invests in type revelation, and the other makes a down-payment. Put differently, the fact that interaction in both games is strategic does not make life more complicated for the parties. On the contrary, it allows them to solve both problems.

At first reading, this may seem surprising. For in a single-shot game, it would not be possible to solve the chicken game by agreement. Let us see why. There are two possible ways to design the agreement. In the first case, the sequence of moves is the following:

1 Nature draws type.
2 E and A agree on the investment and side-payment.
3 The non-investing player pays.
4 The other player invests.

In this scenario, the non-investing player cannot know for sure whether the other player will actually invest. He will do so only if keeping the side-payment brings about a smaller gain than the gain expected from trade after investment. This depends on p and $\bar{p}$, which are both private knowledge.

The alternative sequence of moves does not fare better:

1 Nature draws type.
2 E and A agree on the investment and side-payment.
3 Investment.
4 Payment upon revelation.

The non-investing party is indeed safe under this agreement. But the investment in type revelation or in the transmission of type information is sunk. It is strictly transaction-specific. The investing party can put it to no other use. If the non-investing party is rational, it will thus exploit the investing party and offer to renegotiate the contract. If the investing party is rational, it will accept any offer that leaves a trifle more than the full cost of investment. Since the investing party anticipates such opportunism by the other party, it will not conclude such a contract.

Things change, however, if one takes the specific features of the first-level game into account. Again, there is a good deal of potential agreements that will not work out. The matrix in Figure 3.19 shows the

		Investing player	
		E	A
Sequence	Investment first	⊖	⊕
	Payment first	⊖	⊕

Figure 3.19. Ego and Alter jointly: options for agreed upon investment.

theoretical options. In this figure, ⊖ indicates that the scheme does not work out. ⊕ indicates a possibility of success. Let us look at the flawed designs first.

The upper left cell of the matrix implies the following sequence of moves:

1 Nature draws type.
2 E and A agree on the investment by E and side-payment.
3 E invests and teaches A to be beneficial.
4 A does (not) make a side-payment.
5 E does (not) co-operate.
6 A co-operates.

This works out, since E can sanction A at step 5. Another way of saying why it works stresses that beneficial actors never act opportunistically. But E cannot be sure at the outset that A is beneficial. If A is not, the game looks like this:

1 Nature draws type.
2 E and A agree on the investment by E and side-payment.
3 E invests and teaches A to be detrimental.
4 A does not make a side-payment.
5 E defects, but loses the full cost of revelation.

Let us move to the lower left cell of the matrix. Here the sequence of moves is:

1 Nature draws type.
2 E and A agree on the investment by E and on the side-payment.
3 A pays (not).
4 E invests (not).
5 E co-operates (not).
6 A has no possibility to sanction if E does not co-operate.

The explanation of failure in the lower right cell is again a little more complicated. It works out if Alter is beneficial, as demonstrated by the following sequence of moves:

1 Nature draws type.
2 E and A agree on the investment by A and on the side-payment.
3 E pays.
4 A^+ invests (he always will).
5 E co-operates (he always will).

But the scheme does not work if Alter is detrimental, something Ego does not know when concluding the agreement:

1 Nature draws type.
2 E and A agree on the investment by A and on the side-payment by E.
3 E pays (not).
4 A^- does not invest (he never will) and does not transmit type information.
5 E does not co-operate, but loses the side-payment.

Let us now move on to the successful upper right cell. If Alter is beneficial, the sequence of moves is:

1 Nature draws type.
2 E and A agree on the investment by A and on the side-payment by E.
3 A^+ invests and credibly transmits information about his beneficial type (he always will, since he is at most indifferent).
4 E makes the side-payment.
5 E co-operates.
6 A co-operates (or defects, if E has not made the side-payment)

The scheme also works in the alternative case, i.e. with a detrimental actor:

1 Nature draws type.
2 E and A agree on the investment by A and on the side-payment by E.
3 A^- does not invest (he never does).
4 E does not make the side-payment.
5 E defects.

There are two qualifications, however. A beneficial actor has been defined at the outset as a person who never acts opportunistically. In a way, however, A must act opportunistically in the former case. For if E does break his promise to make a down-payment, A must respond by breaching the original promise to co-operate in the performance game. But this does not seem to be a strong qualification of the behavioural assumption. For this breach is conditional upon E's breach in the second-level game. Legally speaking, A then has recourse to reprisals. In public international law, they are defined as the exceptional right to breach another promise in response to being the victim of a breach of obligations. Psychologically speaking, one need not even point to the – empirically fairly strong – punishing sentiments.[121] It suffices to point out the difference between breaching a promise out of the blue, and breaching one in response to being victim in another game, nested to the former. Another interpretation of the scheme just presented is the following: when they design their mechanism, the players explicitly give Alter the right to sanction Ego, should Ego breach the agreement underlying the mechanism. In accord with that interpretation, Alter has never promised not to sanction Ego. Consequently, sanctioning is not at variance with the behavioural assumption characteristic for this type.

The behavioural assumptions for the beneficial actor even help solve an additional problem. Were both parties fully rational, the mechanism would only work if Alter's cost for transmitting type information were common knowledge. For otherwise Alter would have an incentive to state that the cost is higher than it actually is. He would then make a profit in the predictability game. According to the assumptions in the game analysed here, a detrimental actor would be willing to exploit such an opportunity. But he has no chance to do so. He may induce Ego to conclude an agreement that overstates the cost of type revelation. But Ego's payment is scheduled after type revelation. He then knows that Alter is detrimental, and will not pay. And a beneficial actor is assumed not to cheat. This behavioural assumption carries over to cases of cheating about the cost of type revelation.

3.3.4   Joint response by interaction partner and actor

Having one party reveal the type, and the other contribute to the cost, is not the only co-operative option. There are also joint technologies for type revelation. The first analytic steps are the same as those taken when jointly deciding upon the use of individual technologies. The parties will assess the social benefit and compare it with alternative options (a). They are also faced with a similar problem of strategic interaction (b). In principle, joint technologies can have three advantages. The effect can be qualitative or quantitative, or it can help the parties make credible promises (c). The existing technologies can roughly be characterised as being either contractual (d) or organisational (e).

(a) Social benefit   When they consider joint technologies for type revelation, rational players will engage in cost–benefit analysis.

---

[121] See above 2.2.7.

They will thus compare the expected outcome of remaining inactive with the (larger) outcome expected when the type is revealed. As demonstrated in the previous section, hypothetically, asking a social planner to make the choice helps generate this benchmark.

If they use one of the technologies for jointly generating and distributing type information, this comes at the cost c_{E+A}^{TR}. Note that c_{E+A}^{TR} is not related to either c_A^{TR} or c_E^{TR}. It can be either less or more than either of these, depending on the technology employed by the community of the parties.

If they do have recourse to one of the technologies sketched out below, they will not co-operate with a detrimental actor. Accordingly, investment is rational in isolation if

$$2\underline{p}g - c_{E+A}^{TR} > 0. \tag{34}$$

But rational parties will compare this with the expected social gain under inactivity, which is expressed in Equation 25:

$$2\underline{p}g + (1 - \underline{p})(gg - l) > 0.$$

By transformation, investment thus pays if

$$-(1 - \underline{p})(gg - l) - c_{E+A}^{TR} > 0. \tag{35}$$

The fictitious social planner will also compare the joint technology with a joint choice for one of the technologies available to either Ego or Alter in isolation. He will thus opt for a joint technology only if

$$c_E^{TR} - c_{E+A}^{TR} > 0, \tag{36}$$

and if

$$c_A^{TR} - c_{E+A}^{TR} > 0. \tag{37}$$

The social planner will thus be guided by the matrix in Figure 3.20.

(b) Strategic interaction   If the parties consider relying on a joint technology for type revelation, they are caught in a chicken game regarding who bears the cost. It has the same structure as that depicted in Figure 3.15. The only difference concerns the cost parameters. Instead of c_E^{TR} and of c_A^{TR}, it is written c_{E+A}^{TR}. The ensuing matrix is shown in Figure 3.21.

The chicken game that arises regarding individual technologies for type revelation could be overcome by agreement between the parties. They could agree that Alter engages in type revelation, and have Ego

Social assessment	Inactivity	Type revelation
E	$2\underline{p}g + (1 - \underline{p})(gg - l)$	$2\underline{p}g - c_E^{TR}$
A	$2\underline{p}g + (1 - \underline{p})(gg - l)$	$2\underline{p}g - c_A^{TR}$
E+A	$2\underline{p}g + (1 - \underline{p})(gg - l)$	$2\underline{p}g - c_{E+A}^{TR}$

Figure 3.20. Options compared: social assessment inactivity and type revelation: Ego, Alter, joint.

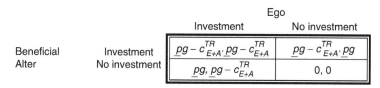

Figure 3.21. Second-level game over cost of type revelation.

make a side-payment after Alter has revealed his type. The scheme works, since it can exploit a feature of the first-level game. A beneficial actor always reveals his type if he can, and a detrimental actor never will. Whether a similar solution is available here depends on the character of the joint technology. It would imply that Alter will take care of all the specific effort needed to get the joint scheme going. It is virtually a matter of definition whether one is still willing to call such a scheme a joint technology of the two parties. If this solution is not available, the parties must find other ways to make their mutual commitments credible. Put differently, they then must embed their solution in a richer context.

(c) Effects of joint technologies for type revelation Joining forces can have three beneficial effects: it can affect quality; it can affect quantity; and it can help to make commitments credible.

The qualitative effect is straightforward: the parties can jointly employ technologies to reveal types that they would not be able to use individually. In a language sometimes used in economics: joining forces pushes the production frontier outwards. One possibility that exists has already been introduced under a different rubric. If the parties agree that Alter is to do the type revelation and Ego is to make a side-payment upon revelation, this does not just solve the chicken problem in the second-level game. It is also a technology for type revelation in the first place. In all but one extreme case, a detrimental actor will not sign such an agreement. If he does, he is worse off than under inactivity. To see why, have another look at the sequence of moves under this agreement:

1 Nature draws type.
2 E and A agree on the investment by A and side-payment by E.
3 A⁻ does not invest (he never does).
4 E does not make the side-payment.
5 E defects.

The present value of this agreement for a detrimental actor is 0. He will not invest. He thus will not incur a cost. But Ego will not co-operate either, meaning that r is also 0. Hence rgg is 0 as well.

The quantitative effect of joining forces has also been investigated earlier. When the parties decide individually, the expected individual gains from trade limit their willingness to invest in type revelation. Figure 3.18 on p. 127 shows the limits.

By joining forces, the settlement range increases. How much so becomes visible from the second, lower part of the matrix. All the necessary calculations can be taken from section 3.3.3(a) above.

The third beneficial effect of joining forces concerns the credibility of commitment. As demonstrated in the sections on the individual options of Ego and Alter, there is no credibility problem if Ego can learn by inspection what type of actor he is dealing with. Likewise, there is no problem if Alter can transmit type information such that it is observable for Ego. But whenever they rely on indirect means, i.e. whenever they have recourse to a mechanism, the credibility problem must be solved. Unilaterally sinking cost is the only possibility. The following sections illustrate how joining forces can help to do this.

(d) Contract   This section looks at joint options for Ego and Alter. In a colloquial way, this option can be called a contract. Legally minded readers should, however, be reminded that this section explicitly assumes away any form of outside intervention. We are thus not talking about a legally binding agreement. Put differently, fulfilment of contractual obligations cannot be taken for granted.

One standard topic of the law and economics literature[122] concerns the means for generating credibility in such an agreement. For an isolated individual, sinking cost is the only option. Put differently, the investment must be transaction-specific. The parties acting jointly can do this too. By mutually sinking cost, they can generate a stalemate, a

---

[122] The standard text is Williamson 1985.

balance of terror. But what counts for credibility is not the investment itself. It is the vulnerability it generates. This vulnerability need not originate in the risk of an out-of-pocket cost. Among fully rational players, the opportunity cost connected with defection is an equally strong incentive. The risk of losing gains from trade can thus replace a costly *ex ante* investment. This, of course, presupposes a credible promise. But the successful mechanism described in section 3.3.3(c) demonstrates that such promises can be feasible for the parties acting jointly, and without sinking cost.

Generating vulnerability becomes even easier in a repeated game (section 3.3.2(e)) and in a nested game (section 3.3.2(f)). These transformations make it possible mutually to bring the players under a shadow of the future. Again, vulnerability results from the loss of opportunities for future gains, not from currently sinking cost.

(e) Organisation Depending on definitions, a repeated, and even more a nested game, can already be considered a solution that transcends contract. This section, however, uses a different conceptual lens, bringing more context in. Institutional economics speaks of relational contracts and of organisations.[123]

In the literature, relational contracts are typically seen as a hybrid between a mere spot contract and outright organisation, i.e. the incorporation as a firm.[124] Speaking of hybrids is not particularly helpful analytically. There is a legalistic way out of this ambiguity. It sees a contract as relational if it comes at two levels: a framework contract has a legal impact on the individual contracts embedded into this framework. Of course, a legalistic approach is not appropriate for this context. But the general idea can be exploited by analogy. In the following, a contract is treated as relational if the predictability game organises more than one performance game. The performance games are not necessarily identical. The framework contract can thus organise a nested game, not only a repeated game. Why is it easier for the parties to overcome the predictability problem in a relational contract thus defined? More precisely even, why can they do better here than when there is mere repetition? The answer comes at two levels. The scheme increases the sanctioning power for Ego. And it generates additional opportunities

---

[123] The classic text on organisation is Coase 1937. The idea of relational contracts was originally formulated by MacNeil 1971. Both ideas are combined in a stimulating way by Williamson 1985.

[124] Characteristic, and combining insights from law and economics, are Jickeli 1996; Rohe 1998; Kulms 2000.

to access type information. In the terminology introduced above, a relational contract thus has a qualitative effect, and an effect on the generation of credibility.

As demonstrated above, mere repetition already makes the players more vulnerable. For this brings them under the shadow of the future. If a player defects in earlier rounds, he risks losing the gains from trade in later rounds. Defection thus has an opportunity cost. It has also been shown that this effect, among fully rational players, rests on some degree of uncertainty about the end of repetition.[125] In a relational contract, as defined here, the parties gain additional degrees of freedom. They can expressly forbid exit. They can make exit conditional upon an event, e.g. some behaviour of the other player. They might, for instance, foresee that exit is only allowed if the other party has defected more than once. Such a rule would neutralise the effects of a mere mistake by one party.[126] The parties might also use the framework contract to introduce sanctions short of exit. They may, for instance, stipulate an obligation for Alter to make Ego whole, should he defect in one round. Under that rule, Ego would not only receive g, i.e. the opportunity cost of Alter's defection. He would also be compensated for the additional loss Alter has inflicted on him. He would thus also be reimbursed for the additional out-of-pocket cost. Formally, it consists of $l - g$. Since he is made whole in the concrete instance, the rule would oblige Ego to continue playing.

The direct effects of the shift to a relational contract for type revelation are even more important. For Ego can now use technologies for type revelation that would not have been available to him otherwise. The difference can be quantitative and qualitative. In quantitative terms, the defined minimum duration of the interaction plays itself out. It makes for an opportunity to exploit economies of scale. If there is a costly inspection technology, it can become available to Ego. This is particularly important if Alter's type is stable throughout the game. In that case, learning this type early on pays in all later rounds. But even if type changes are possible, a defined minimum duration is of help. Ego can now afford more costly technologies for repeated inspection. Put differently, in a relational contract, the investment in inspection technologies is no longer specific to a single performance game, but to the whole series. The investment shifts from a contract-specific investment to a relation-specific investment.

---

[125] See above 3.3.2(e).
[126] Of course, this is already a deviation from the assumption of full rationality on both sides.

The qualitative option rests on two grounds. The first opportunity originates in the difference between a repeated and a nested game. Since the parties are free to go for the latter solution, they can artificially generate divergent contexts. This helps if they reckon that, in at least some of these contexts, a detrimental actor is forced to generate signals about his type. The second design pushes the idea even one step further. The parties create some sort of an assessment centre at the outset of the game, meant to generate type information. Within a strict rational choice framework, the value of these two options should not be overstated. A rational actor of detrimental type will foresee all this. Specifically, in the interest of generating type information, the parties cannot use low stakes in earlier rounds or in the assessment stage. If he knows that later rounds have higher stakes, a rational actor of the detrimental type will forgo opportunities to exploit Ego in earlier rounds. He will see this opportunity cost as an investment, generating opportunities for larger gains in the future.[127]

The additional options inherent in a relational contract only help the parties if they are credible. The predictability contract must thus be self-enforcing. This is not easy to bring about without third-party involvement. Again, making each other vulnerable is the only possibility. The vulnerability must be precisely tailored to the respective risk of defection. Since the whole game is built on an asymmetry in vulnerability, Alter must make himself artificially more vulnerable than the structure of the game has him. Practically this means that he must sink cost to a degree that creates a balance in vulnerability.

In a relational contract, as defined here, the relationship is strictly confined to what is necessary to get the performance game going. Of course, the parties are not restricted to this solution. They can make their relationship even denser. In reality, they will often not only have the predictability problem to solve. They will have more reasons for co-operation, be they commercial or charitable. In rational choice terminology this implies a change in the assumptions. Ego and Alter are then assumed to have richer utility functions. In the interest of clarity, this option will therefore not be further pursued here.

If the only problem they want to solve remains the predictability problem, denser forms of co-operation must make behaviour more predictable. Denser co-operation thus is another option for institutional

---

[127] A relational contract is much more valuable, if one softens the assumptions and allows for a limited ability of Alter to control his behaviour, be it because of cognitive or motivational limitations. In that case, bringing more context in makes involuntary type revelation much more likely; see below 4.3.8(e).

design. Rational players will compare this option with strict relational contracts. They will assess both the increased potential for type revelation and the extra transaction cost. They will opt for the solution if this balance is positive.

There are several ways of saying how organisation differs from contract. Again, an analogy to law is helpful. The law defines a contract by the fact that the parties keep their goals separate. Each contracting partner may pursue whatever ultimate goals he deems fit. The contract only obliges him to a well-defined exchange of goods or services. Organisation, however, is legally defined by the definition of a joint goal. The underlying contract obliges the parties to further this goal. The contract may, but need not, define the efforts by which this is to be done. Even if the effort is defined, what it actually means in concrete situations is legally derived from the joint goal. Put differently, since the parties have agreed on a goal, an organisational contract sets up a governance structure to reach this goal while the organisation exists. Again, for our purposes, none of this must be laid down legally. The ties between the parties can be fully informal. The parties may even have left the joint goal vague, merely understood, without being explicit. The important difference is the common understanding that this relationship is not only about the exchange of defined goods and services at defined points in time.[128] In the terminology of political science, the term organisation is thus not confined to corporate actors here. It also comprises collective actors.[129]

As with a relational contract, organisation helps the parties overcome the predictability problem in both indirect and direct ways. The indirect ways rely on additional vulnerability. This vulnerability is generated by the discretion necessary for implementing the joint goal while the organisation is operative. Examples from commercial organisations, i.e. firms, illustrate the point. A worker can be transferred to a less attractive position. In a partnership, one partner can be excluded from the next, more profitable endeavour. Interventions can be very subtle: for example, simply conveying the feeling to a person that he is no longer part of the inner circle. It is precisely this discretionary power that allows organisations to handle a much higher degree of complexity than contract.[130] The players of the predictability game can make use of this ability of an organisation to invent new sanctioning tools.

---

[128] On the incentive effects of organisation, see the following survey articles: Gibbons 1998; Prendergast 1999; Becht et al. 2002.
[129] On this distinction, see Coleman 1990: chapters 13–19; Scharpf 1997: 54–8.
[130] Stimulating on different classes of complexity is Simon 1962.

The direct effect of organisation on the generation of type information can be quantitative and qualitative. In quantitative terms, exposing Alter to the rich social context of an organisation allows Ego to make many more observations. Since they come together for a joint endeavour, an investment in inspection technologies can exploit even larger economies of scale than a mere relational contract. The qualitative effect rests on the fact that, within an organisation, the context for information generation is not confined to the performance game. An observation from the labour markets illustrates why this is helpful for solving predictability problems. If they need more people in the workforce, companies could just go to the market for human capital. To a surprisingly high degree, they do not. They would rather have an employment bureau bring somebody in. Of course, the services of such bureaux are much more costly than the wages paid to a new worker. In commercial practice, the employment bureau receives more than twice the wage. But this scheme allows the firm to collect many observations about the worker under real life conditions. If they are content with what they see, after a couple of weeks or months, they hire the worker.

Being within an organisation does not only make it possible to make more observations. These observations can also take recourse to what, in information economics, is known as implicit knowledge.[131] Since an organisation is a living social entity, there are many things taken for granted. Other pieces of information are never made explicit, since everybody understands subtle signals. Especially if Ego only needs to know whether Alter is detrimental or beneficial, he has much better opportunities to find this out within such a context.

Like a relational contract, an organisation only helps overcome the predictability problem if Alter cannot step out at will. Specifically, if he does step out, he must be at least as vulnerable as Ego is. Yet solving this credibility problem is typically easier within an organisation than it is within the confines of a relational contract. In reality, this difference often rests on the formal legal character of the organisation's statute. Since at this point we are looking at options without third-party involvement, this element must be ignored. But stepping out of an organisation still typically has a higher cost than breaching a mere relational contract. At closer sight, however, this also turns out to consist of a difference of assumptions, rather than of institutions. For in reality the exit cost associated with leaving an organisation is higher, since there is more at stake in a loss of membership. Again, the scheme thus rests on Alter's

---

[131] On the distinction between explicit and implicit knowledge see Cowan et al. 2000.

artificial vulnerability. It is thus identical to the increased sanctioning power described above.

3.3.5   Third-party involvement

Can Ego and Alter do better if they get third parties involved? At this point, we are only looking at third parties that become involved at the request of at least one of the parties to the game. The third-party involvement discussed in this section is thus voluntary. The third parties here do not want to impose their will on the other parties.[132]

Bringing a third party in is not free of charge. The third party wants to be remunerated for its services. Having a third party on board can also entail an opportunity cost. For instance, keeping information confidential can become more difficult. Accordingly, rational parties will assess this cost, c_{TP}^{TR}, and they will compare this solution with their alternative options (a). Involving a third party only makes sense if this party is able to verify type information. Accordingly, if type information is strictly private or only observable by Ego, third-party involvement is feckless. Whether bringing a third party in can help depends on when this third party is able to verify Alter's type. This can be either before (b) or after Ego's move (c). In the former case, it concerns what we have dubbed the qualitative and the quantitative effects. In the latter, it concerns what we have called generating credibility for promises.

(a) Comparative assessment   Comparing third-party involvement with the other options of the parties is straightforward. It is thus sufficient to enrich the table of expected outcomes. In Figure 3.22, 'third party' is abbreviated as TP. Visibly, the only new element is c_{TP}^{TR}. Apart from this, the calculations are the same as for the individual or joint options of the parties. They are thus the same as in section 3.3.3(a).

(b) Verification ex ante   Bringing a third party in changes the game. One more actor is added. The game goes through one more move. If this verification is *ex ante*, the ensuing game looks like the model represented in Figure 3.23.

---

[132] In the case of a third party hired by Ego, a qualification is warranted. If Alter is of detrimental type, it certainly is not his will that this third party finds this out and informs Alter. Yet this is no different from inspection done by Alter himself. Another reason why such third-party involvement is not classified as imposed becomes visible if one looks at a beneficial actor. For him, the hiring of the outsider by Ego is a way of Ego bearing the entire cost of type revelation.

Individual assessment	Inactivity	Type revelation
E	$pg_E - (1-p)l$	$pg_E - c_E^{TR}$
A⁺	rg_A	$g_A - c_A^{TR}$
A⁻	rgg	-

Social assessment	Inactivity	Type revelation
E	$2pg + (1-\underline{p})(gg - l)$	$2pg - c_E^{TR}$
A	$2pg + (1-\underline{p})(gg - l)$	$2pg - c_A^{TR}$
E+A	$2pg + (1-\underline{p})(gg - l)$	$2pg - c_{E+A}^{TR}$
TP	$2pg + (1-\underline{p})(gg - l)$	$2pg - c_{TP}^{TR}$

Figure 3.22. Options compared: Ego, Alter, joint, third party.

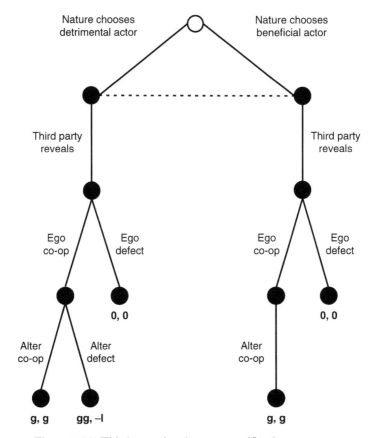

Figure 3.23. Third-party involvement: verification *ex ante*.

The solution to this game is straightforward. It is so, since the third party reveals Nature's move before Ego has to move. If he knows Alter to be beneficial, he employs backwards induction and decides to co-operate. For by doing so, he can now be sure to obtain his fair gain. If, however, Ego learns that Alter is of the detrimental type, he will defect. He thereby prohibits Alter from defecting and imposing a loss on him.

If they hire an intermediary, the parties run into an additional problem. They must predict the intermediary's behaviour. If they expect him to be a utility maximiser, there are two risks for the parties. The intermediary can exert less inspection effort than was agreed to under contract. Or he may receive a side-payment from Alter and make a false statement.[133] This is similar to the original predictability problem faced by Ego and Alter. Actually, predicting the inspection intermediary is typically even more difficult. For the simple model used so far assumes that Ego is certain to learn Alter's type at the end of the game. An opportunistic inspection intermediary, however, will try to hide his bad performance from Ego. A repeated game can be of some help. It means that one of the parties of the original game repeatedly relies on the services of this intermediary. Letting his contractual partner down once might therefore be costly for the intermediary. If his contractual partner doubts his reliability, he might no longer be willing to pay for his services. A nested game, where the intermediary risks his reputation at large by poor performance, is even better. The latter is actually what can be observed in most practical examples. They include credit information bureaux or reporting systems like the one used by eBay.[134]

Hiring an inspection intermediary can be attractive for one of three reasons. The first reason is qualitative. The intermediary has access to information that is inaccessible to Ego. The second reason is quantitative. Ego, Alter, or both jointly, would be able to generate and verify type information. But the intermediary can do the job at a lower cost. The third reason is normative. Technically, Alter would be able to give Ego access to type information in a credible way. But Alter sees this as normatively unacceptable.[135] Let us take these up in turn.

In ideal types, there are two reasons why it may be easier for a third party to generate type information than for Ego. The third party may be able to make more observations, and he may have more generic knowledge at his disposal. The first possibility entails different possibilities of

---

[133] For strict models of this constellation, see Tirole 1986; Kofman and Lawarree 1996; Laffont 1999.
[134] For both an empirical and a theoretical analysis, see Ockenfels 2003.
[135] It is a matter of definition whether one would also ask for Ego to accept the concern in principle.

its own. If the third party is closer to the context from which Alter originates, he may have observed Alter on earlier occasions. He may also be able to rely on observations made by other people who are part of this context. A third party may also be able to compare his observations of Alter with the behaviour of similar actors in comparable contexts. The second asset of a third party is not specific knowledge, but generic knowledge. The third party may have knowledge about what actors typically do in such contexts. He may also know about signals for outliers. Such generic knowledge may come from many sources. It may be statistical, like the information used by life insurance companies. It may result from professional experience, like the information used by doctors. Or it may simply be the upshot of earlier experience in the field.

The quantitative advantage of an inspection intermediary rests on the idea of a division of labour. Of course, we all are forced to become experts in predicting other people's behaviour. If we were not, social interaction would be impossible. But we are only experts in some domains. There will hardly be anybody else who is as good as we are at predicting the behaviour of our spouses and children. But our performance will be rather poor when it comes to predicting the behaviour of an immigrant from a foreign culture. Over time, we can learn. If we live close to Chinatown, some Asian mores will become self-evident to us. But if we want to trade with the Chinese for the first time, it might be easier to rely on the services of a professional agent. If he specialises in intercultural trade, he will be able to generate valuable signals at a much smaller cost. Economically speaking, this superior ability is a matter not of principle, but of production cost. The agent exploits economies of scale and scope.

Finally, there may be a normative reason to bring the third party in. This is best seen if Ego would indeed be able to generate type information at an affordable cost. But both parties agree that this should not be done. Privacy concerns are the main reason for this. Some physical limitations are even evident to a layman. It may be important for Ego to know about them in advance. For instance, a future employer might only look for able-bodied persons. But the future employee would certainly not want to be inspected as is required in military conscription. This is why both parties agree to an examination by a professional doctor. Typically, this doctor is not even allowed to impart any details to the future employer. His examination ends with a mere yes or no: the applicant is able to do the job or he isn't.

Ultimately, Ego is interested in the future behaviour of Alter. Since, psychologically, behaviour results from an interaction between personality and perceived situation, this is hard to identify directly. Typically, the intermediary will not have access to the behavioural dispositions of Alter. This might change in the future, if technologies such as brain-imaging or genetic finger-printing become widespread. But presently the intermediary can typically do no more than collect observations. A credit information bureau might, for instance, certify that Alter has always paid his debt in the past. But he may no longer have the same psychological reasons for keeping his promises that he once had. He may have had a paying routine. But this routine may have come to an end and may have been replaced by calculations along the lines of rational reputation. The present debt may also be booked to a different mental account. Moreover, Alter may now be subject to economic stress, which he did not experience in the past. Despite a stable mental disposition to pay, the psychological situation may therefore have changed in a significant way.

Given such inherent limitations of information generation, the parties may also hire a third party for more moderate purposes. In particular, this would be useful in a Bayesian perspective. If Ego has nothing else, he must start his assessment of Alter's type with subjective beliefs about the distribution of actors in the population. He typically can do much better if he relies on statistical information instead.[136] Such information becomes even more valuable if the intermediary also checks for outliers. It is not certain that he will be able to do so. But he may develop an additional expertise in finding signals that are often correlated with a typical behaviour. A very mundane way of doing so is to form a blacklist. Actors who have defected once in the past are put on this list. This makes sense if they are significantly more likely to defect again, as compared with an average individual.

(c) *Verification* ex post   In the model used here to demonstrate the incentive problems, Alter is certain of his own type. If he is of beneficial type, it is in his interest to inform Ego. For this gives Ego an incentive to co-operate in all cases, rather than to rely on a mixed strategy or on his individual risk preference. But it is difficult for Alter to make this statement credible. Bringing a third party in can make this easier for Alter. The model has a feature that is important in this respect. After Alter has moved, any observer can be certain of his type. If he is a beneficial type, he has co-operated. If he is a detrimental type, he has defected. Verification *ex post* is thus not a concern in this game. This

---

[136] That statistics outperform experts (and even more laymen) has often been demonstrated; see, for example, Meadow and Sunstein 2001.

allows Alter to rely on a third party as a credibility entrepreneur. The resulting game is shown in Figure 3.24.

But third-party intervention is not confined to this situation. It can serve to make any other promise credible. It can thus also be used to back up any co-operative solution. Again, verification *ex post* is not a problem. All the mechanisms investigated above make it patent to any observer whether contractual obligations have been fulfilled or not.

The beneficial actor's statement about his own type becomes credible in the following way. If the third party finds out that Alter has cheated, he is punished. Punishment is effective if, as a result, Alter receives less

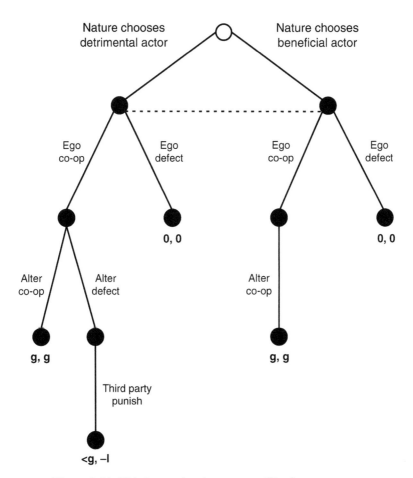

Figure 3.24. Third-party involvement: verification *ex post*.

than he would have had he co-operated. The effective punishment is thus $gg - g + \varepsilon$, where ε is anything above zero.

Note two things. It is not necessary to make Ego whole, should Alter defect. Formally, $gg - g + \varepsilon$ is allowed to be smaller than l. In addition, the fine need not be charged to Ego's purse. It can be cashed in by the third party. Under rationality assumptions, Ego is willing to co-operate nonetheless, if he can be sure that Alter will indeed behave rationally. Rationality thus assumes two things away. Ego need not be afraid that Alter is willing to incur a loss himself if he is able to damage Ego. Emotions like rage or vengeance are thus not a concern. Moreover, Ego can be sure that Alter will not make occasional mistakes. Consequently, there is no need for Ego to be insured against the behavioural risk in Alter.

If both parties trust the third party, this verification technology is advantageous. Put differently, the comparative advantage of this third party then rests in its being trusted by both parties of the game. This can help either way. Ego need not worry about the credibility of Alter's statement. And Alter need not worry about Ego taking a side-payment and not co-operating.

More importantly even, with third-party involvement, sinking cost is no longer the only way to make Alter vulnerable. The third party may dispose of many other ways of inflicting a loss upon Alter. One person can be under the spell of another for a host of reasons. It suffices to make type revelation credible if any such technology is at the disposal of the third party. Specifically, the weaker party must believe two things. Firstly, that the third party is able to inflict a sufficiently large loss on the stronger player. As previously, it can also come in the form of an opportunity cost, i.e. a loss of future gains. And secondly, the stronger player must believe that the third party will inflict this cost if the stronger player turns out to breach an obligation at the end of the game. If these conditions hold, a rational Ego is willing to co-operate.

3.3.6   Sovereign intervention

(a) *Introduction*   None of the foregoing has had recourse to government or to the law. How does the picture change once sovereign intervention is taken into account? Bringing the state in can be advantageous in three respects. Sometimes this is technically the only way to bring co-operation between the parties about. More often, technically speaking the parties could solve the problem, be it unilaterally, jointly or by bringing in third parties. But the revelation cost would eat up the gains from trade, or it would diminish them. Finally, the parties may have normative objections to bringing co-operation about without sovereign intervention. They might, for instance, feel that some aspect of type information should remain private.

According to legal doctrines of sovereignty, only legitimate state government is seen as a sovereign power. The following observations do not make that assumption. Any intervention is seen as sovereign if at least one of the parties has not explicitly agreed to it. That way, any form of social power will also come under this rubric.

A sovereign ruler, by definition, is not part of the little economy of Ego and Alter. Since he is sovereign, he can take the funds for rendering the players this service from wherever he deems fit. Specifically, he can take them from the general budget. This is a way of imposing them on the taxpayer. The players will certainly welcome this element of the solution. Since any other solution to the predictability problem comes at a cost, this feature would inevitably make sovereign intervention the cheapest option. Given this element, they might even be willing to submit voluntarily to sovereign intervention. Technically, this would make the sovereign a third party in the sense of the term used in the previous section.

Of greater interest for this study, however, is sovereign intervention that only transcends the little economy of the two players because of the fact of outside intervention, while the cost of intervention is entirely borne by the players. In line with earlier notation, this cost can be written as c_{SV}^{TR}. For an illustration, assume a fee imposed on the parties that is calculated according to the long-term average cost of intervening in similar cases. Under this assumption, comparing sovereign intervention with the other options is as straightforward as in the case of (voluntary) third-party involvement. Again, it therefore suffices to present the enlarged table of options. In Figure 3.25 sovereign intervention is abbreviated as SV. The calculations for comparing these options are shown in section 3.3.3(a).

As with voluntary third-party involvement, sovereign intervention only helps solve the predictability problem if the sovereign ruler can verify Alter's type. Verification is a serious concern in this case. It typically is at least more costly than for a private, voluntary third party. Not so rarely, pieces of information that would be verifiable for such a private third party are entirely unverifiable for government. If one wants an additional term, beyond the categories of merely observable or verifiable information, one might add the category of provable information. The adjective 'provable' points to the main additional restriction. The rule of law rightly imposes a good deal of formality on any governmental infringement on freedom. Neither courts nor administrative

Individual assessment	Inactivity	Type revelation
E	$pg_E - (1-p)l$	$pg_E - c_E^{TR}$
A⁺	rg_A	$g_A - c_A^{TR}$
A⁻	rgg	-

Social assessment	Inactivity	Type revelation
E	$2\underline{p}g + (1-\underline{p})(gg-l)$	$2\underline{p}g - c_E^{TR}$
A	$2\underline{p}g + (1-\underline{p})(gg-l)$	$2\underline{p}g - c_A^{TR}$
E+A	$2\underline{p}g + (1-\underline{p})(gg-l)$	$2\underline{p}g - c_{E+A}^{TR}$
TP	$2\underline{p}g + (1-\underline{p})(gg-l)$	$2\underline{p}g - c_{TP}^{TR}$
SV	$2\underline{p}g + (1-\underline{p})(gg-l)$	$2\underline{p}g - c_{SV}^{TR}$

Figure 3.25. Options compared: Ego, Alter, joint, third party, sovereign.

agencies are allowed to take a decision that is based on a weak factual basis. Specifically, the burden of proof is as regulated as are the means by which a party may prove contested facts. Moreover, court decisions apart, governmental activity is under democratic control.

As with voluntary third-party involvement, the following looks at verification *ex ante* first (b). It then turns to verification *ex post* (c). Both these sections assume the sovereign power to be a legally and democratically controlled government. The last section drops this assumption and looks at functional equivalents, i.e. at forms of involuntary outside intervention by non-state actors (d).

(b) Verification ex ante   Sometimes, government can use its sovereign powers to extract private information directly. Criminal procedure is a case in point. Most legal orders would not convict a person who is mentally unable to control his behaviour. In such cases, the defendant is forced to undergo psychological and medical investigations aimed at providing his behavioural dispositions. For constitutional reasons, however, legal orders are only willing to intrude that far into privacy and human dignity if the cause is severe. The mere chance of bringing about more co-operation between private parties would certainly not suffice to justify this kind of governmental intrusion. Currently, many legal orders are even considering going further. They are talking about prohibiting private parties from generating or using genetic information for purposes such as writing insurance contracts.[137]

---

[137] For an English-language overview of the German discussion, see Simon and Braun 2002.

Legal orders are more open to less direct intervention. Sometimes government itself collects information about earlier behaviour and makes it available to private parties. A case in point is the register of convicted criminals. To a limited degree, private parties are allowed to receive information from this register if government believes that they have a legitimate concern. For instance, a future employer may have the right to learn about the criminal convictions of the applicant if they are connected to the job.

The next option is identical to one of the main options for regulatory intervention if one drops the rationality assumption on the part of Alter. It will be further investigated below.[138] If government succeeds in patterning behaviour, this also creates an informational advantage. Behaviour is no longer random. It suffices if Ego identifies two things: the pattern, and the situation in which it is likely to apply. In the terminology from information economics used thus far, identifying the situation then is a signal. Depending on how strong the correlation is, it allows Ego to make a better educated guess. Technically speaking, it allows prior beliefs to be updated.

In principle, there are three options for institutional design. The actor can be obliged to send a signal in the first place. Government can help the signal become more credible. And government can intervene in the interest of increasing the correlation between the signal and the information sought.

Again, examples must wait until a later part of this book. By way of illustration, only one shall be mentioned. Government can oblige actors to become part of an organised collectivity. A case in point would be the liberal professions. To be admitted to them, one has to go through university education and pass state exams. Those who follow these professions must regularly co-operate with their peers. The collectivity has a rule-making and a rule-applicatory power. Members are under regular peer review. Under such conditions, learning that an individual is part of that collectivity is a powerful signal of his behaviour in the professional domain.

(c) Verification ex post As with voluntary third-party involvement, verification by the state can also help the parties if it occurs after the fact. In the simplified model used for the rational choice part of the book, such verification is trivially possible. For by defection, Alter reveals his type. This piece of information is obviously also available to a court or to a governmental agency. No conflict with

---

[138] See below 4.3.2(c).

the rule of law or with democracy is to be found. Sovereign intervention can help the parties in three ways. It can force a reluctant party to submit to a mechanism for type revelation. It can impose a distribution of the revelation cost on the parties or on outsiders. And it can make Alter fully vulnerable to state intervention. Let us take these issues up in turn.

Revelation cost and its distribution apart, it is in the interest of a beneficial actor to participate in a voluntary scheme that credibly reveals his type. This would only be wrong in a theoretical case in which an interaction partner believed the population to consist only of beneficial actors. Of course, in this context, a detrimental actor will not want to participate in a revelation scheme. But since they are assumed to be rational, all beneficial actors will. Accordingly, in the language of mechanism design, there is no participation constraint at the outset.

The picture differs, however, once a revelation cost is introduced. Alter will not participate in information revelation if the cost of making his statement credible is prohibitive. This occurs when this cost is larger than his fair gain g. Under the same condition, Ego will not want to invest in a mechanism for type revelation. As demonstrated above, this is only half the truth, however. For the entire gains from trade are $2pg$. Since both parties stand to gain, any revelation cost below $2pg$ is worthwhile. But the parties may fail to agree on the distribution of the cost between themselves, given that, concerning the distribution of the investment cost, the parties are engaged in a chicken game. It has been demonstrated above that the parties themselves are able to avoid this trap if they have Alter reveal his type, and Ego make a side-payment. Under a strict principle of subsidiarity, government would therefore not intervene. But no industrialised country applies the subsidiarity principle that strictly. Moreover, government might intervene, claiming that its intervention is cheaper, or more reliable.

At closer sight, the first and the second option for governmental intervention turn out to be linked. Forcing one of the parties to participate is only a concern since the revelation cost must be distributed in some way. Given this relationship, government also has another intervention option. It can restrict itself to attributing the revelation cost. An indirect way of doing this is by imposing a sequence of moves in the predictability game. As we have seen, the first-mover advantage then determines which of the parties is going to pay for revelation.[139] If government believes in utilitarian values, it could even shift this cost to outsiders. From a utilitarian perspective, the only thing that counts is

---

[139] See above 3.3.3(c).

the overall welfare. As mentioned, one group of such outsiders are the taxpayers. Put differently, government can shoulder this cost itself.

Finally, it is easy for government to save the bonding cost. For sovereignty means that the entire wealth of every citizen is in principle under the aegis of government. It therefore is impossible for an actor to be insufficiently vulnerable to sovereign intervention. Accordingly, there is no need to make Alter artificially vulnerable by having him sink cost.

The unlimited character of sovereign powers also allows government to keep the cost of its own intervention low. Instead of actually enforcing its will on the parties, government can content itself with setting up pertinent rules. Rational actors will believe that government is able and willing to enforce these rules, should they not abide. Of course, this presupposes that non-obedience is easy to verify. But in the simple game analysed here, this is not a concern.

(d) Sovereign intervention without government   In a legal context, sovereignty is linked to legality. Constitutional doctrine and public international law are not oblivious to the possibility of illegitimate power. But such power will be fought if it tries to emancipate itself from sovereign control. This book, however, is interested in understanding the function of institutions. It must therefore start from a context that is not (fully) constitutionalised. It therefore must take power exercised by non-state actors into account.[140] Such power differs from voluntary third-party involvement if a private person interferes with at least one of the parties against his will. Since what counts is factual impact, it does not matter whether this ability rests on economic or on social grounds.

Sovereign governmental power is not only legally unlimited; to a large extent it is also factually unlimited. The same does not necessarily hold true for private forces. If they are more limited, they are also less operational. This weakness can, however, often be outweighed given that private rulers have easier access to information. In particular, such private forces are typically not bound by the rule of law or by the principle of democracy. This allows them to use information that is merely verifiable, not provable in the sense of the terms established above.

When sovereign states conclude treaties, they face a problem similar to the one analysed here. They cannot fully predict *ex ante* whether the

---

[140] Increasingly, lawyers are themselves interested in understanding such private governance, or hybrid forms of governance, combining public and private inputs. For an overview, see Engel 2001c, 2001d, 2004a.

other states will fulfil their contractual obligations. There is no sovereign superior to the sovereign states who could force a deviant state to co-operate. A frequent way out is the following. A larger group of states concludes a framework treaty. Within that treaty, each contracting partner promises all other partners that it will not breach its obligations under secondary treaties. If country A later breaches a secondary obligation to country B, this then constitutes a breach of its primary obligation vis-à-vis all members of the framework treaty. Accordingly, all members of this large community are entitled to afflict reprisals on country A.

Although elegant, this construction is not watertight. For why should country C be willing to help country B? It is individually best off if all the other members of the framework treaty bear the enforcement cost. For country C is interested in the threat power inherent in membership of the framework treaty. But in the terms of economics, enforcement activity is a public good shared by all the contracting partners. Rational choice theory would expect under-provision of this good.[141] But there are ways to get around this. If the other parties can observe the enforcement effort, they might themselves become unwilling to intervene on behalf of country C, should this country get into trouble.

There is a link between this collective mechanism and reputation.[142] This holds if reputation is not individual, but linked to a formal or informal group. Examples are the reputation of a profession or the reputation of a network of franchisees. Such a collective reputation is a powerful tool for making credible promises. For if one member of the group violates the legitimate expectations of outsiders, the reputation of the whole group is at risk. For that reason, all other members of the group must be entitled to sanction such behaviour. The parallel goes even further. For within such a group, the same incentive problem exists. Each individual member is best off if the others bear the enforcement cost.

Finally, the parties can even bilaterally create the functional equivalent to sovereign powers. This is the case if they have an opportunity to agree on a mechanism for type revelation before Nature draws. When this is done, Alter does not know whether Nature will make him beneficial or detrimental when it comes to interaction. The parties thus design the

---

[141] This is a standard problem of a related field, the control of management by the shareholders of a company. Classic texts are Berle and Means 1932; Jensen and Meckling 1976.

[142] Reputation was mentioned earlier during the analysis of nested games; see above 3.3.2(f).

mechanism for type revelation 'under the veil of ignorance'.[143] This need not imply that both prepare for worst cases. A rational reaction would be to design the institution according to their prior beliefs about type distribution in the later population. This can be seen in the extreme case in which both parties believe that the future population will be entirely composed of beneficial actors. In that case, any effort to adduce type revelation would be futile. The revelation cost would be wasted. But the calculation changes if at least Ego thinks it sufficiently likely that there will be quite a number of detrimental actors. Specifically, the willingness of Alter to conclude such an agreement depends on his beliefs about actor distribution. His willingness will be greatest if he believes that he is very likely to be a beneficial type later.

If the parties can design the mechanism for type revelation before Nature moves, it helps them decisively. They then are able to avoid the chicken element in the investment game. For they then can agree on any split of the revelation cost *ex ante*. Promises at this stage are credible, since both parties can make their willingness to play the ensuing game dependent upon the other having paid or having put their share of the revelation cost at the other's disposal.

3.3.7   The problem of linking

Within the model used here, predictability is a strictly specific problem. The model fully specifies the players, the possible actor types, the sequence of moves, the distribution of information and the pay-offs. Yet even within such a well-behaved environment, the response is not necessarily tailor-made. The parties may think it wise to switch to a repeated or nested game. Third parties may render similar services to the players of other predictability games. Sovereign intervention may target classes of behaviour, rather than individual cases. In any of these cases, the resulting predictability is no longer customised. Put differently, the intervention does not bring about local predictability, but global predictability. There may be a number of reasons for such a link across issues or players (a). If such links are present, a number of additional governance problems emerge (b).

(a) Reasons   Linking can be voluntary. It then is usually called bundling. But often the players or the outsiders do not have a choice.

---

[143] This is a term famous in public choice theory, Buchanan 1965, and in social philosophy, Rawls 1999. (The authors do not use the term in the same way; but the differences are not of importance here.)

They must take the link as a given. Put differently, it results from indivisibility. Let us start with the latter.

There can be one of three reasons for indivisibility: customisation can be technically impossible, prohibitively costly or ruled out for normative reasons.[144] Technical impediments mean that there is no technology for generating better-customised predictability. In the strongest case, nobody is able to do so. This type of impediment can only be overcome by technological innovation. The impossibility can also be limited to the parties. In that case, the problem could be overcome by third-party involvement, maybe also by learning. Within the model, this would imply that the parties cannot achieve customised predictability on the spot. It presupposes that one of the parties will make an investment in learning.

Similar considerations apply to the second reason for indivisibility. Prohibitive transaction cost is not an absolute, but a relative impediment. The maximum rational parties are willing to invest in predictability is a little less than the aggregate gains from trade. In the stronger case, this sum is smaller than the cost for customising predictability by whoever would do it. Again, there is a softer case. In that scenario, neither of the parties alone nor both of them together can customise the intervention at a less than prohibitive cost. But outsiders can. This is a typical situation if running the institution for bringing predictability about has economies of scale or scope.

The third reason for indivisibility is normative. In such cases, there is a technology for customisation. It is not prohibitively costly either. But it clashes with the normative convictions of at least one of the parties. Likewise, it might clash with values that an outside actor is willing and able to enforce on the parties. The typical case is a legal prohibition against using a technology to bring predictability about. For instance, many legal orders do not allow the use of lie detectors.[145]

The foregoing has already considered one reason why the parties might forgo better customisation. They might not want to allow for third-party involvement. Bundling can thus be an issue of design, rather than necessity. There are more reasons for this. An individual player may shy away from the sure loss of transaction cost, and rather accept a somewhat less appropriate solution to neighbouring predictability problems. When negotiating a joint solution, or burden sharing, strategic

---

[144] Not by coincidence, the three reasons are identical to the ones that can prevent property rights from being better specified. By implication, global predictability shares the problems inherent in attenuated property rights. On this, see Eggertsson 1990.

[145] From the rich literature, see, for example, Fiedler et al. 2002.

interaction may have brought the parties into this suboptimal equilibrium. The latter is particularly likely. If institutional design involves strategic interaction, it is driven by a struggle over distribution.[146]

(b) Problems What are the additional problems inherent in linking predictability across issues or players? The first point is straightforward. Such an intervention can go beyond what is necessary. It may cover cases with no predictability problem whatsoever. More likely even, the intervention may extend to cases with a tolerably small predictability problem. Such a variance in predictability is probable, since behaviour results from both personality and perceived situation.

The opportunity cost of a link across issues can even be higher. For, as demonstrated, greater predictability is not always a good thing. There are games where the opposite is beneficial.[147] A second type of opportunity cost starts from the observation that the future is never fully certain. Put differently, individuals do not face absolutely identical situations very often in life. Now if the next situation is somewhat different from the previous ones, individuals must be mindful of their ability to adapt. The more strongly an intervention is linked across issues, the greater the risk that this need will be ignored. Evolutionary theorists call this overfitting. Precisely because the response perfectly fits the original case, it risks being inappropriate for later cases.[148]

Links across persons carry a risk of externalities. Welfare economists speak of negative externalities if a bad is inflicted on a non-consenting outsider. They speak of positive externalities if an outsider receives a benefit without the consent of its provider. Both can happen if intervention aimed at predictability is not fully customised.

Let's deal with negative externalities first. They can come at three levels. At the first level, the intervention itself has a detrimental side-effect on outsiders. Take an employer who knows that a small number of his employees steal. If he installs surveillance cameras, all honest employees suffer alike. At the second level are negative side-effects resulting from greater predictability. A classic example is a cartel. Amongst themselves, all participants want to be sure that the other participants do not cheat. Cheating would mean that they sell below the price which the cartel has agreed. Such deals are individually rational if all others abide by the cartel. Defection then makes it possible to attract additional demand. But greater behavioural predictability within the cartel is to

---

[146] This is the basic tenet of Knight 1992.   [147] See above 3.2.3(c).
[148] See again Weigend 1994.

the detriment of the demand side of the market. At the third level, the externality is about predictability itself. Making behaviour predictable in one area can mean that it becomes less predictable in another.[149] A likely instance is the following. The easier it is to create predictability artificially, the easier it is for individuals to liberate themselves from social embeddedness. Many believe that the Internet in particular might show this. It offers technologies that make behaviour between total strangers tolerably predictable. The example of eBay has already been mentioned.[150] This might make it easier for people to leave their professional or social context of origin. Those who are not equally versatile technology-wise could be left behind.

One might think that positive externalities are not a policy concern. Why should one be opposed to outsiders receiving a good or service for free? Yet providers will anticipate the effect. If too much of the benefit goes to outsiders, the insiders' remaining willingness to pay may diminish too much. Put differently, a technology for bringing predictability about may become prohibitively costly, although the aggregate willingness to pay would have been large enough to bear the production cost.

Another problem is evolutionary. There can be a trade-off between better predictability in the case at hand, and a healthy evolution, both of technology and of institutions. For evolution needs variety. It works by picking what looks promising for the future from many occasional deviations. Progress may come either as an entirely new good, or as a more elegant way of providing a good that has already been known before. Strong devices for making behaviour predictable do make it fool-proof. This is likely to reduce variety. The evolutionary problem can be couched as an externality. The ordinary rate of failure has a positive externality. Reducing it cuts this externality back.

If the two parties to the base game solve the predictability problem bilaterally, they face a severe distribution problem. It has been analysed as a chicken game. Using a less well-tailored technology for bringing predictability about can help the parties solve their distribution problem. They can now try to shift part of the burden to other participants. But the new participants will not necessarily applaud this. They may be better off participating than they are avoiding the scheme. But they might prefer a different distribution of the cost. Finally, whenever a problem of distribution is present, there is also a risk of conflict. During

---

[149] In another monograph, I have further developed the idea, and dubbed it regulatory externalities; see Engel 2002a: 307–8.
[150] See again Ockenfels 2003.

the struggle, one of the participants may inflict further losses on some of the others.[151]

3.3.8   The problem of power

(a) *Understanding power*   Taming government: the difficulty of doing this is one of the reasons why almost all states of the world now have written constitutions. Government must be powerful, otherwise it cannot do its job. But power can be abused. Democratic countries have found highly divergent ways of balancing these two goals.[152] But they all rely on (political) institutions for this purpose. Accordingly, power must be a concern if the predictability problem is to be solved by sovereign intervention.

But the problem of power is not confined to this response. One way of modelling the polity makes this obvious. There is a long-standing philosophical tradition of justifying government by a fictitious contract. In a hypothetical state of nature, all individuals by contract submit to later governmental intervention. The idea goes back as far as Thomas Hobbes.[153] It is present among modern thinkers like John Rawls[154] and James Buchanan.[155] In the rational choice framework used in this chapter, the original contract creates a principal–agent relationship. Those governed are the principals. Government is the agent. The model captures the fact that the people can at best partly control government. Government retains considerable leeway, both legally and factually.[156] Now principal–agent relationships are not confined to the study of political institutions. On the contrary, to apply the model to government at all, one needs – with something like an intellectual sleight of hand – to introduce a hypothetical constitutional contract. The principal–agent model applies directly if the original contract is not fictitious, but real. This is the case if the parties solve the predictability problem using voluntary third-party involvement. The principal–agent model also applies directly if the parties respond by creating a form of organisation.

---

[151] For an analysis in greater detail, see Engel 2003a.
[152] Understanding these differences, and how they came about, is the mission of comparative politics. For an overview, see Apter 1996; Mair 1996.
[153] Hobbes 1651.
[154] Rawls 1999.
[155] Buchanan and Tullock 1962; for a most stimulating, comparative analysis of the contractual argument, see Kersting 1994.
[156] For an overview of principal–agent-modelling in political science, see Alt and Alesina 1996.

Principal–agent models were originally even developed to clarify the interaction between shareholders and management.[157]

Detecting the power element in a purely bilateral, one-shot game is not as easy. Of course, one can see an asymmetry in the outside options or in the information distribution as a source of power.[158] But this kind of power is of no additional concern for the parties. The problem of power has already been addressed in the above analysis. A legal concept is central to understanding the additional power problem, not covered as yet. In principle, private law holds the parties to a contract bound by their promises.[159] But, to a greater or lesser extent, the law makes an exception if it considers a promise to be involuntary.[160] Illustrations are the legal protection given to tenants, workers and consumers. Typically, a legal order also contains a general clause, allowing the courts to invalidate a contract if one partner has exploited the other in a grossly unfair manner.

Three standardised examples demonstrate why the additional problem of power is not visible in the model of the original predictability game. Tenants are arguably vulnerable because of a difference in sunk cost. It typically is very costly for a tenant to move to a new apartment. He will not only calculate the actual switching cost, but also the need to re-establish a social network in the new neighbourhood. As long as apartments are sought after, it is fairly easy for the landlord to find a new tenant. Similar considerations apply to the contractual relationship between an employer and his employee. In the case of consumers, in rational choice language, the core problem can be described as a difference in economies of scale and scope. The producer or the seller frequently interacts with more or less similar buyers. It thus makes sense for them to specialise in this type of transaction. A consumer, however, buys hundreds of different goods from many different sources. It would not be rational for him to invest an equal amount of money in swiftly handling each of these transactions. The legal general clause can thus be interpreted as a precautionary measure for other elements of context that result in a significant asymmetry of negotiation power. From this, an analytically clear definition of the additional power problem results.

---

[157] See again Berle and Means 1932; Jensen and Meckling 1976.
[158] This is done in a stimulating way by Knight 1992: chapter 3.
[159] Actually, continental and common law differ substantially in this respect. In continental law, in principle, promise is binding as such. In common law, promise is only binding if given 'in consideration of' something. In the common law perspective, contract is thus interpreted as a tool for mutual exchange only. For a comparative view, see Kötz 1996: § 4.
[160] For a comparative analysis, see Kötz 1996: § 8 I–III.

The problem is present whenever elements of the larger context play themselves out in an additional and significant difference of negotiation power.

(b) *Addressing power* Parties with prevoyance will be aware of the power risk, and they will try to address it in advance. In principle, there are two possible ways to do this. The parties can try to bind power before it originates. This implies a long-term relationship. It will work out particularly well if this original framework contract is concluded under a fairly dense veil of ignorance.[161] The other option is outside intervention. This need not be prepared a long time in advance. The party being threatened by the other party's power brings in additional support. A classic example is workers' unions, organised in order to parry employers' power. Government intervention into private exchange has the same effect. The already mentioned legal rules on behalf of tenants, workers and consumers can thus be understood as sovereign forms of intervention aiming at giving the weaker party countervailing power.

The legal discourse about constitutional issues has found precise terms for the concerns to be addressed by institutions controlling power. These concerns are liberty, democracy and the rule of law. In its stronger form, liberty means that some individual action parameter is entirely fenced off from sovereign intervention. Translated into our context, it implies an *ex ante* limitation of power such that it is prevented from affecting one action parameter. For instance, most democratic countries forbid capital punishment and torture, whatever the regulatory aim. A less intense limitation of power makes its exercise dependent upon properly balancing the goal of intervention with the degree of intrusion into freedom. This is the predominant approach in the constitutional protection of basic rights and fundamental freedoms. The constitution typically does not give its addressees absolute protection. But government must justify any intervention in reference to the proportionality principle. Every act of intervention must serve a legitimate aim. It must be conducive to this aim. The institution chosen must be compared with alternatives. Under this test, the intrusion into private rights is illegal if government could have used an equally effective, but less intrusive alternative. Finally, the act of intervention may not be out of proportion, given the regulatory aim. This last test calls for an open balancing exercise.[162]

---

[161] See again Buchanan 1965, and in social philosophy, Rawls 1999.
[162] More from Engel 2003b.

Democracy and the rule of law mean that government may exercise its sovereign powers only within the confines of organisational and procedural rules. Those who exercise sovereign powers must have come into office in a democratically controlled way. Practically, this means that they must be appointed by the democratically elected government. Any intrusion into freedom or property must be justified by statute. Thereby the substance of the intervention is also subsumed under democratic control.[163] The rule of law is a complex concept, partly also a historically contingent one.[164] For the present purposes it is sufficient to point out its basic effect. When government addresses individuals, it must go through a host of procedural limitations.

All this can in principle be transposed to non-governmental power. The parties are well advised to consider similar safeguards if solving or diminishing the predictability problem brings them under the aegis of some sort of power. Designing such safeguards, however, can be difficult if the source of power is informal. This is precisely why constitutionalisation is a good thing.[165]

3.3.9   Institutional choice

Sometimes the parties have no choice. If they want to overcome the predictability problem, they have just one option. They are in a take-it or leave-it situation. The most important reason for such a narrow choice space is the character of the necessary information. If this information is strictly (only) observable, bringing outsiders in is of no help. But often, conditions are not that tight. If not, the parties must choose rationally. If sovereign intervention is feasible, the outside actor also must decide rationally whether intervention is justified. Such rational means of choosing between several regulatory options comes under the realm of cost–benefit analysis.[166] The strict analysis within the confines of the rational choice model has been the topic of previous sections. But before real-life actors rely on this knowledge, they are well advised to

---

[163] These two aspects of democratic legitimacy, the personal and the substantial, are part of the constitutional principle of democracy, as guaranteed by the German Basic Law; see e.g. Maunz and Dürig 1958-Herzog Art. 20 GG, R II.46.

[164] An overview of the richness is provided by Kunig 1986; Sobota 1997.

[165] Constitutionalisation currently is a key issue in international relations; see Frowein 2000. With respect to private and hybrid governance, a similar discussion is slowly commencing; for an overview, see Engel 2001c, 2004a.

[166] Cost–benefit analysis is legally imposed on most independent regulatory agencies in the USA. This explains why there is a rich legal and interdisciplinary discussion on the pros and cons of the tool in that country. See Breyer 1993; Sunstein 1996; McGarity 1998; Adler and Posner 2000; Symposium 2000.

take additional elements into account. These concerns are listed in the following, starting with benefits (a). They are contrasted to costs (b). In many instances, one or both of these elements is uncertain (c). Taking both benefits and costs into consideration typically makes it advisable to go for soft, not hard predictability (d), i.e. for narrowing down the behavioural space of the actor, without reducing it to just one option.

(a) Benefit In a rational choice perspective, assessing the benefit of the available institutional options is not a very demanding exercise.[167] The parties introduce the institution in the first place precisely because they face a predictability problem. The benefit of the institution consists of its ability to overcome or at least alleviate this problem. A repeatedly mentioned concern is whether the information necessary for making the institution operational is observable, verifiable or provable. There is a long list of further considerations. Whether they play themselves out or not basically depends on how much context is needed to make the institution work. Since no specific institution is being analysed here, suffice it merely to list these considerations.[168] One option may reach the degree of predictability sought after by the parties precisely. Another may be further off this mark. One option may be a causal therapy. Another may only be able to alleviate the symptoms. One option may be open to customisation. Another may only be able to offer a standardised solution. One option may give the parties a choice as to who bears the regulatory cost. Another may always impose it on one player. One option may cut in faster than another. One option may be more robust to disturbances or changes in the environment than another. One option may be available for single predictability problems. Others may work only if applied to a whole class of issues or actors.

(b) Cost Rational parties are aware that making an actor's behaviour more predictable is costly. Their goal is thus not maximum predictability, but optimal predictability. When assessing institutional options, they thus compare costs and benefits. They may be willing to trade better performance for a cheaper solution.

The cost of the individual institutional options comes in three instalments. The first is the transaction cost of the intervention itself. The second consists of the detrimental effects of linking. The third is the risk of uncontrolled power. All this has been analysed above.

---

[167] At least not in principle. Quantification can be a very different matter.
[168] For a more in-depth analysis of these considerations, see Engel 2002a: 100–11.

(c) Uncertainty Regulators typically decide under conditions that are largely uncertain.[169] They often do not even fully understand the regulatory problem. This part of the uncertainty is assumed away in the original model. Both parties know precisely the confines of the predictability problem. The second part of the regulatory uncertainty concerns the effect of intervention. Typically, at best the regulator makes an educated guess about what will happen after intervention.[170] He cannot really know how the addressees will perceive the intervention. They may react in unpredicted, surprising ways. In particular, they have the ability to be innovative. And the environment may change while the rule is still in force. Again, most of this is assumed away by the simplicity of the original model. But at least some of this uncertainty returns through the backdoor. The more contextual the institution, the greater the uncertainty. And fully decontextualised solutions are sometimes unavailable. In other instances, the parties may consider them too costly.

(d) Soft predictability If one only looks at the original model, the parties seem to face a dualistic choice. Either Alter is predictable, or he is unpredictable. In the latter case, Ego decides according to his prior beliefs whether the risk of co-operation seems larger than the expected gains from trade. Yet this model has been introduced only in order to explain the underlying incentive problems. In reality the predictability problem is much more complex. As demonstrated in the second chapter of this book, the predictability problem has many facets. In principle, all these facets could be portrayed in reference to different actor types. But even if both parties are assumed to be fully rational, this variance would overwhelm them. According to the behavioural assumptions, they would still be able to handle all this complexity. But the transaction cost for doing so would explode. Even within a strict rational choice context, full predictability is thus typically not within reach. The most the parties can realistically achieve is soft predictability.[171] The variance

[169] More from Spiecker gen. Döhmann 2001.
[170] For a stimulating analysis of the reasons, see Wegner 1996.
[171] The point has occasionally been alluded to in literature. Cf. Gehlen 1960: 72: 'wenn auch die Institutionen uns in gewisser Weise schematisieren, wenn sie mit unserem Verhalten auch unser Denken und Fühlen durchprägen und typisch machen, so zieht man doch gerade daraus die Energiereserven, um innerhalb seiner Umstände die Einmaligkeit darzustellen, d.h. ergiebig, erfinderisch, fruchtbar zu wirken'; cf. also Jackman and Sniderman 2002: 10: political institutions do not determine voters, they narrow their choice spaces down. Cf. further Schimank 1992: 184: 'dass Erwartungssicherheit und ihr Gegenteil – Anomie – graduelle Zustände sind'. One may also bring Glimcher 2003: 273 and *passim* under this rubric. He stresses that human behaviour is not deterministic at all; there are only different degrees of probability.

in Alter's behaviour is reduced, but not to zero. The same limitation holds for any act of sovereign intervention. Here, the cost is typically even higher than for the parties. This follows precisely from the fact that outside intervention needs at least verifiable, if not provable information.

The following may be viable approaches. Behaviour becomes predictable for standard situations, but not for unusual or new contexts. The degree of possible deviation from a standard expectation may also be reduced. Another option would consist of developing institutions that do not affect standard behaviour, but leave it its original variance. But institutions generate signals for the likelihood of behavioural outliers. Yet another option introduces time. The actor remains free to change behavioural patterns. But if he does, the increased risk of change becomes visible to Ego.

3.4   Subsidy/tax

Restrictive assumptions have a value if they make us see things we wouldn't have seen otherwise. The rational choice model of predictability problems serves this purpose in several respects.[172] Yet another implication of the rational choice model is the topic of the following sections. They point to strategies other than type revelation that are at the disposal of the parties or of outsiders. This section looks at a subsidy or tax scheme. Section 3.5 investigates an insurance solution, while section 6 considers the payment of a risk premium.

Within the language of the rational choice model, the difference between a subsidy/tax scheme and a type revelation scheme can be fleshed out precisely (3.4.1). This solution can be employed by Ego (3.4.2) and by Alter unilaterally (3.4.3). But the parties can also have recourse to it jointly (3.4.4), or outside actors can pick it up (3.4.5).

3.4.1   Characterising the solution

Type revelation is a way of diminishing the predictability problem. A tax or a subsidy leaves the predictability problem untouched and purports to bring co-operation about otherwise (a). The idea works (fully) only if both parties are rational utility maximisers (b). The solution can be advantageous in a number of respects (c). Finally, a related solution will be mentioned. It does not make defection irrational. But it makes the gain from defection so small that there is some empirical likelihood that co-operation will become prevalent (d).

---

[172] See in particular 3.2.3; 3.3.3(b); 3.3.3(c).

(a) Interaction despite the predictability problem   An apparently far-fetched parallel helps explain how a tax or a subsidy differs from type revelation. The climate change negotiations are divided over mitigation versus adaptation. Mitigation is the attempt to reduce carbon dioxide emissions that are thought to be responsible for global warming. The adaptation strategy takes global warming as a given, but tries to implement measures that help nations adapt to a changing climate. From the perspective of the predictability problem, type revelation is a mitigation approach. Predictability increases. A tax or a subsidy takes unpredictability as a given. It strives for a situation where predictability no longer matters. This is feasible since, within the confines of the model, Ego ultimately is not striving for predictability. Increasing his own utility by efficient co-operation is what he is after. Yet another way of making the point is the following. If the parties implement a tax or a subsidy, they treat the predictability problem as an exogenous risk. They deliberately ignore the possibility of generating type information in a credible way. This is feasible if, as a result of the tax or the subsidy, it becomes irrational for a detrimental actor not to co-operate.

These features bring a subsidy and a tax into a class of solutions that are frequently recommended by economists. Economists stress that the intelligence often lies in the institutions, not in the individuals.[173] They posit that institutions should be designed such that they need know as little as possible about the behaviour of agents acting within them.[174] They strive for situations where it does not matter whether the subjects are aware of the rationalising effect of institutions.[175] They are content if subjects act 'as if' they were rational.[176] According to them, institutions, not humans, should be rational.[177]

There is also a psychological way of making the point. As outlined above, behaviour is, roughly speaking, the outcome of the interaction between personality and situation.[178] A tax or a subsidy can be seen as a way of changing the situation, rather than as a way of learning more about the personality of Alter. This gives rise to a further implication. With respect to personality, a tax or a subsidy is a worst case solution. It works even if Alter actually is detrimental, i.e. even if he is an opportunistic *Homo oeconomicus*.

---

[173] Alchian 1950: 216; Becker 1962: 4–6, 12; see also the provocative title of Gode and Sunder 1993: 'Allocative Efficiency of Markets with Zero-Intelligence Traders. Market as a Partial Substitute for Individual Irrationality'.
[174] Heiner 1983: 580.
[175] Smith 1991: 880.
[176] Coleman 1987: 184; Smith 1991: 894.
[177] Gode and Sunder 1993: 119, 134–5.   [178] See above 2.5.3–4.

Finally, there is a legal way of understanding how a tax or a subsidy works. It is a tool to make Alter's commitment credible. Given a credible obligation to pay a tax upon defection, it becomes irrational for an actor not to co-operate. Likewise, if he receives a sufficiently large subsidy when co-operating, defection no longer pays for him. Put differently, because of the tax or the subsidy, the contract becomes self-enforcing.[179]

(b) Behavioural assumptions   A sufficiently large and credible threat of a tax brings co-operation about, even if Alter is detrimental. A credible promise of a sufficiently large subsidy has the same effect. In this respect, a tax and a subsidy can thus be said to be behaviourally robust solutions. But the robustness has limits. It relies on the assumption that Alter is indeed rational. For ease of treatment, type revelation has been illustrated with two types of actors: a beneficial one and *Homo oeconomicus*. But the type revelation model could also be used if actor types were more extreme. Specifically, the detrimental actor could even be willing to inflict harm on Ego if this were not his individually best response. The type revelation model is thus open to envious, greedy or silly actors. With these actors, a tax or a subsidy would no longer work. For the threat of a tax or the promise of a subsidy only changes the behaviour of rational actors in a predictable way.

The second limitation of a tax or a subsidy is subtler. In reality, people sometimes stop behaving in a socially responsible way if they realise that they are treated as rational egoists. This is the topic of some contentious literature on how intrinsic motivation is crowded out by extrinsic impulses.[180] A tax or a subsidy does exactly this. It makes it irrational, by economic standards, not to co-operate. Actors who would have been willing to co-operate without further ado might therefore not only become egoistic. They might even react in irrational, destructive ways. If one takes this risk seriously, switching to a tax or a subsidy can even be counterproductive. This potential effect is not covered by the following rational choice analysis.

(c) Comparative assessment   There are three reasons why using a subsidy or a tax can appear more attractive than type revelation. Firstly, sometimes type revelation is just not available. This is particularly likely to be practical if either Ego or Alter wants to act unilaterally. Ego may

---

[179] Self-enforcing contracts are a standard concept in institutional economics; see e.g. Furubotn and Richter 1997: IV.4.2.
[180] Deci and Ryan 1985; Sansone and Harackiewicz 2000; Frey and Jegen 2001; Janssen and Mendys 2004.

just not have a technology for generating information about Alter's type at his disposal. Alter may simply lack an opportunity to transmit information about what type of an actor he is in a credible way. Secondly, type revelation can be available. But the transaction cost of the feasible technologies for type revelation can exceed the cost of a tax or a subsidy. Finally, type revelation can be normatively unacceptable. In a weaker case, a tax or a subsidy can appear less questionable, normatively speaking. Neither is unlikely, given that type revelation inevitably involves some intrusion into privacy. Since a tax or a subsidy disregards type information altogether, no privacy concerns are present here.

The following analysis focuses on the second of these elements, i.e. the comparison of cost. This is not to say that the other two reasons are less important, practically speaking. But the apparatus of the rational choice model is not particularly well suited to assessing the normative desirability of technologies for bringing co-operation about. One has to weigh numerous normative concerns from entirely different backgrounds for that purpose. The first concern, i.e. the non-availability of type revelation, can, of course, easily be dealt with in rational choice terms. But here the analysis is trivial. If there is no technology for successful type revelation, the parties must look for a substitute. Comparing cost, however, is what the rational choice model is made for.

(d) *Artificial low-cost situation*   If the tax or the subsidy is sufficiently high, defection becomes plainly and simply irrational for Alter. Does this imply that a smaller tax or subsidy is just futile? If so, the parties would be well advised to avoid false negatives. Some false positives would certainly be a lesser concern.[181] The intervening actor would tend to overshoot and choose an amount of tax or subsidy that has some likelihood of exceeding the original incentive to defect.

The picture might change, however, if one allows for a somewhat richer model. Economists surmise that people behave differently in 'low-cost situations'.[182] In such situations, it seems much more likely that people will follow social norms or that they will be guided by their idiosyncratic moral standards. Institutional design can exploit this fact. It can drive the cost of moral behaviour to an artificially low level, without making it just irrational to behave immorally.

---

[181] For philosophical background, see Lübbe 2002.
[182] Kirchgässner 1992, 1996; Kirchgässner and Pommerehne 1993.

3.4.2   Unilateral response by Ego

Like the section that dealt with type revelation, this section looks at options Ego has unilaterally. It then makes the additional assumption that Alter will remain inactive. We know that this is a strong assumption. For it is also in the interest of Alter to bring co-operation about. Within the language of the model, this is a result of the fact that g is defined to be larger than the outside option 0. Note that even the detrimental actor wants co-operation. The worst outcome for Alter is if Ego shies away from co-operation because of the risk of being exploited. Alter is willing credibly to oblige himself not to go for gg if this is the price for obtaining g.

On first reading, it may seem surprising that a subsidy is seen as a solution here. But Ronald Coase has demonstrated in a seminal paper that taxes and subsidies are perfect substitutes.[183] Both have the same effect on incentives. The following two technologies are thus equivalents: imposing a tax on Alter, should he defect; promising Alter a subsidy, should he co-operate. Both technologies obviously differ in terms of distribution. Under a tax scheme, Alter pays the bill, be he beneficial or detrimental. Under a subsidy scheme, Ego bears the entire transaction cost of getting co-operation going. But this does not matter for incentive correction, and hence efficiency.

The foregoing has an interesting implication. The Coase theorem is typically used to understand the problem of externalities.[184] Externalities result from the incompleteness of property rights. In case of a negative externality, the property right of the victim is not complete enough to prevent the aggressor from intrusion. Likewise, in the case of a positive externality, the provider of a good or service is not fully entitled to prevent outsiders from appropriation.[185] The uncertainty about Alter's type can accordingly also be described the following way: the property right of Ego in his own input into the joint endeavour is incomplete. He runs a risk of providing the detrimental actor with a positive externality.

It becomes irrational for a detrimental actor to defect if he is better off co-operating. If Alter defects after Ego has co-operated, he gains gg. If he co-operates too, he gains g. Thus $gg - g$ is how attractive defection is for Alter. Accordingly, the subsidy must be $gg - g + \varepsilon$.

---

[183] Coase 1960.
[184] Pigou 1932 is a basic text on externalities; for a recent treatment, see Cornes and Sandler 1996.
[185] For an in-depth analysis of the concept of property rights, see Eggertsson 1990.

We are considering here a situation where Ego wants to act unilaterally. There is no third party and no state available. This generates a serious problem of credibility. Of course, Ego could pay the subsidy up front. But if Alter is detrimental, this leads to a nightmare. Alter cashes the subsidy in, but he still defects in the last round. That way he obtains the subsidy plus the unfair gain *gg*. Ego will anticipate this, and he will be unwilling to pay up front.

If Ego pays only after Alter has co-operated, he is safe. But now Alter has a problem. Since Ego is rational, he no longer has any interest in paying the subsidy after he is able to cash in his fair gain *g*. For he must pay this subsidy out of his gain. If he breaches his promise at the last moment, he receives co-operation for free. A rational actor will anticipate this. He will not be willing to rely on the promise of a subsidy in the first place.

The reason why a mere promise does not work is as follows. If Ego breaches his promise at the last moment, he is no longer vulnerable to Alter. If he acts strictly unilaterally, the only way out for Ego consists of making himself artificially vulnerable. He can do so by a transaction-specific investment.[186] Because of the strict specificity, this investment would be lost if this particular interaction did not take place. Strict specificity is generated by sinking cost. This term signifies that the investment would lose all its value in any alternative context.

But at closer sight, this does not help either. As a result of the specific investment, Alter is now safe. But Ego cannot be certain that Alter is not abusing what was only meant as a collateral. He can now impose new negotiations on Ego. It is rational for Ego to agree on any redistribution of outcome that leaves him a tiny fraction of his investment, and shifts the rest of it to Alter. By the transaction-specific investment, Ego has thus brought himself into a classic hold-out situation.[187] The parties can overcome the problem bilaterally if Alter makes himself vulnerable the same way.[188] But there is nothing Ego can do unilaterally.

The following must thus make an additional assumption. An unspecified element from the context makes Ego sufficiently vulnerable. Richer contextuality thus allows him credibly to promise a subsidy upon co-operation.

Under which conditions does it pay for Ego to promise a subsidy? The answer comes in two parts. The cost of a subsidy may not be prohibitive. And this cost must be lower than the expected cost of alternative moves.

---

[186] More on degrees of specificity in investment from Furubotn and Richter 1997: IV.2.
[187] More from Williamson 1985: 1.4 and *passim*; Schweizer 1999: VI.
[188] More from Williamson 1985: chapter 8.

A subsidy only changes the detrimental actor's problem if it is actually paid upon co-operation. Part of the cost of this solution is thus the subsidy or $gg - g + \varepsilon$. Moreover, the scheme only works if some element from the context makes Ego sufficiently vulnerable. This can be either an out-of-pocket cost or an opportunity cost, denoted here as c_E^{Tx}. The total cost thus is $gg - g + \varepsilon + c_E^{Tx}$. Ego must pay this out of his gain g. Basic transformation yields the condition laid down in Equation 38:

$$2g - gg - \varepsilon - c_E^{Tx} > 0. \tag{38}$$

The charm of the subsidy scheme is that it generates certainty. If Ego can be sure that Alter is rational, the credible promise of the subsidy yields the fair gain g for sure. But, as is visible from Equation 38, this is a very costly solution. Even if it is available, Ego may consider it too expensive. He may be willing to accept some risk, rather than losing that much money for sure. Within the rational choice framework, taking this decision is a matter of calculus. In its standard form, the model assumes risk neutrality. Ego then is indifferent when faced with the certain prospect of getting a sum x and the same expected value of a gamble. The latter is the product of the (subjective) probability times the outcome. A risk-neutral agent is thus indifferent when choosing between obtaining \$10 for sure and a gamble with a 10 per cent probability of gaining \$100. Psychologically, this is extremely unlikely. The French economist Maurice Allais showed half a century ago that most people value certainty much higher than even the faintest element of uncertainty.[189] The prospect theory from Daniel Kahneman and Amos Tversky has further refined the finding.[190] This implies that many uninformed actors will find the subsidy solution more attractive than the following mathematical exercise shows. Note that the earlier comparisons between potential solutions were not plagued by the certainty effect. For the subsidy scheme is the first solution that guarantees the fair gain g, at least if Alter can be taken to be rational.

If Ego takes no safeguard, his expected outcome can be taken from Equation 4, which is repeated here for convenience:

$$pg_E - (1 - p)l > 0.$$

With subjective probability p, Ego expects his fair gain g. With corresponding subjective probability $1 - p$, he expects the loss l. Ego thus interprets the risk of a loss as an implicit price for the chance of obtaining

---

[189] Allais 1953.   [190] Kahneman and Tversky 1979.

Individual assessment	Inactivity	Type revelation	Subsidy
E	$pg_E - (1-p)l$	$pg_E - c_E^{TR}$	$2g - gg - \varepsilon - c_E^{Tx}$

Figure 3.26. Options compared: individual assessment, Ego: inactivity, type revelation, subsidy.

the fair gain. Accordingly, he will prefer the subsidy scheme only if the expected value of taking the risk of being exploited is smaller. Formally,

$$2g - gg - \varepsilon - c_E^{Tx} > pg_E - (1-p)l \Rightarrow$$
$$2g + (1-p)l - gg - \varepsilon - c_E^{Tx} - pg_E > 0. \tag{39}$$

Obviously, the decisive element in this equation is the subjective probability p. The more optimistic Ego is about Alter's type, the less willing he will be to incur the high cost of the subsidy solution.

Along the same lines, Ego will compare the subsidy scheme with his third option, which is a unilateral investment in type revelation. The expected value of type revelation is $pg_E - c_E^{TR}$. The subsidy scheme will only be attractive if it yields more than this expected value. Formally

$$2g - gg - \varepsilon - c_E^{Tx} > pg_E - c_E^{TR} \Rightarrow$$
$$2g + c_E^{TR} - gg - \varepsilon - c_E^{Tx} - pg_E > 0. \tag{40}$$

In this case, two elements drive the comparison. In the subsidy scheme, the gain is certain; type revelation only prevents the loss from happening. Moreover, both strategies have different costs.

All in all, if he takes the subsidy scheme into consideration, Ego must choose between the three options assembled in Figure 3.26.

3.4.3   Unilateral response by Alter

A detrimental actor will never reveal his type. But he may want to commit to a tax, should he defect. This may be surprising on first reading. But it becomes understandable once one takes the subsidiary function of type revelation into account. Learning Alter's type has no value for Ego on its own. It only helps him assess whether co-operation pays. A tax scheme allows Ego to reckon with gains from trade, at least if he is convinced that Alter will behave rationally. A rational actor anticipates this effect on Ego. A tax scheme makes sense, since it shifts the equilibrium from the outside options to both obtaining the fair gain g.

Since a subsidy and a tax are perfect substitutes, the necessary and sufficient tariff is $gg - g + \varepsilon$. However, if Alter intervenes unilaterally, he faces the same problem as Ego. Within the scarce environment of the model, there is no way of making his promise credible without risking a hold-out situation. The scheme thus rests on some element of the larger context making Alter sufficiently vulnerable. This element enters the model as the cost parameter c_A^{Tx}.

If Ego wants to bring co-operation about in a Pigouvian manner, he must actually pay the subsidy. Not so for Alter, irrespective of his type. It suffices if Ego believes the promise that the tax will be paid, should Alter defect. The characteristic difference between positive and negative sanctions does thus play itself out. As one observer once put it: 'A single gun may suffice to scare off a crowd, but a single cheque will pay for only one successful bribe.'[191] This asymmetry is a result of the fact that Alter can just forgo the opportunity to exploit Ego. It is the uncertainty about Alter's response that puts the co-operative solution of the game at risk. The model used here invites yet another way of making the point. It portrays the uncertainty about Alter's move as an asymmetry in the information about his type. The fact that Ego must actually pay the subsidy can therefore be interpreted thus: given the make-up of the model, Alter has an informational advantage. The subsidy is a way of making sure that Alter obtains the information rent. Specifically, the subsidy scheme can ignore type information, since even the worst type of actor receives his full information rent.

Given the informational advantage of Alter, his cost for a tax scheme thus boils down to the use of the contextual elements that make him sufficiently vulnerable. As with a subsidy scheme, the tax scheme is sure to generate co-operation. Accordingly, the value for this option is $g_A - c_A^{Tx}$. Going for this option is locally rational for Alter if this term is positive. The cost of making the scheme credible may thus not be higher than the gains from trade, or formally

$$g_A - c_A^{Tx} > 0. \tag{41}$$

Alter must compare this option with the other two options investigated so far. In this comparison, the two actor types re-enter the scene. If Alter is beneficial and remains inactive, he expects rg_A, where r is the subjective probability of Ego co-operating.[192] A tax scheme pays for such an actor if it yields a higher outcome. Formally,

---

[191] Scharpf 1997: 152.   [192] For a formal definition, see Equation 14.

$$g_A - c_A^{Tr} > rg_A \rightarrow$$
$$g_A - rg_A - c_A^{Tx} > 0. \tag{42}$$

Alter must thus compare a certain outcome at a certain cost with an uncertain outcome. If the certainty effect is ignored, as with Ego, the subjective probability of Ego co-operating anyhow is decisive.

The equivalent calculation of the detrimental actor differs slightly. In case Ego co-operates anyhow, this actor expects not only the fair gain g, but the unfair gain gg. Accordingly, his problem is

$$g_A - c_A^{Tx} > rgg \Rightarrow$$
$$g_A - rgg - c_A^{Tx} > 0. \tag{43}$$

A detrimental actor will thus be somewhat less inclined to rely on a tax scheme.

At first sight, one might think that this generates a signalling problem. The fact that Alter offers a tax scheme is a weak signal for his being beneficial.[193] Yet under a credible tax scheme, Ego is safe anyhow. He will thus rationally ignore the signal and co-operate.

Finally, Alter also has the option to engage in type revelation unilaterally. Since this would be irrational for a detrimental actor, however, the following comparison can be confined to beneficial actors. For such an actor, the expected benefit from type revelation is $g_A - c_A^{TR}$. Accordingly, Alter's comparative problem reads

$$g_A - c_A^{Tx} > g_A - c_A^{TR} \Rightarrow$$
$$c_A^{TR} - c_A^{Tx} > 0. \tag{44}$$

The problem is thus straightforward. Alter prefers the tax scheme if the transaction cost of doing so is smaller than the cost involved in type revelation.

Summing up, Alter thus faces the choices laid down in Figure 3.27.

Individual assessment	Inactivity	Type revelation	Tax
A$^+$	rg_A	$g_A - c_A^{TR}$	$g_A - c_A^{Tx}$
A$^-$	rgg	-	$g_A - c_A^{Tx}$

Figure 3.27. Options compared: individual assessment, alter: inactivity, type revelation, tax.

[193] More on the signalling problem see above 3.3.2(d).

3.4.4   Joint response by Ego and Alter

If they act unilaterally, Ego and Alter deliberately ignore the fact that the other co-operation partner might also contribute to the solution. This statement has two implications. If one of the partners solves the problem unilaterally, the other receives a free lunch. Moreover, they jointly might have more powerful technologies at their disposal for bringing co-operation about. Both have relevance for the subsidy/tax scheme.

A first option for joining forces would consist of picking one of the unilateral solutions, but sharing the cost. This could be either a subsidy or a tax. In the tax case, the assessment of the social benefit is straightforward. This solution pays socially under the conditions laid down in Equation 45:

$$2g - c_A^{Tx} > 0. \tag{45}$$

Both parties obtain their fair gain g. From this collective gain from trade, they must pay the cost for making Alter's promise credible. Since we at this point are considering Alter's unilateral options, the ability to make a credible promise again is dependent on some additional element from the context.

In the unilateral case, a subsidy scheme has been demonstrated to be much more costly. In that case, the cost has two elements: the cost for making the promise credible, and the cost of the actual subsidy. In a social perspective, however, the cost of a subsidy scheme is exactly the same as the cost of a tax scheme. Equation 45 thus applies as well. Of course, for a subsidy to work Alter must still receive $gg - g + \varepsilon$ upon co-operation. But socially speaking, this is only a way of distributing the gains from trade. If the parties go for the subsidy solution, this means that Alter keeps the lion's share.

This is not, however, where the advantage of joining forces stops. It also makes a more powerful technology available for bringing co-operation about. As explained earlier, both the tax and the subsidy scheme rest on the ability to make promises credible. Within the confines of the base model, none of the parties can do so unilaterally. But bilaterally, this is feasible. If both sink cost, the parties can generate a stalemate.[194] They can thus generate sufficient vulnerability in an artificial way. They no longer rely on the contingent context for the purpose.

Both parties prefer co-operation over their outside options. But both would rather have the other pay the bill for bringing co-operation

---

[194] The idea is further developed in Williamson 1985: chapter 8.

Social assessment	Inactivity	Type revelation	Subsidy/tax
E	$2\underline{p}g + (1 - \underline{p})(gg - l)$	$2\underline{p}g - c_E^{TR}$	$2g - c_E^{Tx}$
A	$2\underline{p}g + (1 - \underline{p})(gg - l)$	$2\underline{p}g - c_A^{TR}$	$2g - c_A^{Tx}$
E+A	$2\underline{p}g + (1 - \underline{p})(gg - l)$	$2\underline{p}g - c_{E+A}^{TR}$	$2g - c_{E+A}^{Tx}$

Figure 3.28. Options compared: social assessment, Ego, Alter, joint: inactivity, type revelation, subsidy/tax.

about despite the uncertainty about Alter's type. In the chapter on type revelation, the ensuing chicken game was analysed. It was demonstrated that merely switching from a simultaneous to a sequential game does not help, given the uncertainty about Alter's type. The only way out was the direct mechanism described above.[195] With a tax or a subsidy scheme, overcoming the chicken problem is easier. This is a result of the fact that Alter's type does not matter. Accordingly, the parties can switch to a sequential game. Practically speaking, they can negotiate about sharing the burden of bringing co-operation about.

Whether the parties jointly opt for a tax or subsidy solution also depends on comparatively assessing the cost of it. Figure 3.28 displays the options.

It does not seem necessary to go through all the calculations. Suffice it to highlight the most important implications. Comparing an individual subsidy or tax with a joint tax scheme is problematic. For only the joint scheme can solve the credibility problem autonomously. If credibility is not a concern in the concrete case, comparing these three options is straightforward. It depends on the cost for making the relevant promise credible. The difference between a subsidy/tax and type revelation is the same socially as it had been individually. Type revelation makes sure that Ego does not suffer a loss. But it does not bring co-operation about if Alter is revealed to be detrimental. Accordingly, under type revelation the parties lose some co-operation. Put differently, the cost involved in a tax scheme can be higher. How much so is shown in Equation 46:

$$2g - c_{E+A}^{Tx} > 2\underline{p}g - c_{E+A}^{TR} \Rightarrow$$
$$2g - 2\underline{p}g + c_{E+A}^{TR} - c_{E+A}^{Tx} > 0 \tag{46}$$

Finally, inactivity is plagued by the additional problem that Ego runs a risk of loss. From a social perspective, this loss is relevant since l by

---

[195] See above 3.3.3(c).

definition is larger than gg. For a social planner, this loss, multiplied by its agreed-upon subjective probability $1 - \underline{p}$, is the implicit cost of in-activity. When they seek a normative benchmark, the parties will thus first compare inactivity and type revelation. The gain from both solu-tions is $2\underline{p}g$. The comparison can therefore be confined to the cost side. Inactivity will be more attractive than type revelation, if its implicit cost is lower. Formally,

$$(1 - \underline{p})(gg - l) - c_{E+A}^{TR} > 0. \tag{47}$$

Depending on which option fares better in this comparison, it is com-pared with the tax scheme, which is sure to generate co-operation. If inactivity is preferable to type revelation, the ensuing calculation is as follows:

$$2g - c_{E+A}^{Tx} > 2\underline{p}g + (1 - \underline{p})(gg - l) \Rightarrow$$
$$2g - 2\underline{p}g(1 - \underline{p})(gg - l) - c_{E+A}^{Tx} > 0. \tag{48}$$

Under this condition, a tax scheme is the parties' best option.

3.4.5   Response by outside actors

As with type revelation, the parties can bring in an outsider in the interest of improving a tax scheme. It is hard to imagine how a tax imposed by an outsider could be qualitatively different from a credible promise to be taxed by the other party. The crucial advantage of volun-tarily submitting to a third party is, however, in the area of credibility. The future subsidy can be handed over to a third party at the outset of the game. This will make it much easier for Alter to believe that he will actually receive it upon co-operation. Likewise, the tax can be given to the third party at the beginning of the game. This will make it easy for Ego to believe that Alter will actually be taxed should he defect.

If the third party is itself rational, it will not provide this service for free. Bringing this person in thus has an out-of-pocket cost. Moreover, the parties are entering into a contractual relationship with an outsider. This outsider might abuse his position. The parties thus run the risk of an additional principal–agent relationship. This can be interpreted as the opportunity cost of bringing the third party in. Both add to the cost of using the third party c_{TP}^{Tx}. Accordingly, the expected benefit of bringing the third party in is $2g - c_{TP}^{Tx}$. The enriched table of options for the parties is shown in Figure 3.29.

Finally, a sovereign ruler can intervene. It can impose two things on the parties: any tax or subsidy it deems fit, and any distribution of the

Social assessment	Inactivity	Type revelation	Subsidy/tax
E	$2\underline{p}g + (1 - \underline{p})(gg - l)$	$2\underline{p}g - c_E^{TR}$	$2g - c_E^{Tx}$
A	$2\underline{p}g + (1 - \underline{p})(gg - l)$	$2\underline{p}g - c_A^{TR}$	$2g - c_A^{Tx}$
E+A	$2\underline{p}g + (1 - \underline{p})(gg - l)$	$2\underline{p}g - c_{E+A}^{TR}$	$2g - c_{E+A}^{Tx}$
TP	$2\underline{p}g + (1 - \underline{p})(gg - l)$	$2\underline{p}g - c_{TP}^{TR}$	$2g - c_{TP}^{Tx}$

Figure 3.29. Options compared: social assessment, Ego, Alter, joint, third-party inactivity, type revelation, subsidy/tax.

Social assessment	Inactivity	Type revelation	Subsidy/tax
E	$2\underline{p}g + (1 - \underline{p})(gg - l)$	$2\underline{p}g - c_E^{TR}$	$2g - c_E^{Tx}$
A	$2\underline{p}g + (1 - \underline{p})(gg - l)$	$2\underline{p}g - c_A^{TR}$	$2g - c_A^{Tx}$
E+A	$2\underline{p}g + (1 - \underline{p})(gg - l)$	$2\underline{p}g - c_{E+A}^{TR}$	$2g - c_{E+A}^{Tx}$
TP	$2\underline{p}g + (1 - \underline{p})(gg - l)$	$2\underline{p}g - c_{TP}^{TR}$	$2g - c_{TP}^{Tx}$
SV	$2\underline{p}g + (1 - \underline{p})(gg - l)$	$2\underline{p}g - c_{SV}^{TR}$	$2g - c_{SV}^{Tx}$

Figure 3.30. Options compared: social assessment, Ego, Alter, joint, third-party, sovereign: inactivity, type revelation, subsidy/tax.

burden. If the sovereign ruler does not shift any cost to outsiders, this again implies both an out-of-pocket cost and an opportunity cost. The ruler will charge the parties a service fee. And the parties run the classic public choice risk that sovereign powers will be abused. These two components add up to cost c_{SV}^{Tx}. The social benefit of sovereign intervention accordingly is $2g - c_{SV}^{Tx}$.

The possibility of sovereign intervention further enriches the list of options which can be seen in Figure 3.30.

3.5   Insurance

Type revelation and a subsidy or tax scheme are not the only options the parties have for bringing co-operation about. The rational choice model brings yet another option to light that ignores type information: Ego can be insured against the risk of being exploited by Alter (3.5.1). Although this may sound surprising, Ego can also insure himself (3.5.2). Alter can insure him (3.5.3). The parties can jointly implement an insurance plan (3.5.4). Or they can bring in an outside actor (3.5.5).

3.5.1 Characterising the solution

In many respects, insurance is similar to a tax or subsidy. The parties deliberately ignore type information. They stick to the pooling equilibrium, and do not try to reach at the separating equilibrium. They treat the predictability risk as exogenous. It is an adaptation strategy, not a mitigation strategy.

Yet insurance differs from tax in the following respects. Insurance has an impact on the incentives of Ego, not Alter. Ego is made whole, should the risk of Alter defecting in the last round materialise. Specifically, the incentives of Ego are changed *ex ante* by a credible promise that he will be made whole *ex post* should the risk materialise.[196]

Under a tax scheme, the tax has to be slightly higher than the potential gain of Alter from defection. It has to be $gg - g + \varepsilon$. There is no similar need to promise a payment of $l + \varepsilon$, should Alter defect. It suffices if Alter is sure to receive compensation should that happen. This difference results from the structure of the game. Gaining $gg - g$ is a positive incentive for Alter. Ego's positive incentive consists of gaining his fair outcome g. The insurance is only needed in order to remove the disincentive inherent in Ego's original calculation. This calculation is contained in Equation 4, which is repeated here for convenience:

$$pg_E - (1 - p)l > 0.$$

This reminder of the original problem of Ego also formally demonstrates why insurance is a worst-case solution. It not only ignores type information. It also does away with any second-guessing about Ego's subjective probabilities. Should Alter defect, Ego is made whole. Formally speaking, the solution ignores the fact that Ego only attaches probability $1 - p$ to Alter being detrimental. This probability can never be larger than 1. If it is 1, Ego holds an extreme belief. He expects the entire population of actors to be detrimental. By implication, a credible promise of $(1 - p)l$ would have the same effect. It would, however, add a new element of uncertainty. Alter could only be certain of co-operation if he had correctly second-guessed the subjective probabilities of Ego. This is why this line of thought is not further pursued here.[197]

By definition, l is larger than gg. Accordingly, the tax, or $gg - g + \varepsilon$, must be smaller than the insurance payment l. If the promised sum is actually paid, insurance is therefore more costly than a tax or a subsidy.

---

[196] This distinguishes insurance from the *ex ante* payment of a risk premium; see below 3.6.
[197] There is a second reason further established below: if the promise to make Ego whole is issued by Alter, l is actually never paid; see below 3.5.3.

As we will see, however, such payment normally does not take place. This difference therefore is of little practical relevance.

A last difference, however, is practically important. A tax and a subsidy only give Ego certainty if Alter actually is rational. This qualification does not hold for an insurance scheme. It makes Ego safe, even if Alter is envious, greedy or silly. Insurance is therefore a more robust solution. If there is a serious risk that Alter will act irrationally, however, the former difference also plays itself out. For in that case, damages must actually be paid. They do not exclusively work by changing incentives.

As with tax and subsidy, there are half-way solutions. One possibility consists of promising a payment smaller than l if Alter defects. This is identical to one of the solutions offered above. It makes sense if Alter thinks he can second-guess p. More interesting is the other half-way solution, probabilistic insurance. Under such a scheme, the original risk is not extinguished, but diminished. The original gamble is replaced by one that is more favourable to the recipient. Although theoretically interesting, this is not likely to be a practical option for the parties. First of all, the very problem in the case at hand stems from the fact that Ego does not know the probability of Alter being detrimental *ex ante*. Alter could thus only guess whether Ego views his offer as favourable. Moreover, and in contrast to the tax case, this half-way solution cannot profit from psychological backing. On the contrary, probabilistic insurance has been one of the test cases for demonstrating that ordinary people do not treat risk rationally. They are not indifferent when choosing between full insurance and probabilistic insurance with the same expected value. Again, a certainty effect is present. That explains why probabilistic insurance is extremely rare in practice.[198]

3.5.2   Unilateral response by Ego

Insurance affects Ego's incentives. He will no longer shy away from co-operation, given the risk of Alter defecting. How is it possible that Ego himself can have recourse to this solution? Mustn't it, by definition, originate with Alter?

Stepping outside of the boundaries of this presentation for a second, it is possible to show plausibly why this is not the case. Ego might find a professional insurer. This company would ask for a risk premium in exchange for the promise of making Ego whole should the defection risk materialise.[199] We must thus again retain a separation between

---

[198] Kahneman and Tversky 2000c: 23–5.   [199] See below 3.5.5.

allocation and distribution. If Ego pays the risk premium, he takes on the cost of establishing the co-operation with Alter. But the technology to do so has an impact on Ego's incentives, not on the incentives of Alter.

The same possibility also exists if Ego does not bring a third party in. He can 'self-insure'. Insurance works by pooling risks. A professional insurer typically pools risks that are sufficiently similar in kind. That allows actuarial mathematics to be applied. The law of large numbers makes this a viable business model. But this is not the only option for pooling. In the end, all one needs is a possibility to cross-subsidise damage in one instance with surplus in others. Accordingly, Ego can decide to generate a risk pool himself. Since there is no need to sell anything on the market, it makes no difference whether he just pools some risks, or whether he pools all the risks he faces in life. Once one has seen this, it is clear that self-insurance turns out to be exactly the same as risk-bearing. It is just another interpretation of Ego's co-operation without a further safeguard. Equation 4 formally states the conditions under which this is a rational decision:

$$pg_E - (1 - p)l > 0.$$

This insight has a number of implications. First of all, from the isolated perspective of Ego, self-insurance is a cheap technology. There is no additional cost involved. Nobody receives an insurance premium. This explains, for instance, why government typically does not buy insurance plans on the open market. Since the state budget covers so many and such divergent risks, it is cheaper to pay an occasional damage out of the general budget. Secondly, risk-bearing can also be interpreted as trusting Alter. Consequently, trust can be interpreted as a decision to self-insure.[200] Thirdly, the distributional difference between subsidy and tax repeats itself for insurance. If a rational actor credibly promises to make Ego whole upon defection, he will not defect. If Ego self-insures, he runs a true risk of being exploited. This risk is the implicit cost of the insurance strategy for him.

Is it rational for Ego to self-insure? He will not if the expected value is negative. Equation 4 shows why this might be the case. Either the difference between g and l is too large or p is too small. Moreover, a rational interaction partner will compare self-insurance with his other options. He will rely on Figure 3.31 for the purpose.

Obviously, insurance and inactivity are identical. The calculations will therefore be confined to the alternatives of type revelation and subsidy.

---

[200] Dunn 1988: 85; Ripperger 1998: 44–6; Engel 1999.

Individual assessment	Inactivity	Type revelation	Subsidy/tax	Insurance
E	$pg_E - (1-p)l$	$pg_E - c_E^{TR}$	$2g - gg - \varepsilon - c_E^{Tx}$	$pg_E - (1-p)l$

Figure 3.31. Options compared: individual assessment, Ego: inactivity, type revelation, subsidy/tax, insurance.

Insurance is preferable to type revelation under the conditions laid down in Equation 49:[201]

$$pg_E - (1-p)l > pg_E - c_E^{TR} \Rightarrow$$
$$c_E^{TR} - (1-p)l > 0. \tag{49}$$

In neither case can Ego be sure that Alter will co-operate. The comparison is thus one of the explicit costs for type revelation, with the implicit cost of being exposed to a loss in the case of self-insurance.

Insurance is preferable over a subsidy under the conditions laid down in Equation 50:[202]

$$pg_E - (1-p)l > 2g - gg - \varepsilon - c_E^{Tx} \Rightarrow$$
$$pg_E + gg + \varepsilon + c_E^{Tx} - 2g - (1-p)l > 0. \tag{50}$$

By opting for self-insurance, Ego thus expects the original rate of co-operation, and he need not pay the subsidy. But he loses co-operation in those cases in which Alter could have been expected to defect. And he runs the risk of a loss in those cases.

3.5.3   Unilateral response by Alter

An insurance plan promise by Alter is straightforward. Since Ego cannot be certain about Alter's type, there is some risk that Ego will not co-operate. This is to the detriment of Alter, irrespective of what type of actor he is. For even a detrimental actor prefers the fair gain g to his outside option zero. If Ego is insured, the disincentive of a potential loss no longer exists. Since Ego is assumed to be rational, he will thus co-operate. For the fair gain g is also more attractive to him than the outside option zero.

For Alter, insurance is a cheap technology for bringing co-operation about. For once he credibly promises to insure Ego, he loses any interest

---

[201] Note that Equation 49 reverses Equation 8.
[202] Note that Equation 50 reverses Equation 39.

in defection. For by definition l is larger than gg. Accordingly, a rational actor will never defect. The only cost he incurs is the cost of making his promise credible. Credibility is, however, a serious concern here. For the reasons laid out in the parallel case of tax, Alter has no unilateral opportunity to make such a promise credible. This technology is thus only at his disposal if an element of the larger context makes him sufficiently vulnerable.[203]

Under the conditions laid down in Equation 51, insurance is a rational strategy for Alter:

$$g_A - c_A^{In} > 0. \tag{51}$$

Alter is certain to obtain his fair gain g. But he must pay the cost for making his promise credible. Note that this assessment is irrespective of the type of actor being dealt with. This is because of the fact that insurance ignores type information.

Of course, Alter will compare this option with his alternatives. He will thus be guided by the calculations summarised in Figure 3.32.

The comparison between insurance and tax is straightforward. Neither damages nor the tax will actually be paid. Accordingly, it is irrelevant that l is by definition larger than $gg - g$. Only the respective cost for making the promise credible matters. If this cost is smaller for tax than for insurance, it is rational to prefer tax. In this comparison, Alter's type is irrelevant, since neither solution exploits type information.

Comparing insurance with type revelation is equally straightforward. Detrimental actors never reveal type. Accordingly, such actors will always prefer insurance. Beneficial actors must again compare transaction costs. This has an interesting implication. Even beneficial actors may prefer insurance. This is the case if the cost for making an insurance promise credible is smaller than the cost for credibly revealing type.

Finally, for a beneficial actor, insurance is preferable to inactivity under the conditions laid down in Equation 52:

Individual assessment	Inactivity	Type revelation	Subsidy/tax	Insurance
A+	rg_A	$g_A - c_A^{TR}$	$g_A - c_A^{Tx}$	$g_A - c_A^{In}$
A−	rgg	-	$g_A - c_A^{Tx}$	$g_A - c_A^{In}$

Figure 3.32. Options compared: individual assessment, Alter: inactivity, type revelation, subsidy/tax, insurance.

---

[203] See above 3.4.3.

$$g_A - c_A^{In} > rg_A \Rightarrow$$
$$g_A - rg_A - c_A^{In} > 0. \tag{52}$$

Accordingly, a beneficial actor will not only take into account the out-of-pocket cost of making the insurance promise credible. He will also deduct the opportunity cost inherent in the expectation that Ego would co-operate anyhow, with the subjective probability r.

The parallel problem for a detrimental actor is laid down in Equation 53:

$$g_A - rgg - c_A^{In} > 0. \tag{53}$$

Accordingly, a detrimental actor is somewhat less likely to offer insurance. For his opportunity cost is higher. With subjective probability r, he expects not only his fair gain g, but also the unfair gain gg. Once insured, it becomes irrational for him to defect.

3.5.4   Joint response by Ego and Alter

As before, an isolated insurance solution by either Ego or Alter is unlikely. It is individually only rational if one party assumes the other will remain inactive. Joining forces has a number of advantages. From the perspective of Ego, the most important advantage is that his risk of running a loss disappears. Once Alter participates in the solution, it becomes irrational for him to defect. That would only reduce the social gain, without being beneficial to him individually. He has more to gain if he imposes most of the cost of insurance on Ego. Put differently, if they join forces, only the distribution problem remains. This has the same effect as a tax or a subsidy scheme. If Ego individually relies on subsidy, he must actually pay the subsidy at the end of the game. If the parties join forces, he need no longer do this.[204]

The second advantage is a larger settlement range. If Alter intervenes individually, he must pay the cost for making the insurance promise credible from his fair gain g. Ego must even pay the implicit cost of a risk of loss from pg. If he does not hold the extreme belief that all actors in the population are beneficial, this is less than g. If they join forces, however, they both will certainly receive their fair gain g. Accordingly, much more expensive technologies for making an insurance promise credible become affordable. Formally,

---

[204] See above 3.4.4.

$$2g - c^{In} > 0. \tag{54}$$

The third advantage of joining forces is equally important. When acting unilaterally, it is difficult for Alter to make his insurance promise credible. This is feasible only if the larger context makes him vulnerable. If they interact, however, the parties can both sink cost and make themselves mutually vulnerable.

With the other regulatory options, there have always been three possibilities for the parties: they could settle for a joint technology, but they could also jointly agree to one of the parties doing the job. In the latter case, the agreement will be confined to sharing the costs. In principle, the same options are available here, too. But in practical terms the unilateral technologies do not make much sense in this context. What the parties want to do is to make Ego safe. They will therefore jointly agree to pay damages to him should Alter defect.

When choosing between regulatory options, the parties should put themselves into the shoes of an outside social planner. For him, the costs and benefits of the four options are as shown in Figure 3.33. Visibly, the only difference between subsidy/tax and insurance is the respective cost of each. Accordingly, for comparisons, the reader can be referred to the section on subsidy/tax.[205]

3.5.5 Response by outside actors

For two reasons, voluntarily bringing a third person in can help the parties. This person can either be the insurer himself, or he can be someone who will help the parties make promises credible.

Under type revelation, one of the reasons for bringing a third party in is to carry out an inspection. This capacity can also be exploited by a

Social assessment	Inactivity	Type revelation	Subsidy/tax	Insurance
E	$2\underline{p}g + (1 - \underline{p})(gg - l)$	$2pg - c_E^{TR}$	$2g - c_E^{Tx}$	$2g - c_E^{In}$
A	$2\underline{p}g + (1 - \underline{p})(gg - l)$	$2pg - c_A^{TR}$	$2g - c_A^{Tx}$	$2g - c_A^{In}$
E+A	$2\underline{p}g + (1 - \underline{p})(gg - l)$	$2pg - c_{E+A}^{TR}$	$2g - c_{E+A}^{Tx}$	$2g - c_{E+A}^{In}$

Figure 3.33. Options compared: social assessment, Ego and Alter joint: inactivity, type revelation, subsidy/tax, insurance.

[205] See above 3.4.4.

third party that offers insurance. But in commercial practice, insurance companies typically do rely on actuarial accounting, rather than inspection. When they do so, the insurer exploits his capacity to pool similar risks. He relies on the law of large numbers. This can work for predictability risks as well, provided individual instances are statistically independent.

Finally the third party can help Ego or Alter to make promises credible. Specifically Alter could make a deposit of l. The insurer could promise to pay this sum to Ego, should Alter defect. After Alter has co-operated, the insurer would pay the deposit back to him.

Whether it is worthwhile to bring the third party in depends on the considerations mentioned earlier. It may not be possible for the parties to solve the problem on their own. Or one of them might not want the available solutions for normative reasons. Or involving the third party might be cheaper. To assess costs and benefits comparatively, the parties should have recourse to Figure 3.34. As with joint action by Ego and Alter, the only difference from a subsidy or a tax scheme is in the potential cost of bringing the third party in. Accordingly, for comparisons, the reader can be referred to the section on subsidy and tax.[206]

While bringing a third party in can help start the insurance scheme going, sovereign intervention does not offer many additional possibilities. As usual, it can make any credibility problem disappear, and it can impose an arbitrary distributional outcome on the parties. Apart from that, the only interesting addendum is compulsory insurance. This can artificially create a pool of risks, and hence make actuarial statistics easier to apply. This presupposes, however, what is empirically questionable: that predictability risks are sufficiently similar.

Social assessment	Inactivity	Type revelation	Subsidy/tax	Insurance
E	$2pg + (1 - \underline{p})(gg - l)$	$2pg - c_E^{TR}$	$2g - c_E^{Tx}$	$2g - c_E^{In}$
A	$2pg + (1 - \underline{p})(gg - l)$	$2pg - c_A^{TR}$	$2g - c_A^{Tx}$	$2g - c_A^{In}$
E+A	$2pg + (1 - \underline{p})(gg - l)$	$2pg - c_{E+A}^{TR}$	$2g - c_{E+A}^{Tx}$	$2g - c_{E+A}^{In}$
TP	$2pg + (1 - \underline{p})(gg - l)$	$2pg - c_{TP}^{TR}$	$2g - c_{TP}^{Tx}$	$2g - c_{TP}^{In}$

Figure 3.34. Options compared: social assessment, Ego, Alter, Ego and Alter, third party: inactivity, type revelation, subsidy/tax, insurance.

[206] See above 3.4.5.

Social assessment	Inactivity	Type revelation	Subsidy/tax	Insurance
E	$2\underline{p}g + (1-\underline{p})(gg-l)$	$2\underline{p}g - c_E^{TR}$	$2g - c_E^{Tx}$	$2g - c_E^{In}$
A	$2\underline{p}g + (1-\underline{p})(gg-l)$	$2\underline{p}g - c_A^{TR}$	$2g - c_A^{Tx}$	$2g - c_A^{In}$
E+A	$2\underline{p}g + (1-\underline{p})(gg-l)$	$2\underline{p}g - c_{E+A}^{TR}$	$2g - c_{E+A}^{Tx}$	$2g - c_{E+A}^{In}$
TP	$2\underline{p}g + (1-\underline{p})(gg-l)$	$2\underline{p}g - c_{TP}^{TR}$	$2g - c_{TP}^{Tx}$	$2g - c_{TP}^{In}$
SV	$2\underline{p}g + (1-\underline{p})(gg-l)$	$2\underline{p}g - c_{SV}^{TR}$	$2g - c_{SV}^{Tx}$	$2g - c_{SV}^{In}$

Figure 3.35. Options compared: social assessment, Ego, Alter, Ego and Alter, third party, sovereign: inactivity, type revelation, subsidy/tax, insurance.

By definition, sovereign intervention is not a choice of the parties. But if government decides to intervene, it should compare this solution with solutions the parties can voluntarily implement. Costs and benefits are certainly not the only considerations when making this decision. But they should have a bearing on it. For this purpose, government should consult Figure 3.35.

Since sovereign intervention differs from third-party intervention only in regard to the cost parameter, there is no need to go through the comparative cost–benefit calculations.

3.6 Risk premium

The game theoretic model unveils a final option. Like an insurance plan, this intervention aims at changing Ego's incentives for co-operation. But while insurance is paid *ex post*, here the payment is up front. This is what happens if Ego receives a risk premium (3.6.1). Surprising as it is, Ego himself can use a functional equivalent (3.6.2). The risk premium idea is straightforward if unilaterally employed by Alter (3.6.3). It is also possible for the parties jointly to agree on a risk premium (3.6.4). Finally they can bring in outsiders for the purpose (3.6.5).

3.6.1 Characterising the solution

If no intervention takes place, Ego faces the by now well-known problem:

$$pg_E - (1-p)l > 0.$$

Since Ego is assumed to be fully rational, he will co-operate whenever this term is positive. In turn, whenever the term is negative, he will prefer to defect at the beginning of the game. As a consequence, Alter runs a certain risk of losing his fair gain g. It is therefore in the interest of Alter to make co-operation more likely. He can do so by paying a side-payment s up front. If he does, Ego's problem changes to

$$pg_E - (1 - p)l + s > 0. \tag{55}$$

By comparing this with Equation 4, one sees that a rational interaction partner will now co-operate more frequently. For, as a result of s, the term is more often positive. How large s must be to insure co-operation depends on the difference between g and l and on p.

The foregoing also makes it possible to calculate precisely the minimum side-payment necessary to bring co-operation about. It can be derived from Equation 55 by transformation. The side-payment is irrelevant if

$$pg_E - (1 - p)l > 0.$$

If

$$pg_E - (1 - p)l < 0,$$

Ego co-operates whenever

$$s > (1 - p)l - pg_E.$$

3.6.2   Unilateral response by Ego

A beneficial actor and Ego have a similar interest in increasing the likelihood of co-operation. Both lose the fair gain g if Ego shies away and defects. It can therefore make sense for Ego to take on some or all of the burden of bringing this co-operation about, as long as this burden is lower than g. But can he also do so by unilaterally employing a risk premium? In the case of insurance, such a surprising unilateral solution has turned out to be feasible.[207] The difference between insurance and a risk premium consists in the time of the payment. Damages are paid *ex post*, whereas a risk premium is paid *ex ante*. In the case of insurance, the difference between inactivity and self-insurance has turned out to be just a matter of interpretation. The payment under inactivity is implicit. It consists of the willingness of Ego to take on a certain risk of loss. Consequently, this exercise in construction can even be pushed one step further. One can interpret Ego's inactivity as a premium paid to himself

---

[207] See above 3.5.2.

Individual assessment	Inactivity	Type revelation	Subsidy/tax	Insurance	Risk premium
E	$pg_E - (1-p)l$	$pg_E - c_E^{TR}$	$2g - gg - \varepsilon - c_E^{Tx}$	$pg_E - (1-p)l$	$pg_E - (1-p)l$

Figure 3.36. Options compared: individual assessment, Ego: all options.

for taking on the risk. The premium then is pg. The present value of the gain is taken as the premium that makes it acceptable for Ego to accept the ensuing risk of loss. His problem then is the same as in Equation 4:

$$pg_E - (1-p)l > 0.$$

If Ego compares all the options he has for acting unilaterally, the table will be as in Figure 3.36. Since, from Ego's perspective, there is no difference between insurance and a risk premium, there is no need to go through the comparative calculations again.

3.6.3   Unilateral response by Alter

If he remains inactive, a beneficial actor expects rg_A. A detrimental actor expects rgg. If they pay a side-payment s up front, their problem changes to

$$\bar{r}g_A - s > 0 \tag{56}$$

for the beneficial actor, and to

$$\bar{r}gg - s > 0 \tag{57}$$

for the detrimental actor. r is defined as in Equation 14, which is repeated here for convenience:

$$r = prob\{\bar{p}g_E - (1-\bar{p})l > 0\}.$$

In this equation, $\bar{p}$ signifies the subjective probability for Ego that Alter will be beneficial, as second-guessed by Alter. If Alter makes a side-payment upfront, Ego's problem changes as in Equation 55. This is what Alter must second-guess. Accordingly $\bar{r}$ denotes Alter's expectation of Ego's willingness to co-operate after he has received the side-payment. Formally,

$$\bar{r} = \bar{p}g_E - (1-\bar{p})l + s > 0. \tag{58}$$

Note an implication: the assumption is that the side-payment will not change the subjective beliefs of Ego about Alter's type. This seems plausible, since a side-payment helps not only a beneficial actor, but also a detrimental one. For it makes co-operation more likely without offering any collateral against exploitation by a detrimental actor. Actually, a detrimental actor has even more to gain from side-payment. For by definition gg is larger than g. One might therefore even defend the idea that Ego will take the side-payment as a weak signal that Alter possesses a detrimental character. In that case $\bar{p}$, and consequently also $\bar{r}$, would have to be somewhat corrected downwards.

If Ego is fully rational, no credibility problem arises. Alter runs no risk that Ego will just cash in the side-payment. Neither must he be afraid that Alter will now defect, nor that Alter will just stick to the original likelihood of co-operation. The first holds as long as s remains smaller than pg. For as long as that is the case, Ego would lose by defection. The second implication is straightforward for a rational player.

Is paying a risk premium Alter's best response? This depends on the comparison of this option with the other technologies that are at his disposal for bringing about co-operation (see Figure 3.37).

A comparison of risk premium and inactivity is straightforward. There is a somewhat higher likelihood of co-operation. It comes at the cost of the side-payment. For a beneficial actor, the remaining comparisons all follow the same scheme. Type revelation, tax and insurance are sure to generate co-operation. But each has its cost. For a beneficial actor, paying a risk premium is thus only attractive if the cost of all other options is significantly higher. For a risk premium only increases the likelihood of co-operation; it is not certain to generate it. For a detrimental actor, the comparison is somewhat more demanding. Both tax and insurance are certain to generate co-operation. But under both regimes, the detrimental actor only receives the fair gain g. However, if he pays the risk premium, he retains the chance of obtaining his unfair gain gg. This finding also increases the signal value of offering a risk premium. Although Ego cannot be certain, there is certainly a likelihood that such an actor will indeed turn out to be detrimental.

Individual assessment	Inactivity	Type revelation	Subsidy/tax	Insurance	Risk premium
A⁺	rg_A	$g_A - c_A^{TR}$	$g_A - c_A^{Tx}$	$g_A - c_A^{In}$	$\bar{r}g_A - s$
A⁻	rgg	-	$g_A - c_A^{Tx}$	$g_A - c_A^{In}$	$\bar{r}gg - s$

Figure 3.37. Options compared: individual assessment, Alter: all options.

3.6.4   Joint response by Ego and Alter

The prime advantage of a risk premium is that Alter can use this technology without facing a credibility problem. He pays up front. Accordingly, Ego runs no risk of losing the premium. And if Ego is rational, the side-payment makes co-operation more likely. There is thus no need for Alter to control Ego's move. There are, however, two qualifications. If the side-payment is larger than Ego's expected gains from trade, he has an incentive to keep the side-payment and defect. Formally, s must be smaller than pg. Moreover, Ego can interpret the side-payment as a weak signal that Alter is detrimental. If so, he corrects his original belief about actor distribution and becomes more pessimistic. If Alter wants to remove these two elements of uncertainty, he can conclude a contract with Ego. In that contract, Alter promises a side-payment, and Ego promises co-operation. With this type of agreement, a joint technology can be more powerful than unilateral action by Alter. Of course, joint action only makes sense for the parties if their reciprocal promises are credible. Since Alter still pays up front, for his part, he faces no credibility problem. The parties must therefore see to it that Ego is sufficiently vulnerable, such that his promise to co-operate becomes credible. In the absence of outside intervention and of elements from the context to exploit, this must be done via sinking cost.

The side-payment changes Ego's problem. But from the perspective of a fictitious social planner, the side-payment is irrelevant for welfare. Its effect is purely distributional. Some of the joint gains from trade are shifted to Ego.

The implicit risk premium paid by Ego himself does not change the original problem. Accordingly the social evaluation can directly be derived from the evaluation made when the parties remain inactive. The social value remains the one shown in Equation 25. Assessing the social value of an actual side-payment is more demanding. A unilateral payment by Alter makes it more likely that Ego will co-operate. If Ego and Alter conclude a contract, co-operation even becomes certain. But Ego's co-operation is not a social value as such. It is a good thing if Alter is beneficial. It is not only individually, but also socially bad, if Alter is detrimental. For in that case the outcome is $gg - l$, which by definition is negative. Accordingly, increasing the likelihood of co-operation is only socially beneficial if Ego has been too pessimistic. Pessimism must, of course, be determined *ex ante*. It is thus not important whether Ego actually gets it right. The beliefs held by an unbiased observer serve as the relevant benchmark. This is exactly what $\underline{p}$ means. Formally, pessimism can thus be characterised as $p < \underline{p}$.

By implication, a risk premium makes the little economy of the two players worse off if Ego was too optimistic anyhow. Formally, this is a situation where $p > \underline{p}$. But social welfare also decreases if $p = \underline{p}$. In this case, Ego makes the normatively correct assessment of actor distribution in the population. Since the side-payment makes him co-operate more often, the likelihood of a welfare loss increases beyond the *ex ante* adequate risk.

Since the social value of a risk premium depends on the prior beliefs of Ego, no formal calculable description can be given that could be compared with the other social options.

3.6.5   Response by outside actors

As with other technologies, bringing a third party in can help the players to make commitment credible. It can thus be certain to help generate Ego's co-operation. The same effect could also result from sovereign fiat. Whether any of this is socially beneficial, however, again depends on the relationship between p and $\underline{p}$. Accordingly, again no abstract assessment of the expected value can be given. Consequently, no comparisons can be calculated.

3.7   Summary

This part of the book has applied the most powerful conceptual tool from the social sciences to the predictability problem: the rational choice model. Predictability is a cognitive problem. The rational choice model exclusively addresses motivation. Information asymmetries are an intellectual trick to translate a cognitive problem into a motivational one. Here, the private information concerns an actor's behavioural dispositions. Two further simplifications help to make the predictability problem tractable in rational choice terms. It is assumed that there are only two types of actors: detrimental and beneficial ones. And it is assumed that actor types are given by nature, not strategically chosen by the actors themselves.

This model makes the strategic character of the predictability problem visible. If Alter is unpredictable (since he can be of either type), this obviously is a problem for Ego. But if both actors are rational, Alter's unpredictability is a problem for Alter as well. For he anticipates that Ego anticipates the unpredictability. Mutually beneficial trade does not take place, or its size is smaller than both parties would ideally want.

In principle, therefore, it is in the interest of both parties to overcome the predictability problem. Each of them has unilateral technologies for

Individual assessment	Inactivity	Type revelation	Subsidy/tax	Insurance	Risk premium
E	$pg_E - (1-p)l$	$pg_E - c_E^{TR}$	$2g_E - gg - \varepsilon - c_E^{Tx}$	$pg_E - (1-p)$	$pg_E - (1-p)l$
A⁺	rg_A	$g_A - c_A^{TR}$	$g_A - c_A^{Tx}$	$g_A - c_A^{In}$	$\bar{r}g_A - s$
A⁻	rgg	-	$g_A - c_A^{Tx}$	$g_A - c_A^{In}$	$\bar{r}gg - s$

Social assessment	Inactivity	Type revelation	Subsidy/tax	Insurance	Risk premium
E	$2pg + (1-\underline{p})(gg-l)$	$2pg - c_E^{TR}$	$2g - c_E^{Tx}$	$2g - c_E^{In}$	$2\underline{p}g + (1-\underline{p})(gg-l)$
A	$2pg + (1-\underline{p})(gg-l)$	$2pg - c_A^{TR}$	$2g - c_A^{Tx}$	$2g - c_A^{In}$	indeterminate
E+A	$2pg + (1-\underline{p})(gg-l)$	$2pg - c_{E+A}^{TR}$	$2g - c_{E+A}^{Tx}$	$2g - c_{E+A}^{In}$	indeterminate
TP	$2pg + (1-\underline{p})(gg-l)$	$2pg - c_{TP}^{TR}$	$2g - c_{TP}^{Tx}$	$2g - c_{TP}^{In}$	indeterminate
SV	$2pg + (1-\underline{p})(gg-l)$	$2pg - c_{SV}^{TR}$	$2g - c_{SV}^{Tx}$	$2g - c_{SV}^{In}$	indeterminate

Figure 3.38. All actors, all options compared.

this. But each of them also is best off if the other takes care of the predictability problem. The first-level dilemma inherent in the predictability problem has therefore a second-level complement. Rational parties are divided over who should bear the cost of bringing fully beneficial co-operation about.

Within the framework of the rational choice model, a 'causal therapy' invites itself: Alter reveals his type in a credible way. If the parties design it cleverly enough, they can indeed set up a mechanism for the purpose. In the alternative, they can also bring a third party in for the purpose, or government can impose itself on them. But there are three more solutions. All of them are more indirect in character. They leave the predictability problem as is, but nonetheless get co-operation going. Here, the translation of the cognitive into a motivational problem bears fruit. The first option is changing relative prices, be it by a subsidy or a tax. The second is insuring Ego against the predictability risk. In this case, Ego is made whole *ex post*, should the predictability problem indeed materialise. The third option is Alter paying *ex ante* a risk premium to Ego if the latter is willing to engage in trade. All these indirect options are costly. But so is making type revelation credible. Rational parties will thus compare the relative cost of all solutions, and choose the one with the best cost–benefit ratio.

In formal language, the parties' choice problem is summed up in Figure 3.38.

4   Behaviourally informed responses

4.1   Introduction

There is no way to escape the trade-off between parsimony and fit.[1] Parsimonious models are sharp lenses. They make it possible to see details that would remain concealed to the unaided eye. But their sharpness comes at a cost – namely a narrow field of vision. Institutional design is about taking action. It profits from the details uncovered by rational choice modelling. But before intervening, the institutional designer must have a second look at his object from a greater distance. This is the external limitation of (rational choice) models, resulting from their limited fit to reality.

Internal limitations are added to this. Some of them are inherent in all rational choice models. The most important is the decisive role of a uniform normative currency, like price. The rational choice model is made for marginal analysis. It is most powerful when describing how the alteration of one parameter plays itself out in other parameters. This capacity of the model was exploited in chapter 3 when the expected utilities of the several options available to the parties were compared. Such calculations become difficult, if not impossible, if there is not one normative currency with which to compare the several parameters. A case in point is the following: the model is hard to apply if Ego cares for Alter's co-operation for reasons other than the gains from trade. He might, for instance, have a strong dislike for being the sucker, since he sees that as a violation of his self-esteem.[2] The problem can be kept within the standard rational choice model if Ego has a shadow price for violations of self-esteem. In that case he attaches a higher negative value to a loss. Within the formal language of the model, l is larger than the money lost if Alter defects in the last round. For the rational choice model, however, things become much harder if Ego is subjectively unwilling to trade a risk of being a sucker against some likelihood of

[1] Harless and Camerer 1994: 1285.
[2] On self-esteem see above 3.2.7.

192

obtaining the fair gain g. It still is possible to write a utility function with different, non-tradable arguments. But the rational choice model loses much of its elegance and power as a result.[3]

The third limitation is subjective. It results from the limited ability of Ego to handle the intricacies of the rational choice model. Chapter 3, based on formal analysis, makes it obvious that there is something to this problem. For chapter 4, however, such subjective limitations are still assumed away. They are taken up in chapter 5. Ultimately, the remaining assumption of full rationality on the part of Ego is not satisfactory. But dropping the rationality assumptions one by one makes it possible to address the predictability problem in a much more controlled way. Specifically, a comparison of chapters 3 and 4 shows that there are many more institutional responses to the psychological predictability problem than just type revelation.

A fourth limitation is to be distinguished from this. Even if Ego is assumed to possess unlimited cognitive abilities, he has to take into account that reality is much more complex than assumed in the rational choice part of this book. Most sources of unpredictability will generate many more than just two types of actors. In Alter, a whole universe of sources for unpredictability can play itself out. If Ego is concerned about predictability, he must address all these potential or real sources of unpredictability at once. To generate predictability in one given situation, he may consider more than one act of institutional intervention. But even if he does, he must take into account that several sources of unpredictability may be entwined. Likewise, his intervention may have unpredicted results if it has to cater for more than one behavioural disposition at a time. It is possible that there are situations in which there are nonetheless acts of intervention that can precisely target one deviation from the rational choice model. But in practice, even a fully rational agent would often prefer to employ entire institutional arrangements, rather than customised intervention. He then opts for a much more sweeping approach. This becomes even more attractive if the transaction cost of diagnosis and therapy is properly taken into account.

In chapter 3, Alter has been treated as a rational *Homo oeconomicus*. This statement can be seen to hold for a detrimental actor. But at closer sight it can also be seen to hold for a beneficial actor. This may sound surprising, since the beneficial actor has been defined in reference to a deviation from the standard assumptions for *Homo oeconomicus*. But

---

[3] Once a third party is introduced, the rational choice approach can even result in outright circularity; classic texts are Condorcet 1785; Arrow 1963; for a recent voice see List and Goodin 2001.

this deviation has been modelled as exogenous. Technically, it has been Nature, not Alter himself, which has chosen to make him beneficial. Given this external fiat, a beneficial actor has behaved rationally. A beneficial actor has thus been modelled as a behaviourally restrained rational actor.

In this chapter, the assumption that Alter is rational is dropped. This brings two things to light: an additional problem for co-operation (4.2), but also additional possibilities for bringing co-operation about (4.3). In the rational choice part of this work, addressing the behavioural uncertainty required type revelation. This turned out not to be the parties' only option. They could use a subsidy/tax scheme, insurance or a risk premium instead. The parties thus had to choose between two strategies: i.e. between reducing the behavioural uncertainty, or deliberately ignoring it. In a behaviourally informed perspective, a similar option exists. The parties can forgo the opportunity to make Alter's behaviour more predictable and change the character of the original task instead (4.4).

4.2   The limited ability of actors to comply

4.2.1   The problem

Rational choice is about incentives. Psychologically speaking, it is a pure theory of motivation. Actors are implicitly assumed to possess an unlimited ability to comply. If they commit to an action, the model is concerned about the credibility of the promise; Alter's ability to comply is taken for granted. Yet one with a behaviourally informed perspective must admit that this ability is often lacking. To this extent, the rational choice recommendations to the parties can be questioned. Even if, after intervention, any other reaction is irrational for Alter, Ego can still not be sure that Alter will follow this course of action. Generating predictability by changing incentives is not always psychologically feasible. Consequently, any commitment to making behaviour more predictable generates a second-order predictability problem. Ego must assess Alter's ability to comply with his own promise. Or, in the language of institutional economics: because of his limited ability to comply, Alter's property right in making his own behaviour more predictable is attenuated.[4]

Predictability has been found to differ across individuals in the first place.[5] The same must hold for the second-order predictability problem,

---

[4] On the concept of property rights, see again Eggertsson 1990.
[5] See above 2.5.4.

i.e. the ability to comply. When deciding upon acts of intervention aimed at bringing co-operation about, Ego must therefore assess the ability of his specific partner to comply.

For Ego, the limited ability of Alter to comply generates a second-order predictability problem. From this classification it follows that the psychological reasons limiting the ability to comply are basically the same ones that generate the first-order predictability problem. When it comes to complying, Alter can be driven by mental tools other than conscious and deliberate decision-making.[6] There are two situations in which this is likely. In the first case, compliance is expected some time in the future or in a new, richer context. If this is the case, it is likely that the behaviour of Alter at the moment of expected compliance will be guided by simple heuristics or by routines. Compliance would then presuppose that he override these behavioural dispositions and switch to conscious decision-making. Depending on the character of the situation, this can be hard to do or at least unlikely.

In the second case, compliance presupposes overriding a mental tool that is not fully conscious, since it is seen to be socially detrimental.[7] A classic example is automatic behaviour.[8] But intervening routines can also be hard to override. This would presuppose a process of unlearning and new learning. More generally, a second-order predictability problem is likely when the behavioural expectations change more quickly than the ability of Alter to adapt. This can also be a result of the abstract character of the behavioural expectation if the original behaviour was controlled by contextual behavioural dispositions. A last element is particularly likely when the partners have recourse to recommendations from rational choice. For many of them invite the parties to take a certain risk. An illustration is the direct mechanism that would free the parties from third-party intervention for type revelation.[9] If both parties behave like rational actors, Alter will not run a risk by making a side-payment up front. Ego knows that Alter can defect in the last round and deprive him of his fair gain. But if Alter does not take the rationality of Ego for granted, he himself faces a behavioural risk. In chapter 2 it has been demonstrated that behaviour under perceived risk tends to be particularly unpredictable.[10] Accordingly, Ego can be less certain than the rational choice model assumes about the success of the direct mechanism.

---

[6] On the plurality of mental tools, see above 2.2.2.
[7] Cf. Strack and Deutsch 2002: 21: direct perception–behaviour links are hard to control through reflective intervention.
[8] Bargh et al. 1996: 241.   [9] See above 3.3.3(c).   [10] See above 2.2.10.

There are also a series of cognitive reasons for low predictability at the implementation stage. Some of the implications of rational choice are mind-boggling. For the uninitiated reader it may even have been difficult to follow them, let alone to generate them without outside help. Commitment is therefore likely to be plagued by a competence/difficulty gap.[11] Even if Alter is in principle able to deliver on his promises, the moment of expected commitment may lapse from his attention.[12] Even if he acts with the best of intentions, he may incorrectly perceive his commitment or the situation in which it is expected.[13] Often, correct implementation presupposes that Alter retrieves information from memory. This can be the recollection of the promise itself, or of any contextual factor needed to get the response right. In these cases, the characteristic limitations of human memory can play a role. It is possible that associative processes will intervene.[14] Memory is typically reconstructive, not photographic.[15] Proper commitment will often conflict with self-perception. Most people overestimate their own abilities[16] and underestimate the power of consciously uncontrolled drives.[17] Consequently a person's subjective predictability tends to be significantly larger than his objective predictability.[18]

Finally, there are many motivational reasons for the second-order predictability problem. Even if Alter commits to plans with the best of intentions, when it comes to fulfilling them, he may be driven by temptation, addiction, fear or enmity and the like.[19] Self-control is conspicuously shaky.[20]

4.2.2   Solutions

The limited ability of actors to comply generates a second-order predictability problem. In principle it could thus be treated the same way as the first-order predictability problem. The whole rational choice analysis laid down in chapter 3 could be applied to it. But this analysis has been based on the assumption that Alter, Nature's initial move apart, is

---

[11] This is the basic conceptual tool used by Heiner 1983: 562 and *passim*.
[12] More on attention above 2.2.3(a).
[13] More on perception above 2.2.3(b).
[14] More from Strack and Deutsch 2002: 24.
[15] More from Strack and Deutsch 2002: 11.
[16] Brocas and Carillo 2002.
[17] Korobkin and Ulen 2000: 1115.
[18] Mischel and Peake 1982: 748.
[19] See above 2.2.8
[20] From the rich literature see, for example, Thaler and Shefrin 1981; Schelling 1984; Baumeister 1998; Smith 2003.

rational. In theory, one might, of course, make a similar assumption here. The second-order predictability problem itself would be exogenous. But Alter would be fully aware of it, and he would react to it in a fully rational way. Yet this is obviously a pretty hard assumption.

If one does not make it, one must assess which of the solutions offered in the rational choice part of this book will also work if Alter is not fully able to predict his behaviour at the moment of expected commitment. This renders useless all technologies for type revelation that assume Alter has the ability to predict his future behaviour correctly. Practically speaking, Ego can still inspect Alter or rely on outsiders for the purpose. If he does so, he can use the knowledge uncovered that way to update his prior beliefs about Alter's type.[21] A subsidy or a tax relies on the assumption that Alter will behave fully rationally.[22] This technology is thus not available. This is different with insurance. This technology is robust for any behaviour that Alter exhibits.[23] A risk premium makes no assumptions about Alter's behaviour whatsoever. It thus can also be used here.[24] And, of course, Ego can co-operate without safeguards, meaning that he bears the behavioural risks.

4.3   Behaviourally informed responses

4.3.1   Introduction

From the last section it follows that there are rational responses, even if one takes Alter's limited ability to comply into account. But are the parties well advised if they have recourse to these solutions? Are they not better off if they strive for behaviourally informed responses?

Can the parties thus do better by exploiting psychological knowledge? Can institutional intervention help them do so? Can the institutional designer himself exploit the generic knowledge about behaviour? Do existing institutions reflect such knowledge? Are they thus carriers of earlier experience in society with the predictability problem and its solution? Can rational choice responses and behaviourally informed responses go hand in hand? Can a behaviourally informed step thus increase the power of rational choice interventions? To what extent are rational choice interventions and behaviourally informed interventions substitutes? If they are substitutes, what is the comparative cost and benefit of relying on behaviourally informed solutions?[25]

---

[21] See above 3.3.1(b).   [22] See above 3.4.1(b).   [23] See above 3.5.1.
[24] See above 3.6.1.
[25] Cf. Conlisk 1996: 671: relying on heuristics can be a way of economising deliberation cost.

These are the questions to be answered in this section. Given the enormous richness of human mental dispositions, none of these questions can be exhausted here.[26] But this book aims to go beyond the existing literature on debiasing.[27] It agrees that, in some contexts, changing behaviour so that it deviates less from the norms of rational choice can be beneficial. It also agrees that preventing actors from using simple heuristics can be a good thing in some contexts. But rationality is not always the right norm. Specifically, this is a book about predictability, not about rationality. Making behaviour more rational can be a way of making it more predictable. But it is not the only way of doing so, and often it is not the best policy. Moreover, the debiasing approach is narrow in that it exclusively targets systematic deviations from the rational choice norms. The behaviourally informed approach advocated here is open for any behavioural disposition. It considers intervention that aims at changing behavioural dispositions, as well as intervention that aims at changing the context so that it matches unaltered behavioural dispositions. It wants to explore the extent to which the parties themselves or outsiders can match these dispositions in their interest in making behaviour more predictable. A further implication concerns the direction of intervention. Predictability does not necessarily presuppose a change in behavioural dispositions. It can be sufficient to reduce the variability of behaviour.

In principle, any behavioural disposition could be matched by institutional intervention. The following looks at three options in somewhat greater detail: exploiting the plurality of mental tools (4.3.2), using the cognitive (4.3.3) and the motivational route (4.3.4). Not everything that is technically feasible is desirable. Before taking action, the institutional designer should take countervailing psychological mechanisms into account (4.3.5), and he should check for opposing normative values (4.3.6). Once the goal is determined, the institutional designer can choose from among a rich array of mechanisms for intervention (4.3.7), and he can choose among psychological paths for getting there (4.3.8). The goal and the mechanism chosen determines who is able to take on the task of institutional design. As with rational choice interventions, there are in

---

[26] Consequently, the list of institutions could even be much richer. Two examples that are not further pursued are the following. Individuals themselves, or outsiders, can impose simple rules on them, like Nancy Reagan's 'just say no' campaign when it comes to drugs. Or government can increase the predictability of economic action by offering no more than non-binding guidelines. This is what, in the French discussion, has been called 'indicative planning'; more from Meade 1970.

[27] An overview of this literature is provided by Conlisk 1996: 671; Klein 2001: 114–15; from the legal literature see, for example, Jolls et al. 1998.

principle five options: Ego, Alter, both jointly, a third party brought in by the co-operating partners and a sovereign (4.3.9). A last step is operationalisation, addressing additional requirements like the speed of intervention or its robustness (4.3.10). Based on all this, behaviourally informed institutions can be sketched out. They can be formal or informal (4.3.11). This section concludes by depicting one important practical avenue for institutional intervention in somewhat greater detail: the impact on the choice of mental tools (4.3.12).

4.3.2   *Exploiting the plurality of mental tools*

(a) *Introduction*   Humans possess a rich array of mental tools. They can be roughly grouped in three classes: deliberate decision-making, routines, and rigorously simple and contextualised heuristics.[28] Institutions can have an impact on the choice among them.[29] They can emphasise and de-emphasise the use of any of them. A de-emphasis can be of different degrees. The most radical form of intervention is outright erasure. A behavioural disposition is then eradicated from an actor's behavioural repertoire. An illustration is shock therapy with phobics. By exposure to the situation that triggers the phobic reaction, the therapist hopes to remove this reaction from the patient's mind. More generally, erasure implies unlearning. Blocking is less radical. The disposition remains part of the actor's repertoire. But, metaphorically speaking, it is locked behind a door. The actor must use the right key to unlock it. One example would be an irascible child who is taught to control his temper better. He does not thereby lose his ability for choleric reactions. But outbreaks become rare in ordinary contexts.[30] An even lesser degree of de-emphasis occurs with masking. The behavioural disposition remains, and it is as accessible as before. But in the concrete case, the impulse to rely on it is overridden by a competing, stronger impulse. An illustration of this is public commitment. It has been demonstrated to reduce the attitude/behaviour gap significantly. The effect is explained by impression management. Since Alter knows that his reputation is at risk, he more often overrides competing drives and sticks to his promise.[31]

---

[28] For an overview see above 2.2.2.

[29] Payne et al. 1997: 182 allude to the possibility.

[30] An example at the pico level is provided by Hebb 1949: 145–9: at the outset, in humans the density of associations with one specific sensory input is low. But 'in assemblies of cells that are frequently active at the same time, fractionation eliminates from each the transmission units whose action is interfered with or controlled by others' (148).

[31] Stults and Messe 1985.

Masking competing behavioural dispositions can also be interpreted as a way of emphasising one disposition that now becomes dominant. Consequently, a behavioural disposition is also emphasised if a pre-existing mask is removed. The following is an example. As a part of his upbringing a person has learned to be polite to the elderly. Later in life, he follows this routine without further ado. If he takes on a job as a travelling salesman, his peers will probably quickly teach him to see the elderly as easy prey and to act accordingly. This is a way of removing the old behavioural routine, and replacing it with rational utility maximising. Like de-emphasising, emphasising can also be more profound. The functional equivalent of blocking an unwanted disposition consists of freezing a desired behavioural trait. A member of a fire brigade learns to do this: he learns a number of routines that help the brigade to be as effective and as responsible as possible in an emergency, even if it requires putting otherwise worthy impulses in check. Finally, there is a functional equivalent to erasure. Institutional intervention can aim at enriching the behavioural repertoire of the addressee. In that case, the addressee acquires behavioural dispositions that did not exist before. The separation of waste fractions in households provides a graphic illustration. By a fairly complex institutional arrangement, most Germans have now internalised this routine.[32]

Let us have a closer look at the ensuing options: i.e. rationalisation (b), routinisation (c) and automation (d).

(b) Rationalisation   The term rationalisation should not be misunderstood. As explained earlier, when humans decide 'rationally', they typically do not follow the norms of rational choice theory. Typical ways of choosing include reason-based choice and narrative reasoning.[33] What is meant by rationalisation is a shift to deliberate and conscious decision-making.[34] It is generally expected that humans will largely be able to replace heuristics and routines by deliberate and conscious decision-making. One can even see the evolutionary advantage of deliberate decision-making in this very ability.[35]

Rationalisation cannot itself be an act of rational decision-making. The goal of this form of intervention is not to change rational decision-making

---

[32] The story is told from a behavioural perspective by Lüdemann 2004.

[33] See above 2.2.9.

[34] See also Goldstein and Weber 1997; 596: 'the relatively slow, laborious following of rules that are stored in explicit declarative form is probably a large part of analytic decision making'.

[35] The idea goes as far back as Bartlett 1932: 206, 208: consciousness as a way to override schemata. More from Stanovich and West 2000: 662–3.

once it takes place, but to bring it about in the first place. But choosing among mental tools can itself be seen as a decision. This explains why the basic building blocks of a deliberate decision are also present in this second-order decision about mental tools. The decision-maker's attention must be directed to the fact that there is a second-order choice to be made. Once the individual is made aware of this, the outcome of this second-order decision depends on how the individual perceives the situation. Deliberate decisions are much more laborious than the use of routines or even simple heuristics. When the individual considers using the deliberate mode, he is thus likely to be influenced by motivational concerns. Let us take them up in turn.

In some contexts, heuristics and routines even fare better than deliberate decision-making.[36] But in many contexts, the performance of deliberation is not worse from the outset. It only implies much more mental effort. This economising effect of routines and heuristics would be thwarted if the individual permanently took second-order decisions about the use of mental tools. Accordingly, the individual typically does not even consider deliberate decision-making. This is different only if a task is brought to the forefront of the individual's attention.[37] If the individual is expected to decide in a non-deliberate way, institutions must thus work as de-routinisers.[38] They must generate a surprise,[39] inducing the individual to make a deliberate meta-choice in the selection of his mental tools.

One example would consist in placing the individual into an unusual context. For instance, under German law, land can only be traded before a notary public. Among the reasons used to justify this rule is that it leads the parties to think twice before the deal becomes binding.[40]

The meta-choice among mental tools is a true choice task. If the institutional designer wants to bring rationalisation about, generating attention is only a necessary condition, not a sufficient one. The individual might have a quick look at the problem, and decide to stick to his

---

[36] More above 2.2.2.

[37] In a stimulating way, this meta-choice among mental tools follows the same logic as the political process: an issue must make it to the agenda; the decision problem must be defined in a way that calls for deliberate decision-making; this mental tool is actually chosen; it performs (called implementation in the political science literature); there is feedback, teaching the individual how to make similar choices in the future (called assessing outcomes in political science). A standard source for the policy cycle model is May and Wildavsky 1978.

[38] The English language does not seem to lend itself to a similar term for taking an individual out of decision-making by heuristics. A neologism would be 'de-automatiser'.

[39] For a different purpose, a sub-field of sociology, cultural theory, has developed an elaborate theory of surprises; Thompson et al. 1990: 69–82.

[40] See (from a comparative law perspective) Kötz 1996: 121–2.

earlier routine or heuristic. It is therefore important that the individual see the task as one that he ought to solve deliberately. At this point, the individual must thus assess the expected performance of the available mental tools. It may well seem reasonable not to override a heuristic or a routine. Actually, demonstrating the power of heuristics is the programme of a whole school in psychology.[41] If the institutional designer nonetheless wants deliberate decision-making, he must frame the decision problem such that the individual is inclined to see rationalisation as an advantage. A frequent practical strategy consists of obliging the individual to give reasons for his decisions.[42] This strategy is not watertight. The individual may construct reasons *ex post* for a decision taken non-deliberately. The psychological research on memory demonstrates how good individuals are at that.[43] But the more elaborate the justification requirement, the less likely it is that the context of decision-making and the context of justification will entirely fall apart.[44]

For scientists, it is to be hoped that thinking is a pleasure. But even scientists do not have unlimited time for thinking. If they spend too much of it on trivial tasks, too little capacity is left over for what they really care about. Economically speaking, deliberate decision-making has a fairly high opportunity cost. And others might see most thinking as annoying or painful in the first place. Accordingly, the individual is well advised to choose carefully the tasks he reserves for deliberation. Institutional designers can exploit this feature and add motivations for selecting conscious decision-making.

The classic response consists of increasing the stakes. Subjects are then much more likely to decide consciously.[45] In many contexts, this also improves performance.[46] This even holds for cognitive tasks, like predicting the outcome of an election.[47] But in other contexts, the effect is more dubious.[48] This might be a result of the fact that higher stakes make people focus all their efforts on what they know they are good at. They tend to neglect the broader search for alternatives that might perform even better.[49] In this context, however, this could be welcome

---

[41] For a programmatic treatment, see Gigerenzer et al. 1999.
[42] Payne et al. 1997: 182; Gigerenzer et al. 1999: 165; Strack and Deutsch 2002: 26–7.
[43] On the constructive character of memory see Anderson 2000b: 285–9; see also Turner 2001 on the power of blending.
[44] The interaction between justification and decision-making is a highly contested field of research; see, for example, Tetlock 1985, 1999; Tetlock et al. 1989; Lerner and Tetlock 1999.
[45] Hogarth et al. 1997: 247.
[46] Smith and Walker 1993; Frey and Eichenberger 1994.
[47] Forsythe et al. 1991.
[48] Rostain 2000: 985–6.   [49] Hogarth et al. 1997: 247.

news. For the normative goal here is not that the individual adapt to his environment, but that behaviour be predictable. Precisely because high stakes make people focus on what they see as the core issue, rationalisation might improve predictability.

Money is not the only motivator.[50] Alternative motivators can be exploited by institutional design as well. A particularly promising approach consists of targeting self-esteem. It might explain the following finding: in an experiment with low stakes, but a clear competitive frame, rationalisation occurred.[51] The result is interesting for institutional designers, since increasing self-esteem is often cheaper and easier to bring about than higher money incentives.

(c) Routinisation Rationalisation helps Ego, since it makes it more likely that Alter will pursue his best interest. But the opposite strategy is at least as powerful in generating predictability. By institutional intervention, behaviour is patterned.[52] This can reduce behavioural variance in several respects. A person can have an observable behavioural repertoire. In that case, variance across situations is reduced. In a given situation, most people follow one and the same routine or a narrow set of behavioural programmes. When they do, variance across persons is reduced. A practically important sub-class of the latter is interaction with one specific partner. The predictability problem for this person is heavily reduced if most actors treat him similarly.

Patterning behaviour works by generating behavioural clusters. The plasticity of human behavioural dispositions is reduced if entire scripts unroll. There are several ways to explain how this might come about. One idea is that it depends on associative links.[53] An old concept is the generation of a schema.[54] The most appropriate explanation, however, seems to be what in psychological jargon is called expertisation.[55] With

---

[50] On other motivators see above 2.2.7.

[51] Apesteguia et al. 2003.

[52] The idea has come up in many contexts. Psychological sources date back to Newcomb 1929 and include Mischel and Peake 1982: 749; Mischel and Shoda 1995: 252; Anderson 2000b: 319–20. Economic sources include Heiner 1983 on rule-based behaviour, and Vanberg 2002 on programme based behaviour. From sociology, see e.g. Thompson et al. 1990: 57: individuals neither make up their preferences from scratch, nor are they fully determined by society. They must choose between existing preference patterns. From political science, see Jackman and Sniderman 2002: political parties work by narrowing down voters' choice spaces to manageable packets.

[53] Strack and Deutsch 2002: 7.

[54] Bartlett 1932: 206.

[55] Anderson 2000b: chapter 9; for a formal model, see Anderson et al. 2004: 1038; see also Strack and Deutsch 2002: 21.

growing exposure to and experience in a context, the individual learns. He no longer repeats all the deliberative steps necessary when first acting within that context. Rather, he aggregates them to a more or less fixed behavioural programme. The individual no longer sees the single steps as his problem. He is able to react to his environment at a much higher level of aggregation. If these aggregates retain some plasticity, a routine emerges. This outcome can be brought about by institutional intervention such as imposed training or merely repeated exposure to a standardised context.

(d) *Automation*   Routines retain some plasticity. They can be seen as standardised problem-solvers, combined with a quick check for applicability in the context at hand. If the context looks a little different, another, equally ready-made solution might be tried. The degree of standardisation in heuristics is even higher. They are entirely cue-based. They guide behaviour in a quasi-automatic way.[56] How individuals acquire heuristics is still very much an open question. But given the general plasticity of human behavioural dispositions, it does not seem very likely that many of them are acquired by birth. If not, acquisition must be the result of learning.[57] In principle, any learning mechanism could be used. Since the heuristic links a response to a cue, classic conditioning might work. It is a non-conscious mechanism by which the individual establishes a stable association between a conditioned stimulus and an unconditioned response.[58] If the individual uses an appropriate heuristic, he receives a positive response from the environment. If he uses an inappropriate one, the response is negative. This explains why heuristics can also be learned via instrumental conditioning. This is important, since this is also a mechanism for unconscious learning.[59] But heuristics might also be acquired the same way as routines, i.e. by progressive expertisation.[60] Finally, once the heuristic is made explicit, it can be described with the help of a formalised decision tree.[61] The individual can learn it cognitively[62] or by imitating other group members.[63]

---

[56] See above 2.2.2.
[57] Cf. Gigerenzer et al. 1999: 183 distinguishing a learning and an application phase.
[58] More on classic conditioning from Anderson 2000b: chapter 2.
[59] More from Anderson 2000b: chapters 3–4.
[60] See above 4.3.2(c).
[61] For an example see Gigerenzer et al. 1999: 3–5.
[62] More on cognitive learning from Krause 1991, 1992; Collins and Bradizza 2001.
[63] More on social learning from Bandura 1977.

4.3.3   Cognitive route

The simpler the mental tool, the less elaborate cognition. If a heuristic leads to one-reason decision-making, the individual is exclusively concerned about the presence of the cue. But even in that case, the individual must become aware of the cue. The more elaborate the mental tool, the more complex cognition becomes. In its full form, the stages of attention (a), perception (b), elaboration (c), judgement (d), memory (e) and learning (f) can be distinguished. Any of them can be targeted by institutional intervention.

Pure cognitive governance is a hazardous enterprise. It must presuppose the motivational problem to be solved. Of course, this is conceivable. Both parties can be in harmony because their interests are complementary, or because they are driven by the same identity. A sufficiently strong outside power may override opposing motivation, without leaving a problem for the parties themselves. A sufficiently large degree of uncertainty can make a conflict of interests irrelevant.[64] But none of this is common. Typically, cognitive governance is therefore part of a richer institutional arrangement. The cognitive part accompanies a second intervention, targeting motivation. Or the intervening actor can engage in two-level governance, starting with the cognitive level.

(a)   Attention   Attention management has already been presented as a tool for rationalisation, i.e. for a switch to deliberate decision-making.[65] It can also help Ego if Alter is likely to engage in deliberate decision-making in the first place. For attention is typically selective.[66] Intervention increases predictability if it makes some elements from the environment salient.[67] There are also more indirect effects. Ego may piggy-back one risk on another by presenting it as essentially identical to the salient one.[68] Or, on the contrary, in the interest of preventing a reaction, he can purposefully downplay an element from the context. This is what the municipality of Oak Park, close to Chicago, did. It wanted to maintain the cohabitation of Caucasians and Afro-Americans in neighbourhoods. It achieved its goal

---

[64] This is the idea behind the metaphor of a veil of ignorance, as used by Buchanan and Tullock 1962. (Rawls 1999 uses a similar metaphor, but only as a conceptual benchmark, not as a statement about fact.)

[65] See above 4.3.2(b).

[66] See, for example, Bohner 2001: 268; Gifford 2001.

[67] Heiner 1983: 561; Payne et al. 1997: 184, 199; a graphic example is provided by Shavitt and Fazio 1991; cf. also Conlisk 1996: 670: subjects tend to exaggerate the importance of vivid over pallid evidence.

[68] Noll and Krier 2000: 344.

by prohibiting the posting of 'for sale' signs.[69] This prevented segregation from gaining momentum. Generating salience is easier, the greater the cultural background that Ego and Alter share. The more common this background is, the more Ego can rely on shared mental models.[70]

(b) *Perception*   The governance effect of institutions rests on how they shape the taken-for-granted, says Arnold Gehlen.[71] This explains in sociological language why governance can effectively target perception. Again, this is feasible for decision-making that employs heuristics and routines.[72] But the more decontextualised the mental tool, the greater the impact of perception.

People tend to use the information in the way it is presented.[73] This explains why representation matters. If one tries to understand the non-normative responses of subjects in experiments, one often finds that they have been logical responses to some other problem representation.[74] And untrained individuals are much better at handling some problem representations than others.[75] For instance, most people are bad at handling statistical data correctly. But they do fairly well if the same numbers are presented in the format of natural frequencies.[76] For all these reasons, Ego is well advised to tend to the representation of Alter's problem.

Editing has been demonstrated to be a serious source of unpredictability.[77] Therefore it helps if outsiders succeed in influencing how Alter edits his task. In so doing they can exploit the fact that some interpretations of choice problems appear more natural to individuals than others.[78] A graphic example goes to the core of the research programme on biases. The term 'loss aversion' offers one way of expressing the essence of prospect theory.[79] The effect decreases, however, with market experience. It is minuscule when the object is money. And it almost entirely disappears for professional sellers. For them, all goods are apparently like tokens, to which they are not attached psychologically.[80] Outsiders can exploit these insights by imposing more experience and transferring interaction to an organised market.

---

[69] Dixit and Nalebuff 1991: 241–5.   [70] Mantzavinos 2001: 103.
[71] Gehlen 1960: 71–2.   [72] Cf. Cosmides and Tooby 1992: 208.
[73] Payne 1997: 199.
[74] Fiedler 2000; Stanovich and West 2000: 655–6.
[75] Cosmides and Tooby 1994: 330.
[76] Gigerenzer 2000b with more material.
[77] See above 2.2.3(c).
[78] More from Thaler 1999: 197–202.
[79] For a basic treatment see Kahneman and Tversky 1979.
[80] Tversky and Kahneman 1991.

Editing can be seen as a special instance of framing. Many have proffered the idea of institutions,[81] and law specifically, as framers.[82] Outsiders can aim at imposing a standardised frame on an issue or a conflict. For that reason, disclosure laws have been criticised. It has been observed that they run the risk of remaining futile if they only say that information is to be provided. Given framing, they also ought to state how the information is to be disclosed.[83] In other instances, it may appear attractive to frame a situation so that the blame is placed on Nature. The sluggish reaction of suppliers to external shocks that make a commodity much scarcer offers one practical example. *Homo oeconomicus* would raise prices. In reality, this is a rare phenomenon. Typically, suppliers keep prices more or less stable and implement some form of rationing.[84] This can be interpreted as a framing effect. For actually, by rationing they decide to the detriment of those who come later, even if their need for the commodity is stronger. But in public perception, this effect is imputed not to the supplier, but to Nature. Framing cannot only be induced or changed. It can sometimes also be overcome by advice.[85] To the extent that this is feasible, deframing can serve as one form of rationalisation.

Anchors are particularly powerful perceptual tools.[86] The person who is able to set the anchor has some sort of a psychological first-mover advantage. This can be exploited by Ego. An illustrative case is an attorney general's proposal of a sentence to the judge. This is very likely to give the judge a reference point.[87]

(c) Elaboration Elaboration has been demonstrated to be a source of particularly low predictability.[88] The best way that outsiders have to respond to this is the following. They can offer an actor ready-made tools with relatively low plasticity: mental models, instead of blending; schemata, instead of mental models; stereotypes, instead of schemata.[89] This is one way of explaining why a relatively stable cultural background dramatically reduces the predictability problem.

---

[81] Cosmides and Tooby 1994: 331; Witt 2000a.

[82] Weck-Hannemann 1999: 85; Korobkin and Ulen 2000: 1104; see also Sunstein 2000c: 2: 'the legal system creates procedures, descriptions, and contexts for choice'.

[83] Jolls et al. 1998: 1536–7.

[84] Frey 1999b: 165–72.

[85] Druckman 2001.

[86] Chapman and Bornstein 1996; Strack and Mussweiler 1997; Chapman and Johnson 1999; Mussweiler et al. 2000.

[87] Englich and Mussweiler 2001.

[88] See above 2.2.3(c).   [89] For details, see above 2.2.3(c).

(d) Judgement Influencing judgement from outside is not easy either.[90] The most promising intervention aims at shifting the mental tools. If Alter uses a simple decision heuristic or a routine, the judgemental element is much smaller, if it exists at all. How such a switch in mental tools can be brought about has been illustrated above.[91] Occasionally, offering judgemental heuristics can help. In that case, Alter still takes a deliberate decision. But for parts of the judgemental element, he uses a heuristic as a shortcut.[92] Finally, outsiders can formalise the process of decision-making. A good illustration is a court procedure. A rich array of procedural rules direct how facts are introduced. Each side has a formalised opportunity to present its cause in the most favourable light. The court is obliged to give explicit reasons. It must state not only the final outcome, but also the facts on which the evaluation is based, and why the court is convinced that these facts were actually present. None of these procedural rules can preclude that the judge's verdict has actually been generated in entirely different ways. But deliberately concealing reasons is no mean feat. It presupposes highly developed rhetorical skills, a certain cold-bloodedness and a good deal of criminal energy. There are not many with such a nature.

(e) Memory In most decision-making, memory is involved. This presents an additional source of low predictability.[93] But it may also be strategically exploited by outsiders. By training obligations, they have a good chance of enriching the memory of actors. Specifically, they can increase the base rate of access to a chunk. This increases the probability of retrieval. For retrieval is governed by both base rates and recent activation.[94] Outsiders can also try to have an impact on the second component of retrieval, recent activation. An example consists of exposing Alter to a real or hypothetical outcome that renders this information more accessible.[95] Making an element from the context salient can have the same effect. That way, attention management and an impact on memory are linked.[96]

(f) Learning Learning is itself not a particularly problematic source of unpredictability. If Ego were not able to observe Alter's learning history, he might not be able to assess the robustness of the

---

[90] On judgement, see above 2.2.4.   [91] See above 4.3.2(c) and (d).
[92] For examples of judgmental heuristics, see above 2.2.4.
[93] For details, see above 2.2.5.
[94] More on retrieval from Anderson 2000b: chapter 8.
[95] Ross et al. 1977b.   [96] On attention management, see above 4.3.3(a).

learning result.[97] This may be important for predicting Alter's reaction in the more distant future. It can also be a problem if Ego thinks the concrete context is unusual or surprising. If any of this is sufficiently important, Ego can respond by trying to affect the learning mechanism. He might, for instance, design a training ground such that a cognitive component is present. This typically makes learning results more robust.

More important is imposed learning, which is one way Ego can try to reduce predictability risks resulting from other sources. Given the high plasticity of human behavioural programmes, it is particularly attractive to design institutions such that they set controlled learning processes in motion.[98]

4.3.4 Motivational route

Governance inspired by the rational choice model is purely motivational. In the part of this book on the limited ability to comply, the limitations of this approach have already been highlighted.[99] One aspect neglected by rational choice is cognition. Other attempts at pure motivational governance are open to the same criticism. They must assume all cognitive problems to be solved. Accordingly, in practice, acts of intervention will typically have a cognitive and a motivational component. This is one reason why practical intervention typically relies on richer institutional arrangements.

Most motivators are open to institutional intervention. This is obvious for money, and for utility more generally. This is what rational choice analysis is about. And in many contexts, changes in the absolute or relative price do indeed have an impact on behaviour. This is true the more that price is salient. An obvious example is suppliers' decisions under workable competition. Accordingly, organising a market and commercialising an issue are likely to make behaviour more predictable.[100]

But there is more to motivation than price. In reality, sanctions are often perceived not as changes in the set of restrictions, but as educational tools.[101] Moreover, institutions in general,[102] and the law in particular, can generate desires that did not exist in the first place.[103] This should not be surprising for any observer of advertising and marketing more generally. A specific way of changing preferences

---

[97] For details, see above 2.2.6.
[98] The idea has been proffered in political science, see e.g. Knill and Lenschow 1999: 10.
[99] See above 4.2.1.
[100] More on organising markets below 4.3.12(a).
[101] For an illustrative account, see Ostrom 1990: 187.
[102] Bohner 2001: 240.   [103] Sunstein 1998.

consists of exposing the individual to a situation that creates cognitive dissonance.[104] One way of reducing this dissonance is to change one's own desires. This is particularly likely if the individual has submitted to light pressure. For then the individual is aware that he might have resisted.[105] Sales people intuitively know this when they apply the 'foot in the door technique'. The small favour of letting the salesperson in makes the future customer much more approachable.[106]

Outsiders can appeal to happiness, rather than utility.[107] An illustrative example is motivation by luxury. A golden pen or a weekend in a posh hotel is not cheap. But compared with how much motivation they generate, they are much cheaper than the monetary equivalent of the effect. Nonetheless, their motivating effect is strong. At the outset, this effect can be put down to a cognitive phenomenon, mental accounting. Although the addressee would easily be able to pay for such luxury, he or she is not likely to do so. For such treats are mentally booked on an account that has a smaller budget.[108] But the effect also has a motivational facet in happiness. Addressees care since an experience far exceeding their mental allowance makes them happier.[109]

A related motivator is self-esteem. It is fairly easy for outsiders to exploit it. This is why governments decorate public servants and firms hail the 'worker of the month'. This also explains why the pillory is such a powerful sanction, and why outsiders can trigger Alter's remorse.[110]

Outsiders often also successfully invoke social norms.[111] A nice example dates back to the days of English King Henry IV. He first promulgated a statute prohibiting jewellery being worn in public. Hardly anybody obeyed the law. This changed dramatically once Henry IV edicted an exception to the earlier rule in accord with which thieves and whores were exempted.[112] A frequent technique is an example of two-level governance. By a first governance impulse, addressees are induced to form a new attitude. At step two they are induced to reason

---

[104] For a basic treatment, see Festinger 1957.   [105] Festinger and Carlsmith 1959.
[106] Freedman and Fraser 1966; Beaman et al. 1983; see also Dillard et al. 1984, offering a cognitive explanation of the effect.
[107] On happiness, see above 2.2.7.
[108] Thaler 1999: 195–6.
[109] Cf. Kahneman 2000b: 686–9 on the effect that visiting an unexpectedly luxurious restaurant has on happiness; see also Brickman and Campbell 1971 on the 'hedonic treadmill'.
[110] See already Smith 1790: II.ii.III.4: remorse is a natural safeguard against the plasticity of human behavioural programmes.
[111] See Mantzavinos 2001: 117 on their combined cognitive and motivational effects, resulting in 'socially developed sentiments'; Elster 1989: 1 and *passim* sees social norms even as the exclusive institution for overcoming predictability problems.
[112] Homann and Suchanek 2000: 62.

explicitly. This makes it pretty likely that they will now act in conformity with the attitude.[113] Likewise, outsiders can appeal to fairness norms.[114]

Relying on motivators other than utility is often of the utmost practical importance. A classic example stems from environmental policy. It goes by the name of substitution of harmful substances. The more environmental policy sanctions the use of one substance, the stronger the incentive of firms to replace it with other potentially even more harmful substances.[115] In such situations, normativity is of utmost importance. The law thus exploits the willingness of its addressees to abide by the spirit, not only the letter of the law.[116] This is feasible only if the law can appeal to the addressees' identities as members of a society, not just as utility maximisers.

4.3.5   Countervailing psychological mechanisms

The previous sections demonstrate that there is considerable room for behaviourally informed acts of intervention that aim at making Alter more predictable. Before he takes action, however, Ego, or any other outside actor, is well advised to see whether the intervention is not counterproductive in practice. This qualification even holds if Ego narrows the goal of intervention down to the generation of higher predictability. Actually, predictability is typically no goal in and of itself. It matters for Ego since he sees successful co-operation as beneficial.[117]

There are many reasons why targeting one source of unpredictability is counterproductive. Checking for a socially detrimental heuristic or routine will often make the individual switch to deliberate decision-making. Behaviour is no longer patterned. It becomes even harder to predict than before. This is particularly likely if individual creativity has been triggered.[118] Often, the individual in such cases will perceive uncertainty and risk. As demonstrated, behaviour under perceived risk is particularly difficult to predict.[119]

One psychological mechanism has received particular attention. Generating financial incentives can backfire. Instead of improving the situation as expected, the overall outcome can create a situation even worse than the one that existed before.[120] The key hypothesis is that

---

[113] See the experiment by Snyder and Swann 1976.
[114] On the plurality of fairness norms, see above 2.2.7.
[115] More from Markovits 1996: 320.
[116] Another illustrative example for the difference is provided by Verweij 2000.
[117] Of course, Ego might also care for Alter's predictability for reasons other than gains from trade. But such instances are considered in a later part of the book, see chapter 6.
[118] This is the main claim of Wegner 1996.   [119] See above 2.2.10.

intrinsic motivation might be crowded out by extrinsic incentives. There is lively controversy over this hypothesis.[121] To a considerable degree, the effect seems to depend on framing.[122] It can also be linked to the already mentioned phenomenon of reducing cognitive dissonance.[123] This is important, since dissonance between self-perception and the treatment by outsiders[124] can also result in reactance.[125] Instead of subduing an urge, the individual might mobilise resources to resist what he perceives as a violation of his self-esteem. Obviously, reactance can result from the exposure not only to incentives, but to any other attempt to make an actor more predictable.

The foregoing can also be translated into a piece of advice. When designing the institutional intervention, the regulator ought not only be concerned with matching the specific behavioural source for unpredictability. He should also shape his intervention such that it is easy for Alter to digest, both cognitively and motivationally.

4.3.6   Opposing values

There is hardly anything in life without a cost. Institutional intervention in the interest of making behaviour more predictable is no exception. In principle, behaviourally informed solutions share the drawbacks of acts of intervention inspired by rational choice. They may not sufficiently discriminate between cases and generate unwanted effects in the environment of the target.[126] Another way of making the point is: such intervention may excessively standardise. Moreover, intervention may bring Alter under the spell of Ego or outsiders. Any of these might exploit their power beyond the degree necessary for creating

---

[120] This effect has attracted interest from economics and from the law: Smith and Walker 1993: 251–6; Fehr and Gaechter 2001, 2002; Frey and Jegen 2001; Nyborg and Rege 2001; Fehr and Falk 2002: 713–19; Murdock 2002.

[121] Apart from the authors listed in the previous note, see Deci 1975; Wiersma 1992; Hogarth et al. 1997: 279; Deci et al. 1999, 2001a, 2001b; Sansone and Harackiewicz 2000; Cameron 2001; Cameron and Pierce 2001.

[122] If incentives are used to govern whole groups, differential psychology might also play itself out. Typically, not all addressees can be reached with the same impulse. The incentive can be counterproductive if it makes one group more responsive to regulation, but reduces the willingness of another group to abide by the rule. Illustrative is the case reported by Krüger 1999; Schöch 1999.

[123] See again Festinger 1957.

[124] This is the conceptualisation by Bohner 2001: 264.

[125] For a basic treatment, see Brehm 1966; Brehm and Brehm 1981; for a more recent overview, see Dickenberger et al. 1993.

[126] See above 3.3.7(b).

predictability.[127] But behaviourally informed intervention raises additional normative concerns.

They can just be counterproductive. This is the case if greater local predictability generates global unpredictability. An example is group membership. Group membership can be a credible signal for attitudes. But it also creates the new predictability risks resulting from group dynamics.

In this part of the book, Ego is assumed to be fully rational. From this, it follows that predictability is not a value for him as such. He cares about predictability if and when this increases the expected value of co-operation. Accordingly, Ego will see it as a problem if the price for greater predictability is reducing expected gains from co-operation. This is not an unlikely event. The following examples illustrate the point. If Ego successfully transposes co-operation into an organised market, Alter's behaviour is typically more predictable.[128] But on markets, strong disincentives for not playing the market game make it fairly likely that Alter will become more selfish. This is something Ego may dislike if he previously was the beneficiary of more pro-social behaviour. Ego may in particular dread Alter's becoming strategic, with all the drawbacks put into relief by game theory.

Likewise, highlighting the stable psychological effects of institutional intervention can have unwanted side-effects. As reported above, anchors are particularly robust to admonition and even outright training. They do not create full predictability. But Ego can feel fairly certain that the anchor will serve Alter as a reference point in making quantitative judgements under uncertainty.[129] This may make Ego cautious not to drop anchors that might be far off the mark. And he might become even more suspicious if the anchor comes from a chance outsider.

A third example is addiction. It by definition creates fairly stable behavioural expectations. For the addict cannot easily overcome the drive, even if he consciously decides to do so. And quite a number of addictions can be generated from outside. This possibility is a long-standing social concern, well known from examples like smoking and drug use. But even if Ego is completely selfish, he may dislike interaction with a future addict. For those areas of behaviour within the grip of the addiction, negotiation becomes a risky enterprise. In one of his clear moments, Alter may be willing to promise socially beneficial action. But the addiction is likely to hamper fulfilment.

---

[127] See above 3.3.8(a).
[128] For more on the rationalising power of organised markets see below 4.3.12(a).
[129] See above 2.2.3(b).

All the foregoing can be seen as a way of counselling Ego or an intervening outsider. Once they become aware of these potential downsides, they are likely to engage in better informed institutional design. The remaining drawbacks, however, have a conflictual element. They are drawbacks only from the perspective of the addressee of institutional intervention, not from that of its author. The obvious problem with any behaviourally informed institutional design is paternalism.[130] The designer deliberately ignores Alter's stated will. Depending on the character of the intervention, Alter may not even notice the intrusion into his behavioural dispositions.[131] If the intervention comes from government, one may also ask whether government has a constitutional mandate to educate the electorate.[132] There is also a repercussion on the control of power,[133] and on the principal–agent relationship between the electorate and government more specifically.[134] If the intervention goes unnoticed, it is particularly difficult for the citizens to control governmental action. The ensuing information asymmetry is particularly pronounced. Finally, a very general concern is applicable. Greater predictability of behaviour also generates higher 'regulability'.[135] The borderline between government and the citizenry is shifted.

In the rational choice part of the analysis, soft predictability turned out to be the proper benchmark.[136] In a behaviourally informed perspective, this holds even more. For, as demonstrated, the potential cost of such intervention is even higher. This does not preclude Ego or outsiders from having recourse to such tools. But, given the cost, it will not normally be advisable to aim at full predictability. The intervention should rather purport to reduce the degree of the original predictability problem.

4.3.7   Mechanisms for intervention

Behaviourally informed intervention purports to affect the behavioural dispositions of Alter. It aims at either changing or enriching Alter's behavioural repertoire. Or it changes the context such that the context

---

[130] From the rich literature, see, for example, Van De Veer 1986; Rachlinski 2003.

[131] Debiasing is a topic at the crossroads of psychology and institutional design; see, for example, Keren 1990; Arkes 1991; Hirt and Markman 1995; Sanna and Schwarz 2003; see also Jolls 2000: 299: 'but is it proper for government to make use of this error in citizens' perception?'.

[132] More from Lüdemann 2004.

[133] On that aspect, see above 3.3.8.

[134] On principal–agent models, see above 3.2.1.

[135] The term 'regulable' has been coined by Lessig and Resnick 1999: 423.

[136] See above 3.3.9(d).

predictably matches the behavioural dispositions of Alter. If Alter consents, both can be seen as second-order decisions to make his behaviour more predictable.[137] Some of these acts of intervention can be ad hoc (a). Typically, however, at least a learning process is required (b), if not intervention at the developmental stage (c) or even an evolutionary change (d).

(a) Ad hoc Some behaviourally informed intervention can be ad hoc. Changing a behavioural disposition on the spot is typically not feasible. But, as demonstrated, most dispositions are not deterministic. The individual is able to override them if a sufficiently powerful stimulus is presented.

The classic case is rationalisation.[138] It is a shift in mental tools. Rather than relying on simple heuristics or routines, Alter shifts to conscious and deliberate decision-making. Rare examples such as the reflexes or addiction notwithstanding, humans can do that for almost any task. Rationalisation increases predictability. Even if human rationality does not obey the norms of rational choice analysis, in many contexts it is fairly calculable what a conscious decision will look like.[139]

But rationalisation is not the only option. Emotionalisation can often be at least as powerful in generating greater predictability. If Ego succeeds in making Alter furious, serene or flabbergasted, this can reduce the variability of Alter's reaction dramatically.

Ad hoc intervention is not confined to bringing about a switch in mental tools. The intervention can also target elements of one mental tool that remain untouched as such. A case in point is rhetoric. 'The rhetorician . . . invites the members of the audience to recruit from their background cognition resources . . . What can be recruited . . . depends on social and cultural location.'[140]

(b) Learning The human ability to learn can itself be a source of unpredictability.[141] But this ability is also one of the practically most promising ways of overcoming predictability problems. Such learning can have objects of very different reach. The most fundamental goal would be the acquisition of an entirely new behavioural disposition, like a new heuristic. The most cautious goal would consist of merely learning

---

[137] More on the idea of second-order decisions is Sunstein and Ullmann-Margalit 2000: in particular 187.
[138] More on rationalisation below 4.3.12(a).
[139] On bringing rationality to human scale see above 2.2.9.
[140] Turner 2001: 153.   [141] See above 2.2.6.

facts, which then change the effect of an existing mental disposition. In between these two extremes would be the learning of a new mental model, attitude, schema or stereotype.[142] Learning, however, only helps if the behavioural disposition creating unpredictability is sensitive to it.[143]

In principle, greater predictability can result from the use of any learning mechanism, be it classic or operant conditioning, imitation or open instruction.[144] Some illustrations must suffice. Experience can help reduce biases,[145] and hence increase predictability, if the original bias has been a source of unpredictability. Experts in many areas perform more predictably than laymen.[146] This has, for instance, been demonstrated for bankers' decisions taken under conditions of uncertainty.[147] But there are also sources of behavioural variability that seem to resist training. This has been reported for sunk cost. The term characterises an effect of issue-specific investment. If the investment cost is sunk, it loses all its value once the issue changes.[148] According to the norms of rational choice, investors should ignore sunk cost. Their decision should be entirely forward-looking. Actually, however, for people's decisions, sunk costs matter. It seems that this deviation from rational choice also holds for experts.[149]

(c) *Development*   A child does not come to earth with a fully equipped brain. In contrast to the lower species, the role of instinct in determining human behaviour is small. For the most part, human behavioural dispositions must be developed in childhood and adolescence.[150] Via enculturation, we 'become complex, multi-layered, hybrid minds, carrying with ourselves, both as individuals and societies, the entire evolutionary heritage of the past few million years'.[151] Or in the words of Adam Smith: 'This natural disposition to accommodate and to assimilate, as much as we can, our own sentiments, principles and feelings, to those which we see fixed and rooted in the persons with

---

[142] On these see above 2.2.3(c).
[143] An example of a behavioural disposition that cannot be improved by training is presented by Friedman 1998: 942.
[144] On learning mechanisms see Domjan 1998; Anderson 2000b; and above 2.2.6.
[145] Frey and Eichenberger 1994: 224–5; for an example see Garvin and Kagel 1994.
[146] Stanovich and West 2000: 651–2.
[147] Shoemaker 1982: 555; Machina 1987: 128.
[148] More on sunk cost from Furubotn and Richter 1997: IV.2.
[149] More from Arkes and Blumer 1985.
[150] For a fascinating story of what happens to the brain in childhood, see Hebb 1949.
[151] Donald 1999: 16.

whom we are obliged to live and converse a great deal, is the cause of the contagious effects of both good and bad company.'[152]

Consequently, behaviour can also be made more predictable via the developmental route.[153] Many formal and informal institutions do exactly this. The most obvious is mandatory schooling. But the exposure to standardised interaction in groups coalescing around informal codes can have a similarly strong effect.

   (d) Evolution   Even if the brain of a newborn exhibits incredible plasticity, it is not empty. Unlike many animals, the behavioural programmes of young children are not ready-made. But there are genetic predispositions. They make it easier to learn some elements than others.[154] Accordingly, making humans more predictable could in principle also occur via the evolutionary path. The ethical objections are patent. But even if a policy-maker were willing to ignore them, this would not be a useful thing to do. Had this been a way of increasing the reproductive success of human genes, natural selection would long ago have made men more predictable. Obviously, the opposite is true. The predictability problem must therefore at least be seen as a price willingly paid by Nature in exchange for a reproductive advantage. And it is not difficult to name it. Precisely because of the enormous plasticity of their behavioural programmes, humans are able to adapt to a rich variety and a quick change of environments. But in all likelihood, the idea of a trade-off is misleading. In a reproductive perspective, the low genetic predictability of humans is an advantage, not a drawback. Put differently, the principal claim of this book can also be made in evolutionary terms. Nature has not only left the human mind without many fixed traces. It has also endowed human beings with the ability to generate the predictability necessary for co-ordination otherwise, namely by institutions. Since institutions are much more malleable than genes, this alone gives humans a strong competitive advantage over other species.

4.3.8   *Psychological paths*

Happily enough, controlled mutation is out of the question for humans. But how can outsiders affect development, learning and the ad hoc

---

[152] Smith 1790: VI.ii.I.17; see also V.ii.2.
[153] Cf. Ayton 2000: some biases are present only in adults, not in children.
[154] This insight is not new. See e.g. Bartlett 1932: 212–13: humans are not born with ready-made schemata. But they bring a quadrangle of appetites, instincts, interests and ideals which help build and select schemata.

access to mental tools? Given the astounding richness of the human mental apparatus, it is not surprising that a huge array of potential psychological paths open up. The following is thus by no means exhaustive. It tries to generate some order among the options, with an eye to institutional design based on this.

One rough cut through the material organises the possibilities in accord with the directness of intervention. Directness is greatest if an outsider imposes training on Alter (a). Imposing formality alone is a more cautious approach (b). A duty to rely on outsiders may be seen as fairly intrusive from the ultimate perspective of behaviour. But it leaves the mental processing of Alter entirely untouched (c). Any of the previous implies some form of communication. But outsiders may content themselves with just talking to Alter (d). Finally, they can restrain themselves to shaping context, rather than the reaction of Alter to it (e).

(a) Imposed training   In public discourse, education is not popular these days. It is obvious that children need it. But once individuals are of legal age, imposed education seems patently at variance with the idea of the people being sovereign. Previous centuries thought differently. This even held for proclaimed liberals, like Adam Smith. For him it was obvious that people permanently needed education.[155] Of course, the power of government to impose education can easily be abused, and the twentieth century has seen some of the worst instances of this.[156] But even modern, democratic states sometimes impose some form of education on newly arrived immigrants. And they can impose training for activities such as driving a car or hunting.

The debiasing movement ennobles education anew.[157] It calls for 'educating them [the decision-makers] about their tendencies'.[158] To the extent that behavioural dispositions resist training, the movement recommends helping actors develop what one might call countervailing mental powers. A case in point is anchoring. It can be prevented from becoming behaviourally relevant if an actor possesses his own subjective theories about the conditions under which anchoring thwarts their judgement. They then can consciously correct what they initially thought to be the right estimate.[159]

[155] See, for example, Smith 1790: III.iii.7, III.iv.12, III.v.1.
[156] For a lucid, but scary look at this, see, Neumann 1942; Arendt 1951.
[157] See again Keren 1990; Arkes 1991; Hirt and Markman 1995; Sanna and Schwarz 2003.
[158] Kelman et al. 2000: 73.
[159] Strack and Deutsch forthcoming: part 8.1.

(b) Imposed formality Many legal and non-legal acts of intervention that aim at making behaviour more predictable impose some kind of formality.[160] It can come in two forms. The effect on predictability is straightforward if the behavioural outcome is standardised.[161] But imposing some form on how to generate this outcome can also be of help. In that case, the actor is obliged to go through a certain procedure, or to be embedded in a certain context.

There are many ways of making procedure more formal. In most countries, buying and selling land must be done via a notary public. A marriage can only be concluded following culturally contingent procedures: it requires going to church in Christian cultures, or circling an open fire seven times in the Sikh religion. In most countries a judge is supposed to sit in a formally decorated courtroom, and to wear a robe.

Psychologically speaking, such obligations work first and foremost as attention managers. They signal that this is not day-to-day business. Addressees are pretty likely to switch to conscious and deliberate decision-making. Moreover, such formality is a compressed signal of a whole set of social expectations. The form is likely to trigger scripts that the actor has learned on earlier occasions. Formality thus affects perception, and it does so by relying on memory. It can also have an impact on motivation. The marriage ceremony in a church is meant to vitalise our sense of responsibility. When we buy a piece of land, the notary public should rather sharpen our attention. The presence of the notary public is meant to cool our emotions down, whereas the presence of the priest in marriage is meant to cheer us up.

An obligation to give reasons is one particular kind of procedure. This is frequent in law. Exceptions such as jury trials notwithstanding, in the court system judgments have to be accompanied by reasons. In many countries, the administration is under the same obligation. Sometimes, the law also obliges private parties to offer justifications for their actions. A case in point in German law is the landlord's requirement when giving a tenant notice. He is allowed to do so only if he wants a property back for personal use, and he must explain why this is the case. For an actor who is determined to be selfish, the justification requirement is not much more than a rhetorical exercise. He takes his decision on whatever grounds he likes, and cooks up reasons that are socially or legally acceptable. But in reality, this is a rather rare event. At the very least, knowing the norms for justification makes the actor

---

[160] Cf. Sunstein and Ullmann-Margalit 2000: 192 on legal formalism as a second-order decision.
[161] On this see Sunstein and Ullmann-Margalit 2000: 190.

think twice. Typically, the repercussions of the anticipated justification stage go even beyond this. The justification requirement highlights social control.[162] The effect is even stronger if the actor is obliged explicitly to state counter-arguments to his own position. This has been demonstrated to be a functional tool for overcoming overconfidence[163] and the hindsight bias.[164] From here, it is only one step further to outright cost–benefit analysis,[165] which can also serve as a tool for rationalisation.[166] The effect is even increased if the procedure is such that two contradictory positions fight for approval, as is typical in litigation. In a parallel field, a tournament of experts has been demonstrated to be a tool for overcoming framing effects.[167]

(c) Duty to rely on outsiders   Many of the forms of imposing formality can also be brought under a different rubric. They also oblige Alter to tolerate or even proactively bring in an outsider. But this is not the only way that behaviour is made more predictable by partly or entirely reducing Alter's decision-making authority.[168] Alter can also be obliged to consult an expert before deciding.[169] A rule from German criminal law illustrates why mere consultation matters. One of the requirements for a legal abortion is that the pregnant woman undergo consultation with a 'pregnancy conflict bureau'. This bureau is obliged by law to inform the woman of what abortion would mean for the foetus.[170] Such consultation generates salience for the issue. And it openly strives to affect mental models. Another institution that works the same way is the obligation to seek mediation, as in labour law conflicts.

A related possibility is the obligation to rely on some technology to prepare the actual decision-making. Apparently, thus far the tool has not been taken up by regulation. In education, computers are already used as powerful learning tools. For instance, algebra trainers target the individual performance of the pupils, rather than an average level of a class. This not only speeds up learning. It makes 'mastery' a realistic

[162] This is the key element in the evolution of the Ajzen and Fishbein theory of attitudes into the 'theory of planned behaviour'; Ajzen and Fishbein 1980; Ajzen 1991.
[163] Koriat et al. 1980.
[164] Slovic and Fischhoff 1977.
[165] From the rich literature on this tool see Sunstein 1996, 2000b; Adler and Posner 1999, 2000; R. Posner 2000; Sunstein 2000b; Symposium 2000.
[166] Sunstein 2001.
[167] Druckman 2001: 65, 79.
[168] On this technology, see Kelman et al. 2000: 73.
[169] More from Druckman 2001: 62–82.
[170] § 219 *Strafgesetzbuch*; see also *Schwangerschaftskonfliktgesetz*, for the details of this consultation.

goal. By this term, pedagogues mean that each and every pupil is brought to a level where he actually masters a predefined task, such as how to solve algebraic functions.[171]

Finally, an obligation to become part of a larger organisation or group can also be interpreted as a way of imposing outside intervention. The only formal difference is membership. It typically gives Alter voice.[172] This gives him some handle on the overall policy of the organisation. Typically, membership is psychologically more powerful than is mere exposure to outside intervention. For organisations aim at creating an identity. This makes it easier for them to affect their member's cognition. They often also successfully shape some values, meaning that they also influence motivation.

(d) Communication   For a trained game theorist, communication is just 'cheap talk'.[173] Experiments, however, show that in many contexts communication matters.[174] It conveys information, despite the credibility problem. It helps Ego give meaning to Alter's behaviour.[175] It activates attitudes and social norms. If the partners engage in serious discourse, this brings them into a problem- solving mood that often helps creatively shape effective solutions.[176]

(e) Shaping context   All the foregoing can be seen as an attempt to influence Alter's personality and how it plays itself out in the case at hand. As demonstrated, personality is only one of two sources for behaviour. The equally important second source is perceived situation.[177] This explains why an alternative approach to making behaviour more predictable is contextual.[178] Actually, many institutional arrangements that aim at generating greater predictability target personality and perceived situation alike.

Practically speaking, contextual governance works by standardising the context for interaction. This can be done by mere exposure, or by

---

[171] More from Anderson 2000b: chapter 11.
[172] On voice as a tool for controlling the management of an organisation, a classic treatment is from Hirschman 1970.
[173] For an overview, see Farrell and Rabin 1996.
[174] Crawford 1998; Forsythe et al. 1999; Brosig et al. 2003.
[175] Cf. Wright and Mischel 1987: 1173: perception is moulded by communication.
[176] The latter point is stressed in political science work on arguing; for an overview see Risse 2000.
[177] See above 2.5.3.
[178] In literature, the point is made by, for example, Hogarth et al. 1997: 278–9; Payne et al. 1997: 201; Rostain 2000: 985; Stanovich and West 2000: 662–3; see also Turner 2001: 91.

an outright obligation to transfer the interaction into that prefabricated environment. One way to do this is again by making Alter a member of an organisation.

A fixed context can in many ways make behaviour more predictable. Heuristics are powerful tools since they are ecological. They are adapted to a fairly defined context.[179] Consequently, standardising context helps: it makes it more likely that actors will indeed rely on context-specific heuristics. Likewise, a stable context invites individuals to become experts in that field. Put differently, they develop context-specific routines.[180] This in turn makes it easier to predict their behaviour. Standardising context also helps if Alter relies on more elaborate mental tools. Context shapes perception. It can provide a frame.[181] In some contexts some elements from the environment are much more salient than others. For instance, in an organised market, participants will focus on quality and price, rather than on the charm or eloquence of the seller. A familiar context often improves the quality of decision-making. What would be hard to solve as a problem in the abstract becomes tractable.[182] Actors learn how to avoid characteristic deviations from rational decision-making. Or they at least exhibit characteristic biases, which then become predictable.[183] Last, but not least, a stable context is a better learning environment. The more likely repetition is, the more learning effort pays. Also, frequent experience generates more feedback and thereby makes inference easier.[184]

4.3.9   Institutional designers

Who is best situated to seize these opportunities for bringing about co-operation? In principle, the same options exist as were discussed in the rational choice part of this book: Ego can take action unilaterally (a), as can Alter (b). Ego and Alter can join forces for the purpose (c). They can

---

[179] For a basic treatment, see Gigerenzer et al. 1999; see also Goldstein and Weber 1997: 586. If Ego knows (or shapes) the context, it becomes easier to predict the mental tool used by Alter.

[180] More from Anderson 2000b: chapter 9.

[181] See Turner 2001: 101–11, on playing a game as a frame: players understand that the goal is interdependent decision-making, based on the goal of maximising individual utility.

[182] Goldstein and Weber 1997: 577 on a particularly prominent fallacy, the solution of Wason selection tasks, that disappears in familiar contexts.

[183] See Ritov and Baron 2000: 172: omission bias is particularly pronounced in agents, for the likelihood of being held liable for harm resulting from commission is much greater than for harm resulting from omission.

[184] Hogarth et al. 1997: 279.

voluntarily bring in a third party (d). And there can be some form of sovereign intervention (e). But the comparative advantages of these institutional designers look significantly different from a behaviourally informed perspective. Moreover, a behaviourally informed scientific observer cannot but call for modesty. Generating predictability is such a demanding task that the institutions actually serving this purpose are often, at most, partly designed and much more evolved (f).

(a) Ego In a behaviourally informed perspective, Ego has additional options. This does not, however, preclude him from treating the predictability problem as an information problem. The solutions developed in the rational choice part of this work thus do in principle remain available. Ego can aim at bringing type revelation about; he can use a subsidy scheme; he can self-insure and he can see the expectation of gains from trade as an implicit risk premium.[185] The only limitation is the potentially limited ability of Alter to comply.[186] It has the greatest impact on subsidy. Depending on the technology employed, it can also have repercussions on type revelation. Insurance and risk premium are not affected.

In a behavioural perspective, the main comparative advantage of Ego is his ability to customise intervention to his relationship to Alter. He typically knows more about this relationship than any outsider. Ego can play this advantage out more, the more stable this relationship is. If the interaction is long-term, he may have recourse not only to those technologies available ad hoc, but also to learning mechanisms. In very long-term relations, such as in a family or some working environments, he might even have an opportunity to have an impact on Alter's development. In a stable relationship, Ego can unilaterally change context such that co-operation becomes more likely. He has a good chance to expose Alter to communication and discourse. All this is much more difficult if the interaction with this specific actor is sporadic.

If he acts unilaterally, Ego cannot as such impose his will on Alter. The only power he has consists in threatening Alter with defection. In a rational choice perspective, this is a rather powerful tool. In a behaviourally informed perspective, however, it is significantly weaker. It works if it is sufficient for Ego to exert power on Alter ad hoc. Longer-term acts of intervention, however, are hard to bring about that way. This would presuppose Alter's willingness to undergo a longer-term encroachment before the actual co-operation ever starts.

---

[185] On all these, see above 3.3–6.   [186] See above 4.2.

(b) Alter   In the rational choice part of this book, unilateral intervention by Ego and by Alter looked fairly similar. In this part of the book, the similarity is substantially reduced. This result is, however, largely an artefact of research design. This chapter is deliberately asymmetric. It retains the rationality assumption for Ego, but drops it for Alter. Accordingly, Alter's ability to respond must also be seen through the behavioural lens. Consequently, the limited ability to comply with rational choice intervention *mutatis mutandis* carries over. This does not preclude any unilateral action by Alter. He may still sit back and decide to undergo training. He may think it wise to subject his behaviour to some kind of formal procedures. He may believe that outsiders are better situated than he is to overcome one of his limitations. He may seek out opportunities for communication and discourse, believing that this might be to his long-term advantage. And he might unilaterally change an element of his context, with the expectation that this will make co-operation more likely in the future. But all this does not only presuppose a willingness and an ability to reason about future action. It is also more likely to be a long-term endeavour. It is especially difficult for Alter unilaterally to bring about on-the-spot-changes of behavioural dispositions and changes in how they play themselves out. Basically, the only strategy that has some likelihood of working is a switch to conscious and deliberate decision-making. The more important Alter perceives the issue to be, the more likely he is to work harder, albeit not necessarily smarter, on it.

(c) Ego and Alter jointly   If Ego and Alter sit together, this can have a number of advantages. One initial potential gain is on the cognitive side. If they have to agree on a solution, they will naturally engage in discourse. This can be used not only as a tool for making co-operation more likely in and of itself. More importantly, it makes misunderstandings less likely. It also gives both sides an opportunity to signal their good intentions.

In a rational choice perspective, joining forces is particularly relevant since it allows for open trade. Each party can offer the other a favour in exchange for that party's willingness to agree to the solution. In a behaviourally informed perspective, this advantage takes on a slightly different hue. If Ego has an opportunity to make himself understood, reactance on the side of Alter is less likely.

Jointly, Ego and Alter may also enjoy greater freedom to reshape context such that it becomes more favourable to co-operation. They may, for instance, agree to transfer their relationship into the confines of an organised group, or they may both undergo some kind of training.

(d) Third party   Third-party intervention differs from sovereign intervention in that its activity rests entirely on the joint will of the parties. In a behaviourally informed perspective, such third parties can, in particular, muster two resources that are typically not available to the parties themselves. They can exploit economies of scale and scope, and they can act under a longer time horizon. Both sometimes allow them to exploit technologies that would be hard for the parties themselves to use. This is particularly helpful if learning or even development looks promising. Alter can, for instance, agree to undergo formal training, organised by such an outsider. They can both agree to become part of an organised group for the purpose. Alter and Ego can bring an experienced outsider in as a mediator. Or they can implant their interaction into a richer context managed by a third party. Finally, the third party can specialise in generating and applying generic behavioural knowledge that would not be affordable in an individual interaction.

(e) Sovereign intervention   The additional resource available in cases of sovereign intervention is the ability to override the opposing will of Alter. Government can just send the child to school, even if the child or his parents would prefer that he play or work. Government can make a driver's licence conditional upon attending a driving school and passing the driving test. It can make professional training a condition for exercising a profession. Government can impose formality, a duty to engage an intermediary or to communicate intensely. It can shape the context on a large scale and make it mandatory for the parties to expose themselves to it.

If the outsider who imposes his will is government, an additional advantage stems from well-developed mechanisms for generating legitimacy. In a rough way, they can be classified into input and output legitimacy.[187] The former splits up again. Democracy theory typically stresses the representation element. Any representative is supposed to speak for the whole constituency, not just for the interests of his own voters.[188] But legitimacy can also result from participation. In line with this view, those being addressed by intervention have a say about its shape.[189] Output legitimacy, however, rests on perceived problem-solving quality.[190]

---

[187] The distinction goes back to Easton 1965. It has been further developed by Scharpf 1999: chapter 1.1.

[188] The idea goes back to Rousseau 1763 and his distinction between a healthy *volonté générale* and a pernicious *volonté de tous*: II.iii.

[189] More on participation from Engel forthcoming: II.3.d.

[190] Output legitimacy thereby is linked to another category central to political science, namely problem-solving capacity; see Scharpf 1998.

(f) Evolved institutions   Historically, almost all institutions have been considered as having grown, not as having been designed. This remark has even held for law. People have obeyed 'good old law'. Having a long tradition was the strongest way of establishing the legitimacy of a rule. This changed with the advent of legal positivism.[191] Thereafter, the prime criterion for legitimacy was not tradition, but adequacy in coping with a perceived social problem. Consequently, the legislator was empowered to generate new law at his will. More generally, institutional design became an independent social function. Even rules that society inherited were now formally treated as enacted by way of legislative fiat.

Many of the institutions to which this part of the book has alluded, and this applies even more to the examples treated more extensively below, are, however, not legal institutions. Sometimes, a legal rule is part of an institutional arrangement. A case in point is the legal obligation not to drive a car unless possessing a driver's licence. But in such cases the law only provides the sanction. The actual behavioural effect stems from going to the driving school. More often than not, greater predictability is thus generated not by formal, but by informal institutions. As the example of the driving school demonstrates, informal institutions can be designed as well. But often they are not. Or better: they may have a designed component. But the actual effect on behaviour relies on many more causes than the ones that have been purposefully set in motion.

It would therefore be an overstatement to maintain that generating predictability is a social task that is beyond purposeful control. But one should be aware that informal, grown institutions may be highly relevant. Accordingly, the policy problem may often call not for design from scratch, but for modest and careful moves that give existing institutional arrangements a slightly different shape.

In the introduction, one of the caveats concerned political process. In principle, it is not covered here. But as an aside, an implication of the foregoing for policy-making should be mentioned. This book makes a strong normative claim: predictability is a serious social problem, largely overlooked both by institutional analysis and by politics. But if policy-makers are attentive to this message, they should act with care. If they strive for grand design, they run a serious risk of getting things wrong, if not making them worse. A piecemeal approach is in place. Small and tentative steps are more likely to lead to social betterment.

---

[191] The struggle is best visible in von Savigny 1814. For a modern overview see Adomeit 2003.

4.3.10   Operationalisation

Institutional designers do not only consider how a defined problem can be effectively solved. They typically have to keep a series of framework conditions in mind. These additional conditions limit and direct the choice among potential acts of intervention.[192] In this context, the following framework conditions warrant particular attention. How stable is the effect of intervention (a)? Can the intervention be customised to the peculiarities of the case at hand (b)? Must it rely on the participation of Alter or Ego (c)? Does it have the character of one neat intervention, or does it require a richer institutional arrangement (d)?

(a) Stability   Stability of intervention can mean several things. A first criterion is the predictability of institutional impact. In a rational choice framework, this is virtually a non-issue. As long as all actors optimise, any act of intervention will automatically trigger those moves that now are in the players' interests. In a behaviourally informed perspective, this would usually be an overly optimistic expectation. Typically, all the intervention can bring about is a probabilistic, not a deterministic effect.[193] The larger the remaining probability that behaviour will not be of the expected kind, the stronger the second-order predictability problem. Despite intervention, Ego cannot be certain about Alter's behaviour.

Another facet of stability consists of the fact that the effect is dependent on the presence of the intervention stimulus. A classic example of the issue is learning, if it results from classic or operant conditioning.[194] The conditioned behaviour does not directly fade away once the unconditioned stimulus or the reinforcer is no longer present. But after a while the conditioned response is extinguished.[195] This is not the case for cognitive learning. Here the effect does not rest on a mere association. Rather, the subject establishes a new mental model during the learning phase. Forgetting this insight, i.e. the weaknesses of memory, is the only source of disturbance then.[196]

Finally, stability can mean robustness in the face of outright disturbances. In that event, the subject is exposed to a stimulus that might

---

[192] For a richer presentation of such conditions, see Engel 2002a: 100–11.

[193] On the distinction between probabilistic and deterministic effects, see e.g. Goldstein and Hogarth 1997: 7.

[194] On these two learning mechanisms, see above 2.2.6.

[195] More on the underlying mechanisms from Domjan 1998: 79–82, 168–72.

[196] Anderson 2000b: 11; see also Anderson 2000b: chapter 7 on forgetting; cf. also Bohner 2001: 254, more generally on the stability of learning results.

counteract the earlier intervention. New information makes Alter see the situation differently. A new opportunity presents itself. Alter undergoes a change of mood, i.e. emotions intervene. On this account, the mental tool used by Alter in the new situation should matter. As long as the cue is still present, a heuristic should still work. A routine might cushion the blow. In deliberate reasoning, Alter might override the intervening stimulus.

(b) Customisation   The ideal intervention is tailor-made. It exhibits neither false positives nor false negatives.[197] Yet such a fully customised tool is rarely available. Typically the tool either misses cases which it should affect. Or it overshoots and has an impact on individual freedom in cases where there was no reason for this to happen. Undershooting and overshooting can occur both with respect to contexts and with respect to actors. In the latter case, outsiders are hit, or potential targets are missed. In a behaviourally informed perspective, one scenario is about as likely as the other. Cognitive abilities and motivation differ across individuals. One and the same individual does not perceive situations purely along the abstract lines that motivated the intervention.

(c) Reliance on participation   All teachers have had the experience: educating a person against his will is at least hard work, if not ineffective. Engaging in discourse with a reluctant communication partner is not very effective either. Imposing formality or a duty to rely on outsiders makes much smaller demands on Alter's willingness to co-operate. And shaping context can do without this willingness entirely. The psychological paths do thus differ with respect to this criterion.

(d) Richness of institutional arrangement   Changing incentives is a straightforward act of intervention. Ego must merely see to a change in relative prices. He offers Alter some money, or he takes some away from him.[198] Behaviourally informed institutions are typically much more complex. Very few of the practical examples are simple institutions;

---

[197] On this old philosophical distinction, relevant for decisions under uncertainty, see Lübbe 2002.

[198] In reality, however, this often turns out to be more cumbersome. Determining the correct change in prices demands access to information the regulator often has a hard time obtaining. And implementing a Pigouvian tax presupposes constant monitoring of the taxed activity. For both reasons, the actual institutions also tend to be fairly rich institutional arrangements.

they tend to be richer institutional arrangements.[199] Examples further
analysed in the following section include the organisation of markets,
professionalisation and culture.

Institutional complexity also has a temporal dimension. Behaviourally
informed intervention is typically not ad hoc. It rather comes as a
process. A learning process, or even an impact on development, takes
time. They are only likely to be effective if many acts of intervention add
up over time. Even if the actual intervention is ad hoc, it can be necessary to prepare for it with experiments.[200] But again, not all potential
intervention fares alike on this scale. For instance, formality can often be
imposed without further ado.

In a behavioural perspective, an entire institutional arrangement
has a number of important advantages. As mentioned earlier, Ego's
predictability problem typically has more than one source. Moreover
each of these sources is typically able to generate a whole array of
behaviour, not only one well-defined deviation from the rational choice
model. A full institutional arrangement is usually better situated to
address the multiplicity of potential behavioural effects. Metaphorically
speaking, Ego uses a rake, rather than a pair of tweezers, to pick
the leaves from the lawn in autumn. Since such an arrangement is a
multi-purpose tool, Ego can also exploit what economists would call
economies of scale and learning effects. It makes sense for him to shape
this tool carefully, and to learn from experience the contexts, and the
ways, in which it is best employed. Finally, the impact of a rich institutional arrangement on Alter is likely to be more robust. This effect
can again be a result of learning. Moreover, it is more likely that Alter
will retrieve the arrangement, and what it means for him, from memory.
For retrieval is largely facilitated by multiplying mental access points,
i.e. by the richness of the elements.[201]

4.3.11 Formal and informal institutions

(a) Formal institutions   Institutional intervention can be either
formal or informal.[202] The quintessential formal institution is the law.
In modern constitutional states, the standard procedure for generating
law is a statute. The common law countries traditionally put greater

---

[199] A similar point is made by Slembeck and Tyran 2002: 2, 18 and *passim* for the specific
case of interventions overcoming the 'three-doors-paradox'.
[200] 'The laboratory as a testing ground for institutional design' is one of the messages from
Smith 1994: 115; see also Smith et al. 1988; Smith 1991: 886.
[201] More on the likelihood of recall in Anderson 2000b: 279–84.
[202] This distinction is found in, e.g., North 1990: 3.

stress on judge-made law.[203] But neither of these implies that every legal intervention meant to increase predictability must come from sovereign intervention. Older forms such as customary law remain,[204] giving social forces a subsidiary power to generate new law. More importantly, state law largely empowers private parties to generate legal obligations. This is true for contract law. Recently, many legal orders have also opened themselves up to the idea of private regulation and found legal forms for that.[205]

The economic analysis of law treats the law as a set of restrictions.[206] In accord with that, the law affects predictability as described in the analysis in the rational choice part of this book. But the effect of the law does not stop here. It also serves as a mechanism for shaping social norms,[207] and for reminding the addressees of them.[208] The law also has a pronounced cognitive component. This is a result of the fact that legal rules are not just on the books. They are implemented in a formal procedure of rule application. This application stage provides a natural opportunity for discourse between the application authority and the addressee. The authority learns how the addressee sees the problem, and the normative expectations of this. The authority can quarrel with the addressee. At the least, at the end of the procedure the addressee knows how this authority sees the problem and how he reads the rule. Not so rarely, the authority will also be able to change how the addressee himself sees the world. This is particularly a result of normativity. A legal rule is not just a restriction to which the addressees react by reoptimising. It is a social demand. It tells the addressees what government sees as good and bad behaviour.[209] Typically, the addressee is not faced with a legal rule that is merely applicable to an isolated temporal event. If the addressee expects to be confronted with this rule over a longer period, the process of rule application is also likely to work as a learning mechanism. The addressee gradually learns how best to accommodate the normative demand of the rule.

---

[203] A standard reference for comparing the two families of legal orders is Zweigert and Kötz 1998.
[204] For more background, see Glenn 1997.
[205] For overviews and background see Kirchhof 1987; Engel forthcoming.
[206] See, for example, the classic pieces by R. Posner 2003; Cooter and Ulen 2004.
[207] On the interaction between the law and social norms see E. Posner 2000a.
[208] The latter is stressed by a school of thought that goes by the name of 'expressive law'; see Tyler 1990; Cooter 1998; Adler 2000; Anderson and Pildes 2000; McAdams 2000; Bohnet and Cooter 2001.
[209] More on the cognitive component of the law, and on its interaction with normativity at Engel 2001a.

Law is the most important, but not the only formal institution. As a result of the proliferation of computer networks, code is increasing in importance. The governance effect of code is enshrined in technology. The classic example is the Internet. If an addressee dislikes the TCP/IP protocol, he must stay away from the Internet. If he is to use the Net, he simply cannot avoid abiding by this protocol.[210] The basic Internet protocol is meant to be as light-handed as possible. But based on it, much more intrusive code can be written. A much-studied example is digital rights management.[211] An illustration is Acrobat Reader. It allows the author to determine technically whether the text can be printed, saved or copied. Code is above all else a powerful restriction; for ordinary users it is even an insurmountable one. But code is also able gradually to shape worldviews.[212] Code therefore is a powerful tool for making behaviour predictable.[213] Because of the extremely low flexibility of this tool, there is even a serious danger of overfitting.

A last formal institution consists of the change in relative prices brought about by governmental intervention in markets.[214] This is what happens in a subsidy or a Pigouvian tax,[215] and with tradable permits.[216] Visibly, these are above all changes in monetary incentives. These tools are typically advocated by economists. But even money can have an impact on behavioural dispositions that goes beyond utility. The most important psychological effect of the monetarisation of an issue is on loss aversion. As reported, typically losses loom larger than gains. If ordinary subjects once possess an object, they are reluctant to trade it against its monetary equivalent.[217] The effect fades away, however, if the traded good is perceived as a token. The standard token is money.[218] Moreover, monetary interventions can be designed such that a decision is transferred from one mental account to another.[219] The effect is particularly likely if, by institutional intervention, what the addressees had perceived as a long-term decision is transformed into a gradual stream of payments. Most people psychologically book permanent payments into a different mental account from investments. Intervention of

---

[210] The classic study highlighting this governance effect is Lessig 1999.
[211] More from Bechtold 2002.
[212] More from National Research Council 2002.
[213] Teubner and Karavas 2003.
[214] There are, of course, more formal institutions. For an overview, see Engel 2001a: 17–23. This section is thus by no means exhaustive.
[215] On these tools, see above 3.4.
[216] More from Bonus 1981; Tietenberg 1982; and more generally Tietenberg 1998.
[217] More on loss aversion above 2.2.3(b).
[218] Thaler 1999: 6; Kahneman et al. 2000a: 213.
[219] For a basic treatment, see Thaler 1999; see also Jolls 2000: 294–7.

this kind can increase predictability if there is better generic knowledge about behaviour in the altered psychological situation.

(b) Informal institutions Informal institutions have become a fashionable topic in the social sciences.[220] The exact borderline with formal institutions has always been disputed.[221] At this point it suffices to consider the power of some obviously informal institutions to increase predictability.

If one presents the predictability problem to an uninitiated interlocutor, the standard response is: the problem is cooked up. It is solved by culture.[222] Unfortunately, culture is an extremely vague term. Only its contrast to genetics is unequivocal.[223] Some theorists use culture as virtually equivalent to informal institutions.[224] Others equate it to social norms.[225] Still others stress the cognitive aspect and link culture as to the shaping and transmitting of mental models.[226] Finally, culture is seen as a mechanism for the transmission of heuristics to a new generation.[227] All of this is indeed able to make behaviour more predictable.

Despite the vagueness of the concept, linking the solution of the predictability problem to culture is important. For culture cannot be designed. It must grow. This is not to say that planned action has had no impact on culture. But no individual actor, and not even a well-organised group, is able to reshape culture at will. Accordingly, an important part of solving the predictability problem is outside the realm of purposeful design. The most design can do in this respect is prevent the existing culture from being altered such that the predictability problem increases dramatically. Or it can give an impulse for cultural change, without being certain about the effect.

Custom is a much more precise informal tool than culture. As one observer put it: 'Custom . . . shapes habits and convictions, sways emotions and cognitions, and influences motivation and action.'[228] Custom thus is a powerful tool for generating greater predictability.

---

[220] From the rich literature, see in particular Geiger and Rehbinder 1987: 128; North 1990: in particular chapters 1 and 5; Ellickson 1991; Knight and Sened 1995; Stiglitz 2000; Eisenberg 2001.
[221] All the authors cited in the previous footnote offer definitions.
[222] In literature the point is, for instance, made by Gehlen 1960: 70–1; Ripperger 1998: 104; Langevoort 2000: 146.
[223] This is indeed how Gehlen 1960: 70–1 uses the term. See also Boyd and Richerson 1994 on the distinction between genes and (cultural) 'memes'.
[224] Granovetter 1985: 486 stresses the point.
[225] That is the way the term is used by Goldstein and Weber 1997: 600.
[226] Mantzavinos 2001: 103; see also Wagenaar et al. 1997: 560.
[227] Gigerenzer et al. 1999: 92.   [228] Schlicht 1998: 1.

Since custom is less global than culture, purposeful design may have a chance. But in custom the unplanned component is also often significant. Typically, the power of custom is weaker than the power of formal institutions. There is no formal sanction if one violates a custom. Ostracism is a severe sanction, but it is not common.[229] Because of this, custom is a practical tool for bringing soft predictability about.[230]

This is not true of taboos.[231] Groups define themselves by shared taboos. Punishing those who break a taboo is a powerful social adhesive. Consequently, a taboo is highly instrumental in bringing predictability about. Any other group member can be almost certain that nobody will break the taboos. But this comes at a high price. Not only individual freedom is trumped. The evolutionary potential for the group is reduced along with this.

Ideology is between a mere custom and a taboo.[232] Not everybody must adhere to it. There can be ideological opposition in a society. But the potential cost of opposition is significant. Opponents run the risk of losing many opportunities if they do not face outright sanctions. The ideological mainstream is likely to fight hard for the maintenance and the propagation of the official ideology. The predictability effect of ideology depends on its internal coherence. Since ideology is a tool for integration,[233] coherence is typically not the highest value. Nonetheless, those who visibly adhere to the dominant ideology send a highly informative signal. The signal is credible since other partisans are often likely to prosecute when there are deviations.[234]

4.3.12 Becoming concrete: institutional impact on the choice among mental tools

All the foregoing had to be kept more or less abstract. In order to demonstrate what practical implications might look like, this last section will be more concrete. It depicts in somewhat greater detail how one of the most important sources for unpredictability could be matched by institutional intervention: the plurality of mental tools.[235] Institutions can indeed have an impact on this choice. They can serve as rationalisers (a), routinisers (b) and automatisers (c) respectively.

---

[229] Gruter and Masters 1986.
[230] On the goal of soft predictability see above 3.3.9(d).
[231] For background, see Webster 1942; Jones 1999.
[232] For an analysis of ideology, see North 1990: chapter 5.
[233] On integration, more from Smend 1968.
[234] For a stimulating formal analysis of 'preference falsification', see Arce and Sandler 2003: 145–52.
[235] See above 2.2.2.

(a) Rationalisers   Human rationality does not obey the norms of rational choice theory. But conscious and deliberate decision-making is predictably distinct from the use of routines or simple heuristics.[236] The predictability gain can even be increased if the institutional arrangement does two things at a time: i.e. if it ensures that its addressees switch to deliberate reasoning, and affects how this happens. This is true for the two most prominent examples: the market and political elections.

Many have observed that markets rationalise behaviour.[237] The most important effect of transferring interaction to a market is motivational. Acting on a market visibly raises stakes.[238] Markets do not only offer opportunities for gains. Psychologically, the threat of loss or even bankruptcy is even more important. For, as demonstrated, psychologically, losses loom larger than gains.[239] Ironically, however, the perceived risk of a large future loss can even make market participants more risk neutral or even risk prone. They learn that avoiding risk now can mean dropping out of the game in the foreseeable future.

Markets also shape motivation. If they are to survive, market participants must keep irrational emotional reactions under control.[240] Strong pro-social motivation is not likely to survive.[241] But in markets, outright selfishness or even irrational anti-social behaviour does not pay either. Markets therefore also serve as training grounds for the basic rules of social interaction.[242]

Markets also have an impact on cognition. The stronger the market experience, the more the divide between the willingness to accept and the willingness to pay diminishes.[243] Loss aversion thus dwindles away. In markets, people do also become more likely to ignore sunk cost, and they thus come closer to the norms of rational choice.[244]

---

[236] See above 2.2.9.

[237] See, for example, Becker 1962: 8: 'households may be irrational and yet markets are quite rational'; Plott 1986; Arrow 1987; Camerer 1987: 982.

[238] Vernon Smith has amassed evidence for this point: Smith 1989, 1991, 1994; Smith and Walker 1993; implicitly, Gebhard Kirchgässner makes the same point in his theory of low cost decisions, Kirchgässner 1992, 1996; Kirchgässner and Pommerehne 1993.

[239] On prospect theory, see above 2.2.3(b).

[240] Farnsworth 2000: 311: 'markets may reduce the incidence and significance of . . . acrimonious attitudes'.

[241] Hoffmann and Spitzer 1985; Fehr and Tyran 1996, both on the diminishing role of fairness orientations.

[242] See the impressive anthropological study by Henrich and Boyd 2001: the closer a population was to market interaction with outsiders, the higher the co-operation rate internally.

[243] Kahneman et al. 2000a: 220; List 2000.   [244] Plott 1986.

Raising stakes is a direct result of competitive pressure. But many of the cognitive effects just listed do not result from competition. They result from the fact that transactions happen on a formally or informally organised market.[245] In such an institutional setting, the situation is strongly standardised. Egos learn a small, well-defined number of signals. They know that they are all striving for the same thing: to make a profit. Organisation is also responsible for defining the area of inter-action, i.e. the product.[246] Consequently, not all markets are alike. Whether behaviour is moulded in some way or other often depends on the specifics of market organisation. For instance, auctions are affected by anchoring. They are executed against a previous 'reference price'. If futures are traded, however, the problem is overcome.[247] Likewise, allowing for direct comparisons with competitors strongly increases the rationalising effect. This is done in rank-order competition within a firm. It allows other workers to see much more clearly how they comparatively fare than if they only have the noisy signal, indicating how much they earn.[248]

Markets also have long-term effects on behaviour. They allow market participants to acquire experiences in a controlled setting.[249] They can observe their competitors and thus learn by imitation.[250] And they can learn explicitly by buying advice or information.[251] A final effect, however, is a borderline case. As a result of market pressure, error-prone actors may find it advisable to delegate market-relevant decisions to intermediaries.[252] And markets can have a selection effect, weeding out those who are least able to live up to market discipline.[253]

A similar rationalising effect results from election.[254] There is also competition. If a party does not see to the next elections, it stands to lose power, if not to fall into oblivion altogether. Stakes are thus visibly high. Votes also serve as a uniform currency: they make the efforts of parties easy to compare. A rich set of legal rules and of informal mores organises this market for votes. Market discipline here is even

---

[245] On the market as an organisation, see Engel and Schweizer 2002.
[246] The latter fact is stressed by market sociology; see e.g. White 1992; Rosa et al. 1999; Engel 2004b.
[247] Jolls et al. 1998: 1496–7.
[248] Mookherjee 1990.
[249] Camerer 1987: 981–2.
[250] Camerer 1987: 982.
[251] Camerer 1987.
[252] Sunstein and Ullmann-Margalit 2000: 193.
[253] Camerer 1987: 982.
[254] Ostrom 1998: 2; see also Satz and Ferejohn 1994: 80.

stronger than in ordinary markets. For in the commercial world there is always the possibility of growth, resulting in an easing up of competitive pressure. When there is innovation, companies can open up entirely new markets, or substitutes for existing products can find their niches. None of this is possible in the market for votes.[255] Elections are strictly a zero-sum game.[256] Actually, it is even worse. No more than one party or coalition can be in power at a time. This turns an election into something like an auction where only the highest bidder obtains the desired good. This is an extreme way of raising the stakes. Parties know that a last-minute impression can be as important as long-term performance. Consequently they specialise in campaign management. Of course, political parties are not individuals, but corporate actors.[257] Attempts to understand how the experimental evidence for individual actors carries over to corporate actors are still very much in their early stages.[258] But the rationalising effect works on individual and corporate actors alike. Moreover, the considerations directly apply if individual candidates compete for office.

(b) *Routinisers* Routines result from expertisation. An individual gains experience in a domain. He no longer needs do things step by step. He can rely on more and more aggregate, ready-made mental building blocks. Mental effort can be confined to the assessment of the fit of these building blocks to the concrete situation, and to the appropriate combining of them.[259] This ready-made character also helps Ego. As long as Alter perceives situations to be sufficiently similar, he is likely to behave in comparable ways. It makes sense for Ego to accumulate experiences with this particular actor.

Professionalisation does exactly this.[260] It is a rich institutional arrangement. Its most important formal component is a legal barrier to market entry. More and more professions have come under this regime. Being a doctor, a dispensing chemist, an architect, a structural engineer, an attorney or a notary public: all this requires formal

[255] The only remote parallel to this is a political party aiming at increasing the turnout.
[256] More on zero-sum versus positive-sum games (resulting from growth) from Sandler 2001: 34–6.
[257] The concept of corporate actors is familiar in political science; see Scharpf 1997: 54–8.
[258] See e.g. Kunda and Nisbett 1988; Bone et al. 1999. Much more developed is research into group dynamics; see e.g. Baron and Kerr 2003.
[259] See again Anderson 2000b: chapter 9.
[260] Gehlen 1960: 71; Goldstein and Hogarth 1997: 29 on doctors; Jolls et al. 1998: 1486; Battaglini et al. 2002; see also Frey and Eichenberger 1994: 224: medical doctors commit fewer errors of diagnosis than inexperienced medical students.

admission.[261] In Germany, the same holds for almost all crafts.[262] The admission requirement makes it possible to impose formal training on future professionals. Moreover, the professions are organised in chambers.[263] This brings professionals under the purview of a formally organised peer group.[264] Both training and peer group control allow for a dense net of informal rules, dos and don'ts and standards of best practice. Moreover, within professions, social status is closely linked to obedience to these rules, and to participation in their implementation. Sociologically speaking, being a member of a profession is a fairly elaborate and a clearly distinct role.[265] None of this strictly standardises behaviour. But it largely narrows down variability. Professionalisation is thus a very apt tool for generating soft predictability.[266]

An element of professionalisation is group membership. It can also be used in isolation to make behaviour more predictable. Group members' cognition is likely to be influenced by the prevailing worldview in the group. Cognitive tools pervasively used in the group will be easily activated by members, even if those members disagree with the dominant view. Moreover, group norms are likely to influence members' judgement. Groups also provide members with a salient tool for distinguishing the interior and the exterior. They thus help classify psychological situations.[267] This explains why being a member of a family[268] or of a functional group is able to increase one's predictability.[269]

Corporatisation is a borderline case. It implies that individuals transfer interaction to the interior of a corporate actor. This has often been reported to be a way of making behaviour more predictable.[270] But one can interpret this as a switch of Alter, rather than as a tool for making individual behaviour more predictable. Organisation affects behaviour in many ways. At the interior of an organisation, discretionary power can be exercised.[271] This raises the stakes in that positive and negative sanctions are easy to muster. Organisations are islands of specialised

---

[261] An overview of German regulation on professions is given by Pitschas 1996.
[262] For an overview of regulation see Czybulka 1995.
[263] For details of the German regulation, see Czybulka 1995; Pitschas 1996.
[264] On the behavioural effect of this, see Battaglini et al. 2002.
[265] For an overview of role theory, see Biddle and Thomas 1979; Biddle 1986.
[266] See above 3.3.9(b).
[267] A graphic illustration of the effect is Robert Ellickson's study on how Shasta County farmers settle disputes. Among themselves, they persistently use group norms and custom, whereas they rely on formal law for conflicts with strangers. Ellickson 1991.
[268] Gehlen 1960: 71.
[269] Gehlen 1960.
[270] Thaler 1999: 19; Kahneman and Lovallo 2000: 394: narrow framing can be overcome by corporate design; see also Simon 1976.
[271] The point has been powerfully made by Simon 1962.

custom.[272] They do not only entail expectations, they also work as a cognitive filter. They affect how members see the world, both inside and outside the organisation.

A last example of the routinising effect of institutions goes back to the sphere of politics. Political scientists have long wondered how the electorate can ever have an actual impact on policy-making. Rational choice analysis has had an easy time demonstrating that the ordinary voter is rationally ignorant.[273] It is so utterly unlikely that he will individually hold the pivotal vote that any effort above zero is irrational. Rationally, he should thus stay at home. This has dealt a serious blow to the idea of democratic legitimacy. If voters who go to the polling booth are irrational, how can they ever exercise any significant control over government? One of the responses to this challenge is psychological. It claims that political parties organise choice spaces for the electorate. They narrow choice down such that it becomes easy enough to manage and the rational choice problem becomes irrelevant. Voters no longer need to exert significant effort to distinguish political positions, or to understand political issues. Voting becomes a meaningful action, despite the fact that the ordinary voter knows extremely little about future political choices.[274] Or put in the terminology used here, party competition is an institution that makes it possible to adopt a voting routine. All the voter does when the next election day arrives is quickly check to see whether he still feels best served by the party he voted for in the last election.

(c) *Automatisers* Quasi-automatic decisions are taken by relying on heuristics. It has already been mentioned that there is fairly little knowledge so far about the way individuals generate or acquire heuristics. Accordingly, it is difficult, at this point, to make strong claims about the impact of institutions on this process. There are, however, institutions that very likely come under this rubric. One example was used earlier. Driving a car is only permitted for those who possess a driver's licence. To obtain the licence, they must take lessons, and they must pass the driving test. The very purpose of this intervention is to endow future drivers with a whole set of very simple decision rules. Stop when the traffic light turns red. Slow down and drive on the shoulder of

---

[272] Schlicht 1998: 6, 207, 248; see also 256: the decisive governance tool within a firm is not command, but custom.
[273] Ferejohn and Fiorina 1974; see also Caplan 2004.
[274] Jackman and Sniderman 2002.

the road if you hear a police siren. Check the mirror before overtaking. Other institutions serve similar purposes. The basic training of soldiers is even more clearly tuned towards the development of heuristics. A last example is taken from a totally different policy area. One of the goals of waste management policy is to ensure a high degree of recycling. For the waste generated in households, this goal can only be reached if households are willing to separate waste into different fractions. By a complex institutional arrangement, German waste management policy has reached compliance rates far above 80 per cent of the population. They could never have done that by simple command and control regulation. The implementation cost would have exploded. What worked was instilling a number of separation heuristics in people's minds. The institutional arrangement is too rich to be reported on here. The basic message consists of a combination of endeavours: for one, taking financial disincentives out; for another, educating people by the use of government messages and advertising campaigns from the recycling industry.[275]

4.4   Changing the character of the task

This chapter has demonstrated that institutional design can exploit the generic knowledge about behaviour. But this is demanding, and the existing stock of generic knowledge is in many respects still far from complete. Before taking action, an institutional designer may therefore want to consider an alternative approach. It aims at initiating interaction while making less stringent demands on getting the behavioural assessment right. This approach works by changing Ego's (4.4.1) or Alter's task (4.4.2).

4.4.1   Ego's task

This chapter is only partly behavioural. It has dropped the rationality assumption for Alter, but has kept it for Ego. Accordingly, before Ego engages in behaviourally informed institutional design, he will do a cost–benefit analysis. On the benefit side, the same elements are present as in the rational choice analysis. The positive incentive consists of obtaining the fair gain from co-operation. The negative incentive consists of the danger of being exploited by a detrimental actor. With this, Ego will compare the expected gain after intervention. He will thus consider the

---

[275] The whole story is told by Lüdemann 2004.

cost of this intervention, and the increase in the expected value from trading with Alter. He will thus be crucially interested in the following questions. How good is the generic behavioural knowledge? How powerful are the available forms of institutional intervention in making behaviour more predictable? How costly is acquiring and applying the necessary generic and specific knowledge? It may well be that the result of this cost–benefit analysis is negative. In that case Ego is better off ignoring the behaviourally informed reactions. In appropriate cases he may still be willing to consider the reactions developed in the rational choice part of this book. But most of them are also plagued by behavioural problems. This is because of the fact that Alter's ability to comply is psychologically limited. Moreover, two of the options considered in chapter 3 crucially rely on behavioural assumptions themselves: namely type revelation and a subsidy. Only insurance and a risk premium are robust to behavioural variability.

When applied by Ego unilaterally, however, they are just identical to remaining inactive. Actually, Ego's choice is thus essentially equivalent to making at least some behavioural assessment, or bearing the predictability risk. Other alternatives fare somewhat better: Ego and Alter jointly, a third party and a sovereign ruler. For them, insurance and a risk premium are not just identical to risk bearing. For them, it accordingly makes sense to compare the cost of either insurance or a risk premium with the cost and the benefit of a behaviourally informed institutional intervention. They will also keep in mind that insurance is not plagued by the asymmetry between beneficial and detrimental actors.

4.4.2   Alter's task

Changing Ego's task is thus tantamount to ignoring the generic behavioural knowledge deliberately. Changing Alter's task is different. It means changing Alter's problem such that the variability of behaviour no longer matters for Ego, or such that it, at least, matters less.

The most radical reaction consists of changing Alter's task enough that it becomes fool-proof, behaviourally speaking. There are various ways of doing that. The decision can be delegated to another person or organisation that is much more predictable.[276] This is particularly likely if the delegate specialises in this kind of decision. His greater experience will make erratic decisions less likely. He will also weigh his reputation capital and consider repercussions of the decision in this one case on his

---

[276] Sunstein and Ullmann-Margalit 2000: 187.

later business opportunities.[277] An even more radical response consists of delegating the decision to technology. Given the advances in computer technology, this is no longer outlandish. On the financial markets, much of the trading is nowadays done via computer-to-computer interaction.[278] An even more radical solution consists of replacing Alter's decision by a lottery.[279]

But there are less extreme responses too. Rather than handling the natural degree of unpredictability, institutional design can aim at transferring an interaction into a setting where Alter's predictability matters less. Design can thus purport to make Alter's task psychologically less demanding. Actually, many of the institutions considered above could also be interpreted this way. For changing Alter's task is just another way of ensuring that institutional intervention aims at changing the perceived situation, rather than at affecting Alter's personality. The only qualification is timing. If a change in the situation is to be classified as a new design of Alter's task, it must be *ex ante*, before interaction between the parties starts. This, for instance, holds for rationalisation via markets, for routinisation carried out by narrowing down choice spaces of voters, and for automatisation achieved by requiring future drivers to pass a driving test.

4.5   Summary

Scientists are well advised not to try everything at once. This book follows the advice and drops the initial rationality assumption in two steps. This chapter has still upheld it for the uninformed actor, called Ego here. But it takes a more realistic view of Alter's behaviour. The chapter thus asks a question that is characteristic for behavioural law and economics: How would an omniscient and benevolent dictator react to the generic knowledge about behavioural dispositions, and to the specific knowledge about how they play themselves out in the specific actor under consideration?

On the most abstract level, there are three insights to be gained. In a behaviourally informed perspective, mere credibility is not enough. Ego should rely on Alter's promises only if Alter can also be expected to possess the behavioural ability to comply. Secondly, behaviourally

---

[277] This is the basic idea of the literature on social capital; for a basic treatment, see Coleman 1990: chapter 12. For my own position, see Engel 1999.

[278] For background and references, see Theissen 2002.

[279] Sunstein and Ullmann-Margalit 2000: 189, 201.

informed reactions are a demanding exercise. Only a small portion of the foreseeable future generic knowledge about behaviour is uncovered as yet. Otherwise psychology would run out of business shortly. In any one context, much more than just one psychological effect is likely to play itself out. Consequently, any intervention is bound to be fairly diffuse. Institutions aiming at making behaviour more predictable tend to be rich institutional arrangements, rather than ad hoc targeted interventions. Thirdly, this being so, changing the actor's task such that the predictability problem matters less may well be preferable.

5 Behaviourally determined responders

Divide et impera is not only good advice for generals; it also serves scientists well. Complex problems often become tractable by being split up. But in the end, the bits and pieces must be assembled anew. This book has used rational choice theory to do the splitting up. In chapter 4 it has partially dropped the strict assumptions of that theory. This chapter closes the circle and drops the rationality assumption for Ego as well.[1] From the perspective of the predictability problem, this can be viewed as even more bad news (5.1). But in some respects, a behaviourally informed view of Ego may also convey a brighter picture (5.2). Both the behavioural weaknesses and the behavioural strengths must be taken into account when designing fully behaviourally informed institutions (5.3).

5.1 Behavioural weaknesses of Ego

5.1.1 Introduction

A behaviourally informed approach runs the risk of designing institutions for demons.[2] It amasses knowledge about behavioural limitations in institutional addressees. But it implicitly assumes that those designing and handling the institutions possess unlimited capabilities. The approach adopted in this book makes this limitation of behavioural analysis patent. For it is not written from the legislator's perspective. Before calling for sovereign intervention, it explores the possibilities of the parties themselves, and of voluntarily introduced third parties. In a legislature, backed by a large ministerial bureaucracy, behavioural

---

[1] This seems a rare approach in literature, but see Bohner 2001: 267, who is concerned about Alter sending out a false signal about his attitudes that might mislead Ego. See also Noll and Krier 2000: 326: policy-makers might do no better than average citizens in risk regulation, since they might be just as affected by the limitations of human risk perception.

[2] The graphic term of rational demons goes back to Gigerenzer et al. 1999: 5.

limitations may not be an obvious concern. But the behavioural limitations become visible at once if one considers the potential reaction of Ego. If his character is not further specified, he will suffer from the same behavioural limitations as Alter. It would thus obviously be misleading to consider reactions or to design institutions that always assume Ego to be fully rational.

To be specific, at this point the predictability problem is not assumed to be symmetrical.[3] For the co-ordination problem it is still important for Ego to predict Alter's behaviour, but Alter need not predict Ego's behaviour. This is the case because, at the outset, only Ego is vulnerable, not Alter.[4] But when it comes to reacting to the asymmetry, Ego comes with the same behavioural endowment as Alter.

The previous chapters have taken into account that most behavioural dispositions are not human universals. Accordingly, behaviour differs not only with respect to situation, but also with respect to personality.[5] Different Egos are no exception. Some people are more intelligent than others. Some are better trained or organised than others. Some dread behavioural risk more than others. Some are more likely than others to react violently to perceived unfairness. This differential component can be ignored if the actual intervention originates in Ego himself, in Alter, or in both of them jointly. But it matters if they bring a third party in, or if the sovereign ruler intervenes. If they are only willing or able to engage in intervention uniformly, they can be forced to trade off some beneficial effect on one group of players for a corresponding detrimental effect on other groups.[6]

5.1.2   Plurality of mental tools

Ego has the same rich mental tools at his disposal as Alter.[7] For him, the ensuing predictability problem is irrelevant. But not all mental tools are equally able to deal with predictability risks. Ironically, human rationality is actually least prepared for that. As reported above, deliberate and conscious human reasoning significantly deviates from rational choice norms. Typically, untrained, non-professional individuals engage in either reason-based choice or narrative reasoning.[8] In the first case, they base their decision on just one reason, i.e. the most convincing one. In

---

[3] On this, see below chapter 6.
[4] For a more precise definition of the asymmetry, see above 3.2.
[5] More above 2.5.4.
[6] For a graphic illustration of this problem, see Krüger 1999; Schöch 1999.
[7] For an overview, see above 2.2.2.   [8] More above 2.2.9.

the second case, they choose between options by building scenarios around them. In both cases, they are very likely to ignore most of the generic knowledge about human behavioural dispositions used above. They are also likely to neglect much of the specific information available that might allow them to update their prior beliefs about the character of Alter. As we will see, interaction routines and decision heuristics can fare considerably better.[9] But their performance is crucially dependent upon contextuality. If Ego gets the context wrong, these tools can be highly misleading.

5.1.3   Cognition

The most profound limitations of Ego in handling the predictability problem are cognitive. They can originate in attention (a), perception (b) and judgement (d). The biggest problem, however, consists in elaboration (c). If Ego tries to find the correct response by deliberation, he is likely to be overwhelmed by complexity.

(a) Attention   Given the enormous plasticity of human mental dispositions, it should not come as a surprise that, in concrete situations, many dimensions of the problem are likely to escape Ego's attention. Solving predictability problems is not a rare event. It is part of day-to-day interaction. People very rationally ignore the problem most of the time. Otherwise pondering about predictability would eat up the mental capacities they need for actual interaction. Consequently, they will only deliberately address a predictability problem if an unusual feature in Alter's behaviour has attracted their attention.[10] That being said, most potential predictability problems will be ignored altogether.

(b) Perception   A second source of cognitive limitations lies in perception. Rationally assessing a predictability problem is a demanding mental exercise. It presupposes that people avoid inappropriate frames and anchors.[11] Ego can make mistakes in editing.[12] An example is the following. Subjects exhibit ambiguity aversion. If they have to choose between the following two prospects, a large majority opts for the first. Prospect 1 allows them to pick a ball from an urn when it is known that the urn contains 50 red and 50 black balls. A red ball wins. Prospect 2 allows them to pick the ball from an urn that contains 100 balls, but in

---

[9] See below 5.2.2.
[10] Cf. Wilder 1978: 281: unpredicted behaviour attracts attention.
[11] On these, see above 2.2.3(b).   [12] On editing, see above 2.2.3(b).

which the proportion of red and black balls is unknown. Of course, according to rational choice norms, both prospects have the same expected value. This aversion disappears if the subjects do not have to choose between two prospects, but are asked to evaluate each prospect independently.[13] In his predictability assessment, Ego can also be intentionally misled by Alter or by outsiders. This is easy, since people tend to use information in the same way as it is presented.[14] People frequently exhibit a false consensus bias. They tend to overestimate the proportion of people in a population who share their own attitudes.[15] The result reverses if they see Alter as a stranger. In that case, they typically believe that a group is better at making predictions about the stranger than the stranger is at making predictions about the group.[16] A further asymmetry has frequently been reported, with what is known as the actor/observer effect. There is a pervasive tendency for actors to attribute their actions to situational requirements, whereas observers tend to attribute the same actions to stable personality dispositions.[17] The assessment of Alter's behaviour is highly sensitive to the degree of Ego's emotional involvement.[18] Ego is likely to be affected by inappropriate perception heuristics. People, for instance, tend to overestimate vivid evidence and underestimate pallid evidence.[19] This is likely here, since most of the generic knowledge on predictability is counter-intuitive. This feature might even induce Ego deliberately to discard generic knowledge. Most of this knowledge can be neither generated nor corroborated by introspection. Ego is likely to replace the existing scientific knowledge with his own, incorrect construction.[20] Even if Ego is sufficiently sensitive to his own limitations, he is likely to engage in positive testing only, thereby missing most of the evidence.[21]

(c) *Elaboration*   An even greater problem is elaboration. Just having a look at the rational choice part of this book should make the problem patent. That part of the book uses a rigorously simplified model. It allows for no more than two players. Alter can be one of only two types: beneficial or detrimental. These types are exactly defined, as is the structure of the game and the information distribution. But even

---

[13] Fox and Tversky 2000: 528.   [14] Payne et al. 1997: 199.
[15] Kunda and Nisbett 1988: 333.   [16] Kunda and Nisbett 1988: 326.
[17] Jones and Nisbett 1972; Baxter and Goldberg 1987: 438, see also 439 for conditions under which the effect tends to vanish.
[18] León and Hernández 1998 distinguish between 'attribution' or 'cold cognition' and emphatic 'appraisal', and explore the framework conditions for both.
[19] Stanovich and West 2000: 647.   [20] Cf. Wright and Mischel 1987: 1172.
[21] Fiedler et al. 1999.

this radically simplified model leads to fairly elaborate and lengthy reasoning. Actually, in almost any real world situation, Ego's problem is much more complex. In principle, a previously unknown Alter could have any of the behavioural traits listed in the opening chapter. In order to be introduced into the rational choice model, each possible combination of all these traits must be construed as a new type of Alter. This makes for thousands of types. Even an almighty observer with unlimited generic knowledge and an unlimited amount of time for observation would be overwhelmed by this complexity. Even more so, any real life Ego.[22]

(d) Judgement Finally, in seeking remedies for the predictability problem, Ego is likely to be affected by the same limitations in judgement as Alter himself. If they are laymen, they will not be able to handle statistical data correctly. They will have to rely on aggregates like stereotypes, schemata, mental models and blending, which all can be misleading in the case at hand. Finally they may rely on inappropriate judgement modes. They may assess alternatives jointly, where separate assessment would be appropriate. And vice versa. They may underestimate knowledge stored in memory, as compared with information taken from the environment. They may rely too much on prototypes, or they may not rely on them enough. And they may use non-normative judgement heuristics.[23]

5.1.4 Motivation

There are also motivational forces that make Ego deviate from the expectations of rational choice theory. The most obvious is a preference for predictability.[24] Fairness norms are also likely to play themselves out,[25] with the ensuing self-serving selection among them.[26] Moreover, Ego can be motivated by self-esteem, rather than utility.[27] All of this can even trigger reactance, i.e. a willingness of Ego to accept a loss if this helps inflict damage on the disliked Alter.[28] There can also be repercussions on cognition. A self-serving bias may result in Ego misperceiving

[22] A similar point is made by Gigerenzer et al. 1999: 10–12; see also Simon 1987, 1990: 6, 1991: 35; Mischel and Shoda 1995: 260.
[23] References for all these effects are to be found above 2.2.4.
[24] References and more details above 2.2.7.
[25] References above, 2.2.7.
[26] Wade-Benzoni et al. 1996; Babcock and Loewenstein 2000: 366.
[27] References and more details above 2.2.7.
[28] Brehm 1966; Brehm and Brehm 1981; Donnell et al. 2001.

Alter's intention and reacting aggressively.[29] Finally, the predictability problem makes interaction risky. If Ego perceives it that way, the peculiarities of risk behaviour become relevant. Specifically, it is likely that Ego will overestimate this risk and shy away from co-operation, even if the expected value of taking the risk is clearly positive.[30]

5.2   Behavioural strengths of Egos

Sometimes, Ego is systematically more rational than Alter. In that case, adopting a behaviourally informed perspective matters less (5.2.1). The more important effect, however, comes from the totally opposite direction. If individuals partly or even entirely neglect normative rationality and take recourse in other mental tools, not so rarely, they even perform better than they would if they acted rationally (5.2.2).

5.2.1   Higher degree of rationality

Sometimes, Ego is better positioned to fulfil the rational choice requirements than Alter. This is particularly likely if Ego is not forced to co-operate with a certain person. He then can privilege some persons and thereby exploit a selection effect. He can also specialise in solving the predictability problem – for instance, since he frequently interacts with one specific person, or with persons who share a certain background. In particular, greater experience might be helpful for finding and assessing signals for predictability and for certain behavioural traits.[31]

5.2.2   Better than rational

For a devoted rationalist, this section heading will sound like provocation. But it is true: in some contexts, by deliberately eschewing attempts at rational reasoning, and using routines or heuristics instead, people perform even better than they would if they acted rationally.[32] This is a result of the fact that most human behavioural dispositions are made for a fundamentally uncertain world.[33] In such an environment, abstraction and calculation are not always the best policy. It is at least as

---

[29] Babcock and Loewenstein 2000: 356.
[30] On decisions under risk, see above 2.2.10.
[31] On signalling, see above 3.2.5.
[32] This is the basic claim of Gigerenzer et al. 1999; the term 'better than rational' originates in Cosmides and Tooby 1994.
[33] For a systematic (and very elegant) model of different worldviews, see Thompson et al. 1990.

important to differentiate important from negligible information, to exploit subtle nuances and to feel comfortable about decisions taken on shaky grounds. Humans are remarkably good at all of these things.[34] The statement holds both for assessment and for action. Humans have a powerful cheater detection mechanism. It exploits subtle, often unspoken information to generate a feeling that an actor behaves in an unusual, suspicious way.[35] Moreover, human behavioural programmes are also particularly well adapted to co-operation tasks. If cheating is perceived, emotionally high-powered punishing sentiments intervene.[36]

Moreover, developing routines is a general human ability. People can rely on this ability to develop interaction routines, be it with one specific actor, or with a whole class of them.[37] If one wants to understand why parsimonious mental tools can perform almost as well as formal rationality, if not better, the most important explanatory factor is context.[38] The secret thus is that these mental tools are 'ecological'.[39] This is helpful, because the human mind is not only a machine for abstract reasoning. It also offers a vast knowledge base.[40] This is particularly helpful when the individual is called upon to make judgements in an uncertain environment. This, for instance, allows individuals to recognise behavioural patterns quickly if they only see a few characteristic elements.[41]

5.3   Fully behaviourally informed institutions

From the foregoing, the following implications for institutional design can be derived. Designers can aim at coping with the behavioural weaknesses of both Alter and Ego (5.3.1). They can, on the contrary, try to exploit the behavioural strengths of Ego (5.3.2). Moreover, all this casts new light on the possibility of changing the character of the task (5.3.3).

5.3.1   Coping with behavioural weaknesses

If one believes in the idea that people can be even better off acting nonrationally than acting rationally, it does not seem very promising to

---

[34] Again, the most comprehensive account is Gigerenzer et al. 1999.
[35] Cosmides and Tooby 1989; Cosmides and Tooby 1992: 193–205; but see Lawson 2002.
[36] Fehr 2000; Price et al. 2002.
[37] On expertisation as the source of routine building, see Anderson 2000b: chapter 9.
[38] For a basic treatment see Brunswik et al. 2001.
[39] Gigerenzer et al. 1999: 5.
[40] Anderson 2000b: 346 and *passim*; Anderson and Lebiere 2003: part 2.4.
[41] Cf. Bone et al. 1999: 76 and *passim*.

repair behavioural weaknesses. Yet not all of the behavioural deviations from rational choice are actually beneficial for the individual. They may in particular be adapted to contexts that have changed over time. Moreover, the remarkably good performance of interaction routines and heuristics is dependent on the ability of Ego to exploit features from his context. Ego cannot tap that capacity in every situation. He may be newly arrived in a community. The context in which he has chosen to live may be liable to frequent changes. If so, Ego may not have enough time to acquire appropriate skills by routinisation, or to generate the knowledge base needed to use heuristics effectively. Even where all this would in principle be possible, the individual or society may not deem it desirable. For the normative implication is that social stability has a high value. In the interest of generating higher welfare, societies may prefer deliberately to allow for more complexity and change.

In principle, the behavioural weaknesses of Ego have the same sources as the low predictability of Alter. Accordingly, the same institutions are in principle able to address these weaknesses. They can aim at improving Ego's attention by making features from the environment salient. By changing the way a situation is represented, they can help Ego better perceive the situation. They can be ad hoc; they can use learning; or they can even try to have an impact on development. They can offer or even impose training on Ego. They can enable or oblige him to rely on an intermediary. They can induce or impose communication. They can change the context and embed the interaction in it, and so forth.[42] Where openness to rapid and unexpected changes in the environment is less important, institutions might also purport to generate routines or even to automatise Ego's behaviour. They can use professionalisation or group membership for the purpose. They can strive to pattern behaviour. And they can have Ego develop the appropriate heuristics.[43] The last would also help overcome the most dramatic stumbling block on the road towards successful co-operation: the vexing complexity of rationally treating Alter's irrationalities.[44]

5.3.2   *Exploiting behavioural strengths*

The opposite strategy does not seek remedies to behavioural weaknesses; it emphasises behavioural strengths, instead. Actually, the difference between both strategies is much smaller than one might expect. For exploiting behavioural strengths by designed intervention is not the same

---

[42] For all these and many more options, see above 4.3.
[43] More above 4.3.12(b)–(c).   [44] See above 5.1.3(c).

as just relying on the human ability to handle problems of co-operation successfully. In many practical instances, the difference is virtually a matter of rhetoric. One and the same intervention can be interpreted as a tool for overcoming a behavioural limitation, or as a tool for exploiting a behavioural strength. That is particularly true for inducing or imposing interaction routines and heuristics. An example would consist of teaching Ego to read more effectively the cultural signals sent out by Alter, be that inadvertently or even purposefully. Helping Ego to professionalise in order to solve some kinds of co-ordination problems comes under the same heading.[45] Honing the cheat detection mechanism is another possibility, as is customising punitive sentiments.[46]

5.3.3 Changing the character of the task

Changing the character of the task such that the predictability problem no longer matters already makes sense from a pure rational choice perspective.[47] It becomes even more attractive if one drops the rationality assumption with respect to Alter.[48] When presenting the latter, a distinction was made between a change in Alter's task and a change in Ego's task. The latter becomes even more compelling in a fully behaviourally informed perspective. As demonstrated, the two options are insurance and a risk premium. In the rational choice part of this book, it has been shown that they differ not only with respect to the distribution effect, but also from a welfare perspective. On both accounts, insurance is preferable.[49] In accord with a behavioural perspective, one more reason can be added. A premium is paid for Ego's willingness deliberately to take a risk. Insurance, however, psychologically neutralises the risk. Since Ego knows that he is indemnified, should the risk materialise, he subjectively need no longer decide under conditions of risk. All the behavioural intricacies inherent in risky choice[50] are overcome.

5.4   Summary

Omniscience is, alas, not part of man's natural endowment. When he chooses how best to respond to Alter's unpredictability, Ego is therefore well advised also to take his own behavioural dispositions into account.

---

[45] Cf. Fox and Tversky 2000: 530: ambiguity aversion disappears in contexts of personal expertise.
[46] For references, see above 5.2.2.   [47] See above 3.4–6.
[48] See above 4.4.   [49] See above 3.5–6.   [50] See above 2.2.10.

Compared with the benchmark of rationality, his reactions may therefore be more modest. In particular, Ego will usually be unable meticulously to perform the cost–benefit calculations suggested in the rational choice part of this book once there is a multitude of potential reasons for unpredictability. However, rationality is not necessarily the most appropriate benchmark for reacting to Alter's limited predictability. There is reason to believe that the human mind is made not for a certain, but for an uncertain world. Part of this uncertainty is the unpredictability of others. When it comes to designing institutions that help Ego cope with Alter's unpredictability, both these insights should be taken into account.

6   Outlook: implications for interaction with higher complexity

The reader who has been willing to read this far in the book will not have retained a view of low complexity. The rational choice part, despite the rigorous simplification of the model, had to rely on mathematics to handle the remaining degree of complexity. The more psychologically inspired chapters gave an account of the universe of findings that are relevant for assessing and containing the predictability risk. And still all this is extremely simplified. The whole book only looks at one class of situations: one informed actor and one uninformed actor have one single opportunity for co-operation. Alter knows everything he wants to about Ego. Only Ego is unable fully to predict Alter's future behaviour. Such situations exist often enough in life. A newly accepted member of a group who interacts with one of the regulars offers one possible example. If the regular follows most of the routine characteristics of the group, Alter may be able to predict Ego's behaviour reasonably well. But Ego may have a much harder time predicting Alter's behaviour. But many situations in life are different. Most of them are inherently more complex.

The predictability problem in situations of higher complexity can in principle also be analysed based on the findings and the structure of this book. This chapter aims to illustrate this potential. But it does so with broad-brush sketches only. There are two reasons for this moderate approach. One is subjective. The book would otherwise have grown out of all proportion. But there is also an objective reason. In this book, it has not been possible to document all psychological effects equally well. But it has nonetheless been possible to collect a fair number of well-established findings for the purpose. Doing the same for situations of higher complexity would sometimes be just impossible. In other instances, the psychological evidence is at least much less developed than for the standard case.

Reciprocal unpredictability. In reality, the predictability problem is often not unilateral. There is not only one co-ordination partner who is not fully predictable to the other. Often the problem is reciprocal. Both partners are to some degree hard for the other to predict. In rational choice terms, this makes an important difference. If the predictability risk is identical on both sides,[1] the game between the partners becomes symmetrical. To deal with this, the whole game theoretic analysis would have to be done anew. If those interacting decided unilaterally, the sequence of moves would become crucial. But because of reciprocity, the opportunities for a deal would improve. Full symmetry will, however, be rare in reality. If the remaining asymmetry is common knowledge, most of the rational choice analysis remains close to what was presented above.

In a behavioural perspective, perception would become crucial. Will the partners see the reciprocity at all? This places high demands on their cognitive abilities. For the reciprocity is not at the ground level, so to speak. It concerns not the exchange of goods and services, but the degree of unpredictability inherent in the deal. Put differently: will each partner just focus on the predictability problem inherent in the other, or will he see both predictability problems as bargaining chips? Yet another way of making the point is: will predictability itself become part of the trade, or will it instil a conflictual element into a trading relationship? Will the punitive sentiments thus cancel out and result in some kind of stalemate? Will they be successfully backed up by mutual cheat detection? Even if both sides consciously experience the mutual predictability risk, will they assess it with conflicting fairness norms? Finally, in rational choice terms, the beneficial effect of reciprocity hinges upon the mutual predictability risk being sufficiently equal. Even if that is the case in terms of subjective expected utility, will the psychological assessment be the same? If not, what looks well balanced in rational choice terms may still turn out to be conflictual from a behavioural perspective.

Repeated interaction. Repeated interaction has been demonstrated to serve as a solution to the predictability problem.[2] In reality, interaction is often naturally repeated. There is thus no need for the parties artificially to commit to repetition. Even if repetition is not certain, one often cannot be sure that interaction will not be repeated. That naturally generates what is known as the shadow of the future. A rational actor will then take account of the detrimental effect that defection might have

---

[1] Specifically, in the neoclassical world, the risk would have to be equally important for each co-operation partner subjectively. Since their *ex ante* endowments and their utility functions can differ, neither the expected damage nor the probability must therefore be the same. What matters is how the risk fares, relative to the *ex ante* position of the respective actor.

[2] See above 3.3.2(e).

on future gains. Depending on the character of the base game, the effect need not be beneficial, however. A well-researched example is competition in a narrow oligopoly. Here, developing a reputation as a tough fighter can individually be very valuable. It thus can pay for a party to be overly aggressive in the first rounds of an encounter, even if that means losing money in the short term.[3]

In accord with a behavioural perspective, a cognitive dimension is to be added. As a result of frequent exposure, Ego may build a larger knowledge base for reading signals about Alter's predictability. Even if he is not able to make that explicit, he may gain implicit knowledge by interacting with this very actor. A second cognitive consideration is framing. Will Ego actually consider each instance of interaction in isolation, or will he look at the whole, long-term relationship with Alter? This might, for instance, matter when judging fairness, and when deciding how to react to Alter's occasional deviations from what he was expected to do. A related point is editing. Will Ego consider utility from this relationship as a stream of income over time, or will he compare each instance with other opportunities for making money at about the same point of time? This difference in framing has been demonstrated to be responsible for a profound difference in evaluation. If Ego looks at the whole stream of income, then the tendency to discount future benefits will at least be reduced, if it does not vanish altogether.[4] The more frequently Ego interacts with Alter, the less likely it is that he will recalculate his action each and every time. It thus becomes probable that this specific interaction itself will become the object of skill acquisition. This can result in a relation-specific interaction routine. This routine, in return, might help standardise the interaction itself. This would be good news for those interested in reducing the predictability problem. For Ego would no longer have to base his assessment of the predictability risk exclusively on Alter's personality. Because of the interaction pattern, the situation would also have partly been standardised. If the routine is not automatic, enough flexibility would be left to enable Ego to react to surprising changes in either the situation or Alter's behaviour.

In accord with a behavioural perspective, repetition is, however, not always a good thing. Actually, in practice everybody has experienced a conflictual long-term relationship.[5] The parties fight tooth and nail, even if that is to their mutual detriment. There are many explanations for this.

---

[3] More from Tirole 1988: 323–52; see also Jickeli 1990: 63–100.
[4] Thaler 1999: 199–200.
[5] For background, see Farnsworth 2000; see also Engel 2003a.

One possibility is the presence of emotions like envy, spite or anger. More specifically, conflict can originate, and then become chronic, as a result of divergent fairness norms. Ego may have perceived earlier defection not only as a utility loss, but as a long-lasting violation of self-esteem. Finally, the parties may develop not only beneficial interaction routines, but also detrimental ones. They may thus get stuck in a pattern of hostile interaction.

Group of informed actors. In reality, Alter is often part of a more or less densely knit group. The more uniform this group is, the better Ego is at predicting Alter's behaviour. In this case, differences across individuals become a crucial concern.[6] Moreover, the bad behaviour of one member of the group has repercussions on other members. Ego will take each individual instance as an opportunity to learn, and he may well shy away from the whole group if he has had too many bad experiences. The effect is even stronger if the group makes it an explicit policy to guarantee that group members will follow certain behavioural standards when interacting with outsiders. In that case the group proactively builds a reputation regarding interaction. Finally, in accord with a rational choice perspective, Ego's problem becomes much easier if he only cares about aggregate outcome. In that case, individual deviations do not matter, as long as interacting with this group remains profitable in the aggregate. Ego is also better off if it is not necessary for him to interact with one given member of the group. If what he cares about is just interaction with one or some members of the group, he can try to improve his situation by selection. He can even impose some sort of competition on group members for this purpose.

In accord with a behavioural perspective, interacting with members of a group is also advantageous. Some of the effects are on Ego. With sufficient experience, he may develop a heuristic that interacting with members of some groups is safe in terms of predictability. Interacting with members of other groups, however, may make the predictability risk highly salient to Ego. The potential impact of the group on its members' predictability is even more important. Groups are powerful agents for socialisation. Members learn interaction routines not only for intra-group behaviour, but also for the interaction with outsiders. Groups are able to frame such interaction. They can instil beneficial stereotypes, schemata, attitudes and mental models in their members. They can even openly impose interaction norms on them. This, for instance, allows them to standardise fairness norms. Group members

---

[6] See above 2.5.4.

are typically motivated to take all of this into consideration. This is not only because of the utility derived from being a member of the group. Individuals also belong to groups because this serves as an additional source of esteem. If they violate group norms, they are likely to lose esteem, if not to be expelled from the group.

There is, however, a downside. Group psychology has long demonstrated the potentially detrimental effects of group dynamics.[7] An individually irrational, conflictual relationship becomes particularly likely if Alter perceives Ego not as an isolated individual, but as a member of an opposing group.[8]

Government as uninformed actor. The relationship between government and the citizenry is typically a special case of Ego interacting with a group of actors. This is because of the fact that democratic constitutions do not want sovereign intervention to be ad hoc. If government is to encroach upon individual freedom or property, it needs a statute allowing it to do so. This statute formulates abstract conditions under which the encroachment is allowed. It thereby generates a group of actors. Not so rarely, statutes target groups that have formed independently in society. But many groups of addressees are tied together by nothing more than a statutory provision. Government can engage in two-level governance and impose some form of corporatisation, in the interest of exploiting this artificially created coherence later. In all these cases, government can use group membership as a tool, and it must be prepared for group dynamics, as a private interaction partner would be. If government does none of this, however, addressing a group of actors only matters in two respects. Government officials may collect experiences related to interactions with this kind of actor. This can result in an informational advantage, e.g. by exploiting signals. And government officials can themselves develop interaction routines and heuristics for this specific task.

Legally speaking, government is just one person. The legal order attaches legal personality to it. Political scientists also sometimes refer to government as one actor. They then treat government as a special instance of a corporate actor.[9] Speaking about corporate actors makes sense if a unit behaves in some unified way, which is not just an aggregate of its members' behaviour. Organisation, procedure, internal discourse and external attribution endow the corporate actor with something like

---

[7] For overviews, see Sedikides et al. 1998; Takacs 2001; Sunstein 2002; Baron and Kerr 2003.
[8] On in-group/out-group effects, see e.g. Hopkins and Murdoch 1999.
[9] On this concept, see Coleman 1990: chapters 13, 20, 21; Scharpf 1997: 54–8.

an autonomous identity.[10] How many of the findings about individual behaviour carry over to the behaviour of corporate actors is still very much an open question.[11] Even less is known about governmental behaviour. This knowledge would be important for an understanding of how government behaves if it assumes the role of the uninformed interaction partner.

The question also has a normative component. If Ego uses intrusive methods to generate knowledge about Alter's personality, the legal order may occasionally intervene. In extreme cases, it may even want to prevent Alter from offering such intrusions himself. But basically, it is for Ego and Alter to decide autonomously what they think is appropriate to solve the predictability problem. Government, however, is endowed with sovereign powers. This explains why all constitutional states limit government activity much more than they limit the equivalent action of citizens. This may prevent government from gaining access to technologies that citizens would be able to use to relieve the predictability problem. In most countries, government is, for instance, not allowed to use a lie detector in court or in administrative procedure.[12] If the issue were not of vital social importance, in democratic countries government would not be allowed to send its citizens to training camps. Neither would governmental brainwashing be acceptable. Such limitations do not only reflect constitutional respect for the dignity of citizens. They are also motivated by an interest in the democratic control of government. In particular, government is not to be allowed to reshape the electorate's attitudes such that it becomes easier to win the next election.[13]

Class of uninformed actors. Often, Ego does not interact with one actor in isolation. If interaction is sufficiently standardised, Ego can be part of a class. This obviously makes efforts to generate higher predictability more valuable. The settlement range with Alter should increase. The class of uninformed actors should be willing to spend more money than an individual actor on bringing predictability about. Yet unfortunately, the distribution problem analysed above for the relationship between Ego and a beneficial Alter then also arises for the uninformed actors' group. Each individual actor is best off if the other members of the class

---

[10] How this can happen in a state is the object of integration theory; for a lucid account, see Smend 1968.

[11] From the growing literature, see in particular Simon 1976; Cohen and Sproull 1995; Messick and Liebrand 1995; Messick et al. 1997; Zhou 1997; Thompson et al. 1999; Kahneman and Lovallo 2000; Langevoort 2000.

[12] Actually the German *Bundesgerichtshof* based this decision on psychological evidence from Fiedler et al. 2002.

[13] More on democratic concerns from Lüdemann 2004.

bear the costs for making behaviour more predictable. If they are successful, the first uninformed actor can free ride, taking advantage of their
efforts.[14] Another way of making the point within rational choice theory
is: the effort to make Alter's behaviour more predictable is a public good,
belonging to all members of the group of uninformed actors.[15] This way
of modelling the problem also brings an important implication to light. A
good is only a public good if it can be appropriated by outsiders. Non-
excludability results from the absence of sufficiently powerful property
rights.[16] The problem disappears if individual uninformed actors succeed in protecting their effort to generate predictability against appropriation. One way of doing this consists simply of keeping this effort
confidential. This, however, only works if Alter co-operates, which is not
in his interest. For if he alerts other uninformed actors to the efforts
of the first, Alter increases his opportunities for successful co-operation.
A more robust possibility consists of adding a sufficiently important
element of specificity to the relationship with an individual uninformed
actor.

In a behavioural perspective, it is less important that the uninformed
actors form a class. Of course, this class may be united by more than
occasional interaction with one and the same informed actor. In this
case, all the group phenomena listed above might well hold for uninformed actors as well. But these phenomena are much less important
here, as long as the predictability problem remains asymmetric. For if
the informed actors form a group, this in and of itself can generate higher
predictability. If the uninformed actors group together, however, that
might only help them to overcome the behavioural limitations involved
in treating a predictability risk. Being a member of that group may, for
instance, help them learn appropriate heuristics or interaction routines.
On a second level, however, forming a proper group can be helpful. For
within a group, overcoming the public goods problem just described can
be easier. For instance, the group may be able to impose an equal or an
otherwise fair contribution on each and every member. A group may also
make an opportunity available for cross-issue trade. If that happens, all
uninformed actors would have to contribute some effort or some payment to the group's budget. The group would, in return, increase
predictability for a whole array of informed actors.

Chance interaction partner. As thorny as it may appear, the bilateral
predictability problem investigated so far still has a comforting element

---

[14] See above 3.3.3(b).
[15] For a basic account of public goods theory see Cornes and Sandler 1996.
[16] More on property rights theory from Eggertsson 1990.

for Ego. He is not forced to co-operate. If he is unable to increase predictability and is risk averse, he can still defect. He then retains his outside option of zero, meaning that he is not worse off than before. Reality is often not that generous. Not so rarely, uninformed actors are forced to co-operate. The classic situation is what lawyers call torts. One potential intruder imposes some form of interaction. All that Ego is able to do is avoid a class of situations altogether. The same effect results from voluntary agreement, if implementation remains uncertain. In such a situation, Alter can still unilaterally make his behaviour more predictable. But this is only rational for him if he otherwise must be afraid that a whole class of uninformed actors will evade contact. Ego himself cannot directly generate higher predictability, nor can Ego and Alter jointly. The possibilities for voluntarily bringing a third party in are also limited. Alter can do so unilaterally. An individual uninformed actor can only entrust the third party with precautionary measures, like the supervision of a whole class of potential informed actors. Accordingly, the choice of institutional designers and, consequently, of institutions is severely restricted.

Put differently, if Ego is not defined *ex ante*, sovereign intervention becomes a very attractive option. Government can basically do two things. It can artificially narrow down contact, be it with respect to persons or situations. In the first instance, an uninformed actor can be certain not to meet informed actors of some kind. In the second case, Ego can be certain not to be exposed to a class of informed actors if he stays away from well-defined situations. The second governmental option directly affects the behaviour of informed actors. This is what tort law does, as well as many public law codes. Since uninformed actors have no chance to avoid contact, informed actors are forced to behave in some predictable way whenever they take action. They, for instance, may drive a car. But they are not allowed to drive on the wrong side of the street, to drive under the influence of alcohol, or to exceed speed limits. Obviously, the predictability effect of such rules decisively hinges upon implementation.[17]

Again, the incentive problems inherent when an informed actor hits upon a chance uninformed actor are dominant. But since not only behaviour, but also the partner is unpredictable, many of the behaviourally informed responses do not work in this context either. Put differently, they only work if and when they also remedy the incentive problem. This is, for instance, the case if professionalisation or corporatisation make Alter more predictable. For this then generates signals

---

[17] On the pervasive problem of an implementation deficit, see Winter 1975; Mayntz 1980, 1983; Windhoff-Héritier 1980.

that are discernible for everybody, at least for every long-term member of a society. One additional element is worth mentioning. If interaction is random, creating generalised trust in a population becomes crucial.[18]

Intrinsic value of predictability. Finally, Alter may have reasons, other than the desire to secure gains from trade, for making his behaviour more predictable. Predictability can thus have intrinsic value for Alter.[19] There are many potential reasons for this. Alter may be concerned not only about the present, but also about future utility, and he may therefore dislike time inconsistency.[20] This would also allow Alter to extend his own planning horizon. He may have experienced, or learned from psychological studies, that individuals are poor predictors of their own future happiness.[21] Alter may expect that he will not be able to resist temptation or addiction, even if that makes him unpredictable. In that case, the classic Ulysses problem comes up.[22] For the individual, becoming more predictable may be tied to self-esteem, or it can result from a sense of social responsibility. Finally, being predictable can be a source of mental comfort to the individual.[23]

If any of these scenarios holds, Alter has an interest in self-paternalism. In practice, this is not a rare phenomenon. People take money to a Christmas savings club that promises, against a charge, not to pay it back before December, regardless of the circumstances.[24] They use stylised commitment technology to limit partially the options available to them in the future.[25] They sign on to Alcoholics Anonymous.[26] Or they even make themselves artificially vulnerable, should they later break their own commitment. For instance, a Denver drug clinic invited patients to write a letter that would do them considerable harm if it got into the wrong hands. The patient entitles the clinic to send the letter out if he actually takes drugs again.[27]

---

[18] For background see Cook 2001; Hardin 2001; Bicchieri et al. 2002; Hardin 2002; McEvily et al. 2002. The question played a particular role in understanding the impact of the Internet on society; see Camp 2000; Bornschier 2001.

[19] Heiner 1983: 573–4.

[20] Thaler and Shefrin 1981.

[21] Kahneman and Snell 1997: in particular 408; see also Loewenstein and Adler 2000: in particular 728–33.

[22] Elster 1979; Heiner 1983: 573–4 links it to predictability.

[23] In the words of Gehlen 1960: 71: 'auf der anderen Seite orientieren sich die Menschen in ihnen [sc.: den Institutionen] zu endgültigen Bestimmtheiten des Tuns und Lassens, mit dem außerordentlichen Gewinn einer Stabilisierung auch des Innenlebens, so daß sie nicht bei jeder Gelegenheit sich affektiv auseinanderzusetzen oder Grundsatzentscheidungen sich abzuzwingen haben'.

[24] Thaler 2000: 283–5.

[25] Laibson 1997: 446.

[26] Sunstein and Ullmann-Margalit 2000: 200.

[27] This and many more examples are reported by Schelling 1984.

Technically, Alter is not the only potential paternalistic institutional designer. Such institutions can also be imposed on Alter by sovereign rulers, be they government or some private regulator. This, however, is normatively a much more demanding situation. Some lawyers interested in behavioural analysis have called for 'anti-anti-paternalism'.[28] But there is obvious reason to be cautious.[29]

---

[28] Sunstein 2000c: 2–3; in the same vein Korobkin and Ulen 2000: 1123 and *passim*.
[29] Rachlinski 2003.

7 Predictability at the crossroads of competing institutionalisms

This has been a book on substance, not on methodology, or on the history of the social sciences. Yet it cannot but make a contribution to the long-standing dispute among institutionalists over the appropriate paradigm.[1] All the many strands of institutionalism are united by their conviction that institutions matter. But they are fiercely divided when it comes to defining institutions, to forging conceptual tools and to drawing normative conclusions. This book cuts across many of the dividing lines. Predictability turns out to be an issue for most strands of institutional thinking. This book demonstrates that it makes sense to combine tools and insights from many institutionalisms,[2] and that this can be done in a methodologically controlled way. Paradigmatically, it shows how, for institutionalists, the interaction with their conceptual competitors can bear fruit.[3]

This is not the place to write yet another summary report on institutionalism.[4] Suffice it to remind the reader of the major catchwords. The most popular typology distinguishes between rational choice, socio-logical and historical institutionalism,[5] to which sometimes an empirical, an international and a societal strand are added.[6] Others prefer a less disciplinary, and a more methodology-driven classification. They distinguish a rational-choice, a social-constructivist and a 'mediated-conflict' version of institutionalism.[7] There is also an uneven willingness to see

---

[1] I am grateful to Margaret McCown for suggesting this epilogue.
[2] This is also claimed by DiMaggio and Powell 1991: 27; Rutherford 1994: 173–81; Hall and Taylor 1996: 955; DiMaggio 1998: 699; Hodgson 1998: 189.
[3] In so doing, it resembles the approach of Sweet 1999: in particular 178–81, albeit for an entirely different issue.
[4] The prime sources are DiMaggio and Powell 1991; Rutherford 1994; Hall and Taylor 1996; DiMaggio 1998; Hodgson 1998; Nee 1998; Peters 1999; Mantzavinos 2001.
[5] It has been introduced by Hall and Taylor 1996; it is also to be found in Immergut 1998: 5 – although this paper is the strongest outlier with respect to classification.
[6] Peters 1999: 19–20 and *passim*.
[7] DiMaggio 1998: 696–7.

the respective 'old institutionalism' as a predecessor:[8] some view it as an adversary, instead.[9]

Some strands of institutionalist thinking have little, if anything, to do with the topic of this book. For instance, Ellen Immergut defines institutionalism by three claims: observed behaviour is not necessarily a translation of 'real preferences'; the aggregation of individual behaviour into collective decisions is problematic; consequently, utilitarianism is no acceptable normative standard.[10] Other institutionalists make claims that seem too strong from the perspective of this book. For instance, Paul DiMaggio holds that institutionalists are tied together by anti-individualism.[11] But most of the richness in conceptualising institutions is helpful, if not necessary, for understanding the role of institutions in generating predictability.

This claim is endorsed by the fact that many institutionalist schools explicitly address predictability. Guy Peters says: 'All the versions of institutionalism argue that institutions create greater regularities in human behaviour than would be otherwise found. At a practical level, institutions do have the capacity to mould individual behaviour and to reduce (but not eliminate) the uncertainty that otherwise dominates much of social life.'[12] Peter Hall and Rosemary Taylor state: 'Both the "calculus" and "cultural" approaches to the relationship between institutions and action observe that institutions affect action by structuring expectations about what others will do.'[13] Victor Nee remarks: 'Institutions reduce uncertainty in human relations. They specify the limits of legitimate action in the way that the rules of the game specify the structure within which players are free to pursue their strategic moves using pieces that have specific roles and status positions.'[14] Ludwig Lachmann is convinced: 'What is particularly required in order to successfully co-ordinate the transactions of millions of people is the existence of institutions. In these institutions, an objectification is achieved for us of the million actions of our fellow men whose plans, objectives,

---

[8] This is most pronounced in Hodgson 1988, 1998, with respect to 'old' economic institutionalism; see also Rutherford 1994 and Mantzavinos 2001.

[9] This is how many political scientists interested in institutions feel; see the overview presented by Peters 1999: 6–9; see also Nee 1998: 1 on 'old' sociological institutionalism.

[10] Immergut 1998: 6–8.

[11] DiMaggio 1998: 696, 699 and *passim*; cf. also Hodgson 1998: 176: 'the explanatory movement is from individuals to institutions, taking individuals as given'; Peters 1999: 141: 'the most fundamental point is that scholars can achieve greater analytical leverage by beginning with institutions rather than with individuals'.

[12] Peters 1999: 141; see also 144, 30 (on routines).

[13] Hall and Taylor 1996: 955; see also 939.

[14] Nee 1998: 8.

and motives are impossible for us to know.'[15] Finally, in the words of Chrysostomos Mantzavinos: 'The institutions, as the rules of the game, stabilise expectations and thus reduce the uncertainty of the agents.'[16]

The deepest divide between institutionalists is methodological. 'New institutional economists' typically are methodological individualists,[17] as are partisans of rational choice analysis in political science[18] and in sociological institutionalism.[19] Pure methodological holists are rare in today's institutionalism.[20] But many institutionalists feel that structure is more important than agency.[21] They insist that, in individual life, institutions come earlier than preferences. Each individual is born into a context that has been heavily shaped by institutions, and in response to which the individual develops his identity.[22] They often also hold that institutions cannot be properly understood without looking at social construction.[23] This book starts with methodological individualism. The psychological part, i.e. chapter 2, is written as the description of a problem for Ego, not as a treatise on the social influences on preference formation. Chapter 3 offers a pure rational choice analysis. But both of these chapters demonstrate that isolated individuals in an institution-free environment would be unable to interact in a meaningful way. Chapters 2 and 3 can therefore also be read as a thought experiment. In a seriously individualistic world, gains from trade are not to be had. It is in the best interest of thorough individualists to allow society to restrict them by developing fairly complex institutional arrangements. This normative insight has its methodological ramifications. At least some of the richer institutional arrangements presented in chapters 4 and 5 are hard to reconstruct in rational choice terms. One needs a methodology that can capture their genuinely social character. This is particularly true for institutions that aim at giving meaning to a complex environment.

The second divide between institutionalists is primarily one of scope, and only secondarily one of method. Rational choice models assume all context away. They are ahistoric. In principle, the same would be

---

[15] Lachmann 1963: 63; I owe this translation to Mantzavinos 2001: 89 note 9.
[16] Mantzavinos 2001: 89; see also 87.
[17] More from Rutherford 1994: 27–50.
[18] More from Hall and Taylor 1996: 945.
[19] Nee 1998; see also Coleman 1990 .
[20] Nee 1998: 3–5 goes back to Emile Durkheim for the purpose.
[21] A summary report of the structure–agency debate is provided by Dessler 1989; on the impact of this distinction for institutionalism, see e.g. Peters 1999: 142–4, Hodgson 1998: 181, 184, 189.
[22] Hodgson 1998: 172.
[23] For a characteristic treatment, see Meyer and Scott 1983; White 1995.

possible for a holistic methodology (and it is indeed characteristic for systems theory).[24] But typically, those interested in explaining institutions from a societal perspective are also willing to take at least some more context on board.[25] They insist that new institutions are created in a world already replete with institutions.[26] Later policy choices may be able to change this path, but only at a rather substantial political cost.[27] The same holds for old, as opposed to new economic institutionalists[28] and, of course, for historical institutionalists in political science.[29] Openness to context does not determine methodology. One need not have recourse to radical opponents of parsimonious modelling, like thick description,[30] for the purpose. There are even attempts at introducing a dynamic or an evolutionary dimension into rational choice modelling.[31] This book addresses contextuality in two steps. It starts out with a context-free, rational choice model. But it demonstrates that, in such an environment, generating predictability would become an insurmountable problem for the actors. Context thus turns out to be key to the solution, not a further complication of the problem.

A third divide is generated by the relative weight of free will. It is absolute in rational choice institutionalism, at least as used by economists. Rational choice sociologists would rather speak of choice within constraints,[32] or of 'context bound rationality'.[33] Other institutionalists stress that institutions do not only have motivational effects. If their effect is more on the cognitive side, they tend to shape what actors take for granted.[34] This effect is typically stressed by the 'cultural', as opposed to the 'calculus' approach in institutionalism.[35] In economic institutionalism, a related divide is often described by the opposition between rationality and rule following.[36] In this respect too, this book

---

[24] For a brief introduction see Luhmann 1986.
[25] For a characteristic, see Peters 1999: 47.
[26] Hall and Taylor 1996: 953; see also DiMaggio and Powell 1991: 10.
[27] Peters 1999: 63.
[28] Hodgson 1998: 176–7, 182–3; see also Denzau and North 1994: 15: 'we may think of culture as encapsulating the experiences of past generations'.
[29] The name-giving book was Steinmo 1992; for summary reports, see Peters 1999: 63–77 and Immergut 1998: 16–25; and see DiMaggio 1998: 697.
[30] Geertz 1973.
[31] Classic sources are Maynard Smith 1982; Axelrod 1984; for a recent summary report, see McKenzie Alexander 2003.
[32] Nee 1998: 4.
[33] Boudon 1987: 64.
[34] DiMaggio and Powell 1991: 10–11; Hall and Taylor 1996: 940.
[35] Hall and Taylor 1996: 939; see also 948.
[36] Rutherford 1994: 51–80.

holds an intermediate position. In the rational choice part, i.e. chapter 3, of course, standard rationality assumptions are made. Chapters 4 and 5 also allow for conscious and deliberate decision-making and judgement. But this is qualified in two respects. Deliberate decision-making significantly deviates from rational choice assumptions. It is seen as typically being either narrative reasoning or reason-based choice.[37] And it is pointed out that humans possess many more decision modes, and that, with respect to the predictability problem, the choice between these modes matters for institutional analysis and design. Specifically, this book stresses the importance of routines and professionalisation. In the institutionalist discussion, both of them are typically addressed in the sociological and historical camps.[38] Even more important is a general finding from institutional phenomenology: very often, predictability is provided by entire institutional arrangements, not by isolated institutional acts of intervention. Now it is next to impossible to introduce a richer institutional arrangement on the spot. Even if all its constituent parts were introduced by purposive design one day, it would only be possible to understand the final specification of the arrangement properly if one were to accept the institution, as such, as an independent causal factor.[39]

Related to this is a fourth divide. While some institutionalists focus on design, others feel that it is more appropriate to study the evolution of institutions. The former is, of course, characteristic for rational choice institutionalism,[40] whereas the latter is more prominent in the sociological and historical schools.[41] As with previous issues, this book tries to strike a balance. It is written by a lawyer, who has been trained to think normatively and thus in categories of institutional design. But it finds that more often than not only entire institutional arrangements are functional. As pointed out, such arrangements cannot be designed on the spot. This implies a pretty high level of evolution, which is not now, or at least not entirely, open to redesign.[42]

---

[37] More above 2.2.9.

[38] See e.g. March and Olsen 1989: 21–26; DiMaggio and Powell 1991: 13, 22; Hall and Taylor 1996: 939.

[39] A similar position is to be found in DiMaggio and Powell 1991: 9; Hall and Taylor 1996: 940; Peters 1999: 141 speaks of 'the fundamental paradox . . . about institutions being formed by human agents but constraining those same actors'.

[40] Peters 1999: 45.

[41] More from Rutherford 1994: 80–128.

[42] Cf. Hall and Taylor 1996: 939: 'without denying that human behaviour is rational or purposive, it [sc: sociological institutionalism] emphasises the extent to which individuals turn to established routines or familiar patterns of behaviour to attain their purposes'.

A minor, fifth divide concerns a matter of style, or language, if you wish. In economics, the quickest way to tell 'old' from 'new' institutionalist work is in reference to mathematics. Old institutionalists decisively avoided the formalisation of economics, whereas new institutionalists are at least open to it, even if they do not proudly boast their mathematical skills.[43] Once more, this book sees value in both approaches. The rational choice part, chapter 3, is (mildly) formal, since this seems both to allow more precision and to make it easier to transmit the message. But handling all the complexity inherent in the psychological findings presented in chapter 2 by way of formal analysis would be mind-boggling. More importantly, it would generate the false impression that rigorous precision is able to capture the essence of the institutional arrangements that generate predictability.

The final divide between at least some of the institutionalist schools is normative. Specifically, new institutionalists in economics tend to believe in markets, whereas their predecessors were highly sceptical.[44] In this respect too, this book is open. In the rational choice part, it seriously investigates the opportunities for self-ordering. But institutional phenomenology suggests that, at least in many instances, the parties need help from outside. Given the complexity of the predictability problem, it is not imaginable that all this help will come at the invitation of the parties themselves and be controlled by them. Finally, the message of this book can be related to one more strand of institutional thinking. As the normative standard, this book calls for soft, not hard predictability.[45] This brings it close to the approach of Friedrich August von Hayek.[46]

This book can thus be related to the perspectives of many strands of institutionalist thinking in the social sciences. It differs from this body of knowledge in two respects: the selection of and ways of combining the elements; and the fact that it adds one more level of analysis, dubbed here behavioural dispositions, or the nano level.[47] It is perhaps not so

---

[43] More from Rutherford 1994.
[44] More from Rutherford 1994: 128–72.
[45] See above 3.3.9(d).
[46] Von Hayek 1967: 56 claims: 'But the rules of which we are speaking generally control or circumscribe only certain aspects of concrete actions by providing a general schema which is then adapted to the particular circumstances. They will often merely determine or limit the range of possibilities within which the choice is made consciously.'
[47] See above 2.1.3. Other institutionalists have occasionally stated that doing this might be productive. See e.g. Hall and Taylor 1996: 950: rational choice institutionalism rests on a 'relatively simplistic image of human motivation'; Hodgson 1998: 167 feels comforted in his habit-based approach by 'significant support from psychology'.

surprising after all that opening the black box of the human mind leads to a position in the middle of the battle lines between institutionalist camps. For institutions work through their effect on human beings. To the extent that an institutionalist position is not bluntly wrong, it must therefore leave some traces on the human mind. Exploring the success institutions have in alleviating one of the most serious problems in social interaction, i.e. predictability, has been the purpose of this book.

Equations

$$gg > g > 0 > -l \tag{1}$$

$$g_E = g_A \tag{2}$$

$$2g + l - gg > 0 \tag{3}$$

$$pg_E - (1 - p)l > 0 \tag{4}$$

$$g - c > 0 \tag{5}$$

$$l - c > 0 \tag{6}$$

$$pg - c > 0 \tag{7}$$

$$(1 - p)l - c > 0 \tag{8}$$

$$P(o|\sigma) = \frac{P(\sigma|o)P(o)}{P(\sigma)} \tag{9}$$

$$p'g - (1 - p')l > 0 \tag{10}$$

$$v = pg - (1 - p)l \tag{11}$$

$$v' = p'g - (1 - p')l \tag{12}$$

$$qv' - v - c_E^s > 0 \tag{13}$$

$$r = prob\{\bar{p}g_E - (1 - \bar{p})l > 0\} \tag{14}$$

$$g_A - c_A > 0 \tag{15}$$

$$g_A - rg_A - c^{TR} > 0 \tag{16}$$

$$\bar{p}'g - (1 - \bar{p}')l > 0 \tag{17}$$

$$r' = prob\{\bar{p}'g - (1 - \bar{p}')l > 0\} \tag{18}$$

$$r'g_A - rg_A - c_A^s > 0 \tag{19}$$

$$r'g_A - rg_A - c^{SQ} > 0 \tag{20}$$

$$r'gg - rgg - c^{SQ} > 0 \tag{21}$$

$$rgg - c^{SQ} > 0 \tag{22}$$

$$\bar{r}'g - \bar{r}g - c^{SQ} > 0 \tag{23}$$

$$gg - g - c^{G2} > 0 \tag{24}$$

$$2\underline{p}g + (1 - \underline{p})(gg - l) > 0 \tag{25}$$

$$2\underline{p}g - c_E^{TR} > 0 \tag{26}$$

$$2\underline{p}g - c_A^{TR} > 0 \tag{27}$$

$$-(1 - p)(gg - l) - c_E^{TR} > 0 \tag{28}$$

$$-(1 - p)(gg - l) - c_A^{TR} > 0 \tag{29}$$

$$c_E^{TR} - c_A^{TR} > 0 \tag{30}$$

$$c_A^{TR} - c_E^{TR} > 0 \tag{31}$$

$$2\underline{p} - p > 0 \tag{32}$$

$$2\underline{p}g - g > 0 \tag{33}$$

$$2\underline{p}g - c_{E+A}^{TR} > 0 \tag{34}$$

$$-(1 - p)(gg - l) - c_{E+A}^{TR} > 0 \tag{35}$$

$$c_E^{TR} - c_{E+A}^{TR} > 0 \tag{36}$$

$$c_A^{TR} - c_{E+A}^{TR} > 0 \tag{37}$$

$$2g - gg - \varepsilon - c_E^{Tx} > 0 \tag{38}$$

$$2g - gg - \varepsilon - c_E^{Tx} > pg_E - (1 - p)l \Rightarrow$$
$$2g + (1 - p)l - gg - \varepsilon - c_E^{Tx} - pg_E > 0 \tag{39}$$

$$2g - gg - \varepsilon - c_E^{Tx} > pg_E - c_E^{TR} \Rightarrow$$
$$2g + c_E^{TR} - gg - \varepsilon - c_E^{Tx} - pg_E > 0 \tag{40}$$

$$g_A - c_A^{Tx} > 0 \tag{41}$$

$$g_A - c_A^{Tx} > rg_A \Rightarrow$$
$$g_A - rg_A - c_A^{Tx} > 0 \tag{42}$$

$$g_A - c_A^{Tx} > rgg \Rightarrow$$
$$g_A - rgg - c_A^{Tx} > 0 \tag{43}$$

$$g_A - c_A^{Tx} > g_A - c_A^{TR} \Rightarrow$$
$$c_A^{TR} - c_A^{Tx} > 0 \tag{44}$$

$$2g - c_A^{Tx} > 0 \tag{45}$$

$$2g - c_{E+A}^{Tx} > 2\underline{p}g - c_{E+A}^{TR} \Rightarrow$$
$$2g - 2\underline{p}g + c_{E+A}^{TR} - c_{E+A}^{Tx} > 0 \tag{46}$$

$$(1 - \underline{p})(gg - l) - c_{E+A}^{TR} > 0 \tag{47}$$

$$2g - c_{E+A}^{Tx} > 2\underline{p}g + (1 - p)(gg - l) \Rightarrow$$
$$2g - 2\underline{p}g - (1 - \underline{p})(gg - l) - c_{E+A}^{Tx} > 0 \tag{48}$$

$$pg_E - (1 - p)l > pg_E - c_E^{TR} \Rightarrow$$
$$c_E^{TR} - (1 - p)l > 0 \tag{49}$$

$$pg_E - (1 - p)l > 2g - gg - \varepsilon - c_E^{Tx} \Rightarrow$$
$$pg_E + gg + \varepsilon + c_E^{Tx} - 2g - (1 - p)l > 0 \tag{50}$$

$$g_A - c_A^{In} > 0 \tag{51}$$

$$g_A - c_A^{In} > rg_A \Rightarrow$$
$$g_A - rg_A - c_A^{In} > 0 \tag{52}$$

$$g_A - rgg - c_A^{In} > 0 \tag{53}$$

$$2g - c^{In} > 0 \tag{54}$$

$$pg_E - (1-p)l + s > 0 \tag{55}$$

$$\bar{r}g_A - s > 0 \tag{56}$$

$$\bar{r}gg - s > 0 \tag{57}$$

$$\bar{r} = \bar{p}g_E - (1-\bar{p})l + s > 0 \tag{58}$$

References

Adler, Matthew D. (2000). 'Expressive Theories of Law. A Skeptical Overview.' *University of Pennsylvania Law Review* 148: 1363–501

Adler, Matthew D. and Eric A. Posner (1999). 'Rethinking Cost-Benefit Analysis.' *Yale Law Journal* 109: 165–247

—— (2000). 'Cost–Benefit Analysis. Legal, Economic and Philosophical Perspectives. Introduction.' *Journal of Legal Studies* 29: 837–43

Adomeit, Klaus (2003). 'Der Rechtspositivismus im Denken von Hans Kelsen und von Gustav Radbruch.' *Juristenzeitung* 58: 161–6

Ainslie, George (1992). *Picoeconomics. The Strategic Interaction of Successive Motivational States within the Person.* Cambridge, Cambridge University Press

Ajzen, Icek (1991). 'The Theory of Planned Behaviour.' *Organizational Behavior and Human Decision Processes* 50: 179–211

Ajzen, Icek and Martin Fishbein (1980). *Understanding Attitudes and Predicting Social Behavior.* Englewood Cliffs, N. J., Prentice-Hall

Akerlof, George A. (1970). 'The Market for "Lemons". Quality Uncertainty and the Market Mechanism.' *Quarterly Journal of Economics* 84: 488–500

Albert, Hans (1978). *Traktat über rationale Praxis.* Tübingen, Mohr

Alchian, Armen A. (1950). 'Uncertainty, Evolution, and Economic Theory.' *Journal of Political Economy* 58: 211–21

Allais, Maurice (1953). 'Le comportement de l'homme rationnel devant le risque. Critique des postulats et axiomes de l'école Américaine.' *Econometrica* 21: 503–46

Allison, J. (1989). 'The Nature of Reinforcement.' *Contemporary Learning Theories. Instrumental Conditioning and the Impact of Biological Constraints on Learning,* ed. S. Klein and R. Mowrer. Hillsdale, Erlbaum: 13–39

Allport, Gordon W., Philip Ewart Vernon and Edwin Powers (1933). *Studies in Expressive Movement.* New York, Macmillan

Alt, James E. and Alberto Alesina (1996). 'Political Economy. An Overview.' *A New Handbook of Political Science,* ed. Robert E. Goodin and Hans-Dieter Klingemann. Oxford, Oxford University Press: 645–74

Anderson, Elizabeth and Richard H. Pildes (2000). 'Expressive Theories of Law. A General Restatement.' *University of Pennsylvania Law Review* 148: 1503–75

Anderson, John R. (2000a). *Cognitive Psychology and its Implications.* New York, Worth Publishers

(2000b). *Learning and Memory. An Integrated Approach.* New York, Wiley

Anderson, John R. and Christian Lebiere (2003). 'The Newell Test for a Theory of Cognition.' *Behavioral and Brain Sciences* 26: 587–640

Anderson, John R., Daniel Bothell, Michael D. Byrne and Christian Lebiere (2004). 'An Integrated Theory of the Mind.' *Psychological Review* 111: 1036–60

Anderson, Simon, Jacob K. Goeree and Charles A. Holt (1998). 'A Theoretical Analysis of Altruism and Decision Error in Public Goods Games.' *Journal of Public Economics* 70: 297–323

Antonides, Gerrit (1996). *Psychology in Economics and Business. An Introduction to Economic Psychology.* Dordrecht and Boston, Kluwer Academic

Apesteguia, José, Martin Dufwenberg and Richard Selten (2003). 'Blowing the Whistle.' Bonn Econ. Discussion Papers 9/2003. ftp://ftp.wiwi.uni-bonn.de/papers/bgse/2003/bgse9_2003.pdf

Apter, David E. (1996). 'Comparative Politics, Old and New.' *A New Handbook of Political Science*, ed. Robert E. Goodin and Hans-Dieter Klingemann. Oxford, Oxford University Press: 372–97

Arce, Daniel G. and Todd Sandler (2003). 'An Evolutionary Game Approach to Fundamentalism and Conflict.' *Journal of Institutional and Theoretical Economics* 159: 132–54

Arendt, Hannah (1951). *The Origins of Totalitarianism.* New York, Harcourt Brace

Arkes, Hal R. (1991). 'Costs and Benefits of Judgment Errors – Implications for Debiasing.' *Psychological Bulletin* 110 (3): 486–98

Arkes, Hal R. and Catherine Blumer (1985). 'The Psychology of Sunk Cost.' *Organizational Behavior and Human Decision Processes* 35: 124–40

Arrow, Kenneth Joseph (1963). *Social Choice and Individual Values.* New York, Wiley

(1987). 'Rationality of Self and Others in an Economic System.' *Rational Choice : the Contrast between Economics and Psychology*, ed. Robin M. Hogarth and Melvin W. Reder. Chicago, Chicago University Press: 201–15

Axelrod, Robert (1984). *The Evolution of Cooperation.* New York, Basic Books

Ayton, Peter (2000). 'Do the Birds and Bees Need Cognitive Reform?' *Behavioral and Brain Sciences* 23: 666–7

Babcock, Linda and George Loewenstein (2000). 'Explaining Bargaining Impasse. The Role of Self-Serving Bias.' *Behavioral Law and Economics*, ed. Cass R. Sunstein. Cambridge, Cambridge University Press: 355–73

Baird, Douglas G., Robert H. Gertner and Randal C. Picker (1994). *Game Theory and the Law.* Cambridge, Mass., Harvard University Press

Baldwin, Richard E. (1989). 'Sunk-Cost Hysteresis.' National Bureau of Economic Research Working Paper 2911

Bandura, Albert (1977). *Social Learning Theory.* Englewood Cliffs, N. J., Prenctice Hall

Banerjee, Abhijt V. (1992). 'A Simple Model of Herd Behavior.' *Quarterly Journal of Economics* 107: 797–817

Bargh, John A., Mark Chen and Lara Burrows (1996). 'Automaticity of Social Behavior. Direct Effects of Trait Construct and Stereotype Activation on Action.' *Journal of Personality and Social Psychology* 71: 230–44

Baron, Robert S. and Norbert L. Kerr (2003). *Group Process, Group Decisions, Group Action*. Philadelphia, Open University Press

Bartlett, Frederic C. (1932). *Remembering. A Study in Experimental and Social Psychology*. Cambridge, The University Press

Bartling, Hartwig (1980). *Leitbilder der Wettbewerbspolitik*. Munich, Vahlen

Battaglini, Marco, Roland Benabou and Lear Tirde (2002). 'Self Control in Peer Groups.' http://papers.ssrn.com/paper.taf?abstract_id=298448

Baumeister, Roy (1998). 'The Self.' *The Handbook of Social Psychology*, ed. Daniel T. Gilbert, Susan T. Fiske and Gardner Lindzey. Boston, McGraw-Hill: 680–740

Baxter, Terri L. and Lewis R. Goldberg (1987). 'Perceived Behavioral Consistency Underlying Trait Attribution to Oneself and Another. An Extension of the Actor–Observer Effect.' *Personality and Social Psychology Bulletin* 13: 437–47

Bayes, Thomas (1738). 'An Essay toward Solving a Problem in the Doctrine of Chances.' *Philosophical Transactions of the Royal Society* 53: 370–418

Beaman, Arthur L., Maureen C. Cole, Marilyn Preston, Bannel Klentz and Nancy Steblay (1983). 'Fifteen Years of Foot-in-the-Door Research.' *Personality and Social Psychology Bulletin* 9: 181–96

Becht, Marco, Patrick Bolton and Ailsa Röell (2002). 'Corporate Governance and Corporate Control.' ECGI Working Paper Series in Finance 02/2002

Bechtold, Stefan (2002). *Vom Urheber-zum Informationsrecht. Implikationen des Digital Rights Management*. Munich, Beck

Beckenkamp, Martin (2003). 'Soziales Dilemma "Umwelt". Spieltheoretische und psychologische Aspekte von Umweltproblemen' (mimeo)

Becker, Gary Stanley (1962). 'Irrational Behaviour and Economic Theory.' *Journal of Political Economy* 70: 1–13

   (1976). *The Economic Approach to Human Behavior*. Chicago, University of Chicago Press

   (1993). *Human Capital: a Theoretical and Empirical Analysis, with Special Reference to Education*. Chicago, University of Chicago Press

Bem, Daryl J. (1967). 'Self-Perception. The Dependent Variable of Human Performance.' *Organizational Behavior and Human Performance* 2: 105–21

   (1972). 'Constructing Cross-Situational Consistencies in Behavior. Some Thoughts on Alker's Critique of Mischel.' *Journal of Personality* 40: 17–26

Bem, Daryl J. and Andrea Allen (1974). 'On Predicting Some of the People Some of the Time. The Search for Cross-Situational Consistencies in Behavior.' *Psychological Review* 81: 506–20

Benz, Matthias and Alois Stutzer (2002). 'Do Workers Enjoy Procedural Utility?' http://papers.ssrn.com/paper.taf?abstract_id=336581

Benz, Matthias, Bruno Frey and Alois Stutzer (2002). 'Introducing Procedural Utility: Not Only What, but also How Matters.' http://papers.ssrn.com/paper.taf?abstract_id=338568

Berger, Peter L. and Thomas Luckmann (1967). *The Social Construction of Reality. A Treatise in the Sociology of Knowledge*. Garden City, N. Y., Doubleday

Berle, Adolf Augustus and Gardiner Coit Means (1932). *Modern Corporation and Private Property*. New York and Chicago, Commerce Clearing House Loose leaf service division of the Corporation Trust Company

Betsch, Tilmann, Henning Plessner, Chistiane Schwieren and Robert Gütig (2001). 'I Like It but I Don't Know Why. A Value-Account Approach to Implicit Attitude Formation.' *Personality and Social Psychology Bulletin* 27: 242–53

Bicchieri, Cristina, John Duffy and Gile Talle (2002). 'Trust among Strangers.' http://papers.ssrn.com/paper.taf?abstract_id=304344

Biddle, Bruce J. (1986). 'Recent Developments in Role Theory.' *Annual Review of Sociology* 12: 67–92

Biddle, Bruce J. and Edwin J. Thomas (1979). *Role Theory. Concepts and Research.* Huntington, N. Y., R. E. Krieger

Bikhchandani, Sushil, David Hirshleifer and Ivo Welch (1992). 'A Theory of Fads, Fashion, Custom, and Cultural Change in Informational Cascades.' *Journal of Political Economy* 100: 992–1026

Blais, Ann-Renee and Elke U. Weber (2001). 'Domain-Specificity and Gender Differences in Decision Making.' *Risk Decision and Policy* 6: 47–69

Bohner, Gerd (2001). 'Attitudes.' *Introduction to Social Psychology*, ed. Miles Hewstone and Wolfgang Stroebe. Oxford, Blackwell: 239–82

Bohnet, Iris and Robert D. Cooter (2001). 'Expressive Law. Framing or Equilibrium Selection?' http://ksghome.harvard.edu/~.ibohnet.academic.ksg/Bohnet_Cooter.doc

Bone, John, John D. Hey and John Suckling (1999). 'Are Groups More (or Less) Consistent than Individuals?' *Journal of Risk and Uncertainty* 8: 63–81

Bonus, Holger (1981). 'Emissionsrechte als Mittel der Privatisierung öffentlicher Ressourcen aus der Umwelt.' *Marktwirtschaft und Umwelt*, ed. Lothar Wegehenkel. Tübingen, Mohr: 54–77

Bornschier, Volker (2001). 'Generalisiertes Vertrauen und die frühe Verbreitung der Internetnutzung im Gesellschaftsvergleich.' *Kölner Zeitschrift für Soziologie und Sozialpsychologie* 53: 233–58

Boudon, Raymond (1987). 'The Individualistic Tradition in Sociology.' *The Micro–Macro Link*, ed. Jeffrey Alexander, Bernard Giesen, Richard Münch and Neil Smelser. Berkeley, University of California Press: 45–70

Boyd, Robert and Peter J. Richerson (1994). 'The Evolution of Norms. An Anthropological View.' *Journal of Institutional and Theoretical Economics* 150: 72–87

Brandenburger, Adam and Barry Nalebuff (1996). *Co-opetition.* New York, Doubleday

Brandts, Jordi, Tatsuyoshi Saijo and Arthur Schram (2002). 'How Universal is Behavior? A Four Country Comparison of Spite, Cooperation and Errors in Voluntary Contribution Mechanisms.' http://papers.ssrn.com/paper.taf?abstract_id=254454

Brehm, Jack Williams (1966). *A Theory of Psychological Reactance.* New York, Academic Press

Brehm, Sharon S. and Jack Williams Brehm (1981). *Psychological Reactance. A Theory of Freedom and Control.* New York, Academic Press

Brennan, Geoffrey and Philip Pettit (2000). 'The Hidden Economy of Esteem.' *Economics and Philosophy* 16: 77–98

Brenner, Thomas (1999). *Modelling Learning in Economics.* Cheltenham and Northampton, Mass., Edward Elgar

Breyer, Stephen G. (1993). *Breaking the Vicious Circle. Toward Effective Risk Regulation*. Cambridge, Mass., Harvard University Press

Brickman, Philip and Donald T. Campbell (1971). 'Hedonic Relativism and Planning the Good Society.' *Adaptation-Level Theory*, ed. Mortimer H. Appley. New York, Academic Press: 287–301

Brocas, Isabelle and Juan D. Carillo (2002). 'Are We All Better Drivers than Average? Self-Perception and Biased Behaviour.' http://papers.ssrn.com/paper.taf?abstract_id=353784

Brosig, Jeannette, Joachim Weimann and Axel Ockenfels (2003). 'The Effect of Communication Media on Cooperation.' *German Economic Review* 4: 217–41

Brown, Donald E. (1991). *Human Universals*. New York, McGraw-Hill

Brunswik, Egon, Kenneth R. Hammond and Thomas R. Stewart (2001). *The Essential Brunswik. Beginnings, Explications, Applications*. Oxford and New York, Oxford University Press

Buchanan, James M. (1965). 'An Economic Theory of Clubs.' *Economica* 32: 1–14

Buchanan, James M. and Gordon Tullock (1962). *The Calculus of Consent. Logical Foundations of Constitutional Democracy*. Ann Arbor, University of Michigan Press

Busemeyer, J. R. and J. T. Townsend (1993). 'Decision Field Theory. A Dynamic Cognitive Approach to Decision Making in an Uncertain Environment.' *Psychological Review* 100: 432–59

Camerer, Colin F. (1987). 'Do Biases in Probability Judgement Matter in Markets? Experimental Evidence.' *American Economic Review* 77: 981–97

  (1995). 'Individual Decision Making.' *Handbook of Experimental Economics*, ed. John H. Kagel and Alvin E. Roth. Princeton, Princeton University Press: 587–703

Camerer, Colin F. and Dan Lovallo (1999). 'Overconfidence and Excess Entry: an Experimental Approach.' *American Economic Review* 89: 306–18

Cameron, Judy (2001). 'Negative Effects of Reward on Intrinsic Motivation: a Limited Phenomenon. Comment on Deci, Koestner, and Ryan (2001).' *Review of Educational Research* 71: 29–42

Cameron, Judy and W. David Pierce (2001). *Rewards and Intrinsic Motivation. Resolving the Controversy*. Westport, Bergin

Camp, Jean (2000). *Trust and Risk in Internet Commerce*. Cambridge, Mass., MIT Press

Caplan, Bryan (2004). 'Rational Ignorance.' *Encyclopedia of Public Choice*, ed. Charles K. Rowley and Friedrich Schneider. Boston, Kluwer

Carpenter, Jeffrey (2002). 'Punishing Free-Riders. How Group Size Affects Mutual Monitoring and the Provision of Public Goods. Middlebury Economics Discussion Paper 02–06. http://www.middlebury.edu/~econ/RePec/papers/02-06.pdf

Chaiken, Shelly and Yaacov Trope (1999). *Dual-process Theories in Social Psychology*. New York, Guilford Press

Chamberlin, Edward (1933). *The Theory of Monopolistic Competition*. Cambridge, Mass., Harvard University Press

Chapman, Gretchen B. and Brian H. Bornstein (1996). 'The More You Ask for, the More You Get. Anchoring in Personal Injury Verdicts.' *Applied Cognitive Psychology* 10: 519–40

Chapman, Gretchen B. and Eric J. Johnson (1999). 'Anchoring, Activation, and the Construction of Values.' *Organizational Behavior and Human Decision Processes* 79: 115–53

Charness, Gary and Ernan Haruvy (2002). 'Altruism, Equity, and Reciprocity in a Gift-Exchange Experiment. An Encompassing Approach.' *Games and Economic Behavior* 40: 203–31

Clark, John Maurice (1961). *Competition as a Dynamic Process*. Washington, D.C., Brookings Institution

Coase, Ronald (1937). 'The Nature of the Firm.' *Economica* 4: 386–405
(1960). 'The Problem of Social Cost.' *Journal of Law and Economics* 3: 1–44

Coglianese, Cary (2002). 'Is Satisfaction Success? Evaluating Public Participation in Regulatory Policymaking.' http://papers.ssrn.com/paper.taf?abstract_id=331420

Cohen, Michael D. and Lee S. Sproull, eds. (1995). *Organizational Learning*. London, Sage

Coleman, James Samuel (1987). 'Psychological Structure and Social Structure in Economics Models.' *Rational Choice. The Contrast between Economics and Psychology*, ed. Robin M. Hogarth and Melvin W. Reder. Chicago, University of Chicago Press: 181–5
(1990). *Foundations of Social Theory*. Cambridge, Mass., Belknap Press of Harvard University Press

Collins, R. Lorraine and Clara M. Bradizza (2001). 'Social and Cognitive Learning Processes.' *International Handbook of Alcohol Dependence and Problems*, ed. Nick Heather and Timothy J. Peters. Chichester, Wiley: 317–37

Condorcet, Marie Jean Antoine Nicolas de Caritat, Marquis de (1785). *Essai sur l'application de l'analyse de la probabilité des decisions rendues à la pluralité des voix*. Paris, Imprimerie Royale

Conlisk, John (1996). 'Why Bounded Rationality?' *Journal of Economic Literature* 34: 669–700

Cook, Karen S., ed. (2001). *Trust in Society*, Russell Sage Foundation series on trust, vol. II. New York, Russell Sage Foundation

Cooter, Robert (1998). 'Expressive Law and Economics.' *Journal of Legal Studies* 27: 585–608

Cooter, Robert and Thomas Ulen (2004). *Law and Economics*. Boston, Addison Wesley Longman

Cornes, Richard and Todd Sandler (1996). *The Theory of Externalities, Public Goods and Club Goods*. Cambridge, Cambridge University Press

Cosmides, Leda and John Tooby (1989). 'Evolutionary Psychology and the Generation of Culture: II. Case Study: a Computational Theory of Social Exchange.' *Ethology and Sociobiology* 10: 51–97
(1992). 'Cognitive Adaptations for Social Exchange.' *The Adapted Mind. Evolutionary Psychology and the Generation of Culture*, ed. Jerome Barkow, Leda Cosmides and John Tooby. New York, Oxford University Press: 163–228
(1994). 'Better than Rational. Evolutionary Psychology and the Invisible Hand.' *American Economic Association Papers and Proceedings* 84: 327–32

Cowan, Robin, Paul A. David and Dominique Foray (2000). 'The Explicit Economics of Knowledge Codification and Tacitness.' *Industrial and Corporate Change* 9: 211–53

Crawford, Vincent (1998). 'A Survey of Experiments on Communication via Cheap Talk.' *Journal of Economic Theory* 78 (2): 286–98

Czybulka, Detlef (1995). 'Gewerbenebenrecht. Handwerksrecht and Gaststättenrecht.' *Öffentliches Wirtschaftsrecht Besonderer Teil 1*, ed. Reiner Schmidt. Berlin, Springer: 111–218

Dalton, Russell D. (1996). 'Comparative Politics: Micro-Behavioral Perspectives.' *A New Handbook of Political Science*, ed. Robert E. Goodin and Hans-Dieter Klingemann. Oxford, Oxford University Press: 336–52

Dawes, Robyn M. (1999). 'A Message from Psychologists to Economists: Mere Predictability Doesn't Matter Like It Should (without a Good Story Appended to It).' *Journal of Economic Behavior and Organization* 39: 29–40

Deci, Edward L. (1975). *Intrinsic Motivation*. New York, Plenum Press

Deci, Edward L. and Richard M. Ryan (1985). *Intrinsic Motivation and Self-Determination in Human Behaviour*. New York, Plenum Press

Deci, Edward L., Richard Koestner and Richard M. Ryan (1999). 'A Meta-Analytic Review of Experiments Examining the Effects of Extrinsic Rewards on Intrinsic Motivation.' *Psychological Bulletin* 125: 627–68

Deci, Edward L., Richard Koestner, and Richard M. Ryan (2001a). 'Extrinsic Rewards and Intrinsic Motivation in Education. Reconsidered Once Again.' *Review of Educational Research* 71: 1–27

Deci, Edward L., Richard M. Ryan and Richard Koestner (2001b). 'The Pervasive Negative Effects of Rewards on Intrinsic Motivation: Response to Cameron (2001).' *Review of Educational Research* 71: 43–51

Dekel, Eddie, Barton L. Lipman and Aldo Rustichini (1998). 'Standard State-Space Models Preclude Unawareness.' *Econometrica* 66: 159–73

Delgado, Jose M. R. (2000). 'Neuronal Imprinting of Human Values.' *International Journal of Psychophysiology* 35: 237–46

Denzau, Arthur and Douglass Cecil North (1994). 'Shared Mental Models. Ideologies and Institutions.' *Kyklos* 47: 3–31

Descartes, René (1664). *De Homine*. Lvgdvni Batavorvm, Officina Hackiana

Dessler, David (1989). 'What's at Stake in the Agent–Structure Debate?' *International Organization* 43: 441–73

Devetag, Giovanna (2000). 'From Utilities to Mental Models. A Critical Survey on Decision Rules and Cognition in Consumer Choice.' *Industrial and Corporate Change* 8: 289–351

Dickenberger, Dorothee, Gisla Gniech and Hans-Joachim Grabitz (1993). 'Die Theorie der psychologischen Reaktanz.' *Theorien der Sozialpsychologie I: Kognitive Theorien*, ed. Dieter Frey and Martin Irle. Berne, Huber: 243–74

Dillard, James, John Hunter and Michael Burgoon (1984). 'Sequential Request Persuasive Strategies. Meta-Analysis of Foot-in-the-Door and Door-in-the-Face.' *Human Communication Research* 10: 461–88

Dilthey, Wilhelm (1923). 'Die Entstehung der Hermeneutik.' *Gesammelte Schriften V*, ed. Wilhelm Dilthey. Leipzig, Teubner: 317–31

DiMaggio, Paul J. (1998). 'The New Institutionalisms. Avenues of Collaboration.' *Journal of Institutional and Theoretical Economics* 154: 696–705

DiMaggio, Paul J. and Walter W. Powell (1991). 'Introduction.' *The New Institutionalism in Organizational Analysis*, ed. Walter W. Powell and Paul J. DiMaggio. Chicago, University of Chicago Press: 1–38

Dixit, Avinash K. and Barry J. Nalebuff (1991). *Thinking Strategically. The Competitive Edge in Business, Politics, and Everyday Life*. New York, Norton

Domjan, Michael (1998). *The Principles of Learning and Behavior*. Pacific Grove, Calif., Brooks/Cole

Donald, Merlin (1999). 'Hominid Enculturation and Cognitive Evolution.' *Cognition and Material Culture. The Archaeology of Symbolic Storage*, ed. Colin Renfrew and Chris Scarre. Cambridge, McDonald Institute for Archaeological Research: 7–17

Donnell, A. J., A. Thomas and W. C. Buboltz (2001). 'Psychological Reactance. Factor Structure and Internal Consistency of the Questionnaire for the Measurement of Psychological Reactance.' *Journal of Social Psychology* 141 (5): 679–87

Druckman, James (2001). 'Using Credible Advice to Overcome Framing Effects.' *Journal of Law, Economics and Organization* 17: 62–82

Dudycha, G. J. (1936). 'An Objective Study in Personality.' *Archives of Psychology* 29: 1–53

Dunn, John (1988). 'Trust and Political Agency.' *Trust. Making and Breaking Cooperative Relations*, ed. David Gambetta. New York, Blackwell: 73–93

Easton, David (1965). *A Systems Analysis of Political Life*. New York, Wiley

Edelman, Murray J. (1964). *The Symbolic Uses of Politics*. Urbana, University of Illinois Press

Eggertsson, Thrainn (1990). *Economic Behavior and Institutions*. Cambridge, Cambridge University Press

Eichberger, Jürgen, David Kelsey and Burkhard Schipper (2003). 'Ambiguity and Social Interaction.' http://with1.awi.uni-heidelberg.de/Publik/social-interaction-dk.pdf

Eichenberger, Reiner (2002). 'Wissen und Information in ökonomischer Perspektive.' *Wissen, Nichtwissen, Unsicheres Wissen*, ed. Christoph Engel, Jost Halfmann and Martin Schulte. Baden-Baden, Nomos: 75–92

Eisenberg, Andrea (2001). *Stabilität and Wandel informeller Institutionen. Selbstorganisation und interdependente Prozesse*. Wiesbaden, Gabler

Ellickson, Robert C. (1991). *Order without Law. How Neighbors Settle Disputes*. Cambridge, Mass., Harvard University Press

Ellsberg, Daniel (1961). 'Risk, Ambiguity, and the Savage Axioms.' *Quarterly Journal of Economics* 75: 643–69

Elster, Jon (1979). *Ulysses and the Sirens. Studies in Rationality and Irrationality*. Cambridge, Cambridge University Press

(1989). *The Cement of Society. A Study of Social Order*. Cambridge, Cambridge University Press

(1998). 'Emotions and Economic Theory.' *Journal of Economic Literature* 36: 47–74

Engel, Christoph (1999). 'Vertrauen – ein Versuch.' Preprints aus der Max-Planck-Projektgruppe Recht der Gemeinschaftsgüter Bonn 1999/12

(2000). 'The Internet and the Nation State.' *Understanding the Impact of Global Networks on Local Social, Political and Cultural Values*, ed. Christoph Engel and Kenneth H. Keller. Baden-Baden, Nomos: 201–60

(2001a). 'Die Grammatik des Rechts.' *Instrumente des Umweltschutzes im Wirkungsverbund*, ed. Hans-Werner Rengeling. Baden-Baden, Nomos: 17–49

(2001b). 'Hybrid Governance across National Jurisdictions as a Challenge to Constitutional Law.' *European Business Organisation Law Review* 2: 569–84

(2001c). 'Institutionen zwischen Staat und Markt.' *Die Verwaltung* 34: 1–24

(2001d). 'Offene Gemeinwohldefinitionen.' *Rechtstheorie* 32: 23–52

(2002a). *Abfallrecht und Abfallpolitik*. Baden-Baden, Nomos

(2002b). 'Die soziale Funktion des Eigentums.' *Bericht zur Lage des Eigentums*, ed. Otto Depenheuer, Christoph Engel and Thomas von Danwitz. Berlin, Springer: 1–107

(2003a). 'Causes and Management of Conflicts.' *Journal of Institutional and Theoretical Economics* 159: 1–15

(2003b). 'The Constitutional Court – Applying the Proportionality Principle – as a Subsidiary Authority for the Assessment of Political Outcomes.' *Linking Political Science and the Law*, ed. Christoph Engel and Adrienne Héritier. Baden-Baden, Nomos: 285–314

(2003c). 'Governing the Egalitarians from Without. The Case of the Internet.' Preprints aus der Max-Planck-Projektgruppe Recht der Gemeinschaftsgüter 2003/10

(2003d). 'Die Internet-Service-Provider als Geiseln deutscher Ordnungsbehörden. Eine Kritik der Verfügungen der Bezirksregierung Düsseldorf.' *Multimedia und Recht* 6, supplement 4: 1–35

(2004a). 'A Constitutional Framework for Private Governance.' *German Law Journal* 5: 197–236

(2004b). 'Marktabgrenzung als soziale Konstruktion.' *Festschrift Immenga*, ed. Andreas Fuchs, Hans Peter Schwintowski and Daniel Zimmer. Munich, Beck: 127–47

(forthcoming) 'Autonomie und Freiheit' *Handbuch der Grundrechte II*, ed. Detlef Merten and Hans-Jürgen Papier. Heidelberg, C. F. Müller

Engel, Christoph and Urs Schweizer (2002). 'Organising and Designing Markets.' *Journal of Institutional and Theoretical Economics* 158: 1–5

Engelmann, Dirk (2001). 'Asymmetric Type Recognition with Applications to Dilemma Games.' *Metronomica* 52: 357–75

Englich, Beate and Thomas Mussweiler (2001). 'Sentencing under Uncertainty. Anchoring Effects in the Court Room.' *Journal of Applied Social Psychology* 31: 1535–51

Epley, Nicolas and Thomas Gilovich (2001). 'Putting Adjustment Back in the Anchoring and Adjustment Heuristic. Differential Processing of Self-Generated and Experimenter-Provided Anchors.' *Psychological Science* 12: 391–5

Epstein, S. (1977). 'Traits are Alive and Well.' *Personality at the Crossroads: Current Issues in Interactional Psychology*, ed. David Magnusson and Norman Solomon Endler. Hillsdale, Erlbaum: 83–98

(1979). 'The Stability of Behavior. I. On Predicting Most of the People Most of the Time.' *Journal of Personality and Social Psychology* 37: 1097–126

Eriksson, Anders and Kristian Lindgren (2002). 'Cooperation in an Unpredictable Environment.' *Artificial Life* 8: 394–99

284   References

Evans, Jonathan St. B. T. (1993). 'Bias and Rationality.' *Rationality. Psychological and Philosophical Perspectives*, ed. K. I. Manktelow and David E. Over. London, Routledge: 6–29

Evans, Jonathan St. B. T. and David E. Over (1997). 'Are People Rational ? Yes, No, and Sometimes.' *Psychologist*: 403–6

Falk, Armin, Ernst Fehr and Urs Fischbacher (2003). 'Reasons for Conflict. Lessons from Bargaining Experiments.' *Journal of Institutional and Theoretical Economics* 159: 171–87

Farnsworth, Ward (2000). 'Do Parties to Nuisance Cases Bargain after Judgement? A Glimpse into the Cathedral.' *Behavioral Law and Economics*, ed. Cass R. Sunstein. Cambridge, Cambridge University Press: 302–22

(2001). 'The Taste for Fairness.' http://papers.ssrn.com/paper.taf? abstract_id=305761

(2002). 'The Economics of Enmity.' *University of Chicago Law Review* 69: 211–61

(2003). 'The Legal Management of Self-Serving Bias.' *University of California at Davis Law Review* 37: 567–603

Farrell, Joseph and Matthew Rabin (1996). 'Cheap Talk.' *Journal of Economic Perspectives* 10: 103–13

Fazio, Russell H. (1990). 'Multiple Processes by which Attitudes Guide Behavior. The MODE Model as an Integrative Framework.' *Advances in Experimental Social Psychology 23*, ed. Mark P. Zanna. San Diego, Academic Press: 75–109

(2001). 'On the Automatic Activation of Associated Evaluations. An Overview.' *Cognition and Emotion* 15: 115–41

Fehr, Ernst (2000). 'Cooperation and Punishment in Public Goods Experiments.' *American Economic Review* 90: 980–94

Fehr, Ernst and Armin Falk (2002). 'Psychological Foundations of Incentives.' *European Economic Review* 46: 687–724

Fehr, Ernst and Simon Gaechter (2001). 'Do Incentive Contracts Crowd out Voluntary Cooperation?' http://papers.ssrn.com/paper.taf?abstract_id=289680

(2002). 'Do Incentive Contracts Undermine Voluntary Cooperation?' http://papers.ssrn.com/paper.taf?abstract_id=313028

Fehr, Ernst and Klaus M. Schmidt (1999). 'A Theory of Fairness, Competition, and Cooperation.' *Quarterly Journal of Economics* 114: 817–68

(2000). 'Theories of Fairness and Reciprocity – Evidence and Economic Applications.' CESifo Working Paper Series No. 403. http://papers.ssrn.com/paper.taf?abstract_id=255223

Fehr, Ernst and Jean-Robert Tyran (1996). 'How Do Institutions and Fairness Interact?' *Central European Journal for Operations Research & Economics* 4: 69–84

Fehr, Ernst and Peter K. Zych (1998). 'Do Addicts Behave Rationally?' *Scandinavian Journal of Economics* 100: 643–62

Fehr, Ernst, Simon Gaechter and Georg Kirchsteiger (1997). 'Reciprocity as a Contract Enforcement Device. Experimental Evidence.' *Econometrica* 65: 833–60

Feldman, Allan M. (1980). *Welfare Economics and Social Choice Theory.* Boston, Martinus Nijhoff

Ferejohn, John A. and Morris P. Fiorina (1974). 'The Paradox of Not Voting. A Decision Theoretic Analysis.' *American Political Science Review* 68: 525–36

Festinger, Leon (1957). *A Theory of Cognitive Dissonance.* Evanston, Ill., Row Peterson

Festinger, Leon and James M. Carlsmith (1959). 'Cognitive Consequences of Forced Compliance.' *Journal of Abnormal and Social Psychology* 58: 203–10

Fiedler, Klaus (2000). 'Beware of Samples! A Cognitive-Ecological Sampling Approach to Judgement Bias.' *Psychological Review* 107: 659–76

Fiedler, Klaus, Eva Walther and Stefanie Nickel (1999). 'The Autoverification of Social Hypotheses. Stereotyping and the Power of Sample Size.' *Journal of Personality and Social Psychology* 77: 5–18

Fiedler, Klaus, Jeannette Schmid and Teresa Stahl (2002). 'What is the Current Truth about Polygraph Lie Detection ?' *Basic and Applied Social Psychology* 24: 313–24

Fischhoff, Baruch (2000). 'Value Elicitation. Is There Anything in There?' *Choices, Values, and Frames*, ed. Daniel Kahneman and Amos Tversky. Cambridge, Cambridge University Press: 620–41

Fishbein, Martin and Icek Ajzen (1975). *Belief, Attitude, Intention, and Behavior. An Introduction to Theory and Research.* Reading, Mass., Addison-Wesley

Fiske, Alan Page (1991). *Structures of Social Life. The Four Elementary Forms of Human Relations: Communal Sharing, Authority Ranking, Equality Matching, Market Pricing.* New York, Free Press and Macmillan

Forsythe, Robert, Forest Nelson, George Newman and Jack Wright (1991). 'The Iowa Presidential Stock Market. A Field Experiment.' *Research in Experimental Economics*, ed. R. Mark Isaac. Greenwich, Conn., JAI Press: 1–43

Forsythe, Robert, Russell Lundholm and Thomas Rietz (1999). 'Cheap Talk, Fraud, and Adverse Selection in Financial Markets. Some Experimental Evidence.' *Review of Financial Studies* 12: 481–518

Fox, Craig R. and Amos Tversky (2000). 'Ambiguity Aversion and Comparative Ignorance.' *Choices, Values, and Frames*, ed. Daniel Kahneman and Amos Tversky. Cambridge, Cambridge University Press: 528–42

Frank, Robert H. (1985). *Choosing the Right Pond. Human Behavior and the Quest for Status.* New York, Oxford University Press

(1988). *Passions within Reason. The Strategic Role of the Emotions.* New York, Norton

Freedman, Jonathan L. and Scott C. Fraser (1966). 'Compliance without Pressure. The Foot-in-the-Door Technique.' *Journal of Personality and Social Psychology* 4: 195–202

Frey, Bruno S. ed. (1999a). *Economics as a Science of Human Behaviour. Towards a New Social Science Paradigm.* Boston and Dordrecht, Kluwer

(1999b). 'The Price System and Morals.' *Economics as a Science of Human Behaviour. Towards a New Social Science Paradigm*, ed. Bruno Frey. Boston: 159–75

Frey, Bruno and Reiner Eichenberger (1994). 'Economic Incentives Transform Psychological Anomalies.' *Journal of Economic Behavior and Organization* 23: 215–34

Frey, Bruno and Reto Jegen (2001). 'Motivation Crowding Theory. A Survey of Empirical Evidence.' *Journal of Economic Surveys* 15: 589–611

Frey, Bruno and Alois Stutzer (2001). 'Beyond Bentham – Measuring Procedural Utility.' CESifo Working Papers 492. http://papers.ssrn.com/abstract=268059.

(2002). *Happiness and Economics*. Princeton, Princeton University Press

Friedman, Daniel (1998). 'Monty Hall's Three Doors. Construction and Deconstruction of a Choice Anomaly.' *American Economic Review* 88: 933–46

Friedman, Milton (1953). *Essays in Positive Economics*. [Chicago], University of Chicago Press

Friedmann, Daniel (1989). 'The Efficient Breach Fallacy.' *Journal of Legal Studies* 18: 1–24

Friedrich, James (2000). 'Fleshing out a Dual-system Solution.' *Behavioral and Brain Sciences* 23: 671–2

Frowein, Jochen A. (2000). 'Konstitutionalisierung des Völkerrechts.' *Berichte der Deutschen Gesellschaft für Völkerrecht* 39: 427–47

Fudenberg, Drew and David K. Levine (1998). *The Theory of Learning in Games*. Cambridge, Mass., MIT Press

Funder, David C. (2000). 'Gone with the Wind. Individual Differences in Heuristics and Biases Undermine the Implication of Systematic Irrationality.' *Behavioral and Brain Sciences* 23: 673–4

Funder, David C. and C. Randall Colvin (1991). 'Explorations in Behavioral Consistency. Properties of Persons, Situations and Behaviors.' *Journal of Personality and Social Psychology* 60: 773–94

Furubotn, Eirik Grundtvig and Rudolf Richter (1997). *Institutions and Economic Theory. The Contribution of the New Institutional Economics*. Ann Arbor, University of Michigan Press

Garvin, Susan and John H. Kagel (1994). 'Learning in Common Value Auctions – Some Initial Observations.' *Journal of Economic Behavior & Organization* 25 (3): 351–72

Geertz, Clifford (1973). 'Thick Description. Toward an Interpretive Theory of Culture.' *The Interpretation of Cultures*, ed. Clifford Geertz. New York, Basic Books: 3–30

Gehlen, Arnold (1960). 'Mensch and Institutionen.' *Anthropologische Forschung. Zur Selbstbegegnung und Selbstentdeckung des Menschen*, ed. Arnold Gehlen. Hamburg, Rowohlt: 69–77

Geiger, Theodor Julius and Manfred Rehbinder (1987). *Vorstudien zu einer Soziologie des Rechts*. Berlin, Duncker & Humblot

Gentner, Dedre and Albert L. Stevens (1983). *Mental Models*. Hillsdale, N. J., Erlbaum

Gentner, Dedre, Keith J. Holyoak and Boicho N. Kokinov, eds. (2001). *The Analogical Mind. Perspectives from Cognitive Science*. Cambridge, Mass., MIT Press

Gérard-Varet, L. A., Serge-Christophe Kolm and J. Mercier Ythier, eds. (2000). *The Economics of Reciprocity, Giving, and Altruism*. Houndmills, Basingstoke, Macmillan; New York, St Martin's Press

Gibbons, Robert (1998). 'Incentives in Organizations.' *Journal of Economic Perspectives* 12: 115–32

Gifford, Sharon (2001). 'Limited Attention as the Bound on Rationality.' http:// papers.ssrn.com/paper.taf?abstract_id=262181

Gigerenzer, Gerd, ed. (2000a). *Adaptive Thinking. Rationality in the Real World*. Oxford, Oxford University Press

(2000b). 'How to Make Cognitive Illusions Disappear.' *Adaptive Thinking. Rationality in the Real World*, ed. Gerd Gigerenzer. Oxford, Oxford University Press: 241–66

Gigerenzer, Gerd, Peter M. Todd and ABC Research Group (1999). *Simple Heuristics that Make us Smart*. New York, Oxford University Press

Glenn, H. Patrick (1997). 'The Capture, Reconstruction and Marginalization of "Custom".' *American Journal of Comparative Law* 45: 613–20

Glimcher, Paul W. (2003). *Decisions, Uncertainty, and the Brain. The Science of Neuroeconomics*. Cambridge, Mass., MIT Press

Gode, Dhananjay K. and Shyam Sunder (1993). 'Allocative Efficiency of Markets with Zero-Intelligence Traders. Market as a Partial Substitute for Individual Irrationality.' *Journal of Political Economy* 101: 119–37

Goffman Erving (1956). *The Presentation of Self in Everyday Life*. Edinburgh, University of Edinburgh Social Sciences Research Centre

Goldstein, William M. and Robin M. Hogarth (1997). 'Judgment and Decision Research. Some Historical Context.' *Research on Judgement and Decision Making*, ed. William M. Goldstein and Robin M. Hogarth. Cambridge, Cambridge University Press: 3–65

Goldstein, William M. and Elke U. Weber (1997). 'Content and Discontent. Indications and Implications of Domain Specificity in Preferential Decision Making.' *Research in Judgement and Decision Making*, ed. William M. Goldstein and Robin M. Hogarth. Cambridge, Cambridge University Press: 566–617

Granovetter, Marc (1985). 'Economic Action and Social Structure. The Problem of Embeddedness.' *American Journal of Sociology* 91: 481–510

Grether, David M. (1980). 'Bayes' Rule as a Descriptive Model. The Representativeness Heuristic.' *Quarterly Journal of Economics* 95: 537–57

(1992). 'Testing Bayes' Rule and the Representativeness Heuristic: Some Experimental Evidence.' *Journal of Economic Behavior and Organization* 17: 31–57

Grunberg, Emile and Franco Modigliani (1954). 'The Predictability of Social Events.' *Journal of Political Economy* 52: 465–78

Gruter, Margaret and Roger D. Masters, eds. (1986). *Ostracism. A Social and Biological Phenomenon*. New York, Elsevier

Guesnerie, Roger (2001). 'The Government and Market Expectations.' *Journal of Institutional and Theoretical Economics* 157: 116–26

Güth, Werner and Hartmut Kliemt (2003). 'Perfect or Bounded Rationality? Some Facts, Speculations and Proposals' (mimeo)

Güth, Werner, Rolf Schmittberger and Bernd Schwarze (1982). 'An Experimental Analysis of Ultimatum Bargaining.' *Journal of Economic Behavior and Organization* 3: 367–88

Hall, Peter and Rosemary C. R. Taylor (1996). 'Political Science and the Three New Institutionalisms.' *Political Studies* 44: 936–57

Hamilton, Walton H. (1932). 'Institution.' *Encyclopedia of the Social Sciences*, ed. Edwin R. A. Seligman and Alvin Johnson. New York, Macmillan: 84–9

Hammond, Daniel J. (1990). 'Realism in Friedman's Essays in Positive Economics.' *Perspectives on the History of Economic Thought. Vol. IV. Keynes, Macroeconomics and Method. Selected Papers from the History of Economics Society Conference*, ed. Donald E. Moggridge. Aldershot, Edward Elgar: 194–208

Hanoch, Yaniv (2002). 'Neither an Angel nor an Ant: Emotion as an Aid to Bounded Rationality.' *Journal of Economic Psychology* 23: 1–25

Hansjürgens, Bernd and Gertrude Lübbe-Wolff, eds. (2000). *Symbolische Umweltpolitik*. Frankfurt, Suhrkamp

Harbaugh, William T. and Kate Krause (2000). 'Children's Altruism in Public Good and Dictator Experiments.' *Economic Inquiry* 38: 95–109

Hardin, Garrett (1968). 'The Tragedy of the Commons.' *Science* 162: 1243–8

Hardin, Russell (2001). 'Conceptions and Explanations of Trust.' *Trust in Society*, ed. Karen S. Cook. New York, Russell Sage Foundation: 3–39

(2002). *Trust and Trustworthiness*. New York, Russell Sage Foundation

Harless, David W. and Colin F. Camerer (1994). 'The Predictive Utility of Generalized Expected Utility Theories.' *Econometrica* 62: 1251–89

Harsanyi, John (1967–68). 'Games with Incomplete Information Played by "Bayesian" Players.' *Management Science* 14: 159–82, 320–4, 486–502

Hartshorne, Hugh, Mark Arthur May, Julius Bernard Maller and Frank K. Shuttleworth (1928). *Studies in the Nature of Character*. New York, Macmillan

Hartwick, John M. and Nancy D. Olewiler (1998). *The Economics of Natural Resource Use*. Reading, Mass., Addison-Wesley

Hastie, Reid and Bernadette Park (1997). 'The Relationship between Memory and Judgement Depends on whether the Judgement Task is Memory-Based or On-Line.' *Research in Judgement and Decision Making*, ed. William M. Goldstein and Robin M. Hogarth. Cambridge, Cambridge University Press: 431–53

Hayashi, Nahoko, Elinor Ostrom, James M. Walker and Toshio Yanagishi (1999). 'Reciprocity, Trust, and the Sense of Control. A Cross-Societal Study.' *Rationality and Society* 11: 27 46

Heath, Chip (1995). 'Escalation and De-Escalation of Commitment in Response to Sunk Costs. The Role of Budgeting in Mental Accounting.' *Organizational Behavior and Human Decision Processes* 62: 38–54

Hebb, Donald O. (1949). *The Organization of Behavior. A Neuropsychological Theory*. New York, Wiley

Heifetz, Aviad, Martin Meier and Burkhard Schipper (2003). 'Interactive Unawareness and Speculative Trade.' http://www.tau.ac.il/~heifetz/interactive_unawareness.pdf

Heiner, Ronald A. (1983). 'The Origin of Predictable Behavior.' *American Economic Review* 73: 560–95

(1985a). 'Origin of Predictable Behavior: Further Modeling and Applications.' *American Economic Review* 75: 391–6

(1985b). 'Predictable Behavior: Reply.' *American Economic Review* 75: 579–85

(1989). 'The Origin of Predictable Dynamic Behavior.' *Journal of Economic Behavior and Organization* 12: 233–57

Henrich, Joseph and Robert Boyd (2001). '"Economic Man" in Cross-Cultural Perspective. Behavioral Experiments in 15 Small-Scale Societies.' http://www.sscnet.ucla.edu/anthro/faculty/boyd/MacGamesBBSFinal.pdf

Hermalin, Benjamin E. and Alice M. Isen (1999). 'The Effect of Affect on Economic and Strategic Decision Making.' University of California, Berkeley, Department of Economics Working Paper: E99/270

Hirschman, Albert O. (1970). *Exit, Voice, and Loyalty. Responses to Decline in Firms, Organizations, and States.* Cambridge, Mass., Harvard University Press

Hirshleifer, Jack (1987). 'On the Emotions as Guarantors of Threats and Promises.' *The Latest on the Best: Essays on Evolution and Optimality,* ed. John Dupre. Cambridge, Mass., MIT Press: 307–26

Hirt, Edward R. and Keith D. Markman (1995). 'Multiple Explanation – a Consider-an-Alternative Strategy for Debiasing Judgments.' *Journal of Personality and Social Psychology* 69 (6): 1069–86

Hobbes, Thomas (1651). *Leviathan, or, The matter, forme, & power of a commonwealth ecclesiasticall and civill.* London, Printed for Andrew Crooke, i.e. Crooke at the Green Dragon in St Pauls Church-yard

Hodgson, Geoffrey Martin (1988). *Economics and Institutions. A Manifesto for a Modern Institutional Economics.* Philadelphia, University of Pennsylvania Press

(1998). 'The Approach of Institutional Economics.' *Journal of Economic Literature* 36: 166–92

Hoffmann, Elizabeth and Matthew L. Spitzer (1985). 'Entitlements, Rights, and Fairness. An Experimental Examination of Subject's Concepts of Distributive Justice.' *Journal of Legal Studies* 14: 259–97

Hoffrage, Ulrich, Gerd Gigerenzer, Stefan Krauss and Larva Mastignan (2002). 'Representation Facilitates Reasoning. What Natural Frequencies Are and What They Are Not.' *Cognition* 84: 343–52

Hogarth, Robin M. and Howard Kunreuther (1997). 'Decision Making under Ignorance. Arguing with Yourself.' *Research in Judgement and Decision Making,* ed. William M. Goldstein and Robin M. Hogarth. Cambridge, Cambridge University Press: 482–508

Hogarth, Robin M. and Melvin W. Reder, eds. (1986). *Rational Choice. The Contrast between Economics and Psychology.* Chicago, University of Chicago Press

Hogarth, Robin M., Brian J. Gibbs, Craig R. M. McKerzie and Margaret A. Marquis (1997). 'Learning from Feedback. Exactingness and Incentives.' *Research on Judgement and Decision Making,* ed. William M. Goldstein and Robin M. Hogarth. Cambridge, Cambridge University Press: 244–84

Holzinger, Katharina (2003). 'The Problems of Collective Action. A New Approach.' http://www.mpp-rdg.mpg.de/pdf_dat/2003_2.pdf

Homann, Karl and Andreas Suchanek (2000). *Ökonomik. Eine Einführung.* Tübingen, Mohr

Honderich Ted, ed. (1985). *Morality and Rehibutive Emotions: a Tribute to John L. Maclire.* London: Routledge

Hopkins, Nick and Neil Murdoch (1999). 'The Role of the "Other" in National Identity. Exploring the Context-Dependence of the National Ingroup Stereotype.' *Journal of Community & Applied Social Psychology* 9: 321–38

Hsee, Christopher K. (2000). 'Attribute Evaluability. Its Implications for Joint-Separate Evaluation Reversals and Beyond.' *Choices, Values, and Frames*, ed. Daniel Kahneman and Amos Tversky. Cambridge, Cambridge University Press: 543–63

Hsee, Christopher K., Jiao Zhang, Fang Yu and Yiheng Xi (2003). 'Lay Rationalism, and Inconsistency between Decision and Predicted Experience.' *Journal of Behavioral Decision Making* 16: 257–72

Hume, David (1739). *A Treatise of Human Nature*. Oxford, Clarendon Press

Immergut, Ellen M. (1998). 'The Theoretical Core of the New Institutionalism.' *Politics and Society* 26: 5–34

Jackman, Simon and Paul M. Sniderman (2002). 'Institutional Organization of Choice Spaces. A Political Conception of Political Psychology.' *Political Psychology*, ed. K. R. Monroe. Mahweh, Erlbaum: 209–24

Jakobs, Günther (1999). *Norm, Person, Gesellschaft. Vorüberlegungen zu einer Rechtsphilosophie*. Berlin, Duncker & Humblot

James, William (1890). *The Principles of Psychology*. New York, H. Holt

Janssen, Maarten W. C. and Ewa Mendys (2004). 'The Price of a Price. On the Crowding out of Social Norms.' *Journal of Economic Behaviour & Organization* 55: 377–95

Japp, Klaus P. (2002). 'Struktureffekte öffentlicher Risikokommunikation auf Regulierungsregime. Zur Funktion von Nichtwissen im BSE-Konflikt,' in *Wissen, Nichtwissen, Unsicheres Wissen*, ed. Christoph Engel, Jost Halfmann and Martin Schulte. Baden-Baden, Nomos: 35–74

Jensen, Michael C. and William H. Meckling (1976). 'Theory of the Firm. Managerial Behaviour, Agency Cost and Ownership Structure.' *Journal of Financial Economics* 3: 305–60

Jickeli, Joachim (1990). *Marktzutrittsschranken im Recht der Wettbewerbsbeschränkungen*. Baden-Baden, Nomos
  (1996). *Der langfristige Vertrag. Eine rechtswissenschaftliche Untersuchung auf institutionen-ökonomischer Grundlage*. Baden-Baden, Nomos

Johnson-Laird, Philip N. (1983). *Mental Models. Towards a Cognitive Science of Language, Inference and Consciousness*. Cambridge, Cambridge University Press
  (1989). 'Mental Models.' *Foundations of Cognitive Science*, ed. Michael Posner. Cambridge, Mass., MIT Press: 469–99

Jolls, Christine (2000). 'Behavioural Economic Analysis of Redistributive Legal Rules.' *Behavioural Law and Economics*, ed. Cass R. Sunstein. Cambridge, Cambridge University Press: 288–301

Jolls, Christine, Cass R. Sunstein and Richard H. Thaler (1998). 'A Behavioral Approach to Law and Economics.' *Stanford Law Review* 50: 1471–550
  (2000). 'A Behavioural Approach to Law and Economics.' *Behavioural Law and Economics*, ed. Cass R. Sunstein. Cambridge, Cambridge University Press: 13–58

Jones, Edward Ellsworth and Richard E. Nisbett (1972). 'The Actor and the Observer. Divergent Perceptions of the Causes of Behavior.' *Attribution.*

Perceiving the Causes of Behavior, ed. Edward Ellsworth Jones. Morristown, General Learning Press: 79–94

Jones, Phil, ed. (1999). *Taboo.* Philadelphia, Jessika Kingsley

Kahneman, Daniel (1986). 'Fairness and the Assumptions of Economics.' *Rational Choice. The Contrast between Economics and Psychology,* ed. Robin M. Hogarth and Melvin W. Reder. Chicago, University of Chicago Press

(1992). 'Reference Points, Anchors, Norms, and Mixed Feelings.' *Organizational Behavior and Human Decision Processes* 51: 296–312

(2000a). 'Evaluation by Moments. Past and Future.' *Choices, Values, and Frames,* ed. Daniel Kahneman and Amos Tversky. Cambridge, Cambridge University Press: 693–708

(2000b). 'Experienced Utility and Objective Happiness. A Moment-Based Approach.' *Choices, Values, and Frames,* ed. Daniel Kahneman and Amos Tversky. Cambridge, Cambrdige University Press: 673–92

(2000c). Preface. *Choices, Values, and Frames,* ed. Daniel Kahneman and Amos Tversky. Cambridge, Cambridge University Press: ix–xvii

Kahneman, Daniel and Dan Lovallo (2000). 'Timid Choices and Bold Forecasts. A Cognitive Perspective on Risk Taking.' *Choices, Values, and Frames,* ed. Daniel Kahneman and Amos Tversky. Cambridge, Cambridge University Press: 393–413

Kahneman, Daniel and Jackie Snell (1997). 'Predicting a Changing Taste. Do People Know What They Will Like?' *Research in Judgement and Decision Making,* ed. William M. Goldstein and Robin M. Hogarth. Cambridge, Cambridge University Press: 393–410

Kahneman, Daniel and Amos Tversky (1972). 'Subjective Probability. A Judgement of Representativeness.' *Cognitive Psychology* 3: 430–54

(1973). 'Availability. A Heuristic for Judging Frequency and Probability.' *Cognitive Psychology* 4: 207–32

(1979). 'Prospect Theory. An Analysis of Decision under Risk.' *Econometrica* 47: 263–91

(1995). 'Conflict Resolution. A Cognitive Perspective.' *Barriers to Conflict Resolution,* ed. Kenneth Joseph Arrow, Robert H. Mnookin, Lee Ross, Amos Tversky and Robert B. Wilson. New York, Norton: 44–61

(2000a). *Choices, Values, and Frames.* Cambridge, Russell Sage Foundation and Cambridge University Press

(2000b). 'Choices, Values, and Frames.' *Choices, Values, and Frames,* ed. Daniel Kahneman and Amos Tversky. Cambridge, Cambridge University Press: 1–16

(2000c). 'Prospect Theory. An Analysis of Decision under Risk.' *Choices, Values, and Frames,* ed. Daniel Kahneman and Amos Tversky. Cambridge, Cambridge University Press: 17–43

Kahneman, Daniel, Paul Slovic and Amos Tversky (1982). *Judgment under Uncertainty. Heuristics and Biases.* Cambridge, Cambridge University Press

Kahneman, Daniel, Jack L. Knetsch and Richard H. Thaler (2000a). 'Experimental Tests of the Endowment Effect and the Coase Theorem.' *Behavioral Law and Economics,* ed. Cass R. Sunstein. Cambridge, Cambridge University Press: 211–31

Kahneman, Daniel, Jack L. Knetsch and Richard H. Thaler (2000b). 'Fairness as a Constraint on Profit Seeking. Entitlements in the Market.' *Choices, Values, and Frames*, ed. Daniel Kahneman and Amos Tversky. Cambridge, Cambridge University Press: 317–34

Kahneman, Daniel, Ilana Ritov and David Schkade (2000c). 'Economic Preferences or Attitude Expressions? An Analysis of Dollar Responses to Public Issues.' *Choices, Values, and Frames*, ed. Daniel Kahneman and Amos Tversky. Cambridge, Cambridge University Press: 642–71

Kandori, Michihiro (2002). 'Introduction to Repeated Games with Private Monitoring.' *Journal of Economic Theory* 102: 1–15

Kaplan, Todd R. and Bradley J. Ruffle (2001). 'The Self-Serving Bias and Beliefs about Rationality.' http://papers.ssrn.com/paper.taf?abstract_id=251308

Kaufman, Bruce E. (1999). 'Emotional Arousal as a Source of Bounded Rationality.' *Journal of Economic Behavior & Organization* 38: 135–44

Kelman, Mark, Yuval Rottenstreich and Amos Tversky (2000). 'Context-Dependence in Legal Decision Making.' *Behavioural Law and Economics*, ed. Cass R. Sunstein. Cambridge, Cambridge University Press: 61–94

Keren, Gideon (1990). 'Cognitive Aids and Debiasing Methods. Can Cognitive Pills Cure Cognitive Ills?' *Cognitive Biases*, ed. Jean-Paul Caverni and Jean-Marc Fabre. Amsterdam, North Holland: 523–52

Kersting, Wolfgang (1994). *Die politische Philosophie des Gesellschaftsvertrags*. Darmstadt, Wissenschaftliche Buchgesellschaft

(1997). 'Methodologische Probleme einer Theorie der sozialen Gerechtigkeit.' *Recht, Gerechtigkeit und demokratische Tugend. Abhandlungen zur praktischen Philosophie der Gegenwart*, ed. Wolfgang Kersting. Frankfurt, Suhrkamp: 213–42

Kiesler, Sara B. (1973). 'Preference for Predictability or Unpredictability as a Mediator of Reactions to Norm Violations.' *Journal of Personality and Social Psychology* 27: 354–9

Kirchgässner, Gebhard (1992). 'Towards a Theory of Low-Cost Decisions.' *European Journal of Political Economy* 8: 305–20

(1996). 'Bemerkungen zur Minimalmoral.' *Zeitschrift für Wirtschafts- und Sozialwissenschaften* 116: 223 51

Kirchgässner, Gebhard and Werner Pommerehne (1993). 'Low Cost Decisions as a Challenge to Public Choice.' *Public Choice* 77: 107–15

Kirchhof, Ferdinand (1987). *Private Rechtsetzung*. Berlin, Duncker & Humblot

Klein, Gary (2001). 'The Fiction of Optimization.' *Bounded Rationality. The Adaptive Toolbox. Dahlem Workshop Report*, ed. Gerd Gigerenzer and Reinhard Selten. Cambridge, Mass., MIT Press: 103–21

Knight, Frank Hyneman (1921). *Risk, Uncertainty and Profit*. Boston and New York, Houghton Mifflin

Knight, Jack (1992). *Institutions and Social Conflict*. Cambridge, Cambridge University Press

Knight, Jack and Itai Sened (1995). 'Introduction.' *Explaining Social Institutions*, ed. Jack Knight and Itai Sened. Ann Arbor, University of Michigan Press

Knill, Christoph and Andrea Lenschow (1999). 'Governance im Mehrebenensystem. Die institutionellen Grenzen effektiver Implementation in der europäischen Umweltpolitik.' Preprints aus der Max-Planck-Projekt-gruppe Recht der Gemeinschaftsgüter Bonn 1999/1. http://www.mpp-rdg. mpg.de/extern/pdf_dat/9808.pdf

Kofman, Fred and Jacques Lawarree (1996). 'On the Optimality of Allowing Collusion.' *Journal of Public Economics* 61: 383–407

Koriat, Asher, Sarah Lichtenstein and Baruch Fischhoff (1980). 'Reasons for Confidence.' *Journal of Experimental Psychology* 6: 107–18

Korobkin, Russell B. and Thomas S. Ulen (2000). 'Law and Behavioral Science. Removing the Rationality Assumption from Law and Economics.' *California Law Review* 88: 1051–144

Kötz, Hein (1996). *Europäisches Vertragsrecht I.* Tübingen, Mohr

Krause, Bodo (1991). 'Components of Cognitive Learning.' *Zeitschrift für Psychologie* 199: 35–44

(1992). 'Kognitives Lernen. Ansätze und experimentelle Befunde.' *Zeitschrift für Psychologie* 200: 199–223

Kreps, David M. (1990). *Game Theory and Economic Modelling.* Oxford and New York, Clarendon Press

Krüger, Hans-Peter (1999). 'Verzicht auf Sanktionsnormen im Straaenverkehrs-recht-ein Beitrag zur Effektivität von Verhaltensnormen?' *Wirkungsforschung zum Recht I. Wirkungen und Erfolgsbedingungen von Gesetzen,* ed. Hagen Hof and Gertrude Lübbe-Wolff. Baden-Baden, Nomos: 223–34

Kühberger, Anton (2000). 'What about Motivation?' *Behavioral and Brain Sciences* 23: 685

Kuhn, Thomas S. (1962). *The Structure of Scientific Revolutions.* [Chicago], University of Chicago Press

Kulms, Rainer (2000). *Schuldrechtliche Organisationsverträge in der Unternehmens-kooperation.* Baden-Baden, Nomos

Kunda, Ziva and Richard E. Nisbett (1988). 'Predicting Individual Evaluations from Group Evaluations and Vice Versa. Different Patterns for Self and Other?' *Personality and Social Psychology Bulletin* 14: 326–34

Kunig, Philip (1986). *Das Rechtsstaatsprinzip. Überlegungen zu seiner Bedeutung für das Verfassungsrecht der Bundesrepublik Deutschland.* Tübingen, Mohr

Lachmann, Ludwig M. (1963). 'Wirtschaftsordnung und wirtschaftliche Institutionen.' *Jahrbuch für die Ordnung von Wirtschaft und Gesellschaft* 14: 63–77

Laffont, Jean-Jacques (1999). 'Political Economy, Information and Incentives.' *European Economic Review* 43: 649–69

Lahno, Bernd (2002). *Der Begriff des Vertrauens.* Paderborn, Mentis

Laibson, David (1997). 'Golden Eggs and Hyperbolic Discounting.' *Quarterly Journal of Economics* 112: 443–77

Laird, John E., Allen Newell and Paul Rosenbloom (1991). 'Soar: an Architec-ture for General Intelligence.' *Artificial Intelligence* 47: 289–325

Langer, Ellen J. (1975). 'The Illusion of Control.' *Journal of Personality and Social Psychology* 32: 311–28

Langevoort, Donald C. (2000). 'Organized Illusions. A Behavioral Theory of Why Corporations Mislead Stock Market Investors (and Cause Other Social Harms).' *Behavioral Law and Economics,* ed. Cass R. Sunstein. Cambridge, Cambridge University Press: 144–67

Langlois, Richard N. (1986). 'Rationality, Institutions, and Explanation.' *Economics as a Process. Essays in the New Institutional Economics*, ed. Richard N. Langlois. Cambridge, Cambridge University Press: 225–55

LaPiere, Richard T. (1934). 'Attitudes vs. Actions.' *Social Forces* 13: 230–7

Lawson, Anton E. (2002). 'The Origin of Conditional Logic. Does a Cheater Detection Module Exist?' *Journal of Genetic Psychology* 163: 425–44

Ledyard, John O. (1995). 'Public Goods. A Survey of Experimental Research.' *The Handbook of Experimental Economics*, ed. J. H. Kagel and A. E. Roth. Princeton, Princeton University Press: 111–94

Lehmann, Jill Fain, John E. Lairdand Paul Rosenbloom (1998). 'A Gentle Introduction to Soar: an Architecture for Human Cognition.' *Methods, Models, and Conceptual Issues, Vol. IV. An Invitation to Cognitive Science*, ed. Don Scarborough and Saul Stemberg: 211–53

León, Immaculada and Juan A. Hernández (1998). 'Testing the Role of Attribution and Appraisal in Predicting Own and Other's Emotions.' *Cognition and Emotion* 12: 27–43

Lerner, Jennifer S. and Philip E. Tetlock (1999). 'Accounting for the Effects of Accountability.' *Psychological Bulletin* 125: 255–75

Lessig, Lawrence (1999). *Code and other Laws of Cyberspace*. New York, Basic Books

Lessig, Lawrence and Paul Resnick (1999). 'Zoning Speech on the Internet. A Legal and Technical Model.' *Michigan Law Review* 98: 395–431

Levinson, Stephen C. (1995). 'Interactional Biases in Human Thinking.' *Social Intelligence and Interaction*, ed. Esther Goody. Cambridge, Cambridge University Press: 221–60

Liebrand, Wim B. and Charles G. McClintock (1988). 'The Ring Measure of Social Values. A Computerized Procedure for Assessing Individual Differences in Information Processing and Social Value Orientation.' *European Journal of Personality* 2: 217–30

Lind, E. Allan and Tom R. Tyler (1988). *The Social Psychology of Procedural Justice*. New York, Plenum Press

Linton, Ralph (1945). *The Cultural Background of Personality*. New York, London, D. Appleton-Century

List, Christian and Robert E. Goodin (2001). 'Epistemic Democracy. Generalizing the Condorcet Jury Theorem.' *Journal of Political Philosophy* 9: 277–306

List, John A. (2000). 'The Effect of Market Experience on the WTA/WTP Disparity. Evidence from a Field Experiment with Sports Memorabilia.' http://papers.ssrn.com/sol3/papers.cfm?abstract_id230007

Loewenstein, George and Daniel Adler (2000). 'A Bias in the Prediction of Tastes.' *Choices, Values, and Frames*, ed. Daniel Kahneman and Amos Tversky. Cambridge, Cambridge University Press: 726–34

Loewenstein, George F. and Drazen Prelec (1992). 'Anomalies in Intertemporal Choice. Evidence and an Interpretation.' *Quarterly Journal of Economics* 107: 573–98

  (2000). 'Preferences for Sequences of Outcomes.' *Choices, Values, and Frames*, ed. Daniel Kahneman and Amos Tversky. Cambridge, Cambridge University Press: 565–77

Loewenstein, George and Richard H. Thaler (1997). 'Intertemporal Choice.' *Research on Judgement and Decisionmaking*, ed. William M. Goldstein and Robin M. Hogarth. Cambridge, Cambridge University Press: 365–78

Loewenstein, George, Elke U. Weber, Christopher, Hsee and Ned Welch (2001). 'Risk as Feelings.' *Psychological Bulletin* 127: 267–86

Lübbe, Weyma (2002). 'Epistemische Pflichten in der "Wissensgesellschaft".' *Wissen, Nichtwissen, Unsicheres Wissen*, ed. Christoph Engel, Jost Halfmann and Martin Schulte. Baden-Baden, Nomos: 145–60

Lüdemann, Jörn (2004). *Edukatorisches Staatshandeln.* Baden-Baden, Nomos

Luhmann, Niklas (1986). *Ökologische Kommunikation. Kann die moderne Gesellschaft sich auf ökologische Gefährdungen einstellen?* Opladen, Westdeutscher Verlag

McAdams, Richard H. (2000). 'A Focal Point Theory of Expressive Law.' *Virginia Law Review* 86: 1649–729

McCaffery, Edward, Daniel Kahneman and Matthew L. Spitzer (2000). 'Framing the Jury. Cognitive Perspective on Pain and Suffering Awards.' *Behavioral Law and Economics*, ed. Cass R. Sunstein. Cambridge, Cambridge University Press: 259–87

McEvily, Bill, Roberto Weber, Cristiná Bicchieri and Violet Ho (2002). 'Can Groups be Trusted? An Experimental Study of Collective Trust.' http://papers.ssrn.com/paper.taf?abstract_id=323223

McGarity, Thomas O. (1998). 'A Cost-Benefit State.' *Administrative Law Review* 50: 7–79

Machina, Mark J. (1987). 'Choice under Uncertainty. Problems Solved and Unsolved.' *Journal of Economic Perspectives* 1: 121–54

McKenzie Alexander, Jason (2003). 'Evolutionary Game Theory.' *The Stanford Encyclopedia of Philosophy*, ed. Edward E. Zalta. Stanford, Stanford University

MacNeil, Ian R. (1971). *Contracts: Exchange Transactions and Relationships.* Mineola, Foundation Press

(1982). 'Efficient Breach of Contract: Circles in the Sky.' *Virginia Law Review* 68: 947–69

Mair, Peter (1996). 'Comparative Politics. An Overview.' *A New Handbook of Political Science*, ed. Robert E. Goodin and Hans-Dieter Klingemann. Oxford, Oxford University Press: 309–35

Mantzavinos, Chrysostomos (2001). *Individuals, Institutions, and Markets.* Cambridge, Cambridge University Press

March, James G. and Johan P. Olsen (1989). *Rediscovering Institutions. The Organizational Basis of Politics.* New York, Free Press

Markovits, Richard S. (1996). 'Monopoly and the Allocative Inefficiency of First-Best-Allocatively-Efficient Tort Law in our Worse-Than-Second-Best World. The Whys and some Therefores.' *Case Western Reserve Law Review* 46: 313–448

Martignon, Laura and Kathryn Blackmond Laskey (1999). 'Bayesian Benchmarks for Fast and Frugal Heuristics.' *Simple Heuristics that Make Us Smart*, ed. Gerd Gigerenzer and Peter M. Todd. New York, Oxford University Press: 169–90

Maslow, Abraham H. (1954). *Motivation and Personality.* New York, Harper

Maunz, Theodor and Günter Dürig, eds. (1958). *Grundgesetz: Kommentar.* Munich, Beck

May, Judith V. and Aaron B. Wildavsky (1978). *The Policy Cycle.* Beverly Hills, Sage

Maynard Smith, John (1982). *Evolution and the Theory of Games.* Cambridge, Cambridge University Press

Mayntz, Renate (1980). *Implementation politischer Programme. Empirische Forschungsberichte.* Königstein/Ts., Athenäum

(1983). 'Implementation von regulativer Politik.' *Implementation politischer Programme II,* ed. Renate Mayntz. Opladen, Westdeutscher Verlag: 50–74

Meade, James (1970). 'The Theory of Indicative Planning.' *The Collected Papers of James Meade, Vol. II. Value, Distribution and Growth,* ed. James Meade. Winchester, Unwin Hyman: 109–57

Meadow, William and Cass R. Sunstein (2001). 'Statistics, not Experts.' *Duke Law Journal* 51: 629–46

Meehl, Paul E. (1954). *Clinical Versus Statistical Prediction. A Theoretical Analysis and a Review of the Evidence.* Minneapolis, University of Minnesota Press

Messick, David M. and Wim B. Liebrand (1995). 'Individual Heuristics and the Dynamics of Cooperation in Large Groups.' *Psychological Review* 102: 131–45

Messick, David M., Don A. Moore and Max H. Bazerman (1997). 'Ultimatum Bargaining with a Group. Underestimating the Importance of the Decision Rule.' *Organizational Behavior and Human Decision Processes* 69: 87–101

Meyer, David E. and David E. Kieras (1997). 'A Computational Theory of Executive Cognitive Processes and Multiple-Task Performance: I. Basic Mechanisms.' *Psychological Review* 104: 3–65

Meyer, John W. and W. Richard Scott (1983). *Organizational Environments. Ritual and Rationality.* Beverly Hills, Sage

Miller, Dale T. and Michael Ross (1975). 'Self-Serving Biases in the Attribution of Causality: Fact or Fiction?' *Psychological Bulletin* 82: 213–25

Mischel, Walter and Philip K. Peake (1982). 'Beyond déjà vu in the Search for Cross-Situational Consistency.' *Psychological Review* 89: 730–55

Mischel, Walter and Yuichi Shoda (1995). 'A Cognitive-Affective System Theory of Personality. Reconceptualizing Situations, Dispositions, Dynamics, and Invariance in Personality Structure.' *Psychological Review* 102: 246–68

Mookherjee, Dilip (1990). 'Rank Order Competition and Incentives. An Organizational Perspective.' *Economic Theory and Policy. Essays in Honour of Dipak Banerjee,* ed. Bhaskar Dutta. New Delhi, Oxford University Press: 194–229

Morgenstern, Oskar (1928). *Wirtschaftsprognose. Eine Untersuchung ihrer Voraussetzungen und Möglichkeiten.* Vienna, Springer

(1935). 'Vollkommene Voraussicht und wirtschaftliches Gleichgewicht.' *Zeitschrift für Nationalökonomie* 6: 337–57

Mui, Vai-Lam (1995). 'The Economics of Envy.' *Journal of Economic Behavior and Organization* 26: 311–36

Mullainathan, Sendhil (2002). 'A Memory-Based Model of Bounded Rationality.' *Quarterly Journal of Economics* 117: 735–74

Murdock, Kevin C. (2002). 'Intrinsic Motivation and Optimal Incentive Contracts.' *Rand Journal of Economics* 33: 650–71

Mussweiler, Thomas, Fritz Strack and Tim Pfeiffer (2000). 'Overcoming the Inevitable Anchoring Effect. Considering the Opposite Compensates for Selective Accessibility.' *Personality and Social Psychology Bulletin* 26: 1142–50

National Research Council (2002). *Global Networks and Local Values*. Washington, D.C, National Academy of Sciences

Nee, Victor (1998). 'Sources of the New Institutionalism.' *The New Institutionalism in Sociology*, ed. Mary C. Brinton and Victor Nee. New York, Russell Sage Foundation: 1–16

Nelson, Richard R. (1995). 'Recent Evolutionary Theorizing about Economic Change.' *Journal of Economic Literature* 33: 48–90

Nelson, Richard R. and Sidney G. Winter (1982). *An Evolutionary Theory of Economic Change*. Cambridge, Mass., Harvard University Press

Neumann, Franz Leopold (1942). *Behemoth. The Structure and Practice of National Socialism*. New York, Oxford University Press

Newcomb, Theodore Mead (1929). *The Consistency of Certain Extrovert-Introvert Behavior Patterns in 51 Problem Boys*. New York, Teachers College Columbia University

Newell, Allen (1990). *Unified Theories of Cognition*. Cambridge, Mass., Harvard University Press

Newell, Allen and Herbert Alexander Simon (1972). *Human Problem Solving*. Englewood Cliffs, N. J., Prentice-Hall

Newstead, Stephen E. (2000). 'Are There Two Different Types of Thinking?' *Behavioral and Brain Sciences* 23: 690–91

Nisbett, Richard E. and Lee Ross (1980). *Human Inference. Strategies and Shortcomings of Social Judgment*. Englewood Cliffs, N. J., Prentice-Hall.

Noll, Roger and James E. Krier (2000). 'Some Implications of Cognitive Psychology for Risk Regulation.' *Behavioral Law and Economics*, ed. Cass R. Sunstein. Cambridge, Cambridge University Press: 325–54

North, Douglass Cecil (1981). *Structure and Change in Economic History*. New York, Norton

  (1990). *Institutions, Institutional Change, and Economic Performance*. Cambridge, Cambridge University Press

Nyborg, Karine and Mari Rege (2001). 'Does Public Policy Crowd out Private Contributions to Public Goods?' http://papers.ssrn.com/paper.taf?abstract_id=292802

Ockenfels, Axel (2003). 'Reputationsmechanismen auf Internet-Marktplattformen. Theorie und Empirie.' *Zeitschrift für Betriebswirtschaft* 73: 295–315

Ofek, Elie, Muhamet Yildiz and Ernan Haruvy (2002). 'Sequential Decision Making: How Prior Choices Affect Subsequent Valuations.' http://papers.ssrn.com/paper.taf?abstract_id=353421

Ostrom, Elinor (1990). *Governing the Commons. The Evolution of Institutions for Collective Action*. Cambridge, Cambridge University Press

  (1998). 'A Behavioral Approach to the Rational Choice Theory of Collective Action.' *American Political Science Review* 92: 1–22

Parsons, Talcott (1951). *The Social System*. Glencoe, Ill., Free Press

Pashler, Harold E. (1998). *The Psychology of Attention.* Cambridge, Mass., MIT Press

Pavlov, Ivan Petrovich and Gleb Vasilievich Anrep (1927). *Conditioned Reflexes. An Investigation of the Physiological Activity of the Cerebral Cortex.* London, Oxford University Press and Humphrey Milford

Payne, John W., James R. Bettman et al. (1988). 'Adaptive Strategy Selection in Decision Making.' *Journal of Experimental Psychology* 14: 534–52

(1992). 'Behavioral Decision Research. A Constructive Processing Perspective.' *Annual Review of Psychology* 43: 87–131

(1997). 'The Adaptive Decision Maker. Effort and Accuracy in Choice.' *Research on Judgement and Decision Making. Currents, Connections, and Controversies,* ed. William M. Goldstein and Robin M. Hogarth. Cambridge, Cambridge University Press: 181–204

Pennington, Nancy and Reid Hastie (1993). 'Reasoning in Explanation-Based Decision-Making.' *Cognition* 49: 123–63

(1997). 'Explanation-Based Decision Making. Effects of Memory Structure on Judgement.' *Research in Judgement and Decision Making,* ed. William M. Goldstein and Robin M. Hogarth. Cambridge, Cambridge University Press: 454–81

Perritt, Henry H. (2000). 'Dispute Resolution in Cyberspace. Demand for New Forms of ADR.' *Ohio State Journal on Dispute Resolution* 15: 675–703

Peters, B. Guy (1999). *Institutional Theory in Political Science. The New Institutionalism.* London, Pinter

Pigou, A. C. (1932). *The Economics of Welfare.* London, Macmillan

Pitschas, Rainer (1996). 'Recht der Freien Berufe.' *Öffentliches Wirtschaftsrecht Besonderer Teil 2,* ed. Reiner Schmidt. Berlin, Springer: 1–126

Plessner, Helmuth (1928). *Die Stufen des Organischen und der Mensch. Einleitung in die Philosophische Anthropologie.* Berlin and Leipzig, W. de Gruyter

Plott, Charles R. (1986). 'Rational Choice in Experimental Markets.' *Rational Choice. The Contrast between Economics and Psychology,* ed. Robin M. Hogarth and Melvin W. Reder. Chicago, University of Chicago Press: 117–44

Posner, Eric A. (2000). *Law and Social Norms.* Cambridge, Mass., Harvard University Press

Posner, Richard A. (2000). 'Cost–Benefit Analysis. Definition, Justification, and Comment on Conference-Papers.' *Journal of Legal Studies* 29: 1153–77

(2003). *Economic Analysis of Law.* New York, Aspen

Poundstone, William (1992). *Prisoner's Dilemma.* New York, Doubleday

Prendergast, Canice (1999). 'The Provision of Incentives in Firms.' *Journal of Economic Literature* 37: 7–63

Presson, Paul K. and Victor A. Benassi (1996). 'Illusion of Control. A Meta-Analytic Review.' *Journal of Social Behavior and Personality* 11: 493–510

Price, Michael E., Leda Cosmides and John Tooby (2002). 'Punitive Sentiment as an Anti-Free Rider Psychological Device.' *Evolution and Human Behavior* 23: 203–31

Priest, George L. (1981). 'A Theory of the Consumer Product Warranty.' *Yale Law Journal* 90: 1297–352

Quattrone, George A. and Amos Tversky (2000). 'Contrasting Rational and Psychological Analysis of Political Choice.' *Choices, Values, and Frames,* ed. Daniel Kahneman and Amos Tversky. Cambridge, Cambridge University Press: 451–72

Quillen, Gwyn D. (1988). 'Contract Damages and Cross-Subsidization.' *Southern California Law Review* 61: 1125–41

Rabin, Matthew (1998). 'Psychology and Economics.' *Journal of Economic Literature* 36: 11–46

(2002). 'A Perspective on Psychology and Economics.' *European Economic Review* 46: 657–85

Rachlin, Howard (2001). 'Behavioural Analysis, Cognitive Analysis, and Economics.' Behavioral and Experimental Economics Nobel Symposium, 4–6 December 2001, at http://www.iies.su.se/nobel/papers/stockholm text3. pdf

Rachlinski, Jeffrey J. (2000). 'A Positive Psychological Theory of Judging in Hindsight.' *Behavioral Law and Economics,* ed. Cass R. Sunstein. Cambridge, Cambridge University Press: 95–115

(2003). 'The Uncertain Psychological Case for Paternalism.' *Northwestern University Law Review* 97: 1165–225

Rapoport, Anatol and Albert M. Chammah (1965). *Prisoner's Dilemma. A Study in Conflict and Cooperation.* Ann Arbor, University of Michigan Press

Rasmusen, Eric (1989). *Games and Information. An Introduction to Game Theory.* Oxford and New York, Basil Blackwell

Rawls, John (1999). *A Theory of Justice.* Cambridge, Mass., Belknap Press of Harvard Univeristy Press

Redelmeier, Donald A. and Amos Tversky (1992). 'On the Framing of Multiple Prospects.' *Psychological Science* 3: 191–3

Ripperger, Tanja (1998). *Ökonomik des Vertrauens.* Tübingen, Mohr

Risse, Thomas (2000). ' "Let's Argue!". Communicative Action in World Politics.' *International Organization* 54: 1–39

Ritov, Ilana and Jonathan Baron (2000). 'Reluctance to Vaccinate. Omission Bias and Ambiguity.' *Behavioral Law and Economics,* ed. Cass R. Sunstein. Cambridge, Cambridge University Press: 168–86

Roberts, Brent W. and Eileen M. Donahue (1994). 'One Personality, Multiple Selves. Integrating Personality and Social Roles.' *Journal of Personality* 62: 199–218

Rohe, Mathias (1998). *Netzverträge. Rechtsprobleme komplexer Vertragsbindungen.* Tübingen, Mohr

Ronis, D. L., J. F. Yates and J. P. Kirscht (1989). 'Attitudes, Decisions, and Habits as Determinants of Repeated Behavior.' *Attitude Structure and Function,* ed. A. R. Pratkanis, S. J. Breckler and A. G. Greenwald. Hillsdale, Erlbaum: 213–39

Rosa, Jose Antonio, Joseph F. Porac, Jelena Runser-Spanjol and Michael S. Saxan (1999). 'Sociocognitive Dynamics in a Product Market.' *Journal of Marketing* 63: 64–77

Ross, Lee and Richard E. Nisbett (1991). *The Person and the Situation. Perspectives of Social Psychology.* New York, McGraw-Hill

Ross, Lee, David Greene and Pamela House (1977a). 'The False Consensus Effect: an Egocentric Bias in Social Perception and Attribution Processes.' *Journal of Experimental Social Psychology* 13: 279–301

Ross, Lee, Mark R. Lepper, Fritz Strack and Julia Steinmetz (1977b). 'Social Explanation and Social Expectation. Effects of Real and Hypothetical Explanations on Subjective Likelihood.' *Journal of Personality and Social Psychology* 35: 817–29

Rostain, Tanina (2000). 'Educating Homo Economicus. Cautionary Notes on the New Behavioral Law and Economics Movement.' *Law and Society Review* 34: 973–1006

Rousseau, Jean-Jacques (1763). *Du contrat social; ou, Principes du droit politique.* n.p

Rutherford, Malcolm (1994). *Institutions in Economics. The Old and the New Institutionalism.* Cambridge, Cambridge University Press

Sandler, Todd (2001). *Economic Concepts for the Social Sciences.* Cambridge, Cambridge University Press

Sanna, Lawrence J. and Norbert Schwarz (2003). 'Debiasing the Hindsight Bias. The Role of Accessibility Experiences and (Mis)attributions.' *Journal of Experimental Social Psychology* 39 (3): 287–95

Sansone, Carol and Judith M. Harackiewicz (2000). *Intrinsic and Extrinsic Motivation. The Search for Optimal Motivation and Performance.* San Diego, Academic Press

Satz, Debra and John A. Ferejohn (1994). 'Rational Choice and Social Theory.' *The Journal of Philosophy* 91: 71–87

Savage, Leonard J. (1954). *The Foundations of Statistics.* New York, Wiley

Scharpf, Fritz Wilhelm (1997). *Games Real Actors Play. Actor-Centered Institutionalism in Policy Research.* Boulder, Colo., Westview Press

(1998). 'Die Problemlösungsfähigkeit der Mehrebenenpolitik in Europa.' *Politische Vierteljahresschrift* 39: 121–44

(1999). *Governing in Europe. Effective and Democratic?* Oxford and New York, Oxford University Press

Scheler, Max (1928). *Die Stellung des Menschen im Kosmos.* Darmstadt, Reichl

Schelling, Thomas C. (1960). *The Strategy of Conflict.* Cambridge, Mass., Harvard University Press

(1984). 'Self-Command in Practice, in Policy, and in a Theory of Rational Choice.' *American Economic Review Papers and Proceedings* 74: 1–11

Schimank, Uwe (1992). 'Erwartungssicherheit und Zielverfolgung. Sozialität zwischen Prisoners' Dilemma und Battle of the Sexes.' *Soziale Welt* 43: 182–200

Schlicht, Ekkehart (1998). *On Custom in the Economy.* Oxford, Clarendon Press

Schmeidler, David (1989). 'Subjective Probability and Expected Utility without Additivity.' *Econometrica* 57: 571–87

Schöch, Heinz (1999). 'Verzicht auf Sanktionsnormen im Straßenverkehrsrecht – ein Beitrag zur Effektivität von Verhaltensnormen?' *Wirkungsforschung zum Recht I. Wirkungen und Erfolgsbedingungen von Gesetzen*, ed. Hagen Hof and Gertrude Lübbe-Wolff. Baden-Baden, Nomos: 235–44

Schulte, Martin (2002). 'Zum Umgang mit Wissen, Nichtwissen und Unsicherem Wissen im Recht – dargestellt am Beispiel des BSE- and

MKS-Konflikts.' *Wissen, Nichtwissen, Unsicheres Wissen*, ed. Christoph Engel, Jost Halfmann and Martin Schulte. Baden-Baden, Nomos: 351–70

Schumpeter, Joseph Alois (1912). *Theorie der wirtschaftlichen Entwicklung.* Leipzig, Duncker & Humblot

Schweizer, Urs (1999). *Vertragstheorie.* Tübingen, Mohr

Sedikides, Constantine, John Schopler and Chester A. Insko (1998). *Intergroup Cognition and Intergroup Behavior.* Mahwah, N. J., Lawrence Erlbaum

Selten, Reinhard (1978). 'The Chain Store Paradox.' *Theory and Decision* 9: 127–59

(1998). 'Features of Experimentally Observed Bounded Rationality.' *European Economic Review* 42: 413–36

Shackle, George L. (1992). 'Risk, Uncertainty and Imagination.' *The Theory of Choice. A Critical Guide*, ed. H. Heap Shaun, Martin Hollis, Bruce Lyons, Robert Sudgen and Albert Wale. Oxford, Blackwell: 51–61

Shafir, Eldar, Itamar Simonson and Amos Tversky (2000). 'Reason-Based Choice.' *Choices, Values, and Frames*, ed. Daniel Kahneman and Amos Tversky. Cambridge, Cambridge University Press: 597–619

Shavitt, Sharon and Russell H. Fazio (1991). 'Effects of Attribute Salience on the Consistency between Attitudes and Behaviour Predictions.' *Personality and Social Psychology Bulletin* 17: 506–17

Sheposh, J. P. and P. S. Gallo (1973). 'Asymmetry of Payoff Structure and Cooperative Behaviour in the Prisoner's Dilemma Game.' *Journal of Conflict Resolution* 17: 321–33

Sherrington, Charles Scott (1906). *The Integrative Action of the Nervous System.* New York, C. Scribner's Sons

Shoda, Yuichi (1999). 'A Unified Framework for the Study of Behavioral Consistency. Briding Person x Situation Interaction and the Consistency Paradox.' *European Journal of Personality* 13: 361–87

Shoemaker, Paul J. (1982). 'The Expected Utility Model. Its Variants, Purposes, Evidence and Limitations.' *Journal of Economic Literature* 20: 529–63

Siebert, Horst (1996). 'Institutionelle Arrangements für die Zuweisung von Opportunitätskosten.' *Festschrift für Ernst-Joachim Mestmäcker*, ed. Ulrich Immenga, Wernhard Möschel and Dieter Reuter. Baden-Baden, Nomos: 309–20

Sil, Rudra (2000). 'The Division of Labor in Social Science Research. Unified Methodology or "Organic Solidarity"?' *Polity* 32: 499–531

Simon, Herbert Alexander (1957). *Models of Man: Social and Rational. Mathematical Essays on Rational Human Behavior in a Society Setting.* New York, Wiley

(1962). 'The Architecture of Complexity.' *Proceedings of the American Philosophical Society* 106: 467–82

(1976). *Administrative Behavior. A Study of Decision-Making Processes in Administrative Organization.* New York, Free Press

(1987). 'Rational Decision Making in Business Organisations.' *Advances in Behavioural Economics 1*, ed. Leonard Green and John H. Kagel. Norwood, Ablex: 18–47

(1990). 'Invariants of Human Behavior.' *Annual Review of Psychology* 41: 1–19

(1991). 'Cognitive Architectures and Rational Analysis. Comment.' *Architectures for Intelligence*, ed. Kurt VanLehn. Hillsdale, Erlbaum: 25–39

(1993). 'Altruism and Economics.' *American Economic Review* 83: 156– 61

Simon, Jürgen and Susanne Braun (2002). 'Legal Aspects of Genetic Data Banking in Germany.' *Eubios Journal of Asian and International Bioethics* 12: 171–6

Simonson, Itamar (2000). 'The Effect of Purchasing Quantity and Timing on Variety-Seeking Behavior.' *Choices, Values, and Frames*, ed. Daniel Kahneman and Amos Tversky. Cambridge, Cambridge University Press: 735–57

Singer, O. (1993). 'Policy Communities und Diskurs-Koalitionen. Experten und Expertise in der Wirtschaftspolitik.' *Policy Analyse. Kritik und Neuorientierung*, ed. Adrienne Héritier. Opladen, Westdeutscher Verlag: 149–74

Slembeck, Tilman and Jean-Robert Tyran (2002). 'Do Institutions Promote Rationality? An Experimental Study of the Three-Door Anomaly.' http://papers.ssrn.com/paper.taf?abstract_id=345721

Slovic, Paul (1995). 'The Construction of Preference.' *American Psychologist* 50: 364–71

Slovic, Paul and Baruch Fischhoff (1977). 'On the Psychology of Experimental Surprises.' *Journal of Experimental Psychology* 3: 544–51

Smend, Rudolf (1968). 'Verfassung und Verfassungsrecht.' *Staatsrechtliche Abhandlungen und andere Aufsätze*, ed. Rudolf Smend. Berlin, Duncker & Humblot: 119–276

Smith, Adam (1790). *The Theory of Moral Sentiments, or, An Essay Towards an Analysis of the Principles by which Men Naturally Judge Concerning the Conduct and Character, First of Their Neighbours, and Afterwards of Themselves. To which is Added, a Dissertation on the Origin of Languages*. London, Strahan

Smith, Eliot R. and Jamie De Coster (2000). 'Dual-Process Models in Social and Cognitive Psychology: Conceptual Integration and Links to Underlying Memory Systems.' *Personality and Social Psychology Review* 4: 108–31

Smith, Trenton G. (2003). 'Obesity and Nature's Thumbprint. How Institutions Make Behaviour Predictable. How Modern Waistlines can Inform Economic Theory.' University of California at Santa Barbara, Working Paper in Economics 18-02, 23 August 2003

Smith, Vernon L. (1989). 'Theory, Experiment and Economics.' *Journal of Economic Perspectives*: 3 (1): 151–69

(1991). 'Rational Choice. The Contrast between Economics and Psychology.' *Journal of Political Economy* 99: 877–97

(1994). 'Economics in the Laboratory.' *Journal of Economic Perspectives* 8: 112–31

Smith, Vernon L. and James M. Walker (1993). 'Monetary Rewards and Decision Cost in Experimental Economics.' *Economic Inquiry* 31: 245–61

Smith, Vernon L., Gerry L. Suchanek and Arlington W. Williams (1988). 'Bubbles, Crashes, and Endogenous Expectations in Experimental Spot Asset Markets.' *Econometrica* 56: 1119–51

Snyder, Mark and William B. Swann (1976). 'When Actions Reflect Attitudes. The Politics of Impression Management.' *Journal of Personality and Social Psychology* 34: 1034–42

Sobota, Katharina (1997). *Das Prinzip Rechtsstaat. Verfassungs- und verwaltungs-rechtliche Aspekte*. Tübingen, Mohr

Spiecker gen. Döhmann, Indra (2001). 'Staatliche Entscheidungen unter Unsicherheit. Juristische und ökonomische Vorgaben.' *Gentechnik im nicht–menschlichen Bereich – was kann und was sollte das Recht regeln?*, ed. Joachim Lege. Berlin, Arno Spitz: 51–88

Stanovich, Keith E. and Richard F. West (2000). 'Individual Differences in Reasoning. Implications for the Rationality Debate?' *Behavioral and Brain Sciences* 23: 645–65

Stark, Oded (1995). *Altruism and Beyond. An Economic Analysis of Transfers and Exchanges within Families and Groups*. Cambridge, Cambridge University Press

Steinmo, Sven, Kathleen Ann Thelen and Frank Longstreth (1992). *Structuring Politics. Historical Institutionalism in Comparative Analysis*. Cambridge, Cambridge University Press

Stephens, David W. and J. R. Krebs (1986). *Foraging Theory*. Princeton, Princeton University Press

Stiglitz, Joseph E. (2000). 'Formal and Informal Institutions.' *Social Capital. A Multifaceted Perspective*, ed. Partha Dasgupta and Ismail Serageldin. Washington, D.C., World Bank: 59–68

Strack, Fritz and Roland Deutsch (2002). 'Reflective and Impulsive Determinants of Social Behaviour' (mimeo)

(forthcoming). 'Urteilsheuristiken.' *Theorien der Sozialpsychologie – Motivations- und Informationsverarbeitungstheorien*, ed. Dieter Frey and Martin Irle

Strack, Fritz and Thomas Mussweiler (1997). 'Explaining the Enigmatic Anchoring Effect. Mechanisms of Selective Accessibility.' *Journal of Personality and Social Psychology* 73: 437–46

Ströbele, Wolfgang (1987). *Rohstoffökonomik Theorie natürlicher Ressourcen mit Anwendungsbeispielen Öl, Kupfer, Uran und Fischerei*. Munich, Vahlen

Stults, Daniel M. and Lawrence A. Messe (1985). 'Behavioral Consistency: the Impact of Public Versus Private Statements of Intentions.' *Journal of Social Psychology* 125: 277–8

Sunstein, Cass R. (1996). 'Legislative Foreword. Congress, Constitutional Moments, and the Cost-Benefit State.' *Stanford Law Review* 48: 247–309

(1998). 'How Law Constructs Preferences.' *Georgetown Law Journal* 86: 2637–52

ed. (2000a). *Behavioral Law and Economics*. Cambridge Series on Judgment and Decision Making. Cambridge, Cambridge University Press

(2000b). 'Cost–Benefit Default Principles.' Chicago, John M. Olin Law & Economics Working Paper 104. http://papers.ssrn.com/paper.taf?abstract_id=247884

(2000c). 'Introduction.' *Behavioral Law and Economics*, ed. Cass R. Sunstein. Cambridge, Cambridge University Press: 1–10

(2001). 'Cost–Benefit Default Principles.' *Michigan Law Review* 99: 1651–723

(2002). 'The Law of Group Polarization.' *Journal of Political Philosophy* 10: 175–95

Sunstein, Cass R. and Edna Ullmann-Margalit (2000). 'Second-Order Decisions.' *Behavioral Law and Economics*, ed. Cass R. Sunstein. Cambridge, Cambridge University Press: 187–208

Svenson, Ola (1981). 'Are We All Less Risky and More Skilful than Our Fellow Drivers?' *Acta Psychologica* 47: 143–8

Sweet, Alec Stone (1999). 'Judicialization and the Construction of Governance.' *Comparative Political Studies* 32: 147–84

Symposium (2000). 'Cost–Benefit Analysis. Legal, Economic, and Philosophical Perspectives.' *Journal of Legal Studies* 29: 837–1177

Tack, Werner H. (2003). 'Kooperative Rationalität in sozialen Situationen.' *Grenzen rationaler Orientierung*, ed. Michael Astroh. Hildesheim, Olms: 103–35

Takacs, Karoly (2001). 'Structural Embeddedness and Intergroup Conflict.' *Journal of Conflict Resolution* 45: 743–69

Tedeschi, James T. (1981). *Impression Management Theory and Social Psychological Research*. New York, Academic Press

Tetlock, Philip E. (1985). 'Accountability. The Neglected Social Context of Judgement and Choice.' *Research in Organizational Behaviour* 7: 297–332

  (1999). 'Accountability Theory. Mixing Properties of Human Agents with Properties of Social Systems.' *Shared Cognition in Organizations. The Management of Knowledge*, ed. Leigh L. Thompson, John M. Levine and David M. Messick. Mahwah, N. J., Lawrence Erlbaum: 117–37

Tetlock, Philip E., Linda Skitka and Richard Boettger (1989). 'Social and Cognitive Strategies for Coping with Accountability. Conformity, Complexity, and Bolstering.' *Journal of Personality and Social Psychology* 57: 632–40

Teubner, Gunther and Vaios Karavas (2003). 'http://www.CompanyName-Sucks.com: Drittwirkung der Grundrechte gegenüber "Privaten" im autonomen Recht des Internet.' *Innovationsoffene Regulierung des Internet*, ed. Karl-Heinz Ladeur. Baden-Baden, Nomos: 249–72

Thaler, Richard H. (1999). 'Mental Accounting Matters.' *Journal of Behavioral Decision Making* 12: 183–206

  (2000). 'Toward a Positive Theory of Consumer Choice.' *Choices, Values, and Frames*, ed. Daniel Kahneman and Amos Tversky. Cambridge, Cambridge University Press: 269–87

Thaler, Richard H. and H. M. Shefrin (1981). 'An Economic Theory of Self-Control.' *Journal of Political Economy* 89: 392–406

Theissen, Eric (2002). 'Floor versus Screen Trading. Evidence from the German Stock Market.' *Journal of Institutional and Theoretical Economics* 158: 32–54

Thompson, Leigh L., John M. Levine and David M. Messick (1999). *Shared Cognition in Organizations. The Management of Knowledge*. Mahwah, N. J., Lawrence Erlbaum

Thompson, M., Richard Ellis and Aaron B. Wildavsky (1990). *Cultural Theory*. Boulder, Colo., Westview Press

Thorburn, W. M. (1915). 'Occam's Razor.' *Mind* 24: 287–8

Tietenberg, Thomas H. (1982). 'Transferable Discharge Permits and the Control of Air Pollution – a Survey and Synthesis.' *Zeitschrift für Umweltpolitik und Umweltrecht* 3: 477–508

  (1998). *Environmental Economics and Policy*. Reading, Mass., Addison-Wesley

Tirole, Jean (1986). 'Hierarchies and Bureaucracies: On the Role of Collusion in Organizations.' *Journal of Law, Economics and Organization* 2: 181–214

(1988). *The Theory of Industrial Organization*. Cambridge, Mass., MIT Press

(2002). 'Rational Irrationality. Some Economics of Self-Management.' *European Economic Review* 46: 633–55

Turner, Mark (2001). *Cognitive Dimensions of Social Science*. New York, Oxford University Press

Tversky, Amos and Dale W. Griffin (2000). 'Endowments and Contrasts in Judgements of Well-Being.' *Choices, Values, and Frames*, ed. Daniel Kahneman and Amos Tversky. Cambridge, Cambridge University Press: 709–25

Tversky, Amos and Daniel Kahneman (1973). 'Availability. A Heuristic for Judging Frequency and Probability.' *Cognitive Psychology* 5: 207–32

(1974). 'Judgement under Uncertainty: Heuristics and Biases.' *Science* 185: 1124–31

(1991). 'Loss Aversion in Riskless Choice. A Reference-Dependent Model.' *Quarterly Journal of Economics* 106: 1039–61

(2000). 'Rational Choice and the Framing of Decisions.' *Choices, Values and Frames*, ed. Daniel Kahneman and Amos Tversky. Cambridge, Cambridge University Press: 209–23

Tversky, Amos and Itamar Simonson (2000). 'Context-Dependent Preferences.' *Choices, Values, and Frames*, ed. Daniel Kahneman and Amos Tversky. Cambridge, Cambridge University Press: 518–27

Tversky, Amos, Shmuel Sattath and Paul Slovic (2000). 'Contingent Weighting in Judgement and Choice.' *Choices, Values, and Frames*, ed. Daniel Kahneman and Amos Tversky. Cambridge, Cambridge University Press: 503–17

Tyler, Tom R. (1990). *Why People Obey the Law*. New Haven, Yale University Press

(1997). 'The Psychology of Legitimacy.' *Personality and Social Psychology Review* 1: 323–44

Underwood, Bill and Bert S. Moore (1981). 'Sources of Behavioral Consistency.' *Journal of Personality and Social Psychology* 40: 780–5

Vanberg, Victor (2002). 'Rational Choice vs. Program-Based Behavior. Alternative Theoretical Approaches and their Relevance for the Study of Institutions.' *Rationality and Society* 14: 7–54

Vanberg, Victor and James M. Buchanan (1989). 'Interests and Theories in Constitutional Choice.' *Journal of Theoretical Politics* 1: 49–62

Van De Veer, Donald (1986). *Paternalistic Intervention. The Moral Bounds of Benevolence*. Princeton, Princeton University Press

Veblen, Thorstein (1919). *The Place of Science in Modern Civilisation and Other Essays*. New York, B. W. Huebsch

Verweij, Marco (2000). *Transboundary Environmental Problems and Cultural Theory. The Protection of the Rhine and the Great Lakes*. Houndmills, Basingstoke, and New York, Palgrave

Von Hayek, Friedrich-August (1967). *Studies in Philosophy, Politics and Economics*. London, Routledge

Von Neumann, John and Oskar Morgenstern (1944). *Theory of Games and Economic Behavior*. Princeton, Princeton University Press

Von Savigny, Friedrich Karl (1814). *Vom Beruf unsrer Zeit für Gesetzgebung und Rechtswissenschaft*. Heidelberg, Mohr and Zimmer

Wade-Benzoni, Kimberly A., Ann E. Tenbrunsel and Max H. Bazerman (1996). 'Egocentric Interpretations of Fairness in Asymmetric, Environmental Social Dilemmas. Explaining Harvesting Behavior and the Role of Communication.' *Organizational Behavior and Human Decision Processes* 67: 111–26

Wagenaar, Willem A., Gideon Keren and Sarah Lichtenstein (1997). 'Islanders and Hostages. Deep and Surface Structures of Decision Problems.' *Research on Judgement and Decision Making*, ed. William M. Goldstein and Robin M. Hogarth. Cambridge, Cambridge University Press: 552–65

Walker, James M., Roy Gardner, Andrew Herr and Elinor Ostron (2000). 'Collective Choice in the Commons. Experimental Results on Proposed Allocation Rules and Votes.' *The Economic Journal* 110: 212–34

Weber, Elke U. and Patrizia G. Lindemann (2002). 'Decision Modes or Choosing How to Choose. Making Decisions with Our Head, Our Heart, or by the Book' (mimeo)

Weber, Elke U., William M. Goldstein and S. Barlas (1995). 'And Let Us not Forget Memory. The Role of Memory Processes and Techniques in the Study of Judgement and Choice.' *The Psychology of Learning and Motivation, 32. Decision Making from a Cognitive Perspective*, ed. J. R. Busemeyer, Reid Hastie and D. L. Medin. San Diego, Academic Press: 33–81

Weber, Max (1976). *Wirtschaft und Gesellschaft. Grundriss der verstehenden Soziologie*. Tübingen, Mohr

Webster, Hutton and H. Milford (1942). *Taboo. A Sociological Study*. Stanford, Stanford University Press; London, Oxford University Press

Weck-Hannemann, Hannelore (1999). 'Rationale Außensteuerung menschlichen Verhaltens – Möglichkeiten und Grenzen.' *Rationale Umweltpolitik - Rationales Umweltrecht. Konzepte, Kriterien und Grenzen rationaler Steuerung im Umweltschutz*, ed. Erik Gawel and Gertrude Lübbe-Wolff. Baden-Baden, Nomos: 67–92

Wegner, Gerhard (1996). *Wirtschaftspolitik zwischen Selbst- und Fremdsteuerung – ein neuer Ansatz*. Baden-Baden, Nomos

Weigend, A (1994). 'On Overfitting and the Effective Number of Hidden Units.' *Proceedings of the 1993 Connectionist Models Summer School*, ed. Michael C. Mozer. Hillsdale, N. J., Lawrence Erlbaum: 335–42

Welch, Ivo (1992). 'Sequential Sales, Learning, and Cascades.' *Journal of Finance* 47: 695–732

White, Harrison C. (1992). *Identity and Control. A Structural Theory of Social Action*. Princeton, Princeton University Press
 (1995). 'Social Networks Can Resolve Actor Paradoxes in Economics and in Psychology.' *Journal of Institutional and Theoretical Economics* 151: 58–74

Wicker, Allan W. (1969). 'Attitudes versus Actions. The Relationship of Verbal and Overt Behavioral Responses to Attitude Objects.' *Journal of Social Issues* 25: 41–78

Wiersma, Uco J. (1992). 'The Effects of Extrinsic Rewards in Intrinsic Motivation. A Meta-Analysis.' *Journal of Occupational and Organizational Psychology* 65: 101–14

Wilder, David A. (1978). 'Effect of Predictability on Units of Perception and Attribution.' *Personality and Social Psychology Bulletin* 4: 281–4

Williamson, Oliver E. (1985). *The Economic Institutions of Capitalism. Firms, Markets, Relational Contracting.* New York, Free Press; London, Collier Macmillan

Wilson, Timothy D., Christopher E. Houston, Kathryn M. Etling and Nancy Brekke (1996). 'A New Look at Anchoring Effects. Basic Anchoring and its Antecedents.' *Journal of Experimental Psychology* 125: 387–402

Wilson, Timothy D., Samuel Lindsey and Tonya Y. Schooler (2000). 'A Model of Dual Attitudes.' *Psychological Review* 107: 101–26

Windhoff-Héritier, Adrienne (1980). *Politikimplementation. Ziel und Wirklichkeit politischer Entscheidungen.* Königstein/Ts., Hain

Winter, Gerd (1975). *Das Vollzugsdefizit im Wasserrecht. Ein Beitrag zur Soziologie des Öffentlichen Rechts.* Berlin, Schmidt

Witt, Ulrich (2000a). 'Changing Cognitive Frames – Changing Organizational Forms: an Entrepreneurial Theory of Organizational Development.' *Industrial and Corporate Change* 9: 733–55

(2000b). 'Genetic Adaptation, Cultural Learning, and the Utilitarian Program in Economics.' Paper prepared for the AEA Panel 'Consilience: the Unity of Knowledge in the 21st Century', Boston, 7 January 2000

Wright, Jack C. and Walter Mischel (1987). 'A Conditional Approach to Dispositional Constructs. The Local Predictability of Social Behavior.' *Journal of Personality and Social Psychology* 53: 1159–77

Yee, Albert S. (1996). 'The Causal Effects of Ideas on Policies.' *International Organization* 50: 66–108

Young, H. Eyton (1994). *Equity. In Theory and Practice.* Princeton, Princeton University Press

Zhou Xueguang (1997). 'Organizational Decision Making as Rule Following.' *Organizational Decision Making*, ed. Zur Shapira. New York, Cambridge University Press: 257–81

Zweigert, Konrad and Hein Kötz (1998). *Introduction to Comparative Law.* Oxford, Clarendon Press

Index

For EU product safety concerns, contact us at Calle de José Abascal, 56–1°, 28003 Madrid, Spain or eugpsr@cambridge.org.

www.ingramcontent.com/pod-product-compliance
Ingram Content Group UK Ltd.
Pitfield, Milton Keynes, MK11 3LW, UK
UKHW012155180425
457623UK00007B/42